Preventing
Violence in
Relationships

Preventing Violence in Relationships

Interventions Across the Life Span

Edited by

Paul A. Schewe

American Psychological Association
Washington, DC

First Printing May 2002
Second Printing July 2004
Third Printing October 2009

Published by
American Psychological Association
750 First Street, NE
Washington, DC 20002
www.apa.org

To order
APA Order Department
P.O. Box 92984
Washington, DC 20090-2984
Tel: (800) 374-2721; Direct: (202) 336-5510
Fax: (202) 336-5502; TDD/TTY: (202) 336-6123
Online: www.apa.org/books/
Email: order@apa.org

In the U.K., Europe, Africa, and the Middle East, copies may be ordered from
American Psychological Association
3 Henrietta Street
Covent Garden, London
WC2E 8LU England

Typeset in Goudy by Page Grafx, Inc., St. Simons Island, GA
Printer: Data Reproductions, Auburn Hills, MI
Cover Designer: Naylor Design, Washington, DC
Technical/Production Editor: Kristen R. Sullivan

The opinions and statements published are the responsibility of the authors, and such opinions and statements do not necessarily represent the policies of the American Psychological Association.

Library of Congress Cataloging-in-Publication Data
  Preventing violence in relationships : interventions across the life span / edited by
  Paul A. Schewe.
      p.   cm.
   Includes bibliographical references and index.
   ISBN 1-55798-911-7 (alk. paper)
    1. Family violence—Prevention. 2. Conflict management. 3. Violence—Prevention.
  4. Interpersonal conflict—Prevention. I. Schewe, Paul A.
   HV6626 .P734 2002
   616.85'822'0651—dc21

                                                                                      2002018497

British Library Cataloguing-in-Publication Data
A CIP record is available from the British Library.

Printed in the United States of America

CONTENTS

Contributors vii

Introduction. New Directions in Preventing
Interpersonal Violence   3
Paul A. Schewe

Chapter 1.   School-Based Child Sexual Abuse Prevention   9
Sandy K. Wurtele

Chapter 2.   Reconceptualizing Child Sexual Abuse as a
Public Health Concern   27
*Keith Kaufman, Michelle Barber, Heather Mosher,
and Megan Carter*

Chapter 3.   Interventions for Children Victimized by Peers   55
Heidi Gazelle and Gary W. Ladd

Chapter 4.   Dating Violence Education: Prevention and
Early Intervention Strategies   79
Sarah Avery-Leaf and Michele Cascardi

Chapter 5.   Guidelines for Developing Rape Prevention and
Risk Reduction Interventions 107
Paul A. Schewe

Chapter 6.   Rape Avoidance: Self-Protection Strategies
for Women 137
Sarah E. Ullman

Chapter 7.   Fostering Men's Responsibility for Preventing
                Sexual Assault 163
                Alan D. Berkowitz

Chapter 8.   Recent Therapeutic Advances in the Prevention of
                Domestic Violence 197
                *Sabina M. Low, Natalie D. Monarch, Scott Hartman,
                and Howard Markman*

Chapter 9.   Violence and the Elderly Population:
                Issues for Prevention 223
                *Deborah Henderson, Jeffrey A. Buchanan, and
                Jane E. Fisher*

Chapter 10.   Evaluating Prevention Programs: Challenges and
                Benefits of Measuring Outcomes 247
                Paul A. Schewe and Larry W. Bennett

Conclusion.   Past, Present, and Future Directions
                for Preventing Violence in Relationships 263
                Paul A. Schewe

Author Index 267

Subject Index 279

About the Editor 289

CONTRIBUTORS

Sarah Avery-Leaf, PhD, Independent Consultant, Durham, NH

Michelle Barber, BA, Department of Psychology, Portland State University

Larry W. Bennett, PhD, Jane Addams Center for Social Policy and Research, University of Illinois at Chicago

Alan D. Berkowitz, PhD, Independent Consultant, Trumansburg, NY

Jeffrey A. Buchanan, MA, Department of Psychology, University of Nevada, Reno

Megan Carter, BA, Department of Psychology, Portland State University

Michele Cascardi, PhD, Independent Consultant, Glen Ridge, NJ

Jane E. Fisher, PhD, Department of Psychology, University of Nevada, Reno

Heidi Gazelle, PhD, Department of Educational Psychology, University of Illinois at Urbana–Champaign

Scott Hartman, MA, Psychology Department, University of Denver

Deborah Henderson, MA, Department of Psychology, University of Nevada, Reno

Keith Kaufman, PhD, Department of Psychology, Portland State University

Gary W. Ladd, PhD, Department of Family and Human Development and Department of Psychology, Arizona State University, Tempe

Sabina M. Low, MA, Psychology Department, University of Denver

Howard Markman, PhD, Psychology Department, University of Denver

Natalie D. Monarch, MA, Psychology Department, University of Denver

Heather Mosher, BS, Department of Psychology, Portland State University

Paul A. Schewe, PhD, Department of Psychology, University of Illinois at Chicago

Sarah E. Ullman, PhD, Department of Criminal Justice, University of Illinois at Chicago

Sandy K. Wurtele, PhD, Department of Psychology, University of Colorado at Colorado Springs

Preventing Violence in Relationships

INTRODUCTION:
NEW DIRECTIONS IN PREVENTING INTERPERSONAL VIOLENCE

PAUL A. SCHEWE

Although the shootings at American schools over the past several years have focused the country's attention and resources on combating the problem of interpersonal violence, many of the proposed solutions (e.g., installing metal detectors, increasing locker searches, changing gun laws) will do little to change the individual, family, peer group, community, and societal problems that interact to produce situations where violence can and does erupt. All violence is essentially interpersonal. No matter how much aggressors attempt to depersonalize their victims, the fact remains that violence occurs between people. Until educators, policymakers, and researchers come to realize that strong, healthy relationships between individuals are the key to preventing violence, little progress will be made in the effort to promote peaceful coexistence. Nowhere is this more obvious than in the field of intimate partner violence prevention.

The problems of child abuse, bullying, sexual assault, dating violence, spouse abuse, and elder abuse have drawn attention from investigators from the diverse fields of psychology, sociology, public health, social work, psychiatry, women's studies, nursing, and education. Almost without fail, any journal article on these topics has included a section describing the implications of research results for prevention. Until recently, however, most violence prevention efforts have focused on reducing the incidence of assaults by strangers, despite U.S. Department of Justice (1998) statistics that indicate that people are twice as likely to be victimized by an acquaintance,

3

friend, relative, or intimate partner. Efforts to prevent men from assaulting or abusing their partners and efforts to teach young people healthy relationship skills are relatively new approaches to dealing with the age-old problems of sexual assault and spouse abuse. Recent research suggests that these new approaches hold considerable promise.

Attachment researchers inform of the incredible power that the early parent–child relationship has in directing brain development and establishing lifelong patterns of interpersonal behavior. As children grow, interactions with siblings and peers begin to dominate their development. Soon, children begin to develop intimate relationships and may eventually enter into a monogamous lifelong intimate relationship. It is people's experiences within these relationships that shape who they are. People's relationships are at the very core of who they are. Although for a long time we have realized the importance of teaching hygiene, nutrition, and basic safety skills to our children, we have left the development of healthy relationship skills largely up to chance. Children are bombarded every day with hundreds of examples of respectful, caring, and polite behaviors, as well as manipulative, insensitive, selfish, and hurtful behaviors, from parents, siblings, friends, teachers, the media, and others. They see people rewarded for good behavior, and they see people rewarded for bad behavior. Punishments are meted out equally arbitrarily. Children need clear, consistent relationships with caring mentors to provide some stability from which they can make sense of sometimes-nonsensical situations.

When things go wrong, when children are abused or neglected by their caretakers, when they are left with no guide or interpreter for the flood of media messages, when self-gratification is the only goal they know, then their lives will be marked by unhealthy, hurtful, nonsatisfying relationships. Can this be prevented? Can men and women be prevented from abusing their children? Can families, siblings, and peers be taught to solve interpersonal conflicts? Can sons be prevented from raping? Can men and women achieve a respectful and healthy balance of power and control within their relationships? Can our parents be protected from us, as they become old and fragile? It is all about relationships. It is about knowing that violence is never an acceptable solution. It is about knowing that men and women can work together for mutual benefit.

Unfortunately, research regarding the efficacy of preventive interventions has lagged far behind the practice of providing these interventions. Although more and more schools are providing interventions to their students addressing child sexual abuse, bullying, dating violence, and sexual assault, questions regarding the effectiveness of these interventions have only recently begun to be addressed. One dilemma facing researchers is the lack of adequate measures for evaluating the effects of a preventive intervention. Documenting the successful prevention of violence is a much more difficult task than documenting the existence of violence. Many researchers have developed innovative measures to assess prosocial changes in knowledge, attitudes, and behaviors, but the lack of reliable and valid indicators of effectiveness across studies has hampered the usefulness of much of the research on violence prevention. Studies comparing the effectiveness of two or more interventions are just not available at this time in the field of violence prevention. Because of the paucity of well-developed studies and methodologically sophisticated research designs, the recommendations and conclusions offered in some of these chapters are based as much on theory and practice as on sound research. Despite the weaknesses in the existing literature, the field of violence prevention has advanced enormously in the past decade, and it seems appropriate now to summarize what we have learned with the aim of improving existing services and guiding future research.

The goal of this book is to act as a guide for researchers, program directors, educators, clinicians, and social workers who are concerned about preventing violence in relationships at all developmental stages. The authors of these chapters describe both common and innovative interventions. They translate the available research into practical steps for promoting healthy relationships and preventing violence. The explicit focus of this volume is the integration of theory, research, and practice, guided by a vision of developing policies and programs to promote healthy relationships and prevent violence within society. A core question posed by those invested in health promotion and violence prevention is "What can be done from the start and throughout the life course to maximize the probability of children developing in wholesome ways?"

The authors participating in this volume are leading scholars who share my vision of the importance of prevention and of the importance of not placing the responsibility for preventing violence on potential victims. The types of violence covered in the book include verbal, physical, and sexual abuse between acquaintances, dating partners, and married couples, as well as child sexual abuse and elder abuse within families. The book explores the relationship skills and attitudes that males and females need to develop at each developmental stage, from preschool to parenting.

ORGANIZATION OF THIS BOOK

The book begins with chapter 1 by Sandy Wurtele that explores issues related to school-based child sexual abuse prevention efforts. The chapter explores the risk and protective factors associated with child sexual abuse, describes characteristics of effective child sexual abuse prevention programs, and makes recommendations for improving these efforts. Chapter 2, by Keith Kaufman, Michelle Barber, Heather Mosher, and Megan Carter, reflects the application of the public health model to the nuances of child sexual abuse and illustrates several promising approaches that go beyond the traditional school-based, child-directed prevention efforts. Heidi Gazelle and Gary Ladd's chapter 3 reviews theory and evidence regarding individual and interpersonal factors that increase children's vulnerability to peer victimization. This focus on child recipients of victimization stems from a holistic concern for the well-being of these potentially vulnerable children, but is not intended to imply that child recipients of victimization are to blame for their victimization. Efforts to ameliorate individual and relational vulnerabilities aim not only to prevent or terminate peer victimization but also to mitigate the consequences of victimization and to promote the healthy social and emotional development of children who are likely vulnerable to victimization as well as other social and emotional difficulties.

Several chapters in this volume address sexual assault prevention and teenage dating violence. In chapter 4, Sarah Avery-Leaf and Michelle Cascardi identify risk factors that can and should be targeted by programs aiming to prevent teenage dating violence and review program evaluation research documenting the efficacy of school-based dating violence prevention programs. The conclusions they draw are geared toward educators charged with selecting a prevention program for their student population. Similarly, in chapter 5 I report the results of a review of 33 empirical evaluations of rape prevention programs from 1984 to 2000. The chapter provides a set of guidelines that rape prevention educators can use in selecting or developing curricula for use in middle and high schools. Two additional chapters on sexual assault focus on men and women separately. Sarah Ullman's chapter 6 on rape avoidance strategies reviews this area of research and provides recommendations that can enhance women's ability to avoid rape until the broader goal of primary prevention of rape can be effected in society. Alan Berkowitz's chapter 7 provides an overview of the issues involved in men taking responsibility for sexual assault prevention, suggests a philosophy and pedagogy for rape prevention, provides a developmental model for prevention programs, makes recommendations for advancing the field, and reviews promising interventions and strategies.

Adult relationships too, are often marked by violence. Sabina Low, Natalie Monarch, Scott Hartman, and Howard Markman, in chapter 8, review observational studies of interactions between spouses in violent marriages and other research on predictors of marital violence to make recommendations for both primary and secondary prevention programs. In chapter 9 on elder abuse, Deborah Henderson, Jeffrey Buchanan, and Jane E. Fisher discuss popular theoretical explanations for the causes of elder abuse, describe characteristics associated with an increased probability of abuse, identify barriers to identification, and describe effective prevention strategies.

Because of the paucity of research in most areas of interpersonal violence that directly informs preventive interventions and the clear need for more research regarding effective interventions, chapter 10 in this volume provides basic information on why agencies should evaluate their programs and how to design and conduct an evaluation that will provide maximally useful information. My hope is that this book will inspire readers to advance the knowledge of effective prevention efforts and to improve the work that is being done to prevent all types of interpersonal violence across the life span.

REFERENCE

Greefeld, L. A., Rand, M. R., Craven, D., et al. (1998). *Violence by intimates*. U.S. Department of Justice, NCJ–167237.

1

SCHOOL-BASED CHILD SEXUAL ABUSE PREVENTION

SANDY K. WURTELE

This chapter focuses on the serious problem of child sexual abuse (CSA). I briefly review what is known about this problem, including information about the scope and consequences of CSA. I present risk and protective factors associated with CSA, along with their implications for prevention. I then review the relatively brief history of safety education for children and critically examine the evidence for the effectiveness of child-focused programs. Finally, I conclude the chapter with suggestions for the improvement of child education programs, along with a call for the development of alternative approaches to prevention.

SCOPE OF THE CSA PROBLEM

Determining the magnitude of the CSA problem is difficult for several reasons. The term *child sexual abuse* incorporates a variety of activities, ranging from intentionally exposing one's sexual organs to a child to having vaginal or anal intercourse with a minor. Sexual abuse is also a secretive offense; a good portion of victims never disclose their abuse. Thus, no data can tell exactly how many children are victimized each year. Instead, incidence data are based on cases that are disclosed to law enforcement or child protection agencies. In the United States in 1999, an estimated 826,000 children were victims of child maltreatment: 11.3% of them experienced sexual abuse (U.S. Department of Health and Human Services, 2001). Encouragingly, this report shows that the rate of sexual abuse has declined from 1.9 children per 1,000 in 1995 to 1.3 per 1,000 in 1999.

As an alternative to determining the scope of the CSA problem, prevalence studies ask adults if they experienced sexual abuse as children. Sexual abuse rates in retrospective studies range from 7% to 62% for women (with an average of 22% for abuse involving contact with the genitals) and from 3% to 16% for men (with an overall average of 7%; Wurtele & Miller-Perrin, 1992). Prevalence rates that are based on adult samples most likely underestimate the actual extent of the problem, as there may be many more men and women who were victimized as children but do not remember these experiences. Indeed, Williams (1994) followed up with 129 women who, as children, were brought to an emergency room with a primary complaint of having been sexually abused. Over one third (38%) of these women did not recall having been sexually abused. Thus, both incidence and prevalence studies most likely underestimate the extent of CSA. What is clear, however, is that sexual victimization during childhood is not rare.

CONSEQUENCES OF CSA

Research conducted over the past decade has shown that a wide range of psychological difficulties are more prevalent among those who have been sexually abused than among those who have not. These difficulties include depression, anxiety, anger, an impaired sense of self, problems with sexuality, cognitive disturbances (e.g., poor concentration, inattentiveness, dissociation) that can lead to behavioral and academic problems at school, physical problems (e.g., sexually transmitted diseases, urinary tract infections), and interpersonal difficulties (less social competence, more aggression, less trusting, more socially withdrawn). (For recent reviews of the consequences of CSA, see Beitchman, Zucker, Hood, daCosta, & Akman, 1991; Beitchman, Zucker, Hood, daCosta, Akman, & Cassavia, 1992; Briere & Elliott, 1994; Kendall-Tackett, Williams, & Finkelhor, 1993; Miller-Perrin & Wurtele, 1990; Wolfe & Birt, 1995.)

Sexual victimization during childhood is associated with initial and long-term psychological difficulties, but its impact is neither inevitable nor completely predictable. Indeed, a substantial minority of sexually abused children exhibit minimal or no sequelae: Estimated proportions of victims found to be free of symptoms have ranged from 10% to 49% (Briere & Elliott, 1994; Kendall-Tackett et al., 1993). Actual impact may depend on abuse variables (who the perpetrator was, what was done, for how long, whether force was used), child characteristics (premorbid adjustment, age, gender, coping style), family functioning (family composition, parent–child relationship, reaction to disclosure), and community support (reactions to disclosure, availability of resources).

RISK AND PROTECTIVE FACTORS ASSOCIATED WITH CSA

No single risk factor has been identified that provides a necessary or sufficient cause of CSA. Instead, etiological models typically consider individual, familial, and sociocultural factors that may increase the likelihood of this type of child maltreatment.

Wurtele and Miller-Perrin (1992) compiled a list of risk factors thought to increase the likelihood of CSA occurring (see Exhibit 1.1). This list also contains possible protective or buffering factors, factors that may decrease the likelihood that a child will be victimized. Using this model, it is assumed that the more risk factors involved across all systems, the higher the likelihood abuse will occur. Conversely, the more protective or compensatory factors involved across all systems, the lower the likelihood of abuse. This multifactor conceptualization suggests that reduction in the incidence of CSA will be achieved only by developing a comprehensive prevention approach targeting the personal, familial, and environmental conditions that increase and decrease the risks of abuse. The remainder of this chapter focuses on one risk factor for children: their lack of knowledge and skills related to personal safety.

EDUCATION PROGRAMS TO PREVENT CSA

In response to the growing body of knowledge regarding the scope and consequences of CSA, many prevention programs have been developed and widely disseminated since the 1980s. Unlike efforts to prevent the physical abuse or neglect of children (which focus on modifying adult behavior), the focus of CSA prevention efforts has been primarily to alter the knowledge and skills of children through group-based instruction on personal safety, usually conducted in educational settings.

School systems have evolved as the obvious choice for teaching children about sexual abuse, given that their primary function is to inform and educate. School-based prevention programs also have appeal because of their ability to reach large numbers of children of every racial, ethnic, and socioeconomic group in a relatively cost-efficient fashion. A universal primary prevention strategy likewise eliminates the stigma of identifying specific

EXHIBIT 1.1
Possible Risk and Protective Factors Associated With Child Sexual Abuse

Components of CSA	Risk factors	Protective factors
Offender	Male Sexual attraction toward children Lack of empathic concern for children Cognitions or fantasies supporting sexual contact with children Poor impulse control Narcissistic identification with children Use of alcohol/drugs to lower inhibitions History of abuse or betrayal Feelings of inadequacy, loneliness, vulnerability, dependency Poor interpersonal (especially heterosocial) skills High stress (e.g., unemployment, financial problems) Need for power and control (possibly related to early life experience that resulted in feelings of helplessness)	If past history of abuse, has awareness of CSA History of a positive relationship with a good parental role model Good interpersonal skills Respect for children Empathy for, sensitivity to others Good decision-making skills High self-esteem Social support Good coping abilities
Child	Lack of knowledge of appropriate and inappropriate sexual behavior High need for attention or affection Overly trusting Low self-esteem, self-confidence Isolated Emotionally neglected Passive, unassertive Taught to be obedient Poor decision-making or problem-solving skills	Knowledgeable about appropriate and inappropriate sexual behavior Assertive High self-esteem, self-competence Have support persons Good problem-solving, decision-making skills
Child's family	Emotional neglect of children Inappropriate expectations regarding child's responsibilities (e.g., role reversal) Inefficient or sporadic supervision Marital discord Family characterized by secretiveness, poor communication Over- or undersexualized home	Low stress Good social supports Economic security Supportive parents Age-appropriate sexual knowledge Efficient supervision Open climate; good communication patterns Child's sexual development promoted Child's self-esteem promoted

EXHIBIT 1.1 (Continued)

Components of CSA	Risk factors	Protective factors
Child's family (cont'd)	Lack of privacy; household crowding Situations in which offenders have access to victims Power imbalance in marital dyad Self-protective behavior not modeled by parents Inappropriately close or distant parent–child boundaries Stressors in family (unemployment; poverty) Socially or geographically isolated home Father substitute present History of abuse in either parent Exploitation of children to meet the needs of adults Absence of natural parent	Importance of personal safety stressed in home Respect for each other's privacy by adults and children Affectionate parent–child relationship Positive male–female relationships (mutual, symmetrical) Effective problem solving modeled by adults Positive sense of self modeled by adults Appropriate boundaries between adults and children
Community/ society	View of children as possessions Cultural acceptance for deriving sexual satisfaction from children Easy access to victims Easy access to child pornography Portrayal of children as sexual beings in media and advertising Reluctance of legal system to prosecute and punish offenders Sexually restrictive culture Lack of community support for families Strong masculine sexualization (dominance, power in sexual relationships) Patriarchal-authoritarian subcultures Belief that children should always obey adults Few opportunities for male/child nurturant interchanges that contain no sexual component Lack of sexuality education in educational system Devaluation of children Community denial of the CSA problem	Culture opposed to deriving sexual satisfaction from children Quick prosecution and consistent punishment of offenders by legal system Cultural emphasis on equality between males and females Provision of sexuality education for children Community support for families Children highly valued Low tolerance for sexually coercive behaviors Community awareness of the CSA problem and efforts devoted to its prevention Research programs designed to further our understanding of CSA and how to prevent it

Note. From *Preventing Child Sexual Abuse: Sharing the Responsibility* (pp. 48–49), by S. K. Wurtele and C. L. Miller-Perrin, 1992, Lincoln: University of Nebraska Press. Copyright 1992 by the University of Nebraska Press. Reprinted with permission.

children or families as being at risk for sexual abuse and thus avoids costly and intrusive interventions into family privacy (Daro, 1994).

School-based personal safety programs have been rapidly adopted across the United States. National surveys of school administrators have found that 48% to 85% of school districts offer CSA prevention programs (Daro, 1994; Helge, 1992). More than 90% of teachers across the country viewed school-based CSA prevention programs as valuable and effective (Abrahams, Casey, & Daro, 1992), and in a national sample, 96% of elementary school principals rated the provision of CSA prevention education as average to above average in importance (Romano, Casey, & Daro, 1990). Parents have also been found to be supportive of including CSA prevention programs in elementary schools and preschools (Conte & Fogarty, 1989; Wurtele, Kvaternick, & Franklin, 1992). Many children have participated in these programs. In fact, a telephone survey of 2,000 young people between ages 10 and 16 conducted in 1993 found that 67% of respondents reported having participated in a school-based victimization prevention program at some time in their educational careers (Finkelhor & Dziuba-Leatherman, 1995).

The primary focus of CSA prevention programs is to strengthen children's abilities to recognize potentially abusive situations and teach them strategies to resist assault (primary prevention), although the programs often have a secondary prevention focus as well (Miller-Perrin & Wurtele, 1988). The secondary prevention objective is to encourage victims to disclose abuse and to improve adults' responses to these disclosures so children can receive early intervention and protection to reduce the negative consequences of sexual exploitation. Most prevention programs also emphasize that abuse is never the child's fault.

In the past decade, more than 40 evaluations of CSA prevention programs have been published. There have been at least three meta-analyses (Berrick & Barth, 1992; Heidotting & Soled, 1996; Rispens, Aleman, & Goudena, 1997) and several major narrative reviews of this research (Carroll, Miltenberger, & O'Neill, 1992; Conte & Fogarty, 1990; Conte, Rosen, & Saperstein, 1986; Daro, 1994; Finkelhor & Strapko, 1992; Hazzard, 1990; Kolko, 1988; MacMillan, MacMillan, Offord, Griffith, & MacMillan, 1994; O'Donohue, Geer, & Elliott, 1992; Reppucci & Haugaard, 1989; Tharinger et al., 1988; Tutty, 1993; U.S. General Accounting Office, 1996; Wurtele, 1987, 1998, 1999; Wurtele & Miller-Perrin, 1992). Very similar conclusions have been reached by meta-analytic and narrative reviews. A summary of these findings follows.

Knowledge Gains

Both school- and preschool-age children demonstrated enhanced knowledge about CSA prevention concepts following program participation. In their meta-analysis of CSA prevention evaluation studies, Berrick and Barth (1992) reported large effect sizes for both preschool-age children ($d = .86$) and elementary school-age children ($d = .98$). Furthermore, knowledge gains have been shown to be maintained for up to one year (Briggs & Hawkins, 1994; Hazzard, Webb, Kleemeier, Angert, & Pohl, 1991), although knowledge gains tend to fade over time for younger children (Rispens et al., 1997).

Skill Gains

Research also shows that preschool- and school-age children can learn certain preventive skills. Following program participation, children improved their ability to recognize inappropriate touches. This skill has been demonstrated with both school-age children and 3–6-year-old children. With younger children, the ability to discriminate between appropriate and inappropriate touching of the genitals improved more when they were taught to use a concrete rule to protect their private parts as opposed to using feelings to guide their decision making (Blumberg, Chadwick, Fogarty, Speth, & Chadwick, 1991; Sarno & Wurtele, 1997; Wurtele, Kast, Miller-Perrin, & Kondrick, 1989).

The reviews also agree that these programs can enhance children's resistance skills. Most personal safety programs teach some form of self-protection, usually verbal skills (e.g., saying "no," yelling, or threatening to tell) and behavioral skills (e.g., trying to get away or, more rarely, fighting back). After participating in a personal safety program, both preschool- and school-age children demonstrated enhanced behavioral skills (saying "no," trying to get away, telling an adult). In their meta-analysis of school programs, Rispens et al. (1997) found a significant and considerable mean postintervention effect size ($d = .71$) and concluded that victimization prevention programs are successful in teaching children sexual abuse concepts and self-protection skills. Follow-up studies have demonstrated that, as with knowledge gains, skill gains are maintained for as long as a year after program presentation (Hazzard et al., 1991). Preventive skill scores are higher when children participate in active-learning programs that provide multiple opportunities for children to practice the skills during the program (Blumberg et al., 1991; Wurtele, Marrs, & Miller-Perrin, 1987). Rispens et al. (1997) concluded that "programs that focus on skills training, allowing sufficient time for children to integrate these self-protection skills into their cognitive repertoire, are to be preferred" (p. 983). They also suggested that there should be more opportunity for repeated learning.

Another skill objective of most personal safety programs is to encourage children to report past or ongoing abuse. One method of assessing this skill is to ask children whether they would tell someone if they were involved in an abusive situation. After participating in personal safety programs, preschool- and school-age children indicated a greater willingness to tell an adult about an inappropriate touching situation. However, preschool-age children have difficulty describing the abusive situation to the resource person (Ratto & Bogat, 1990; Sarno & Wurtele, 1997; Wurtele & Owens, 1997). Young children's short attention span and their limited metamemory and communication skills make it difficult for them to fully recount the abusive situation. Given that reporting is one of the primary objectives of personal safety programs, program developers and instructors need to emphasize the importance of disclosure and provide ample opportunities for children to practice reporting.

Another way to determine whether these programs are facilitating reporting is to present information on unsolicited disclosures. Unfortunately, very few researchers have reported disclosures occurring during or after the program, despite their importance as a secondary prevention method. Published disclosure rates immediately following the program have ranged from a low of 0% (Gilbert, Berrick, Le Prohn, & Nyman, 1989; Hill & Jason, 1987) to a high of 11% (Kolko, Moser, & Hughes, 1989). The 11% figure is quite impressive, given that few sexually abused children purposefully disclose (Sorenson & Snow, 1991).

Using an alternative strategy to measure resistance skills, Finkelhor and his colleagues telephoned a nationally representative sample of 2,000 young people between ages 10 and 16. The youths were asked about their experiences with and responses to actual or threatened sexual assaults. Among their survey respondents, a surprisingly high number (40%) reported specific instances in which they used the information or skills taught in an antivictimization program to protect themselves (Finkelhor & Dziuba-Leatherman, 1995). Victimized and threatened children were more likely to use self-protection strategies if they had received comprehensive prevention instruction, which included opportunities to practice the skills in class, multiday presentations, and materials to take home to discuss with their parents (Finkelhor, Asdigian, & Dziuba-Leatherman, 1995).

The reviews have concluded that children can learn about sexual abuse and skills that might prove useful in an abusive situation. The programs have also prompted some victimized children to disclose past or ongoing abuse. The reviews have also agreed that concepts and skills can be grasped better when taught with active participation (e.g., modeling or role-playing techniques) than with more passive methods (e.g., films or lectures). Program guidelines recently published by the National Center for Missing and Exploited Children (NCMEC, 1999) reiterate and expand on these recommendations. Specifically, the guidelines suggest that prevention programs (a) be developmentally appropriate with regard to language, content, and teaching methods; (b) use behavior rehearsal, role-playing, and feedback to teach skills; (c) occur on multiple occasions over several years and include periodic reviews and supplemental sessions to reinforce skills; and

(d) include homework and parental involvement. Additional suggestions for effective prevention programs can be found in Exhibit 1.2.

Reducing Incidence of CSA

Critics of CSA prevention programs, along with reviewers of this research, all agree that there is not yet any direct evidence that these programs have been effective in preventing CSA. One way to determine whether these programs actually prevent sexual victimization is to monitor incidence rates; if programs are effective, then CSA incidence rates should decrease over time. As noted earlier, national incidence rates for CSA have declined since 1995, but this decline cannot be definitively attributed to the sexual abuse prevention movement.

Another strategy to determine whether these programs actually prevent sexual victimization is to examine whether rates of victimization differ

EXHIBIT 1.2
Characteristics of Effective CSA Prevention Programs

1. Focus of material matches the specific needs of the community.
2. Program provides guidance for preparing the setting, including the following:
   - Suggests conducting a needs assessment
   - Emphasizes involving individuals and groups in the community prior to program implementation
   - Includes proper training for presenters (for teaching the program and handling disclosures)
   - Promotes parental involvement before, during, and after the program.
3. Content of program does the following:
   - Defines and describes sexual abuse
   - Describes offenders (examples should include authority figures, family members, and strangers)
   - Describes potential victims (examples should include both males and females of all races, ages, and sizes)
   - Helps children distinguish between appropriate and inappropriate touches
   - Helps children identify the private parts of their bodies using correct anatomical terms
   - Teaches children self-protective skills to avoid abuse (say "no," try to get away)
   - Stresses body ownership and self-pride
   - Teaches children decision-making skills
   - Promotes disclosure by instructing children to tell an adult
   - Emphasizes that abuse is never the fault of the child.
4. Process criteria of program include the following:
   - Developmentally appropriate
   - Grounded in theory and research
   - Includes rehearsal, role-play, practice
   - Is sensitive to audience characteristics
   - Includes multiple presentations and periodic reviews
   - Includes homework and parental involvement
   - Includes comprehensive evaluation.

overall between children who have and have not participated in a sexual abuse prevention program. Gibson and Leitenberg (2000) followed this strategy and asked 825 undergraduate women to report their histories of CSA and childhood participation in school-based prevention programs. Nine percent of respondents who reported ever having had a prevention program also reported having been sexually abused; 16% of respondents who never participated in a prevention program reported having been sexually abused. Thus, young women who had not participated in a school prevention program in childhood were about twice as likely to have experienced CSA as those who had participated in a program. Participation in a prevention program was also associated with faster disclosure of sexual abuse. These findings provide the first direct suggestion that sexual abuse prevention programs are indeed associated with the desired outcome of a decreased occurrence of sexual abuse. Further support will come with prospective studies that follow children who have and have not participated in a school prevention program.

Negative and Positive Side Effects

Another criticism of CSA prevention programs has been that they produce negative side effects. Critics of education programs have raised concerns that program participants may become oversensitive to appropriate touch, may become frightened or upset, or may develop negative attitudes toward sexuality.

Reviewers of the side-effects research have found little evidence of these negative effects. For example, few teachers or parents notice signs of behavior problems or emotional distress among program participants. Few program participants have misinterpreted nurturing touches or made false accusations of CSA. No significant increases in anxiety have been found among program participants, although some children reported that the program made them feel worried or scared (Finkelhor & Dziuba-Leatherman, 1995; Garbarino, 1987; Hazzard, Kleemeier, & Webb, 1990). Interestingly, children who reported increased levels of fear and anxiety in the study by Finkelhor and Dziuba-Leatherman (1995) were also the ones who rated the programs most positively and were the ones most likely to use the skills taught in the programs. The authors suggested that these higher anxiety ratings reflect that the children were taking the message of the training seriously, and they urged professionals to refrain "from assuming that reports of increased fear and anxiety are a negative outcome of training programs" (p. 137).

As for critics' concerns that CSA prevention programs will harm children's normal sexual development (e.g., Krivacska, 1990; Melton, 1992), a growing body of literature shows that personal safety programs may actually enhance young children's sexual development. For example, there is evidence that these programs can teach young children the anatomically correct terminology for their genitals (Wurtele, 1993; Wurtele, Melzer, & Kast, 1992). After participating in the program, significantly more children said they like their private parts (suggesting increased body pride) and also said it is acceptable for them to touch their own private parts (Wurtele & Owens, 1997). Further, in their follow-up study of adult women, Gibson and Leitenberg (2000) asked respondents about their current sexual satisfaction and sexual behaviors and found no evidence that participation in CSA prevention programs negatively affects sexual development or sexual satisfaction into young adulthood.

Finally, several researchers have found what might be considered positive side effects of program participation. For example, Finkelhor and Dziuba-Leatherman (1995) found that 95% of youth who participated in a school-based antivictimization program said they would recommend it to other children, and those who reported being victimized or threatened perceived themselves as having been more effective in keeping themselves safe and minimizing their harm. Other researchers have found that after participating in a program, children are more likely to discuss the contents of the program with their parents (Finkelhor et al., 1995; Hazzard et al., 1991; Wurtele, 1990). As I discuss in the next section, increasing parent–child communication about CSA should be a major objective of school-based programs.

CONCLUSIONS AND RECOMMENDATIONS

Extant evaluations suggest that personal safety programs can teach children the knowledge and skills thought to be useful in avoiding sexual assault, and they can do so without increasing children's anxiety, acting out, or confusion about appropriate touch. There is also preliminary evidence that children are able to apply this information in real-life situations. Learning how to value and protect themselves are important lessons; children deserve this instruction. Clearly, school-based personal safety programs play an important part in the effort to keep children safe from sexual victimization. There is also the possibility that these programs may prevent the perpetration of sexual abuse as well as victimization.

All schools should offer some type of program on personal safety. But schools cannot and should not shoulder the full responsibility for preventing CSA. Schools are encouraged to enlist parents as "partners in prevention" (Wurtele & Miller-Perrin, 1992). The impact of a school-based program depends on the support of parents at home.

Parents' first role in prevention efforts is to support their child's participation in the program. Parents who have concerns about these programs or believe they are harmful may not allow their children to participate. Educators need to address parents' concerns about personal safety programs by informing them of the research reviewed in this chapter on negative and positive side effects. Educators also need to debunk the many myths about CSA held by the public in general and parents in particular. For example, parents who believe their children are at low risk for sexual exploitation (Collins, 1996) or who believe children are too young to understand the topic (Wurtele, Kvaternick, & Franklin, 1992) may not support their children's personal safety education. Parents who think child molesters are "social misfits" (Conte & Fogarty, 1989), "dirty old men" (Morison & Greene, 1992), or strangers (Berrick, 1988; Calvert & Munsie-Benson, 1999; Wurtele, Kvaternick, & Franklin, 1992) may believe their children are not at risk for sexual victimization if they do not allow their children to have contact with these types of people. Educators need to inform parents about the characteristics of victims (i.e., that young children are especially vulnerable) and perpetrators (i.e., that perpetrators are often family members, substitute caregivers, or trusted adults who function "normally" in society).

By allowing their children to participate in school-based programs, parents indirectly support prevention efforts. They can also be enlisted to provide more direct support in the role of adjunct teacher of personal safety. Educators should inform parents of the lessons being taught at school so that parents can clarify concepts and correct any misconceptions their children might have. They can also help their children to apply this new knowledge in daily life. Assignments can be sent home with the children to be completed with their parents. When parents are trained to be prevention educators, then their children receive repeated exposure to prevention information in their natural environment, thus providing booster sessions to supplement classroom presentations.

Educators can also teach parents about how to identify child victims and how to respond appropriately to victim disclosures. They can be alerted to the possible risk and protective factors associated with CSA (contained in Exhibit 1.1) and can be encouraged to modify some of the familial conditions that increase and decrease the likelihood of abuse.

Preliminary research supports parental involvement in personal safety education. Several studies have found that parents (when provided with a script, materials, and encouragement) can be very effective instructors for their young children (Wurtele, Currier, Gillispie, & Franklin, 1991; Wurtele, Gillispie, Currier, & Franklin, 1992; Wurtele, Kast, & Melzer, 1992). Also, there is empirical support for the effectiveness of a commercially produced educational video ("What Do I Say Now?"; Committee for Children, 1996) for increasing parent–child communication about CSA (Burgess & Wurtele, 1998). Finally, Finkelhor and colleagues (1995) found that children who had received victimization prevention instruction from their parents (in addition to a school-based program) had substantially more knowledge about CSA, made more use of self-protection strategies, were better able to thwart victimization attempts, and were more likely to disclose victimization.

Given the numerous advantages of and initial successes in enlisting parents as additional instructors of personal safety, researchers are urged to focus their efforts on finding ways to encourage parents (especially fathers) to become more involved. Future research needs to identify effective ways to encourage attendance at parent workshops, to compare different approaches to enhancing parent–child discussions about CSA, and to evaluate the impact of parent-focused education on parents' CSA-related beliefs and behaviors.

It is clearly time to extend preventive efforts and target others, particularly parents, to play a more active part in preventing CSA. Children should not shoulder the full responsibility for prevention.

REFERENCES

Abrahams, N., Casey, K., & Daro, D. (1992). Teachers' knowledge, attitudes, and beliefs about child abuse and its prevention. *Child Abuse and Neglect, 16*, 229–238.

Beitchman, J. H., Zucker, K. J., Hood, J. E., daCosta, G. A., & Akman, D. (1991). A review of the short-term effects of child sexual abuse. *Child Abuse and Neglect, 15*, 537–556.

Beitchman, J. H., Zucker, K. J., Hood, J. E., daCosta, G. A., Akman, D., & Cassavia, E. (1992). A review of the long-term effects of child sexual abuse. *Child Abuse and Neglect, 16*, 101–118.

Berrick, J. D. (1988). Parental involvement in child abuse prevention training: What do they learn? *Child Abuse and Neglect, 12*, 543–553.

Berrick, J. D., & Barth, R. P. (1992). Child sexual abuse prevention: Research review and recommendations. *Social Work Research and Abstracts, 28*, 6–15.

Blumberg, E. J., Chadwick, M. W., Fogarty, L. A., Speth, T. W., & Chadwick, D. L. (1991). The touch discrimination component of sexual abuse prevention training: Unanticipated positive consequences. *Journal of Interpersonal Violence, 6*, 12–28.

Briere, J. N., & Elliott, D. M. (1994). Immediate and long-term impacts of child sexual abuse. *The Future of Children, 4*, 54–69.

Briggs, F., & Hawkins, R. M. F. (1994). Follow-up data on the effectiveness of New Zealand's national school based child protection program. *Child Abuse and Neglect, 18*, 635–643.

Burgess, E. S., & Wurtele, S. K. (1998). Enhancing parent–child communication about sexual abuse: A pilot study. *Child Abuse and Neglect, 22*, 1167–1175.

Calvert, J. F., Jr., & Munsie-Benson, M. (1999). Public opinion and knowledge about childhood sexual abuse in a rural community. *Child Abuse and Neglect, 23*, 671–682.

Carroll, L. A., Miltenberger, R. G., & O'Neill, H. K. (1992). A review and critique of research evaluating child sexual abuse prevention programs. *Education and Treatment of Children, 15*, 335–354.

Collins, M. E. (1996). Parents' perceptions of the risk of CSA and their protective behavior: Findings from a qualitative study. *Child Maltreatment, 1*, 53–64.

Committee for Children (Producer). (1996). *What do I say now? How to help protect your child from sexual abuse* [Film]. (Available from Committee for Children, 2203 Airport Way South, Suite 500, Seattle, WA 98134-2027)

Conte, J. R., & Fogarty, L.A. (1989). Attitudes on sexual abuse prevention programs: A national survey of parents. (Available from J. R. Conte, School of Social Work, University of Washington, Mailstop 354900, 4101 15th Avenue NE, Seattle, WA 98195-6299)

Conte, J. R., & Fogarty, L. A. (1990). Sexual abuse prevention programs for children. *Education and Urban Society, 21*, 270–284.

Conte, J. R., Rosen, C., & Saperstein, L. (1986). An analysis of programs to prevent the sexual victimization of children. *Journal of Primary Prevention, 6*, 141–155.

Daro, D. (1994). Prevention of child sexual abuse. *The Future of Children, 4*, 198–223.

Finkelhor, D., Asdigian, N., & Dziuba-Leatherman, J. (1995). The effectiveness of victimization prevention instruction: An evaluation of children's responses to actual threats and assaults. *Child Abuse and Neglect, 19*, 141–153.

Finkelhor, D., & Dziuba-Leatherman, J. (1995). Victimization prevention programs: A national survey of children's exposure and reactions. *Child Abuse and Neglect, 19*, 129–139.

Finkelhor, D., & Strapko, N. (1992). Sexual abuse prevention education: A review of evaluation studies. In D. J. Willis, E. W. Holden, & M. Rosenberg (Eds.), *Prevention of child maltreatment: Developmental and ecological perspectives* (pp. 150–167). New York: Wiley.

Garbarino, J. (1987). Children's response to a sexual abuse prevention program: A study of the Spider-man comic. *Child Abuse and Neglect, 11*, 143–148.

Gibson, L. E., & Leitenberg, H. (2000). Child sexual abuse prevention programs: Do they decrease the occurrence of child sexual abuse? *Child Abuse and Neglect, 24*, 1115–1125.

Gilbert, N., Berrick, J. D., Le Prohn, N., & Nyman, N. (1989). *Protecting young children from sexual abuse: Does preschool training work?* Lexington, MA: Lexington Books.

Hazzard, A. (1990). Prevention of child sexual abuse. In R. T. Ammerman & M. Hersen (Eds.), *Treatment of family violence: A sourcebook* (pp. 354–384). New York: Wiley.

Hazzard, A., Kleemeier, C. P., & Webb, C. (1990). Teacher versus expert presentations of sexual abuse prevention programs. *Journal of Interpersonal Violence, 5*, 23–36.

Hazzard, A., Webb, C., Kleemeier, C., Angert, L., & Pohl, L. (1991). Child sexual abuse prevention: Evaluation and one-year follow-up. *Child Abuse and Neglect, 15*, 123–138.

Heidotting, T., & Soled, S. W. (1996). *School-based sexual abuse and personal safety prevention programs for children: A meta-analysis.* (Available from Suzanne W. Soled, Department of Educational Foundations, College of Education, 406 Teachers College, University of Cincinnati, PO Box 210002, Cincinnati, OH 45221-0002.) Unpublished manuscript.

Helge, D. (1992). *Child sexual abuse in America—A call for school and community action.* Bellingham, WA: National Rural Development Institute.

Hill, J. L., & Jason, L. A. (1987). An evaluation of a school-aged child sexual abuse primary prevention program. *Psychotherapy Bulletin, 22,* 36–38.

Kendall-Tackett, K. A., Williams, L. M., & Finkelhor, D. (1993). Impact of sexual abuse on children: A review and synthesis of recent empirical studies. *Psychological Bulletin, 13,* 164–180.

Kolko, D. J. (1988). Educational programs to promote awareness and prevention of child sexual victimization: A review and methodological critique. *Clinical Psychology Review, 8,* 195–209.

Kolko, D. J., Moser, J. T., & Hughes, J. (1989). Classroom training in sexual victimization awareness and prevention skills: An extension of the Red Flag/Green Flag people program. *Journal of Family Violence, 4,* 25–45.

Krivacska, J. J. (1990). *Designing child sexual abuse prevention programs: Current approaches and a proposal for the prevention, education, and identification of sexual misuse.* Springfield, IL: Charles C Thomas.

MacMillan, H. L., MacMillan, J. H., Offord, D. R., Griffith, L., & MacMillan, A. (1994). Primary prevention of child sexual abuse: A critical review. Part II. *Journal of Child Psychology and Psychiatry, 35,* 857–876.

Melton, G. B. (1992). The improbability of prevention of sexual abuse. In D. J. Willis, E. W. Holden, & M. Rosenberg (Eds.), *Prevention of child maltreatment: Developmental and ecological perspectives* (pp. 168–189). New York: Wiley.

Miller-Perrin, C. L., & Wurtele, S. K. (1988). The child sexual abuse prevention movement: A critical analysis of primary and secondary approaches. *Clinical Psychology Review, 8,* 313–329.

Miller-Perrin, C. L., & Wurtele, S. K. (1990). Reactions to childhood sexual abuse: Implications for post-traumatic stress disorder. In C. Meek (Ed.), *Post-traumatic stress disorder: Assessment, differential diagnosis, forensic evaluation* (pp. 91–135). Sarasota, FL: Professional Resource Exchange.

Morison, S., & Greene, E. (1992). Juror and expert knowledge of child sexual abuse. *Child Abuse and Neglect, 16,* 595–613.

National Center for Missing and Exploited Children. (1999). *Guidelines for programs to reduce child victimization: A resource for communities when choosing a program to teach personal safety to children.* (Available from NCMEC, 9176 Alternate A1A, Suite 100, Lake Park, FL 33403-1445)

O'Donohue, W., Geer, J. H., & Elliott, A. (1992). The primary prevention of child sexual abuse. In W. O'Donohue & J. H. Geer (Eds.), *The sexual abuse of children. Vol. II: Clinical issues* (pp. 477–517). Hillsdale, NJ: Erlbaum.

Ratto, R., & Bogat, G. A. (1990). An evaluation of a preschool curriculum to educate children in the prevention of sexual abuse. *Journal of Community Psychology, 18,* 289–297.

Reppucci, N.D., & Haugaard, J. J. (1989). Prevention of child sexual abuse: Myth or reality. *American Psychologist, 44,* 1266–1275.

Rispens, J., Aleman, A., & Goudena, P. P. (1997). Prevention of child sexual abuse victimization: A meta-analysis of school programs. *Child Abuse and Neglect, 21,* 975–987.

Romano, N., Casey, K., & Daro, D. (1990). *Schools and child abuse: A national survey of principals' attitudes, beliefs, and practices.* Chicago: National Committee for the Prevention of Child Abuse.

Sarno, J. A., & Wurtele, S. K. (1997). Effects of a personal safety program on preschoolers' knowledge, skills, and perceptions of child sexual abuse. *Child Maltreatment, 2,* 35–45.

Sorenson, T., & Snow, B. (1991). How children tell: The process of disclosure in child sexual abuse. *Child Welfare, 70,* 3–15.

Tharinger, D. J., Krivacska, J. J., Laye-McDonough, M., Jamison, J., Vincent, G. G., & Hedlund, A. D. (1988). Prevention of child sexual abuse: An analysis of issues, educational programs, and research findings. *School Psychology Review, 17,* 614–634.

Tutty, L. M. (1993). Are child sexual abuse prevention programs effective? A review of the research. *Revue Sexologique, 1,* 93–114.

U.S. Department of Health and Human Services. (2001). *Child maltreatment 1999.* Washington, DC: U.S. Government Printing Office.

U.S. General Accounting Office. (1996). *Preventing child sexual abuse: Research inconclusive about effectiveness of child education programs.* Washington, DC: Author.

Williams, L. M. (1994). Recall of childhood trauma: A prospective study of women's memories of child sexual abuse. *Journal of Consulting and Clinical Psychology, 62,* 1167–1176.

Wolfe, V. V., & Birt, J. (1995). The psychological sequelae of child sexual abuse. In T. H. Ollendick & R. J. Prinz (Eds.), *Advances in clinical child psychology* (Vol. 17, pp. 233–263). New York: Plenum Press.

Wurtele, S. K. (1987). School-based sexual abuse prevention programs: A review. *Child Abuse and Neglect, 11,* 483–495.

Wurtele, S. K. (1990). Teaching personal safety skills to four-year-old children: A behavioral approach. *Behavior Therapy, 21,* 25–32.

Wurtele, S. K. (1993). Enhancing children's sexual development through child sexual abuse prevention programs. *Journal of Sex Education and Therapy, 19,* 37–46.

Wurtele, S. K. (1998). School-based child sexual abuse prevention programs: Questions, answers, and more questions. In J. R. Lutzker (Ed.), *Handbook of child abuse research and treatment* (pp. 501–516). New York: Plenum Press.

Wurtele, S. K. (1999). Sexual abuse. In R. T. Ammerman & M. Hersen (Eds.),

Handbook of prevention and treatment with children and adolescents: Intervention in the real world context (pp. 357–384). New York: Wiley.

Wurtele, S. K., Currier, L. L., Gillispie, E. I., & Franklin, C. F. (1991). The efficacy of a parent-implemented program for teaching preschoolers personal safety skills. *Behavior Therapy, 22,* 69–83.

Wurtele, S. K., Gillispie, E. I., Currier, L. L., & Franklin, C. F. (1992). A comparison of teachers vs. parents as instructors of a personal safety program for preschoolers. *Child Abuse and Neglect, 16,* 127–137.

Wurtele, S. K., Kast, L. C., & Melzer, A. M. (1992). Sexual abuse prevention education for young children: A comparison of teachers and parents as instructors. *Child Abuse and Neglect, 16,* 865–876.

Wurtele, S. K., Kast, L. C., Miller-Perrin, C. L., & Kondrick, P. A. (1989). A comparison of programs for teaching personal safety skills to preschoolers. *Journal of Consulting and Clinical Psychology, 57,* 505–511.

Wurtele, S. K., Kvaternick, M., & Franklin, C. F. (1992). Sexual abuse prevention for preschoolers: A survey of parents' behaviors, attitudes, and beliefs. *Journal of Child Sexual Abuse, 1,* 113–128.

Wurtele, S. K., Marrs, S. R., & Miller-Perrin, C. L. (1987). Practice makes perfect? The role of participant modeling in sexual abuse prevention programs. *Journal of Consulting and Clinical Psychology, 55,* 599–602.

Wurtele, S. K., Melzer, A. M., & Kast, L. C. (1992). Preschoolers' knowledge of and ability to learn genital terminology. *Journal of Sex Education and Therapy, 18,* 118–122.

Wurtele, S. K., & Miller-Perrin, C. L. (1992). *Preventing child sexual abuse: Sharing the responsibility.* Lincoln: University of Nebraska Press.

Wurtele, S. K., & Owens, J. S. (1997). Teaching personal safety skills to young children: An investigation of age and gender across five studies. *Child Abuse and Neglect, 21,* 805–814.

2

RECONCEPTUALIZING CHILD SEXUAL ABUSE AS A PUBLIC HEALTH CONCERN

KEITH KAUFMAN, MICHELLE BARBER, HEATHER MOSHER, AND MEGAN CARTER

Child sexual abuse (CSA) can be defined as sexual contact with a child or adolescent that occurs because of coercion or force or within the context of a relationship that is exploitative because of an age difference or caretaking responsibility (Finkelhor, 1992). A broad range of sexual activities may be involved in abuse, from "noncontact" offenses (e.g., voyeurism) to acts of varying physical intrusiveness (e.g., from fondling to intercourse; Walker, Bonner, & Kaufman, 1988). Legal definitions vary from state to state but often include similar elements. Criminal charges are determined based on the ages of the victim and the offender, the victim–offender relationship, the type of sexual act perpetrated, and the frequency of the abuse. Although adult males represent the largest group of child sexual offenders, estimates

The authors express their thanks to colleagues who were willing to provide prevention information as well as comments on a draft of this chapter: Rodney Hammond, PhD, Centers for Disease Control and Prevention; Fran Henry, MBA, STOP IT NOW!; Gail Ryan, MA, Kempe Children's Center; and Joan Tabachnik, MPPM, STOP IT NOW!

suggest that juveniles are responsible for 20%–30% of all rapes and 30%–60% of all cases of CSA committed each year (Becker, Kaplan, Cunningham-Rathner, & Kavoussi, 1986; Brown, Flanagan, & McLeod, 1984; Fehrenbach, Smith, Monastersky, & Deisher, 1986). Evidence also suggests that females perpetrate less than 15% of CSA (Finkelhor, 1984).

The accuracy of CSA rates have long been considered suspect because of concerns related to underreporting as well as wide variation in approaches to detection and the collection of such data. It is clear, however, that CSA is a national problem of immense proportions. Results of the most recent *National Incidence Study of Child Abuse and Neglect* revealed a fivefold increase in reports of sexual abuse between 1980 and 1993 (Sedlak & Broadhurst, 1996). This same report identified 300,200 cases of sexual abuse nationally in 1993. However, other sources suggest that rates are most likely much higher. For example, Elliott and Briere (1995) found, according to a mail survey ($N = 505$), that 30% ($n = 84$) of females and 14% ($n = 32$) of males indicated that they had experienced some form of hands-on sexual abuse.

In addition to the alarming rates of CSA, empirical findings suggest that sexual abuse may be associated with short- and long-term psychological and psychosocial consequences for victims and their families. These effects may include a broad array of problems: internalizing disorders (e.g., depression, anxiety), acting-out behaviors (e.g., prostitution, running away from home), socialization difficulties, parent–child conflict, marital disruption, and sexual dysfunction (Briere & Runtz, 1988; Browne & Finkelhor, 1986; Chandy, Blum, & Resnick, 1996; Kendall-Tackett, Williams, & Finkelhor, 1993).

PREVENTION AS A RESPONSE TO CSA

Recognition of the prevalence and consequences of CSA in the early to mid-1980s led to the development of school-based prevention programs (e.g., Reppucci & Haugaard, 1989; Wurtele, 1987). These programs combined clinical lore, case reports, and descriptive studies of offender characteristics, with methods adapted from the rape prevention movement, and initially provided elementary-age children with skills and information to resist CSA. Program content included a broad array of topics including abuse definition, body ownership, private body part identification, touch continuum, saying "no," disclosing secrets, and reassurance that abuse is always the responsibility of the offender (Conte, Rosen, Saperstein, & Shermack, 1985; Ray-Keil, 1988). A secondary purpose of these programs was to foster disclosure of ongoing abuse in children who otherwise may not have opportunities to reveal abusive situations.

As these initial programs were expanded and refined, their focus broadened to provide programming for children from preschool through junior high. Content was also improved to ensure developmental appropriateness as well as to take advantage of research describing optimal approaches for teaching prevention skills (see Rispens, Aleman, & Goudena, 1997; Wurtele, chapter 1, this volume, for reviews). In sum, programs of this nature have been particularly appealing given their ability to affect a large number of children at a relatively low cost (Wurtele, chapter 1, this volume); demonstrate that children can learn the skills and information being taught (Heidotting & Soled, 1996; Rispens et al., 1997; Wurtele, 1998, 1999); provide programming with an minimum of negative side effects (Hazzard, Kleemeier, & Webb, 1990); avoid stigma by offering information to all children; and encourage disclosure of ongoing abuse (Kolko, Moser, & Hughes, 1989).

Evidence of the positive impact of such programs on "real-world" prevention behavior has been suggested in two different studies. First, Finkelhor and Dziuba-Leatherman (1995) conducted a nationally representative telephone survey of 2,000 children from ages 10 to 16 years regarding prevention program attendance and the use of program content. Their findings revealed that many respondents (40%) had used what they learned in prevention programs to keep themselves safe in situations that posed a threat. Second, research by Gibson and Leitenberg (2000) investigated differences in the incidence of CSA for women who had and had not participated in prevention programs. From a sample of more than 800 undergraduate women, Gibson and Leitenberg found that those women who did not attend a school-based prevention program reported a history of sexual abuse almost twice as often (16%) as those women who participated in such a program (9%).

Although these findings offer some evidence to support the efficacy of school-based sexual abuse prevention programs, they are by no means conclusive. Moreover, the lack of empirical evidence for a direct connection between school-based prevention programs and reductions in the incidence of CSA is particularly troublesome given the field's reliance on this approach for more than 20 years.

A closer examination of the literature, however, reveals concerns about school-based, child-targeted prevention efforts since the mid-1980s. These programs have been sharply criticized for an overreliance on anecdotal clinical information and a lack of empirical support for the prevention techniques used in their curricula (Berliner & Conte, 1988; Conte, 1984; Conte, Wolf, & Smith, 1989). It has also been pointed out that empirical data describing offenders' patterns of perpetration are sorely lacking and that this information needs to be incorporated into prevention programming to ensure its ecological validity (Reppucci & Haugaard, 1989). Concerns have also been expressed regarding the logic underlying the assumption that elementary school-age children are in a position to keep themselves safe from the abusive advances of older teenagers and adults (Reppucci, Woolard, & Fried, 1999). Perpetration of most abuse by a trusted adult reduces children's potential to resist abusive advances. Moreover, obvious differences in cognitive, emotional, and experiential sophistication, as well as discrepancies in physical size, place children at a disadvantage that cannot be breached simply by providing classroom-based information and brief skills training.

Despite the importance of these issues, the greatest challenge to the field is the almost exclusive reliance on school prevention efforts. This focus has resulted in a reluctance to explore a broader array of preventive interventions, target groups, and vehicles for dissemination. As with many areas that have developed because of a critical clinical need, CSA prevention has suffered from the lack of a theoretical framework to organize and guide its trajectory. The call for divergent thinking in CSA prevention is not new (Wurtele & Miller-Perrin, 1992), yet the suggestion of adapting a framework to foster its expansion is recent and holds considerable promise (Mercy, 1999).

CONSIDERING THE PUBLIC HEALTH MODEL

The public health model represents a systematic approach to addressing matters of broad public concern. The Centers for Disease Control and Prevention (CDC) has used this framework since the late 1940s to identify critical risk factors underlying widespread infectious diseases (e.g., tuberculosis, malaria, polio) as well as diseases resulting from risky health behaviors (e.g., lung cancer). The approach has also guided the development of comprehensive interventions to stem the tide of such outbreaks (Epidemiology Program Office, 1999). Successful efforts have been described as owing their efficacy to key elements that include a comprehensive approach; an interdisciplinary focus; and interventions that address attitudes, behaviors, and social norms (Prothrow-Stith, 1995).

Despite this model's effectiveness, nonmedical concerns have been considered within this model only since the mid-1990s. At that time, both the CDC in 1995 (Foege, Rosenberg, & Mercy, 1995) and the World Health Assembly in 1996 identified violence as a public health problem. This designation invited the application of the public health model to both youth violence and violence against women.

Redefining these problems as public health concerns has had significant implications for these areas with regard to public policy, funding, and approach. For example, the federal Violence Against Women Act (1994) reflected the first comprehensive legislative plan designed to set into motion a national agenda for combating violence perpetrated against women. Similar attention to youth violence in the Juvenile Crime Bill (1997) has fostered the development of research and interventions to address various forms of youth violence. In both cases, millions of dollars have been allotted to support research as well as a systematic program of pilot interventions with associated evaluation components. Designation as a public health concern has done a great deal to foster a more systemic approach to the problems of youth violence and violence against women.

ADVANTAGES OF THE PUBLIC HEALTH APPROACH

The public health approach advocates a focus on primary prevention (i.e., interventions to ameliorate the risk factors that lead to a problem). This is in stark contrast to approaches that typically involve intervention after the problem has occurred (e.g., incarceration of offenders, treatment of victims). At the same time, the public health model recognizes that a two-track approach (Mercy, 1993) focusing on both proximal and distal concerns is necessary to eradicate problems of this scope. Such an approach offers opportunities for "comprehensive efforts at all risk levels," which is described by Prothrow-Stith (1995, p. 98) as integral to successful application of the model.

Figure 2.1 graphically represents a comprehensive two-track model. The distal track emphasizes an investment in long-term primary prevention strategies to be directed toward the public at large. The goal is to prevent the development of risk factors associated with the problem. Intervention strategies center on changing attitudes, increasing knowledge, changing behaviors, and influencing social norms. Examples include efforts to foster acceptance of diversity, teach elementary school children nonviolent problem solving, develop peer mentoring programs, enhance parents' child-rearing skills, and advocate reductions in violent television programming.

The proximal track reflects a strong and direct response to the immediate aspects of the problem (Mercy, 1993). Sometimes described as "secondary prevention," efforts of this nature are intended to intervene with groups already identified as displaying risk-related attitudes or behaviors. The goal is to reduce the presence and salience of these risk factors (e.g., tendency to get into fights or "hang out" with delinquent peers, availability of inexpensive handguns) in an effort to avoid the individual's engagement in behaviors of concern (e.g., physical violence, delinquency, handgun violence). Intervention strategies strive to change risky attitudes and behaviors as well as reduce the risks that familial and social conditions (e.g., poor supervision, tolerance of violence) may foster. Interventions may include a variety of services directed toward at-risk groups, including mentoring programs, teenager and caregiver skill building, and modifying teenagers' peer groups (for a comprehensive review and evaluation of 15 such programs, see Powell, Dahlberg, Friday, Mercy, Thorton, & Crawford, 1996).

The proximal track also encompasses "tertiary prevention" strategies intended to enhance the quality of treatment for both offenders and victims. The goals of these programs are to address the impact of victimization, reduce

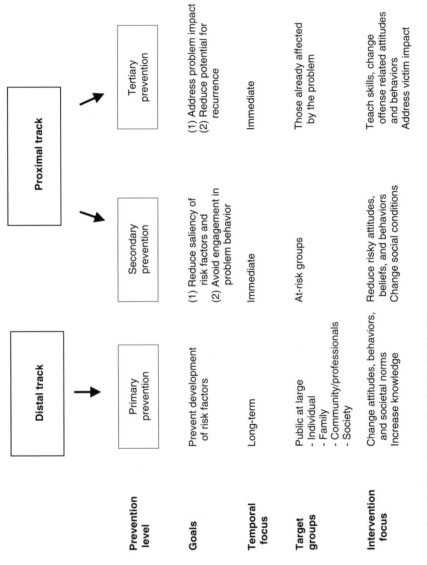

	Distal track	Proximal track	
Prevention level	Primary prevention	Secondary prevention	Tertiary prevention
Goals	Prevent development of risk factors	(1) Reduce saliency of risk factors and (2) Avoid engagement in problem behavior	(1) Address problem impact (2) Reduce potential for recurrence
Temporal focus	Long-term	Immediate	Immediate
Target groups	Public at large - Individual - Family - Community/professionals - Society	At-risk groups	Those already affected by the problem
Intervention focus	Change attitudes, behaviors, and societal norms Increase knowledge	Reduce risky attitudes, beliefs, and behaviors Change social conditions	Teach skills, change offense related attitudes and behaviors Address victim impact

Figure 2.1. A Comprehensive Dual Track Public Health Model.

the likelihood that offenders recidivate, increase the likelihood that victims do not themselves become perpetrators, uncover previously unidentified abuse, and interrupt the intergenerational transmission of violence.

The public health approach draws heavily on scientific methods in identifying critical risk factors and evaluating pilot interventions. In fact, a popular methodology for implementing the primary prevention track of the public health approach (Mercy & Hammond, 1999) includes four dimensions: (a) surveillance (e.g., monitoring incidence and prevalence), (b) identification of risk factors (e.g., factors associated with greater potential for victimization and offending), (c) interventions development and evaluation (e.g., pilot testing of interventions and policies that are based on risk factor research), and (d) wide-scale program implementation (e.g., disseminating nationally, developing guidelines, examining cost-effectiveness, evaluating outcomes). This process guides the development of prevention areas, ensuring progress toward effective interventions that can be disseminated nationally.

In sum, advantages of the public health approach over the justice model include (a) the ability to involve a broader spectrum of individuals, organizations, and institutions in prevention activities; (b) the opportunity to incorporate prevention into everyday settings such as schools, community centers, and neighborhoods; (c) the inclusion of a comprehensive continuum of prevention activities (e.g., primary, secondary, tertiary); and (d) the incorporation of scientifically valid approaches to research design and evaluation.

FRAMING CSA AS A PUBLIC HEALTH CONCERN

Mercy (1999) has suggested that discomfort in addressing sexual issues as well as the perception of CSA as a law enforcement problem has greatly limited the scope of response. He pointed out that society would "spare no expense" (p. 317) to eradicate a childhood disease that affected 20% of girls and 14% of boys; caused intrapersonal, interpersonal, and health-related difficulties; and replicated itself across generations. This description characterizes CSA, but a comprehensive national campaign to address CSA has not been forthcoming. This is particularly curious given that the American Medical Association (Bristow, 1995) has identified CSA as a "violent, silent, epidemic" and that the *Healthy People 2000* report identified CSA as a national priority (U.S. Department of Health and Human Services, 1991).

Only in the past few years has consideration been given to identifying CSA as a public health problem. Henry (1996) framed CSA as a public health problem, citing the limitations of the criminal justice and child protection systems in preventing abuse. McMahon and Puett (1999), in discussing the work of a CDC national task force, described the need for and advantages of framing CSA in this manner. For CSA prevention, the public health approach defines the context of the problem more broadly, with greater potential for involvement by a wider variety of individuals, groups, organizations, and institutions. It also offers the promise of a more systematic approach to creating a comprehensive prevention response to a complex problem of epidemic proportions.

CREATING A TEMPLATE FOR A
PUBLIC HEALTH RESPONSE TO CSA

Application of the public health model to the problem of CSA offers considerable promise. To be successful, however, several changes in the approach to CSA prevention are needed. First, the field will need to encourage the establishment of a national agenda to guide the development of a long-term, systematic response. The CDC has already established a planning task force and developed an initial set of priorities (McMahon & Puett, 1999). This agenda will need to be supported by complementary changes in legislation and public policy (Reppucci, Woolard, & Fried, 1999).

Second, CSA professionals should consider the best means of involving the broadest possible array of individuals, families, organizations, and communities in the prevention process. With greater inclusiveness, the model would predict concomitant increases in preventive effectiveness.

Third, preventive efforts need to recognize and address ethnic and cultural diversity in the establishment of risk factors and the crafting of intervention approaches. Preliminary evidence suggests important ethnic and cultural differences related to CSA, family and community response to abuse, and the need to approach prevention in a culturally sensitive manner (Ahn & Gilbert, 1992; Fontes, 1993, 1995, 1998).

Fourth, the field must adopt a more systematic research methodology that can guide practice. Such an approach should involve the identification of all associated risk factors followed by a comprehensive exploration of potential interventions. Evaluation of these strategies would culminate in the development of effective prevention programs for national dissemination (Mercy, 1993).

Fifth, CSA professionals should view multidisciplinary collaborations as more powerful means of addressing the problem and should be linked to efforts intended to train professionals in the application of the public health model (Yung, Hammond, Sampson, & Warfield, 1998).

Finally, to truly work toward the eradication of CSA, we must initiate and maintain a comprehensive approach addressing all levels of prevention (i.e., primary, secondary, and tertiary).

Figure 2.2 reflects the application of the general public health model to the nuances of CSA with these considerations in mind. To illustrate the

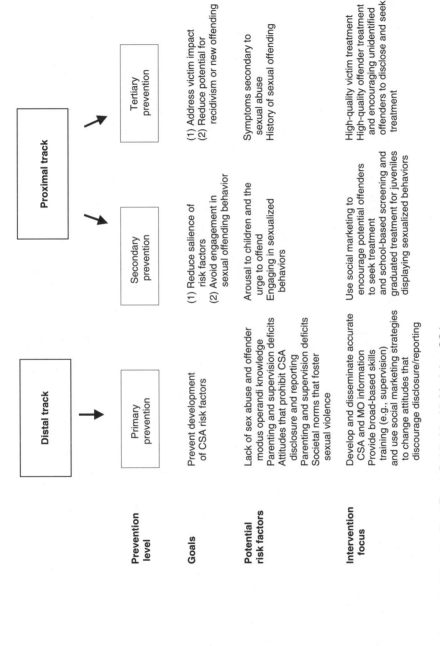

Prevention level	Distal track	Proximal track	
	Primary prevention	Secondary prevention	Tertiary prevention
Goals	Prevent development of CSA risk factors	(1) Reduce salience of risk factors (2) Avoid engagement in sexual offending behavior	(1) Address victim impact (2) Reduce potential for recidivism or new offending
Potential risk factors	Lack of sex abuse and offender modus operandi knowledge Parenting and supervision deficits Attitudes that prohibit CSA disclosure and reporting Parenting and supervision deficits Societal norms that foster sexual violence	Arousal to children and the urge to offend Engaging in sexualized behaviors	Symptoms secondary to sexual abuse History of sexual offending
Intervention focus	Develop and disseminate accurate CSA and MO information Provide broad-based skills training (e.g., supervision) and use social marketing strategies to change attitudes that discourage disclosure/reporting	Use social marketing to encourage potential offenders to seek treatment and school-based screening and graduated treatment for juveniles displaying sexualized behaviors	High-quality victim treatment High-quality offender treatment and encouraging unidentified offenders to disclose and seek treatment

Figure 2.2. Applying the Dual Track Public Health Model to CSA.

potential application of this model, we discuss several promising approaches that go beyond that of the traditional school-based, child-directed prevention efforts below.

DISTAL TRACK INITIATIVES: PRIMARY PREVENTION

Primary prevention efforts represent the hallmark of the public health approach. Although application of such efforts regarding CSA has primarily involved school-based prevention programs, several key directions for expansion are suggested by (a) gaps in existing programs (e.g., the lack of empirical information provided to the public describing offenders' patterns of behavior leading up to sexual offenses), (b) the identification of critical risk factors in related areas (e.g., the importance of supervision and monitoring in differentiating delinquent and nondelinquent juveniles), (c) promising new approaches in the field of child abuse (e.g., changing public attitudes regarding the importance of reporting suspected abuse), and (d) interventions in related areas that may be expanded to include CSA prevention (e.g., efforts to reduce rape-supportive attitudes in college students). Initiatives at this level of prevention may offer the greatest potential to impact the field, largely because of their ability to reach broad segments of the population.

Improving Knowledge: Offenders' Modus Operandi

Parents and caregivers are logical partners in the expansion of CSA prevention efforts (Reppucci, Jones, & Cook, 1994; Wurtele & Miller-Perrin, 1992), yet evidence suggests that they have rarely been included in formalized programs. In fact, Finkelhor and Dziuba-Leatherman (1995) found that only 11% of school-based programs have involved participants' parents, and even then the extent of parental participation varied widely (e.g., from receiving handouts to direct involvement in training).

Parents have expressed a strong interest in educating their children regarding sexual abuse topics (Elrod & Rubin, 1993) yet are often reluctant to discuss sexual issues with their children (e.g., 41%–47% indicated that they did not do so; Finkelhor, 1984; Wurtele & Miller-Perrin, 1992). Parents are also likely to underestimate their own child's risk of abuse (Collins, 1996). When parents do discuss these issues with their children, the content may not be accurate because parents have been found to know little about CSA (Elrod & Rubin, 1993; Finkelhor, 1984; Tabachnick & Dawson, 2000).

Although prevention programs have sought to incorporate available information, empirically based descriptions of abusers' patterns of offending, or modus operandi, have only recently become available. Kaufman and his colleagues (Kaufman, Hilliker, & Daleiden, 1996; Kaufman et al., 1998) reported on a series of large-scale studies of the modus operandi of adult and juvenile sexual offenders. Using questionnaire data that was based on anonymous self-reports, these studies solicited input from offenders in seven states. Findings suggest sophisticated patterns of "grooming" used by juvenile and adult offenders intended to engage victims in sexually abusive behaviors. For example, adult and juvenile offenders reported using approaches designed to "desensitize" the victims to sexualized behavior. In other words, they systematically introduced greater levels of sexual discussion and contact over time. By progressing in small increments and simultaneously engaging in caring, loving behaviors, offenders may be able to normalize sexual behaviors, maintain a caring facade to supervisors, and create frequent opportunities to gauge the potential for discovery. Further, findings revealed juvenile offenders' reliance on pornography to engage victims as well as more frequent use of other modus operandi strategies when compared to their adult counterparts. Offender–victim relatedness was also linked to differences in modus operandi, with extrafamilial offenders relying on substances (e.g., drugs and alcohol), and intrafamilial offenders using gifts to gain compliance in sexually abusive behaviors.

These studies offer a level of detail regarding adult and juvenile sexual offenders' modus operandi that would be of value not only to parents and caregivers but also to family members, professionals, and community members. Information of this nature can be used to alert the public to the common patterns that offenders use to gain access to and manipulate children and ensure their compliance in sexually abusive behaviors. It also offers a means of directly dispelling myths often associated with sexual offending. In many cases, these strategies involve approaches that are observable to family or neighbors but, given the lack of context, they are rarely considered as part of an abusive process.

Continued efforts are warranted to expand the knowledge regarding the nuances of offenders' modus operandi. The CDC is currently funding its first study of risk factors related to CSA (Kaufman et al., 1998). This investigation is designed to examine offenders' modus operandi (and caretaker supervision patterns) across three ethnic and cultural groups (e.g., Hispanic/ Latino, African American, European American) from a variety of perspectives (e.g., adult and juvenile offenders, caregivers of victims) in multiple states. Additional work in this area will be critical to guide the development of pilot intervention programs. At the same time, efforts need to be actively undertaken to disseminate empirically based information describing sexual offense-related risks and offenders' modus operandi.

Improving Knowledge: School-Based Approaches

School-based CSA prevention initiatives offer a unique opportunity to directly access children and teenagers. These programs, however, may be most appropriate for middle and high school students (Reppucci, Woolard,

& Fried, 1999), who are in a better position than younger children to cognitively and emotionally incorporate information of this nature. Content should be expanded to include empirically based information describing offenders' modus operandi. Particular attention should be paid to the patterns intrafamilial offenders use, because evidence suggests that almost 80% of CSA is perpetrated by relatives of the victim (including mother's boyfriends and stepfathers; Martone, Jaudes, & Calvin, 1996).

Rather than making children and teenagers responsible for their own safety, school programs should simultaneously provide information about offenders' modus operandi to parents, caregivers, and other family members. Children should continue to be given explicit permission to disclose abuse, no matter who is the perpetrator. At the same time, programs should make clear that the adults around them are responsible for ensuring their safety. Programs should provide information to older children and teenagers so that they can understand the process of abuse and alert adults to intervene if they become uncomfortable with someone's behavior or suspicious about his or her intent. Adults in the family and the community need permission to act on their suspicions as well as guidance regarding how to proceed. Evidence suggests that programs need to develop approaches to overcome adults' reluctance to report potential abuse as a key barrier to success (Chasan-Taber & Tabachnick, 1999).

Finally, program staff should consider incorporating developmentally appropriate information on healthy relationships and intimacy. This information could serve as a proactive means of shaping positive attitudes that may ultimately lead to reductions in intimate violence. Enhancing adolescents' knowledge may offer more appropriate models for relationships and discourage abusive acts by clarifying the consequences. At the same time, a better understanding of healthy relationships offers children and teenagers an informed perspective that fosters early identification of inappropriate or abusive advances.

Changing Behaviors: Caregiver Supervision and Monitoring

Researchers have highlighted the role of caregivers' supervision and monitoring as a critical factor for inhibiting adolescents' antisocial and delinquent behavior (Fisher, 1983; Forehand, Miller, Dutra, & Chance, 1997; Patterson & Bank, 1986; Patterson & Dishion, 1985; Patterson & Stouthamer-Loeber, 1984). Patterson and his colleagues (Patterson & Bank, 1986; Patterson & Dishion, 1985; Patterson & Stouthamer-Loeber, 1984) referred to *parental supervision* as "monitoring" and defined it as the extent to which a caregiver is aware of the child's whereabouts and deviant behavior in and outside of the home and the extent to which the parent supervises the child's activity (Patterson & Dishion, 1985). Although a variety of parenting variables have been considered (e.g., communication, discipline practices), Forehand and his colleagues (1997) suggest that monitoring is the primary parenting variable in the child-rearing process.

CSA, like most delinquent activity, involves identifiable behaviors that the offender must conceal from responsible adults. Inadequate adult supervision of the juvenile offender or the victim presents an opportunity for the abuse to occur and decreases the potential for detection. Adolescents who are not closely supervised will have many more opportunities to sexually offend than adolescents whose behavior and whereabouts are rigorously monitored. Likewise, children who lack adequate supervision may be targeted as "easy" sexual abuse victims by either juvenile or adult offenders (Finkelhor, 1984).

Consideration should also be given to the ease with which juvenile as well as adult offenders are able to attain positions of authority that afford access to potential victims. Screening of volunteers and employees who work with children (e.g., police background checks) is an important initial step to enhance children's safety. However, organizations and businesses also need policies that create a high level of safety by reducing the potential for staff and volunteers to be alone with the children who participate in their programs. More active approaches to employee and volunteer supervision and better training regarding offenders' modus operandi may also help to reduce the potential for abuse in these contexts.

Changing Public Attitudes: STOP IT NOW!

In 1995, STOP IT NOW!, a nonprofit organization founded and directed by Fran Henry, initiated the first public health campaign designed to change the public's knowledge and attitudes about CSA (Chasan-Taber & Tabachnick, 1999). Borrowing from the models used to promote the prevention of drunk driving, unsafe sex practices, and the incorrect use of child safety seats, STOP IT NOW! used various forms of media to educate the public and change attitudes about CSA. Baseline information describing the general population's knowledge of CSA and their awareness of the problem was collected via telephone interview (random digit dialing). Of a representative sample of 200 Vermont residents, 67.3% agreed to participate in the telephone interview. Results indicated that respondents strongly supported programming that would hold adults, rather than children, responsible for the prevention of CSA. Findings also suggested that respondents had some degree of familiarity with issues related to sexual abuse. However, informational gaps were identified in respondents' ability to define abuse, identify warning signs, and acknowledge that offenders lived in their community.

Over 4 years, STOP IT NOW! used a systematic program of broad media coverage and information provided through organizations working with at-risk families to attempt to educate individuals living in Vermont. This approach involved news programs, public service announcements on television and radio, news stories and editorials in newspapers, bus advertising, an interactive web site, newsletters, guidebooks, and posters. The Vermont population as a whole was targeted through the media, while specific at-risk groups were contacted via community agencies.

Results of a follow-up survey in 1999 (Tabachnick & Dawson, 2000) suggested several dramatic changes in Vermonters' knowledge, including (a) a 40% increase in the number who could define CSA, (b) a 10% increase in the number who could identify at lease one warning sign of abuse (38%), and (c) a 6% increase in the number who recognized that offenders are likely to live in their neighborhood (74%). The same survey, however, uncovered continuing concerns regarding respondents' attitudes about reporting suspected CSA. Only 66% of Vermonters surveyed indicated that they would take some direct action if they suspected abuse. This figure dropped to 43% when the abuser described in the situation was someone that they knew. This was in contrast to 96% of the respondents who stated that they would act if they thought someone was drunk and trying to drive. Also of concern was the fact that 66% of the respondents were themselves victims of sexual assault, yet they had failed to disclose the abuse.

Social marketing efforts used by STOP IT NOW! show great promise for improving knowledge and influencing attitudes about CSA in general. At the same time, their findings indicate the need for more focused efforts to affect attitudes and behaviors related to the disclosure of abuse as well as the reporting of suspected abuse. It is unclear if more positive outcomes could result from increased specificity in the marketing campaigns or if other approaches would have a more significant impact. It does seem likely that changes in social policy that encourage community involvement and protect against litigation may foster increased public involvement when it comes to addressing CSA.

Reducing Socialization to Violence

Familial, community, and societal factors have been linked to violence, despite an almost exclusive focus by prevention programs on risks at the individual level (Hammond & Yung, 1993; Lowry, Sleet, Duncan, Powell, & Kolbe, 1995). Much of the research has targeted juveniles and has related violence to economic distress, exposure to violence in the community, chronic stress, availability of substances, and media representations condoning violence (Guerra, Attar, & Weissberg, 1997; Reppucci, Woolard, & Fried, 1999). The sexual offender literature has also suggested that societal norms sanctioning rape, negative attitudes toward women, and viewing women and children as men's property contribute to the etiology of sexual offending (Schwartz, 1995; White & Koss, 1993). Concerns of this nature underscore the need to address society's acceptance of violence toward women and children.

Prevention approaches to related problems with similar risk factors (e.g., rape) may offer new directions for CSA prevention. For example, rape prevention programs designed for use with college students frequently combine attempts to debunk myths, change attitudes, provide sexual education, and build empathy (Lonsway, 1996; Schewe & O'Donohue, 1993). These programs have demonstrated some ability to change beliefs and attitudes supportive of rape (Hanson & Gidycz, 1993; Lonsway et al., 1998). The format and content of these programs may easily accommodate the inclusion of additional information specific to CSA prevention (e.g., legal consequences of sexual behavior with minors, impact of sexual victimization on children and young teenagers). Systematic efforts are needed to incorporate this information into programs directed at large groups of older teenagers, college students, and young adults. Research designs comparing intervention strategies, program content, and program–recipient fit could clarify the overall efficacy of this strategy and determine how approaches can be tailored to fit the needs of participants.

Advocacy efforts intended to influence policies regarding physical and sexual violence in the media may also be effective in reducing messages that sanction rape, child abuse, and violence toward women. Tabachnick and Dawson (2000) demonstrated that collaboration with the media can result in increased air time for messages intended to inform the public and encourage offenders to seek treatment. However, in a country where violent programming sells advertising and translates into box office hits, carefully designed research to support legislative mandates for change may be needed. It is also important to recognize the need to educate parents and caregivers regarding the importance of these decisions. Movie rating systems and parental warnings on compact discs with explicit lyrics are of little value when parents fail to adequately supervise their children or choose to ignore these warnings. Changing society's socialization to violence must be directed at adults as well as children and teenagers if it is to impact the problem.

PROXIMAL TRACK INITIATIVES: SECONDARY PREVENTION

Limited financial resources, as well as the need to ensure that more potent interventions are offered when indicated, highlight the value of secondary prevention efforts. These initiatives target participants based on the presence of well-defined risk factors. Although some secondary prevention programs have been criticized for creating stigma simply by identifying participants, framing programs as supportive in nature (e.g., "Family Support Center") and targeting large groups of individuals (e.g., families exposed to inner city violence) may reduce the potential for adverse effects (Reppucci, Woolard, & Fried, 1999). Programs at this level have been directed toward adults who may be struggling with deviant arousal to children (i.e., but have not yet offended), juveniles exhibiting sexualized behaviors, and college students with attitudes that may suggest a proclivity toward offending (i.e., acceptance of rape myths).

STOP IT NOW! Outreach to Potential Abusers

As a complement to its primary prevention initiatives, STOP IT NOW! has provided outreach services to individuals who are either at risk to offend or have already perpetrated sexual abuse but have not been detected. This dimension of their program has combined an active social marketing component with a toll-free telephone help line and a social policy change agenda. The social marketing strategy involved provocative ads that highlighted the effectiveness of treatment, encouraged abusers to stop hurting children, urged offenders to get help, and prompted family members to call for assistance (Tabachnick & Dawson, 2000). Information was also disseminated through various community organizations and agencies that worked with at-risk families. The help line was designed to take calls from abusers and potential abusers, as well as other concerned individuals calling for assistance or general information. Self-identified abusers were assigned a confidential identification number to encourage them to contact providers for information on treatment without the fear of being turned in to authorities. This approach was taken to foster abusers' access to information regarding assessment and treatment and to encourage them to work toward disclosure of their offenses. Efforts to change social policy centered on reducing barriers to offender disclosure and supportive treatment intake.

Over the 4 years since its inception, the STOP IT NOW! help line received 657 calls (Tabachnick & Dawson, 2000). Of these calls, 15% were from abusers, 50% were from people who knew an offender or a victim, and 35% were information calls or calls from agency staff. It is impossible to directly track outcomes of abusers who contacted the help line (because of their anonymity), but the State Attorney's office reported that 15 adults and 10 adolescents self-reported CSA to authorities during this time. In addition, clinicians across the state reported that 20 adult offenders self-reported their offense and 98 juveniles entered treatment without a direct victim report.

The outreach strategies of STOP IT NOW! represent the first time that prevention programming has been directed toward sexual abusers. Given the high costs associated with CSA (in human as well as fiscal terms), even conservative estimates regarding program outcomes suggest that this is a strategy in need of refinement, replication, and expansion. Currently, efforts are under way to replicate this model in other cities and further evaluate its efficacy.

Identifying and Responding to At-Risk Behaviors in the School

Sexual education in school has always stirred controversy and created anxiety for parents as well as teachers. School-based sexual education programs have focused mainly on informing children about the physiology of reproduction, but few programs have addressed attitudes, beliefs, or behaviors relevant to the quality of sexual relationships and interactions. Ryan (2000a) reported that many educators do not clearly understand the normal development of childhood sexuality and hence feel uneasy and unprepared to respond to children's sexual behavior. On the basis of these observations, the Kempe Center (Ryan, 2000a) facilitated a review of the literature relevant to childhood sexuality and sexually abusive behaviors to begin identifying sexual behaviors that might be considered "normal" during childhood.

The literature review revealed a paucity of research describing the expected range of sexual behaviors during childhood. Studies did, however, suggest a continuous developmental path for sexuality beginning with arousal in utero and early autoerotic behaviors by toddlers and preschool children (Ford & Beach, 1963; Galenson & Riophe, 1974; Kinsey, Pomeroy, & Martin, 1948; Kinsey, Pomeroy, Martin, & Gebhard, 1953). Despite scientific attempts to acknowledge this continuous process, a denial of childhood sexuality by parents and pediatricians remains the norm. As a result, caregivers as well as professionals who work with children often feel ill prepared to respond to sexualized behaviors.

In 1993, the Kempe Center began piloting a training curriculum to address these issues within Colorado's largest school (Fujioka et al., 1993). The curriculum developed, "Understanding and Responding to the Sexual Behaviors of Children" (Ryan et al., 1988/1993), assists teachers and parents in identifying potentially troublesome behaviors among elementary school-age children. It also teaches professionals the skills and strategies necessary for addressing such behaviors. Curriculum goals regarding the identification of at-risk behaviors are derived from studies identifying common characteristics among sexual abusers (Briggs, 1975; Landry & Peters, 1992; Steele, 1987). These characteristics include (a) the inability to articulate needs and emotions, (b) the inability to read and interpret cues in others that indicate their needs and emotions, and (c) a distorted attribution of responsibility. Professionals are taught to recognize children at risk and intervene to improve children's communication skills, foster their empathy, encourage the verbal expression of their needs, and support them to take responsibility for their actions.

The Kempe Center's approach is not to introduce new information to children but to provide a base of knowledge for adults to facilitate adults' response to what children are doing or saying by rewarding or correcting behavior. The primary goal is to provide progressive levels of intervention, giving children who are exhibiting problematic sexual behaviors multiple opportunities to change those behaviors. Teachers and support staff actively monitor and respond to sexual behaviors exhibited by the children. Those children who do not respond to teacher interventions are invited to participate in a psychoeducational group at the school. If additional therapeutic intervention is warranted after the school-based group is completed, children are referred to a more intensive treatment group at the mental health center. Finally, children whose behavior cannot be brought under control in this fashion are referred to the local Department of Social Services for possible alternative placement.

Successes have been noted in response to the Kempe Center pilot curriculum. Reports have indicated significant changes in behavior, often with minimal interventions (Ryan, 2000a, 2000b). Although preliminary findings are promising, a rigorous evaluation is needed to systematically clarify outcomes that are based on this type of intervention.

Changing Attitudes in At-Risk College Students

As previously mentioned, rape prevention programs on college campuses have sought to reduce attitudes thought to be associated with sexual offending. Although most programs were designed to provide information to the broad range of students on college campuses, at least one study attempted to target students at higher risk (Schewe & O'Donohue, 1993). These authors compared the attitudes of high-risk male college students following an empathy intervention, a "facts" intervention, or a no-treatment control condition. Interestingly enough, this intervention included empathy information regarding victims of CSA as well as rape and sexual harassment. Interventions were found to be effective in reducing high-risk students' potential to commit CSA. However, results indicated that students identified as high-risk for rape also reported fantasizing about sexual play with children significantly more often than did low-risk students. Taken together with previous findings that suggest that a small portion of college students (7%) would abuse a child if there were no chance of being caught (Briere & Runtz, 1989), rape prevention programs for college students reflect an important access point for future CSA prevention efforts.

PROXIMAL TRACT INITIATIVES: TERTIARY PREVENTION

Tertiary prevention efforts are most frequently conceptualized as services provided after the behavior in question has occurred. In the case of CSA, services typically include treatment of identified victims and offenders as well as school-based efforts to encourage unidentified victims to reveal their abuse. Although the public health model advocates for the investment of greater resources at the primary prevention end of the spectrum, it clearly recognizes the importance of providing a comprehensive array of services across the prevention continuum (Prothrow-Stith, 1995). In fact, high-quality treatment of victims and offenders is critical not only for addressing the immediate impact of the abuse and maintaining community safety but also for reducing the potential of intergenerational transmission of abusive patterns. Although few methodologically strong outcome evaluations are available, those that exist seem to offer positive outcomes for both victim and offender treatment.

Treating Sexual Offenders

Programs designed to treat adult and adolescent sexual offenders have grown from a handful in 1975 (Knopp, 1985) to more than 1,000 by the mid-1990s (Freeman-Longo, Bird, Stevenson, & Fiske, 1995). Programs have varied in content but have typically addressed three major areas: (a) the reduction of sexual offense-related factors (e.g., deviant arousal and fantasies, thinking errors); (b) the development of prosocial skills (e.g., anger management, healthy sexuality, dating skills, social skills, relapse prevention); and (c) the establishment of community and family support networks (Hanson & Bussiere, 1998; Worling & Curwen, 2000).

Recent reviews of adult and juvenile sexual offender outcome studies suggest the efficacy of treatment. Hanson and Bussiere's (1998) meta-analysis of 87 studies of almost 29,000 adult sexual offenders over a 4–5-year follow-up period identified sexual recidivism rates of 13%, nonsexual violent recidivism rates of 12%, and an overall recidivism rate of 36%. Juvenile sexual offender recidivism rates across 10 outcome studies (e.g., reported in Worling & Curwen, 2000) averaged 8%, and nonsexual recidivism rates for treated offenders averaged 28%, with follow-up periods ranging from several weeks to 5 years.

Relatively low sexual offense recidivism rates suggest the efficacy of treatment for many sexual offenders; however, several concerns warrant further discussion. First, given the rigor involved with publishing an article in a professional journal, recidivism rates reported in the literature may reflect offenders participating in better quality programs. Treatment standards, such as those provided by the Association for the Treatment of Sexual Abusers (ATSA, 2001), need to be mandated on a national basis to ensure uniformity in the quality of programming.

Second, national trends toward "truth in sentencing" (i.e., requirements that offenders serve complete sentences) have reduced the "good time" (e.g., early release for good behavior and participation in treatment programming) that often motivated offenders to complete treatment. As a result, offenders are reentering communities having never received treatment specifically for sexual offenders. Legislative advocacy is needed to mandate sexual offender treatment for all incarcerated offenders.

Third, group-based services in which all offenders receive the same series of treatment modules are still the norm in sexual offender treatment. Systematic research is needed to determine the optimal mix of offender presenting problems and tailored treatment response (Weinrott, 1996). Greater attention to strategies for tailoring treatment (e.g., including interventions to address nonsexual offending) may also offer a means of reducing relatively high rates of nonsexual recidivism reported in the literature (Hanson & Bussiere, 1998; Worling & Curwen, 2000).

Finally, enhancing juvenile offender treatment programs will require attention to additional issues specific to this population, including the need to differentiate best practices for juvenile as opposed to adult offenders, to assess the value of requiring juveniles to participate in community registration and notification (both in terms of their outcomes and community safety), and to develop strategies to successfully reintegrate incarcerated juvenile sexual offenders into their families and the community.

Treating Victims of Sexual Abuse

Victim treatment initiatives proliferated following the adoption of mandatory child abuse reporting laws in the mid- to late 1970s. Since that time, treatment approaches have varied considerably in their theoretical foundation (e.g., from psychoanalytic to cognitive behavioral) as well as in their mode of service delivery (e.g., individual, group, family; Saunders & Williams, 1996). Despite the passage of more than 20 years, a recent review of the literature was able to identify only 29 victim treatment studies that met basic standards for outcome research (Finkelhor & Berliner, 1995). The review did, however, suggest that victim treatment has been associated with improvements, especially with regard to symptom reduction. The existing literature does not indicate which treatment approaches or modalities result in better treatment outcomes.

Briere (1996), in a commentary for a special issue of *Child Maltreatment* on treatment outcome research, suggested that studies reflecting more sophisticated clinical and methodological approaches represent the future of the field. He advocated the use of experimental designs, random assignment to groups, multiple measures completed by multiple reporters, use of control groups, attention to therapist bias, the clinical significance of study outcomes, and the generalizability of study findings.

In the same issue, Friedrich (1996), commenting on clinical directions for the treatment of CSA, highlighted the importance of abuse-specific therapy (i.e., approaches that target abuse-related symptoms). He pointed to studies in the special issue that demonstrate reductions in posttraumatic stress disorder (Deblinger, Lippmann, & Steer, 1996) and children's fears and anxieties (Berliner & Saunders, 1996) following sexual abuse as supportive of his contention. His conclusions suggest the need to also ensure that all presenting symptoms are addressed as part of an effective treatment response.

Friedrich also noted that enhancing the efficacy of victim treatment will require additional work to clarify intervention-related questions that remain unanswered. First, what treatment modality (i.e., individual, group, family) or combination of modalities is most effective, and with whom? Second, what assessment approaches foster treatment planning as well as offer indicators of treatment outcome? Furthermore, what assessment measures or approaches can be developed for younger children (i.e., younger than age 8 years) who have previously been excluded from testing because of the lack of appropriate instruments? Third, what role should parents and caregivers play in treatment, and how much treatment should be directed toward parents as opposed to victims? Fourth, how should treatment differ for male and female victims? Fifth, how long should treatment last, and what is the role of booster sessions in maintaining treatment gains? As with other developing areas, it seems that interventions with CSA victims will improve steadily as researchers continue to focus on enhanced methodological rigor in outcome studies and incorporate research findings to improve the quality of clinical treatment.

Fostering Children's Reports of Unidentified CSA

Children's propensity to report CSA following school-based trainings remains a largely ignored aspect of prevention programming. Most studies examining school-based programs have failed to report child disclosures. As a result, it is difficult to evaluate the few that have included such reports. Kolko and his colleagues (Kolko, Moser, & Hughes, 1989) reported a disclosure rate of 11%, in contrast to Gilbert and colleagues' finding of no disclosures at all (Gilbert, Berrick, Le Prohn, & Nyman, 1989).

Efforts to foster abuse disclosure merit greater attention, given that school-based programs may represent the only time that a child or teenager is offered an opportunity to reveal abuse in a safe environment. Ideally, schools should be one of several organizations and institutions that are available to children and teenagers to discuss their safety concerns (i.e., including abuse and neglect) and provide supportive solutions. Other community-based settings that could be developed for this purpose include community centers, libraries, and after-school programs.

Steps toward the establishment of disclosure-friendly settings would necessitate the development of (a) materials advertising these settings as places where children and teenagers could go to seek help, (b) protocols to guide staff and volunteers' response to abuse disclosure, (c) networks and referral procedures to address legal aspects, and (d) training modules for individuals who work or volunteer in these settings. Finally, systematic evaluation research would offer insight into program components' efficacy and offer directions for modification and improvement.

CONCLUSIONS AND RECOMMENDATIONS

In this chapter we proposed the adoption of the public health approach to address the problem of CSA. A dual track model focusing on both proximal and distal factors is offered as a template for the expansion of work in this area and as a vehicle for the inclusion of a broader array of individuals, families, organizations, and communities in the prevention process. This model encompasses the complete prevention continuum (i.e., primary, secondary, tertiary) and allows for the incorporation of existing efforts (e.g., school-based education) and approaches (e.g., the criminal justice response). It advocates for a shift in accountability for children's safety from the children themselves to adults in their lives and the community at large. This notion of broader responsibility for children and teenager's safety invites multidisciplinary participation and challenges the field to craft new types of interventions.

Moving beyond a focus on child-based prevention approaches will require considerably more support for models that recognize the ability of prevention programs to augment and reduce the necessity for more expensive tertiary care services. In Vermont, program staff have experimented with and demonstrated some success in shifting statewide resources from tertiary to primary prevention services without increasing expenses (Hogan, 1997). Other states and the federal government need to be encouraged to adopt proactive strategies that make primary prevention a priority, while recognizing the need to address secondary and tertiary concerns as well.

Changing underlying social norms and attitudes related to violence against women and children is critical to a greater national support for prevention initiatives and for reducing the factors that predispose individuals to sexually offend. STOP IT NOW! (Chasan-Taber & Tabachnick, 1999) has demonstrated the ability to join with the media to foster these public health goals. Greater investment is needed in media partnerships that use social marketing strategies to affect large segments of the population. Approaches of this nature can be used to educate, change attitudes, and advocate for social policy change consistent with the prevention of CSA.

Coordination will also be required in the development of primary and secondary prevention strategies intended to improve skills, foster support, and reduce the influence of contextual risk factors. Development of a national agenda to guide and monitor work in this area would maximize resources and minimize duplication of efforts. This agenda would support the broad-based identification of key risk factors related to CSA. Once CSA risk factors are identified, funding would be required to support pilot interventions intended to ameliorate these risks. Strong evaluation components should be included in pilot investigations so that the most effective prevention approaches can be identified. Finally, as the model suggests, strategies for national dissemination of successful prevention programs should be undertaken along with their own integrated evaluation components.

More effective collaboration between professionals who treat victims and those who treat offenders will also be necessary to ensure successful long-term outcomes. The vast majority of offenders know their victims, and an estimated two thirds of offenders are family members. Our challenge will be to develop new strategies for linking victim and offender treatment in ways that make resulting programs better at reuniting families, integrating offenders into the community, and ensuring ongoing community safety. Clinicians and researchers will also need to collaborate in ways that foster the development of more effective intervention programs. Incorporating evaluation components into community-based treatment and modifying approaches that are based on evaluation findings will strengthen our ability to help victims as well as offenders.

The public health approach offers a myriad of possibilities and the promise of the amelioration of CSA. Attaining these goals will necessitate a sustained commitment to collaboration, advocacy, and a comprehensive continuum of prevention services.

REFERENCES

Ahn, H. N., & Gilbert, N. (1992). Cultural diversity and sexual abuse prevention. *Social Service Review*, 66 (3), 410–427.

Association for the Treatment of Sexual Abusers. (2001). *Professional standards for clinical practice*. Portland, OR: Author.

Becker, J. V., Kaplan, M. S., Cunningham-Rathner, J., & Kavoussi, R. (1986). Characteristics of adolescent incest sexual perpetrators: Preliminary findings. *Journal of Family Violence, 1*(1), 85–97.

Berliner, L., & Conte, J. R. (1988). *What victims tell us about prevention?* Chicago: University of Chicago, School of Social Services.

Berliner, L., & Saunders, B. (1996). Treating fear and anxiety in sexually abused children: Results of a controlled 2-year follow-up study. *Child Maltreatment, 4*, 294–309.

Briere, J. (1996). Treatment outcome research with abused children: Methodological considerations in three studies. *Child Maltreatment, 4*, 348–352.

Briere, J., & Runtz, M. (1988). Symptomatology associated with childhood sexual victimization in a nonclinical adult sample. *Child Abuse and Neglect, 12*, 51–59.

Briere, J., & Runtz, M. (1989). University males' sexual interest in children: Predicting potential indices of "pedophilia" in a nonforensic sample. *Child Abuse and Neglect, 13*, 65–75.

Briggs, D. (1975). *Your child's self esteem*. New York: Doubleday.

Bristow, L. R. (1995, November). AMA's guidelines on sexual assault. *American Medical Association* [On-line]. Available: ama-assn.org/public/releases/assault/statemnt.htm.

Brown, E. J., Flanagan, T. J., & McLeod, M. (1984). *Sourcebook of criminal justice statistics—1983*. Washington, DC: Bureau of Justice Statistics.

Browne, A., & Finklehor, D. (1986). Impact of child sexual abuse: A review of the research. *Psychological Bulletin, 99*, 66–77.

Chandy, J. M., Blum, R. W., & Resnick, M. D. (1996). Gender-specific outcomes for sexually abused adolescents. *Child Abuse and Neglect, 20,* 1219–1231.

Chasan-Taber, L., & Tabachnick, J. (1999). Evaluation of a child sexual abuse prevention program. *Sexual Abuse, 11,* 279–292.

Collins, M. E. (1996). Parents' perceptions of the risk of child sexual abuse and their protective behaviors: Findings from a qualitative study. *Child Maltreatment, 1*(1), 53–64.

Conte, J. (1984). Progress of treating the sexual abuse of children. *Social Work, 29,* 258–263.

Conte, J., Rosen, C., Saperstein, L., & Shermack, R. (1985). An evaluation of a program to prevent the sexual victimization of young children. *Child Abuse and Neglect, 9*(3), 319–328.

Conte, J. R., Wolf, S., & Smith, T. (1989). What sexual offenders tell us about prevention strategies. *Child Abuse and Neglect, 13,* 293–301.

Deblinger, E., Lippmann, J., & Steer, R. (1996). Sexually abused children suffering posttraumatic stress symptoms: Initial treatment outcome findings. *Child Maltreatment, 4,* 310–321.

Elliott, D. M., & Briere, J. (1995). Posttraumatic stress associated with delayed recall of sexual abuse: A general population study. *Journal of Traumatic Stress Studies, 8,* 629–648.

Elrod, J. M., & Rubin, R. H. (1993). Parental involvement in sexual abuse prevention education. *Child Abuse and Neglect, 17*(4), 527–538.

Epidemiology Program Office, Centers for Disease Control and Prevention. (1999, December 24). Achievements in public health, 1900–1999: Changes in the public health system. *CDC MMWR Weekly, 45*(50), 1141–1147.

Fehrenbach, P. A., Smith, W., Monastersky, C., & Deisher, R. W. (1986). Adolescent sexual offenders: Offender and offense characteristics. *American Journal of Orthopsychiatry, 56*(2), 225–233.

Finkelhor, D. (1984). *Child sexual abuse: New theory and research.* New York: Free Press.

Finkelhor, D. (1992). Child sexual abuse. In J. M. Last & R. B. Wallace (Eds.), *Public health and preventive medicine* (pp. 1048–1051). Norwalk, CT: Appleton & Lange.

Finkelhor, D., & Berliner, L. (1995). Research on the treatment of sexually abused children: A review and recommendations. *Journal of the American Academy of Child and Adolescent Psychiatry, 34,* 1408–1423.

Finkelhor, D., & Dziuba-Leatherman, J. (1995). Victimization prevention programs: A national survey of children's exposure and reactions. *Child Abuse and Neglect, 19*(2), 129–139.

Fisher, D. G. (1983). Parental supervision and delinquency. *Perceptual and Motor Skills, 56,* 635–640.

Foege, W. H., Rosenberg, M. L., & Mercy, J. A. (1995). Public health and violence prevention. *Current Issues in Public Health, 1,* 2–9.

Fontes, L. A. (1993). Disclosures of sexual abuse for Puerto Rican children: Oppression and cultural barriers. *Journal of Child Sexual Abuse, 2*(1), 21–35.

Fontes, L. A. (1995). *Sexual abuse in nine North American cultures.* New York: Sage.

Fontes, L. A. (1998). Ethics in family violence research: Cross cultural issues. *Family Relations, 47,* 53–61.

Ford, C. S., & Beach, F. A. (1963). Development of sexual behavior in human beings. In R. Grinder (Ed.), *Studies in adolescence* (pp. 433–445). New York: MacMillan.

Forehand, R., Miller, D. S., Dutra, R., & Chance, M. W. (1997). Role of parenting in adolescent deviant behavior: Replication across and within two ethnic groups. *Journal of Consulting and Clinical Psychology, 65*(6), 1036–1041.

Freeman-Longo, R., Bird, S., Stevenson, W., & Fiske, J. (1995). *1994 Nationwide survey of treatment programs and models.* Brandon, VT: Safer Society Press.

Friedrich, W. (1996). Clinical considerations of empirical treatment studies of abused children. *Child Maltreatment, 4,* 343–347.

Fujioka, J., Ryan, G., Robertson, S., Compoz, P., Cantwell, H., Leversee, T., Boscoe, J., & Asafi, I. (1993). *Continuum of response to the sexual behavior of children.* Denver, CO: Kempe Children's Center.

Galenson, E., & Riophe, H. (1974). The emergence of genital awareness during the second year of life. In R. C. Friedman, R. M. Richart, & R. L. Van de Wiele (Eds.), *Sex differences in behavior* (pp. 32–38). New York: Wiley.

Gibson, L. E., & Leitenberg, H. (2000). Child sexual abuse prevention programs: Do they decrease the occurrence of child sexual abuse? *Child Abuse and Neglect, 24*(9), 1115–1125.

Gilbert, N., Berrick, J., Le Prohn, N., & Nyman, N. (1989). *Protecting young children from sexual abuse. Does preschool training work?* Lexington, MA: Lexington Press.

Guerra, N. G., Attar, B., & Weissberg, R. P. (1997). Prevention of aggression and violence among inner-city youths. In D. M. Stoff, J. Breiling, & J. D. Maser (Eds.), *Handbook of antisocial behavior* (pp. 375–383). New York: Wiley & Sons.

Hammond, W. R., & Yung, B. (1993). Psychology's role in the public health response to assaultive violence among young African-American men. *American Psychologist, 48*(2), 142–154.

Hanson, K. R., & Bussiere, M. T. (1998). Predicting relapse: A meta-analysis of sexual offender recidivism studies. *Journal of Consulting and Clinical Psychology, 66*(2), 348–362.

Hanson, K. A., & Gidycz, C. A. (1993). Evaluation of a sexual assault prevention program. *Journal of Consulting and Clinical Psychology, 61*(6), 1046–1052.

Hazzard, A. P., Kleemeier, C. P., & Webb, C. (1990). Teacher versus expert presentations of sexual abuse prevention programs. *Journal of Interpersonal Violence, 5*(1), 23–36.

Heidotting, T., & Soled, S. W. (1996). *School-based sexual abuse and personal safety prevention programs for children: A meta-analysis.* Unpublished master's thesis, University of Cincinnati, Cincinnati, OH.

Henry, F. (1996, November). *Public health, public policy, and sexual abuse*. Paper presented at the Annual Research and Treatment Conference of the Association for the Treatment of Sexual Abusers. Chicago.

Hogan, C. (1997, November). *The human services response to preventing sexual offending*. Keynote address presented at the Annual Research and Treatment Conference of the Association for the Treatment of Sexual Abusers. Chicago.

Juvenile Crime Bill, H.R. 810, 105th Cong. 362 Sess. (1997).

Kaufman, K. L., Hilliker, D. R., & Daleiden, E. L. (1996). Subgroup differences in the modus operandi of adolescent sexual offenders. *Child Maltreatment, 1*, 17–24.

Kaufman, K., Holmberg, J., Orts, K., McCrady, F., Rotzien, A., Daleiden, E., & Hilliker, D. (1998). Factors influencing sexual offender' modus operandi: An examination of victim–offender relatedness and age. *Child Maltreatment, 3*(4), 349–361.

Kendall-Tackett, K. A., Williams, L. M., & Finkelhor, D. (1993). Impact of sexual abuse on children: A review and synthesis of recent empirical studies. *Psychological Bulletin, 133*, 164–180.

Kinsey, A. C., Pomeroy, W. B., & Martin, C. E. (1948). *Sexual behavior in the human male*. Philadelphia: Saunders.

Kinsey, A. C., Pomeroy, W. B., Martin, C. E., & Gebhard, P. H. (1953). *Sexual behavior in the human female*. Philadelphia: Saunders.

Knopp, F. H. (1985). *The youthful sex offender: The rationale and goals of early intervention and treatment*. Syracuse, NY: Safer Society Press.

Kolko, D., Moser, J., & Hughes, J. (1989). Classroom training in sexual victimization awareness and prevention skills: An extension of the Red Flag/Green Flag People program. *Journal of Family Violence, 4*(1), 25–45.

Landry, S., & Peters, R. (1992). Toward an understanding of a developmental paradigm for aggressive conduct problems. In R. Peters, R. McMohan, & V. Quinsey (Eds.), *Aggression and violence throughout the life span* (pp. 1–30). Thousand Oaks, CA: Sage.

Lonsway, K. A. (1996). Preventing acquaintance rape through education: What do we know? *Psychology of Women Quarterly, 20*(2), 229–265.

Lonsway, K. A., Klaw, E., Berg, D., Waldo, C. R., Kothari, C., Mazurek, C. J., Hegeman, K. E. (1998). Beyond "no means no": Outcomes of an intensive program to train peer facilitators for campus acquaintance rape education. *Journal of Interpersonal Violence, 13*(1), 73–92.

Lowry, R., Sleet, D., Duncan, C., Powell, K., & Kolbe, L. (1995). Adolescents at risk for violence. *Educational Psychology Review, 7*, 7–39.

Martone, M., Jaudes, P. K., & Calvin, M. K. (1996). Criminal prosecution of child sexual abuse cases. *Child Abuse and Neglect, 20*(5), 457–464.

McMahon, P. M., & Puett, R. C. (1999). Child sexual abuse as a public health issue: Recommendations of an expert panel. *Sexual Abuse, 11*(4), 257–266.

Mercy, J. A. (1993, Summer). Youth violence as a public health problem. *Spectrum*, 26–30.

Mercy, J. A. (1999). Having new eyes: Viewing child sexual abuse as a public health problem. *Sexual Abuse, 11*(4), 317–322.

Mercy, J. A., & Hammond, W. R. (1999). Combining action and analysis to prevent homicide: A public health perspective. In H. D. Smith & M. A. Zahn (Eds.), *Homicide: A sourcebook of social research* (pp. 297–310). Thousand Oaks, CA: Sage.

Patterson, G. R., & Bank, L. (1986). Bootstrapping your way in the nomological thicket. *Behavioral Assessment, 8*(1), 49–73.

Patterson, G. R., & Dishion, T. J. (1985). Contributions of families and peers to delinquency. *Criminology, 23*, 63–79.

Patterson, G. R., & Stouthamer-Loeber, M. (1984). The correlation of family management practices and delinquency. *Child Development, 55*, 1299–1307.

Powell, L. B., Dahlberg, L. L., Friday, J., Mercy, J. A., Thorton, T., & Crawford, S. (1996). Prevention of youth violence: Rationale and characteristics of 15 evaluation projects. *American Journal of Preventive Medicine, 12*, 3–12.

Prothrow-Stith, D. B. (1995). The epidemic of youth violence in America: Using public health prevention strategies to prevent violence. *Journal of Health Care for the Poor and Underserved, 6*(2), 95–101.

Ray-Keil, A. A. (1988). *Intersect of social theory and management practice in preventing child exploitation*. Seattle, WA: Committee for Children.

Reppucci, N. D., & Haugaard, J. J. (1989). Prevention of child sexual abuse: Myth or reality. *American Psychologist, 44*, 1266–1275.

Reppucci, N. D., Jones, L. M., & Cook, S. L. (1994). Involving parents in child sexual abuse prevention programs. *Journal of Child and Family Studies, 3*(2), 137–142.

Reppucci, N. D., Woolard, J. L., & Fried, C. S. (1999). Social, community, and preventive interventions. *Annual Review of Psychology, 50*, 387–418.

Rispens, J., Aleman, A., & Goudena, P. P. (1997). Prevention of child sexual abuse victimization: A meta-analysis of school programs. *Child Abuse and Neglect, 21*(10), 975–987.

Ryan, G. (2000a). Childhood sexuality: A decade of study. Part I—Research and curriculum development. *Child Abuse and Neglect, 24*(1), 33–48.

Ryan, G. (2000b). Childhood sexuality: A decade of study. Part II—Dissemination and future directions. *Child Abuse and Neglect, 24*(1), 49–61.

Ryan, G., Blum, J., Sandau-Christopher, D., Law, S., Weher, F., Sundine, C., Astler, L., Teske, J., & Dale, J. (1993). *Understanding and responding to the sexual behavior of children* [Trainer's manual]. Denver: Kempe National Center, University of Colorado Health Sciences Center. (Original published 1988)

Saunders, B., & Williams, L. (1996). Introduction to special issue on outcome research. *Child Maltreatment, 4*, 293.

Schewe, P. A., & O'Donohue, W. (1993). Sexual abuse prevention with high-risk males: The roles of victim empathy and rape myths. *Violence and Victims, 8*(4), 339–351.

Schwartz, B. K. (1995). Theories of sex offenses. In B. K. Schwartz & H. R. Cellini (Eds.), *The sex offender: Corrections, treatment and legal practice* (pp. 2-1–2-32). Kingston, NJ: Civic Research Institute.

Sedlak, A. J., & Broadhurst, D. D. (1996). *The National Incidence Study of Child Abuse and Neglect* (Vol. 3). Washington, DC: National Clearinghouse on Child Abuse and Neglect Information.

Steele, B. (1987). Abuse and neglect in the earliest years: Groundwork for vulnerability. *Zero to Three, 7*, 14–15.

Tabachnick, J., & Dawson, E. (2000). *STOP IT NOW! Vermont: 4 year program evaluation (1995–1999)*. Haydenville, MA: STOP IT NOW!.

U.S. Department of Health and Human Services. (1991). *Healthy people 2000: National health promotion and disease prevention objectives* (DHHS Publication No. PHS-91-50213). Washington, DC: U.S. Government Printing Office.

Violence Against Women Act, Title IV of the Violent Crime Control and Law Enforcement Act of 1994, Pub. L. No. 103-322, 103rd Cong., 2nd Sess. (1994).

Walker, C. E., Bonner, B., & Kaufman, K. (1988). *The physically and sexually abused child: Evaluation and treatment*. Elmsford, NY: Pergamon Press.

Weinrott, M. (1996). *Juvenile sexual aggression: A critical review*. Boulder: Center for the Study and Prevention of Violence, University of Colorado.

White, J. W., & Koss, M. P. (1993). Adolescent sexual aggression within heterosexual relationships: Prevalence, characteristics, and causes. In H. E. Barbaree, W. L. Marshall, & S. M. Hudson (Eds.), *The juvenile sex offender* (pp. 182–202). New York: Guilford Press.

World Health Assembly. (1996). *Prevention of violence: Public health priority* (WHA 49, 25). Geneva, Switzerland: World Health Organization.

Worling, J. R., & Curwen, T. (2000). Adolescent sexual offender recidivism: Success of specialized treatment and implications for risk prediction. *Child Abuse and Neglect, 24*(7), 965–982.

Wurtele, S. K. (1987). School-based sexual abuse prevention programs: A review. *Child Abuse and Neglect, 11*, 483–495.

Wurtele, S. K. (1998). School-based child sexual abuse prevention programs: Questions, answers, and more questions. In J. R. Lutzker (Ed.), *Handbook of child abuse research and treatment. Issues in clinical child psychology* (pp. 501–516). New York: Plenum Press.

Wurtele, S. K. (1999). Comprehensiveness and collaboration: Key ingredients of an effective public health approach to preventing child sexual abuse. *Sexual Abuse, 11*(4), 323–325.

Wurtele, S. K., & Miller-Perrin, C. L. (1992). *Preventing child sexual abuse: Sharing the responsibility*. Lincoln: University of Nebraska Press.

Yung, B. R., Hammond, W. R., Sampson, M., & Warfield, J. (1998). Linking psychology and public health: A predoctoral clinical training program in youth violence prevention. *Professional Psychology Research and Practice, 29*(4), 398–401.

3

INTERVENTIONS FOR CHILDREN VICTIMIZED BY PEERS

HEIDI GAZELLE AND GARY W. LADD

Many of the relationships that receive attention in this volume (e.g., spousal and dating relationships) are typically defined by positive qualities such as romantic affection, yet these relationships can also function as contexts for serious interpersonal violence. In contrast, interpersonal harm is the defining characteristic of "bully–victim" relationships among children. Intervention efforts designed to address childhood peer victimization have primarily focused on children who perpetrate aggressive acts against their peers. The importance of intervention for children who victimize peers has been widely recognized and received attention elsewhere (e.g., see Graham & Juvonen, 1998a; Hudley & Graham, 1993; Olweus, 1993a). This chapter focuses on intervention for children victimized by peers—a topic that has received comparatively less attention but that we view as equally important.

In this chapter we review theory and evidence regarding individual and interpersonal factors that increase children's vulnerability to peer

Preparation of this chapter was supported by National Institute of Mental Health Grants 1-RO1MH-49223 and 2-RO1MH-49223 to Gary Ladd, University of Illinois at Urbana–Champaign.

victimization and apply these findings to the conceptualization of intervention goals and corresponding intervention strategies. This focus on intervention for victimized children stems from a holistic concern for the well-being of these vulnerable children. We do not imply that these children are to blame for their victimization. Failure to recognize that some children are more vulnerable to victimization than others may discourage the availability of interventions for vulnerable children and compromise the efficacy of interventions when they are available. We propose that worthy intervention goals include not only prohibiting acts of victimization, but also mitigating individual vulnerability to peer victimization and emotional consequences of peer victimization, and augmenting the support available to vulnerable children through peer friendships.

CONCEPTUALIZATION AND MEASUREMENT
OF PEER VICTIMIZATION

What types of interactions among children qualify as peer victimization? At present, researchers have not achieved a clear consensus about the definition of peer victimization. In traditional definitions, victimization occurs when a stronger child regularly commits unprovoked aggressive acts ranging from physical attacks to verbal taunting against a weaker or otherwise defenseless child (e.g., Smith, Bowers, Binney, & Cowie, 1993). Although unprovoked aggression is often featured in conceptual definitions of victimization, it is difficult to measure whether the aggressor perceives provocation and whether such perceptions may be accurate. Another less restrictive definition is that *peer victimization* occurs when peers (one or many) repeatedly direct aggressive behaviors toward specific children (i.e., victims), including physical (e.g., hitting), verbal (e.g., name-calling, verbal threatening), and relational (e.g., rumor-spreading, harming friendships or other relationships) forms of aggression or harassment (see Kochenderfer & Ladd, 1996b; Perry, Kusel, & Perry, 1988). In this definition, many aggressors (not just bullies or stronger children) can be considered as perpetrators of victimization, and many forms of peer aggression (not just unprovoked) qualify as victimization. We use the less restrictive definition of victimization in this discussion because it matches the way victimization was actually measured in the studies to be reviewed.

Both peer- and self-reports of victimization are frequently used in research with children, and the research we review in this chapter includes work done using both of these methods. Self-report measures ask children to rate how often they have been harassed by peers, and peer-report measures ask children to nominate classmates whom they have seen experience one or more forms of abuse at the hands of peers (e.g., peers identify children who "get picked on," "hit, pushed, or kicked," "called bad names by other kids").

Thus, self-reports typically index the *frequency* with which a child is victimized by peers, whereas peer reports assess the degree of *consensus* among peers that a child is victimized by peers (see Graham & Juvonen, 1998b; Ladd & Kochenderfer-Ladd, in press).

Consistent with the focus on relationships in this volume, this chapter attempts to move beyond the traditional conceptualization of victimization by considering the possibility that victimization consists of more than just the behaviors that aggressors perpetrate against victims. Peer victimization can be understood as occurring in the context of a relationship or role that children develop among peers. When victims can be defined by their role in an ongoing pattern of interaction with aggressors, many researchers are inclined to characterize these bully–victim interaction patterns as relationships (e.g., Ladd, Kochenderfer, & Coleman, 1997; Pierce & Cohen, 1995). Although evidence has suggested that a substantial amount of victimization occurs in dyadic bully–victim relationships (Pierce & Cohen, 1995), not all victimization occurs in this context (for information on group victimization of single children, see Lagerspetz, Bjorkqvist, Berts, & King, 1982). Nevertheless, we propose that a relationship or role perspective may be especially useful in guiding interventions with vulnerable children because research suggests that patterns of peer affiliation and associated social–behavioral characteristics are important determinants of vulnerability.

Our discussion is geared toward repeated or chronic, rather than brief or sporadic, victimization because it has been more closely linked with children's adjustment difficulties (Kochenderfer & Ladd, 1996a; Kochenderfer-Ladd & Wardrop, 2001) and is consistent with the idea that victimization may occur in the context of ongoing relationships. Yet it is also important to note that, as Graham and Juvonen (1998a) argued, a single extreme act of victimization against a child may have substantial emotional consequences. Even so, there may be important distinctions to be made between those who experience chronic as opposed to isolated acts of victimization, both in terms of individual and relational antecedents as well as social–emotional consequences (Kochenderfer-Ladd & Ladd, 2001). Other findings have suggested that victims of brief acts of victimization are less likely to suffer severe or enduring dysfunction when compared to those who experience chronic victimization (Kochenderfer & Ladd, 1996a; Kochenderfer-Ladd & Wardrop, 2001).

With these qualifications in mind, our review and discussion focus on victimization as a repeated, dyadic phenomenon. This approach may offer insights into the development of intervention programs that not only terminate victimization in the short term but also foster long-term prevention of victimization, other relational problems, and internalizing difficulties through the promotion of healthy relationships and social–emotional adaptation for vulnerable children.

LINKS BETWEEN VICTIMIZATION AND ADJUSTMENT

The importance of intervention for childhood victimization has become increasingly clear as many investigators have documented links between victimization and concurrent and later maladjustment. Victimization is associated with concurrent depressive symptoms, loneliness, social dissatisfaction, school avoidance, and dislike of school and predicts increases in loneliness and school avoidance in kindergartners over the course of the school year (Bjorkqvist, Ekman, & Lagerspetz, 1982; Kochenderfer & Ladd, 1996a, 1996b; Ladd et al., 1997).

Perhaps most important, in a growing number of studies researchers have found that many of the negative outcomes linked to victimization persist even after victimization abates. Investigators have found that children victimized in the fall of their kindergarten year who were no longer victimized in the spring of that year nevertheless exhibited elevated rates of loneliness and school avoidance in the spring (Kochenderfer & Ladd, 1996a; Kochenderfer-Ladd & Wardrop, 2001). Similarly, boys who were victimized by peers in middle childhood and adolescence exhibited low self-esteem and elevated depressive symptoms in adulthood (age 23), even though they experienced no more victimization than did other men in adulthood (Olweus, 1993b). Because psychological difficulties linked to victimization may persist long after victimization subsides, there is a need to design interventions that will not only prevent victimization or end ongoing victimization but also mitigate the psychological wounds experienced by victims and strengthen the support available to victims in their personal relationships.

Designing such interventions requires a better understanding of the processes that link victimization to internalizing difficulties. Recent work has begun to address these mechanisms. It has been suggested that victimization, as a concrete expression of negative peer evaluations, may lead to loneliness and depression by influencing children's self-perceptions (Boivin & Hymel, 1997; Boivin, Hymel, & Bukowski, 1995). Another process-oriented investigation suggests that children who make internal, global, and stable attributions for their victimization are especially susceptible to loneliness, depression, and social anxiety (Graham & Juvonen, 1998b). However, additional work is needed on mechanisms that link victimization experiences to internalizing difficulties.

Given that victimization is linked to emotional difficulties and associated with negative self-perception and attributional styles, it is perhaps not surprising that evidence also indicates that victimization contributes to disengaged and maladaptive social behaviors. In a play group study, Schwartz, Dodge, and Coie (1993) found that boys engaged in more solitary behavior after experiencing victimization by play group partners. In another investigation, mothers reported that some victimized children displayed increased externalizing, attentional, and immature/dependent behaviors over time (Schwartz, McFadyen-Ketchum, Dodge, Pettit, & Bates, 1998).

Thus, a substantial body of evidence indicates that peer victimization contributes to child emotional and behavioral problems. But who is most at risk for becoming a target of repeated peer victimization and suffering such consequences?

RISK FOR VICTIMIZATION

Investigations indicate that risk factors for childhood victimization operate at multiple levels, including the school environment, social–behavioral characteristics of the child, and the quality of the child's social relationships with peers and family. We first review the risk factors at each of these levels and then discuss interventions designed to address each level of risk, with particular focus on individual- and peer relationship-level interventions.

School Environment Risk Factors

Contrary to popular belief, Olweus (1993a) reported that most peer victimization of children occurred at school rather than on the way to or from school. Victimization is particularly likely to happen at school when adult supervision is minimal, for instance, at recess. Olweus (1993a) reported a –.45 correlation between the relative teacher–student ratio at recess and the occurrence of victimization. Thus, adult monitoring of children's school activities is an important element of the school environment.

The incidence of peer victimization at school may also be related to the preparedness of school personnel to intervene in victimization. Approximately 40% of elementary school students and 60% of junior high school students in Olweus's (1993a) Scandinavian sample reported that that their teachers rarely intervened in peer victimization. This finding suggests that raising awareness of victimization and providing instruction in prevention and intervention techniques for school personnel may be instrumental in creating school environments that protect children from victimization.

Individual Risk Factors

Although victimization is a product of interpersonal interaction as opposed to individual behavior, it appears that there are social behaviors that render individual children vulnerable to victimization.

Behavioral Risk

Numerous studies have indicated that submissiveness and social withdrawal are risk factors for peer victimization (Gazelle & Ladd, 2002; Hodges,

Malone, & Perry, 1997; Hodges & Perry, 1999; Ladd & Burgess, 1999; Perry et al., 1988; Schwartz et al., 1993; Schwartz, Dodge, et al., 1998). Not only are submissiveness and social withdrawal associated with concurrent peer victimization (Hodges et al., 1997; Schwartz, Dodge, et al., 1998, but they are also predictive of increases in victimization over time (Hodges & Perry, 1999; Schwartz et al., 1993).

Submissiveness and social withdrawal may increase vulnerability for victimization through multiple mechanisms. When submissiveness is exhibited during normal peer play, it may mark the submissive child as a potential "easy mark" for later victimization. In Schwartz et al.'s (1993) play group study, boys who responded submissively to nonaggressive peer actions (e.g., rough-and-tumble play) were subsequently targeted for victimization. Furthermore, submission to aggressors may reward aggressors and encourage future attempts at victimization.

The vulnerability of socially withdrawn children to victimization may be attributed not only to submissive or unassertive social strategies (Stewart & Rubin, 1995) but also to anxious vulnerability (Perry, Kusel, & Perry, 1988), lack of positive peer affiliations, and susceptibility to peer exclusion and rejection (Gazelle & Ladd, 2002), and low self-perceived social acceptance. Behaviors characteristic of anxious–withdrawn children, such as verbal inhibition and "hovering" peer entry style (watching other children play without joining in, a sign of social interest that is blocked by social anxiety), communicate anxious vulnerability and have been linked to victimization (Hodges et al., 1997; Hodges & Perry, 1999). Also, socially withdrawn children may be readily available victims because they often spend time alone (Hodges et al., 1997) and tend to have few friends among classmates (Gazelle & Ladd, 2002), leaving them with few potential peer allies. Additionally, children who are both withdrawn and excluded by peers have especially high levels of peer-reported victimization (Gazelle & Ladd, 2002), perhaps because consensus among peers that these children are not allowed to join their play activities indicates that their vulnerability is especially prominent. On a similar note, Boivin and colleagues (Boivin et al., 1995; Boivin & Hymel, 1997) provided evidence to support a model in which social withdrawal places children at risk for rejection in middle childhood, and the combined forces of social withdrawal and rejection render children vulnerable to victimization. Finally, there is evidence that low self-perceived social acceptance, a characteristic consistently linked with social withdrawal, interacts with behavioral risk to increase vulnerability to victimization (Egan & Perry, 1998). Low self-perceived acceptance may increase withdrawn children's risk for victimization because it is "associated with reduced motivation or ability to assert and defend the self effectively during conflicts with peers," as well as expectation and acceptance of negative feedback (p. 299).

Thus, evidence suggests that anxious solitary behaviors increase children's risk for victimization and, as discussed earlier, that victimization increases the solitary and anxious behaviors that children display over time (Schwartz et al., 1993; Schwartz, Dodge, et al., 1998). These findings are not necessarily contradictory. In many cases, the initial manifestation of anxious solitary behaviors may occur for reasons other than victimization and thus precede victimization. Indeed, there is evidence to suggest that both the quality of early parent–child relationships and early temperament are related to the display of anxious solitary behaviors during the early school years (see Rubin & Burgess, 2001, for a review). Victimization may exacerbate pre-existing anxious solitary behaviors in some children and precipitate the emergence of anxious solitary behavior in other children. These behavioral consequences of past victimization, in turn, may then increase risk of future victimization.

Although the majority of child victims are characterized by submissive and withdrawn social behavior, many investigators have identified a small proportion of aggressive victims within their samples (Ladd & Ladd, 1998; Perry et al., 1988; Schwartz, Dodge, Pettit, & Bates, 1997). These victims may display a mix of socially withdrawn and aggressive behavior. Two recent studies have indicated that aggressive–withdrawn children are more victimized and rejected than other socially withdrawn or aggressive children, as well as normative children (Gazelle & Ladd, 2002; Ladd & Burgess, 1999). There is also evidence to suggest that aggressive victims more often display reactive aggression as opposed to proactive aggression (Schwartz, Dodge, et al., 1998). That is, these victims' aggression is likely to be a quick, angry response to a perceived threat as opposed to a cool, calculated strategy for obtaining a goal. Although aggressive victims are often characterized as "provocative," it is unclear whether this is an accurate characterization if their aggression tends to be primarily reactive. The accuracy with which reactive aggressive victims perceive threat is also relevant to this issue.

Social–Cognitive Risk

Researchers are beginning to explore social–cognitive characteristics that are linked with victimization and are characteristic of reactive–aggressive victims in particular. Victimization may be related to differences in the ways children interpret and respond to peer social behavior. Reactive–aggressive victims seem to display hostile attribution bias, that is, to interpret ambiguous social occurrences as hostile (Schwartz, Dodge, et al., 1998). For instance, when a child is hit with a ball on the playground and there are no obvious clues about the intent of the child who threw the ball, he or she may assume it was done purposefully to hurt as opposed to assuming that it was an accident. It is unclear whether hostile attribution bias is characteristic only of aggressive victims or whether passive victims may also hold such a bias.

Anxious social withdrawal, a characteristic of many nonaggressive victims, is associated with underattributing peer hostile intent in young children (Harrist, Zaia, Bates, Dodge, & Pettit, 1997). Yet, social withdrawal due to peer exclusion is associated with hostile attribution bias in young children (Harrist et al., 1997). Because many excluded, socially withdrawn children also tend to be aggressive in early childhood (e.g., see Asendorpf, 1990), attribution bias in these children may reflect aggressive behavioral tendencies. Another possibility is that being repeatedly excluded and victimized may encourage children to develop hostile attribution bias. Because peers may often intend to harm these children, they may come to expect hostility even when it is not present.

Because many anxious–withdrawn children also appear to be excluded and victimized by peers (Gazelle & Ladd, 2002), they may develop hostile attribution bias after exposure to this mistreatment. Although hostile attribution bias is linked to aggressive behavior in children who have positive expectations for aggressive behavior (i.e., think that their aggressive behavior will be effective in defending themselves or obtaining desired outcomes), this bias may result in submissive behavior in victims who tend to have negative outcome expectations for aggression and assertiveness (i.e., think that their aggression or assertiveness will be ineffective in defending themselves or obtaining desired outcomes; Schwartz, Dodge, et al., 1998; see also Crick & Ladd, 1990; Dodge & Crick, 1990). Along these lines, Egan, Monson, and Perry (1998) found that boys who were victimized evidenced decreased expectations for being rewarded for aggression over the course of the school year. Longitudinal work will be needed to examine whether hostile attribution bias and reactive aggression emerge only after children experience victimization and exclusion, or whether these characteristics precede children's exposure to peer maltreatment. Recent evidence has suggested that externalizing behaviors precede peer victimization in some aggressive victims (Schwartz, McFadyen-Ketchum, Dodge, Pettit, & Bates, 1999).

Physical Risk

Physical weakness is also a well-established concurrent and predictive risk factor for peer victimization in boys (Hodges et al., 1997; Hodges & Perry, 1999; Olweus, 1993b). Boys who are physically weaker than their peers may find it difficult to assertively ward off aggressive attacks due to obvious disadvantages in size and strength. Olweus (1993b) reported that peer-perceived physical weakness is strongly predictive of degree of victimization in boys. Less is known about potential risk factors for victimization that are specific to girls because victimization is more often studied in boys, and existing theories tend to direct attention toward types of victimization that are particularly prevalent among boys (e.g., physical victimization).

Overall, evidence suggests that individual differences in social behavior as well as physical strength place children at risk for victimization.

Children's submissive, withdrawn, aggressive–withdrawn, and reactive–aggressive behaviors and associated social–cognitive characteristics seem to be powerful indices of risk for peer victimization.

Peer Relations Risk Factors

Evidence also suggests that characteristics of children's peer relationships serve as risk or protective factors for peer victimization. It has been proposed that the combination of behavioral and relational risk factors renders children vulnerable to peer victimization (Hodges et al., 1997). Evidence indicates that children with a greater number of reciprocated friendships experience less concurrent victimization, even when they display behavioral risk factors (Hodges et al., 1997). Yet, it seems that friendships deter victimization only to the extent that friends fulfill a protective function. Friendship may only be protective if a victimized child both actively seeks help from friends and has friends who are capable of providing protection. Boys who possess coping strategies for victimization, such as seeking help from a friend, are less likely to be victimized in the future compared to boys whose strategies are to fight back (Kochenderfer & Ladd, 1997). Nonaggressive victims tend to have friends who are not well equipped to protect them because they also tend to be weak, withdrawn, submissive, and victimized themselves (Hodges et al., 1997; Malone & Perry, 1995). Conversely, having aggressive friends tends to reduce children's risk for victimization (Hodges & Perry, 1999).

Similarly, the combination of behavioral risk and peer rejection is linked to peer victimization (Hodges et al., 1997; Perry et al., 1988). Rejection makes a unique contribution to increased victimization over time after accounting for behavioral risks (Hodges & Perry, 1999). Bullies may recognize that rejected children occupy a vulnerable position in the peer group because even nonaggressive peers do not tend to sympathize with rejected children when they are victimized (Hodges & Perry, 1999; Perry, Williard, & Perry, 1990). Additionally, dislike may fuel a bully's desire to harm the victim, and the victim's weak social position may create an opportunity for a bully to assert social dominance. In turn, being picked on by a bully may signal to other peers that it is acceptable to mistreat victimized children.

There is some indication that peer rejection is a stronger predictor of victimization than is a lack of friends (Hodges & Perry, 1999; Pellegrini, Bartini, & Brooks, 1999). Rejection and friendship participation may be linked to victimization through different processes. Schwartz et al. (1999) presented evidence suggesting that rejection may mediate the relationship between behavioral risk and victimization, whereas friendship may moderate this relationship. Overall, it is clear that being negatively regarded by the peer group and lacking supportive peer relationships contribute to children's vulnerability to victimization.

Familial Risk Factors

Factors that increase children's vulnerability for victimization may operate at a family level as well as at an individual and peer relations level. Although our focus is on school-based interventions that address victimized children's peer relationships and emotional well-being, the influence of family on peer victimization is central to our relationship perspective. Evidence from multiple theoretical orientations has linked family relationships to children's victimization among peers, including investigations of caregiver–child attachment, parenting styles, and family systems.

Social–behavioral styles that increase children's vulnerability to peer victimization may be rooted in the quality of children's relational experiences within the family. Children with anxious–resistant attachment to caregivers may be especially likely to display anxious vulnerability, which is linked to risk for victimization (Troy & Sroufe, 1987). Because anxious–resistant children typically have experienced inconsistent parenting (Troy & Sroufe, 1987), their anxiousness may stem from uncertainty about how social partners are likely to respond to them. Also, the link between children's insecure attachment and peer victimization may be partially mediated by children's withdrawn behavior. Children's insecure attachment to caregivers in early childhood is predictive of social withdrawal from peers in middle childhood (for a review, see Rubin & Burgess, 2001). Thus, children's insecure attachment to caregivers may contribute to socially withdrawn behavior in the peer group which, in turn, may increase vulnerability for peer victimization.

There is evidence that parenting style, as well as parent–child relationship quality, is linked with children's vulnerability to peer victimization. Ladd and Ladd (1998) proposed that parenting styles that undermine children's sense of control and personal agency in social interactions increase all children's vulnerability to victimization. In support of this premise, Ladd and Ladd demonstrated that parental intrusive demandingness and unresponsiveness were predictive of victimization in kindergarten for boys and girls.

Whereas intrusive, unresponsive parenting appears to be a risk factor for children of both sexes, many parenting styles linked to peer victimization appear to be gender specific. On a different but not necessarily contradictory note, Finnegan, Hodges, and Perry (1998) proposed that parenting styles that undermine children's display of culturally acceptable gender role behavior are linked to victimization. Indeed, converging evidence has indicated that differential parenting patterns are linked to risk in boys and girls. For boys, maternal overprotectiveness, intense closeness to the mother, father negativity, and poor identification with the father are concurrently and predictively related to victimization (Bowers, Smith, & Binney, 1992, 1994; Finnegan et al., 1998; Ladd & Ladd, 1998; Olweus, 1993b; Smith et al., 1993), perhaps because these parenting styles impede the development of autonomy and independence valued in boys' peer groups (Finnegan et al., 1998). Similarly, parental overprotectiveness and overcontrol are also linked to social withdrawal (for a review, see Rubin & Burgess, 2001), again raising the possibility that social withdrawal may partially mediate the relationship between parental overcontrol and risk for victimization. For girls, maternal rejection is associated with victimization (Finnegan et al., 1998; Rigby, 1993), perhaps because it interferes with the intimate communication and connectedness characteristic of girls' relationships (Finnegan et al., 1998). Thus, parenting styles that undermine children's agency appear to increase vulnerability in all children, whereas the effect of many other aspects of parenting style may depend on their capacity to undermine culturally accepted gender role behavior.

Evidence from a family systems perspective also has linked family characteristics and child victimization. A family systems perspective suggests that children may learn the role of victim, or both the roles of aggressor and victim, within conflictual family relationships. This possibility may be particularly relevant to aggressive victims, who may alternate between aggressor and victim roles. Troy and Sroufe (1987) observed that avoidantly attached children (children who avoid contact with their caregiver after a brief separation), who typically experience rejection from parents, tend to alternate between aggressor and victim roles during peer interaction. Furthermore, Schwartz et al. (1997) reported that boys who were victims of abuse within their families at an early age later became aggressive victims of peer abuse, in contrast to boys who later became aggressive but not victimized by peers. Overall, evidence supports the premise that children's familial relationship histories contribute to their risk for peer victimization.

PROHIBITING ACTS OF VICTIMIZATION

Few investigators have developed or empirically evaluated intervention programs for children who experience peer victimization (Graham & Juvonen, 1998a). Large-scale systematic intervention for peer victimization has occurred to a much greater extent abroad, particularly in Scandinavia, than in the United States. First, we review Olweus's (e.g., 1993a) landmark Norwegian intervention program that was focused primarily at the level of the school environment. Then we consider other intervention strategies that address vulnerabilities at the level of the child and the child's social relationships.

School Environment-Level Intervention

Olweus's large-scale intervention study received substantial support from the Norwegian government and public because of concern about the role that peer victimization seemed to have played in the suicide of several teenage boys. A total of 2,500 students from the fourth to seventh grades participated in the intervention study, and assessments were conducted at three time points: before the intervention program was initiated and 1 and 2 years after the intervention was in place.

The intervention was implemented by school personnel, who were provided with instructional materials about the prevalence and nature of victimization and the program procedures. At the school level, the program included improving adult supervision at recess and forming teacher and parent discussion groups. At the classroom level, the program included regular classroom meetings, student role plays, and establishment of explicit classroom rules about victimization. Classroom rules stipulated that "1. We shall not bully others, 2. We shall try to help those that are bullied, and 3. We shall make a point to include students that are easily left out" (Olweus, 1993a, p. 123). Thus, not only was victimization prohibited, but also peers were encouraged to actively include excluded children and to intervene if they observed victimization. In sum, the program involved raising awareness; providing a concrete policy of action; and stimulating dialogue among all those present, responsible, or concerned with child welfare in the school environment, including school personnel, parents, and children (whether or not they were directly involved in victimization).

Bully–Victim Relationship-Level Intervention

As another important aspect of Olweus's intervention program, teachers were expected to directly intervene in existing bully–victim relationships. Teachers spoke to children involved in bully–victim relationships and their parents to engage all parties in efforts to terminate victimization. The effects of these direct efforts are unknown, as they were not separable from the effects of the overall intervention program.

In Olweus's study, teachers were presented with information about the prevalence of victimization at their school, but it is unclear whether teachers may have been alerted to the presence of specific bully–victim relationships. Awareness of such relationships may be partially achieved though observation of children's interaction, especially during recess, lunchtime, and other relatively unstructured periods of the school day. Children's self- and peer reports of victimization are additional valuable sources of information about the occurrence and prevalence of bullying. Yet, teachers must be sensitive in their use of children's reports about victimization. If school personnel intend to use child-reported information about victimization to target services to particular children, children should be warned that their reports would not be kept confidential. Also, precautions should be taken to prevent bullies from taking revenge on victims or other children for reporting their bullying behavior to teachers.

It is likely that the success of these methods would depend on coordinated effort among teachers, because children are often victimized by older children who are not a part of their classroom (Olweus, 1993a). The teacher discussion groups included in the intervention may have facilitated coordinated efforts to stop bully–victim relationships.

The overall results of this intervention program were impressive. Olweus (1993a) reported an approximately 50% reduction in the percentage of children involved in bully–victim problems after the program had been in place for 20 months. Additionally, evidence suggested that the program reduced the rates of students' overall antisocial behavior. It is likely that the public support that was mobilized for this project was critical to its success. Yet, the demonstrated effects of this program were largely limited to terminating or preventing victimization.

MITIGATING VULNERABILITY TO VICTIMIZATION AND THE CONSEQUENCES OF VICTIMIZATION

Although reducing the incidence of victimization is undoubtedly a laudable achievement, other objectives may be considered important goals for victimization intervention programs, such as mitigating the social–behavioral difficulties and negative emotional consequences associated with victimization and facilitating the development of more adaptive relationships for victims (see Table 3.1 for a summary of intervention strategies and corresponding goals). These goals call for interventions at an individual and relationship level.

Individual-Level Intervention

Because parents and teachers cannot ensure that children are always in protective environments or that environmental-level efforts are sufficient to protect children at high risk for victimization, vulnerable children are likely to benefit from interventions that provide them with self-protective tools. Moreover, intervention is warranted for high-risk children because characteristics that place children at risk for victimization—social withdrawal in particular—are linked to concurrent and later social and emotional difficulties independent of victimization (Hymel, Rubin, Rowden, & LeMare, 1990; Morison & Masten, 1991; Rubin, 1985, 1993; Rubin, Chen, & Hymel, 1993; Rubin, Chen, McDougall, Bowker, & McKinnon, 1995; Rubin & Mills, 1988; Strauss, Forehand, Smith, & Frame, 1986). Also, as previously mentioned, victimized children continue to be at risk for school avoidance, loneliness, and depressive symptoms long after victimization has subsided (Kochenderfer & Ladd, 1996a; Olweus, 1993b). Thus, in the interest of children's overall well-being, interventions could be designed to address

TABLE 3.1
Levels of Intervention for Peer Victimization and Corresponding Intervention Goals

Levels of intervention for peer victimization	Intervention goals
Programs aimed at prevention or termination of victimization	
School environment	
• Assess and disseminate information about prevalence and nature of victimization	• Raising awareness
• Form teacher and parent discussion groups	• Coordinating efforts against victimization
• Improve adult supervision of recess	• Preventing victimization during recess
Classroom environment	
• Establish classroom rules about victimization	• Creating explicit policy on victimization
• Hold classroom meetings	• Discussing victimization, group problem solving
Bully–victim relationships	
• Identify bully–victim relationships and talk with children directly involved and their parents	• Terminating ongoing bully–victim relationships
Programs aimed at mitigating vulnerability and consequences of victimization	
Socially withdrawn and submissive individual characteristics	
• Assertiveness training	• Promoting use of assertive strategies
• Anxiety regulation training	• Reducing social anxiety through interactive means
• Proactive prosocial strategy training	• Initiating positive exchanges with peers
Friendship–relational characteristics	
• Play sessions with potential friends that emphasize features of friendship and structure friendship tasks	• Promoting high-quality friendships, school liking
	• Reducing time spent alone, loneliness
	• Creating peer allies
Internalizing tendencies	
• Self-blaming attribution retraining	• Reducing shame, risk for depression

children's individual and relational vulnerabilities. Such interventions may reduce risk not only for future victimization but also for social and emotional maladjustment linked to both victimization and behavioral difficulties.

Intervention research geared toward ameliorating the social competency of children with peer relations difficulties has been carried out since the late 1970s (for a review, see Ladd, 1999). Early peer relations intervention studies were based on a social skills deficit model that proposed that training children in prosocial skills and guiding the practice of these skills with peer partners would improve children's social skillfulness and, in turn, their peer acceptance. In recent years, intervention studies have been designed according to multiple perspectives that aim not only to promote prosocial behavior but also to deter maladaptive social behavior and transform patterns of social cognition and emotional regulation that may drive maladaptive behavior.

In a related trend, interventions have been increasingly geared toward children with specific social behavioral profiles (e.g., aggressive, withdrawn) that are associated with particular patterns of social cognition and emotional regulation, as opposed to being aimed at heterogeneous groups of children who are rejected by their peers. Although this evolution in intervention studies has been spearheaded by researchers concerned with developing interventions tailored to the needs of aggressive children, interventions are also needed to address the specific difficulties of socially withdrawn and submissive children who are at risk for peer victimization, as well as for a variety of internalizing difficulties. Next, we review research on the few existing interventions developed for withdrawn children and suggest further ways of addressing the vulnerability of these children to victimization and internalizing problems. Although we believe that individual-level intervention is also indicated for children who perpetrate peer victimization, this topic has been covered elsewhere (see Graham & Juvonen, 1998a; Hudley, & Graham, 1993), and we limit our discussion to interventions for children who are likely to be victimized by peers.

Only two sociometric-based interventions have been conducted with withdrawn children to date (Bienert & Schneider, 1995; Csapo, 1983), despite substantial advances in knowledge of the characteristics of socially withdrawn children and the risks associated with social withdrawal since the early 1980s (see Rubin, 1993). In the Csapo (1983) study, third-grade children who had been identified by their teachers as withdrawn and who were in the lowest third of their class in peer-acceptance ratings were trained in skills such as asking questions of peers, offering suggestions and directions to peers, and praising and encouraging peers. Children played with a peer partner and received instructor feedback for an average of 32 sessions. Significant gains in peer acceptance ratings were found after completion of the intervention as well as at a 4-week follow-up. Although this study suggests that training in prosocial skills can improve the short-term peer acceptance of withdrawn children, it did not examine the incidence of victimization or internalizing problems, explicitly address many skills of special relevance to withdrawn children, or include a long-term follow-up.

Anxious–withdrawn children may need training in more than just prosocial skills. For instance, anxious–withdrawn children may require particular emphasis on regulation of social anxiety, being appropriately assertive, and thinking of themselves as equals with their peers (Eisenberg, Fabes, & Murphy, 1995; Stewart & Rubin, 1995; Trower, Gilbert, & Sherling, 1990). Cognitive–behavioral therapists have used relaxation techniques such as breathing exercises and guided imagery with anxious children. Although these techniques appear to help children relax in a protected environment, they may have limited practical application when the child is in the midst of peer social partners. These strategies might actually encourage solitary children to withdraw from peers and focus on themselves, reinforcing their behavioral withdrawal. Anxious–withdrawn children may need to be taught interactive strategies for regulating their social anxiety. More attention was given to such issues of special relevance to withdrawn children in an intervention conducted by Bienert and Schneider (1995).

In Bienert and Schneider's (1995) study, separate interventions were designed and implemented specifically for poorly accepted sixth graders who were identified as either socially withdrawn or aggressive. The intervention designed for socially withdrawn children included proactive prosocial strategies (introducing oneself and joining in), anxiety regulation strategies (dealing with fear and embarrassment, relaxing), assertiveness training (making a complaint), and problem solving (dealing with group pressure). This manualized weekly 10-session intervention took place in the context of small groups of withdrawn children that were led by pairs of clinical graduate and undergraduate students. Procedures included didactic instruction, games, modeling displays, role-play practice, and feedback on role-play performance accompanied with replaying taped role-plays. After completion of this intervention, withdrawn children evidenced significantly diminished withdrawn behavior, higher peer acceptance ratings, and higher self-perceived social acceptance, whereas withdrawn waitlist control children did not evidence these improvements (the latter group participated in this intervention at a later date). Additionally, withdrawn children in this intervention demonstrated more improvement in peer liking and withdrawn behavior than did an additional control group of withdrawn children who received an intervention designed for aggressive children.

Results suggest that an approach tailored to the particular emotional regulatory and social difficulties of withdrawn children produces a broader range of changes in withdrawn children's functioning than do approaches designed for children with different behavioral difficulties (aggression) or based exclusively on prosocial skills (e.g., Csapo, 1983). However, only improvements in withdrawn behavior, but not in peer acceptance or self-perceived social acceptance, were maintained at seventh-grade follow-up, after the transition to secondary school. The investigators suggested that the transition to middle school might have been particularly difficult for withdrawn adolescents, rendering maintenance of improved acceptance and self-perceptions more challenging than in a nontransition year. Another factor that may have weakened the results of this study is the absence of dyadic peer interaction sessions. Because the improvements of withdrawn children had not been established in the context of enduring dyadic peer relationships, the ongoing support for children's maintenance of improvements may have been lacking.

Because neither Bienert and Schneider (1995) nor Csapo (1983) assessed levels of victimization either before or after intervention, it is unknown whether these interventions may have had an impact on victimization of withdrawn children. Yet, it is possible that improving withdrawn children's peer acceptance may decrease their tendency to be victimized. Because low peer acceptance has been implicated in the causal chain leading from social withdrawal to victimization and ultimately to internalizing difficulties (Boivin et al., 1995; Boivin & Hymel, 1997), improved acceptance may interrupt the relational processes that lead to victimization. Additionally, decreasing children's withdrawn behavior, as in the Bienert and Schneider (1995) study, may arrest processes that contribute to vulnerability for victimization at an even earlier stage. We also recommend that additional components be incorporated in interventions for socially withdrawn and other vulnerable children to better address the internalizing and relationship difficulties associated with victimization.

Because there is evidence that children who place blame for being victimized on stable, unchangeable characteristics of themselves (characterological self-blame) are especially likely to experience loneliness and symptoms of anxiety and depression (Graham & Juvonen, 1998b), we suggest that attribution retraining may also be an important component of victimization intervention. Small discussion groups of victimized children could serve as a context for helping children to make more adaptive attributions for victimization (e.g., discouraging self-blame), realize that other children also experience victimization, and engage in role-plays to practice assertive behavior.

Friendship-Level Intervention

There is reason to believe that a friendship-based approach to intervention would be particularly appropriate for withdrawn children, as they tend to have few reciprocated friendships (Gazelle & Ladd, 2002), and withdrawn-low accepted children report wanting help to learn how to make friends at a higher rate than other low-accepted children (Asher, 1993). It has similarly been suggested that friendship interventions may be useful for victimized children in general because children who have few friends are vulnerable to peer victimization (Hodges et al., 1997).

Asher, Parker, and Walker (1996) argued that social skills interventions should be aimed not only at increasing children's peer acceptance but also at encouraging the initiation and maintenance of quality peer friendships. Social skills intervention studies generally do not address the reciprocal nature of social skill and close, high-quality relationships. That is, social skills may not only lead to the formation of positive relationships, but also be learned in the context of close positive relationships.

Interventions could take on a friendship focus if peer partners were chosen according to their potential for becoming friends with the target child, instead of being chosen merely on the basis of being a same-sex peer of a particular social status. For instance, a peer nomination such as "who would you like to get to know as a friend," might be helpful in identifying potential friendship partners. There is some evidence that dyadic interaction in social skills training programs can stimulate friendship. In one study, target children's initial gains in friendship ratings were maintained with training partners but not with other classmates at the 6-weeks follow-up (Bierman, 1986; Bierman & Furman, 1984). Bierman (1986) further suggested that friendship with training partners might eventually translate into additional friendships or improved peer acceptance if training partners facilitate target children's entry into the partner's friendship network.

The content as well as the structure of social skills instruction could be specifically geared toward friendship formation and maintenance of high-quality friendships. Dyadic interaction sessions could be designed to instruct the target child in key features of friendship such as communicating effectively, giving and receiving validation and help, and establishing trust and intimacy (e.g., see Gottman, 1983). Also, interventions could foster the development of friendships with peer partners by building friendship tasks into weekly assignments. Children's "homework" could involve speaking to the partner during recess, calling the partner at home, and inviting the partner home to play (e.g., see Ladd & Golter, 1988; Ladd & Hart, 1992).

Interventions designed to promote victimized children's friendships may reduce risk of victimization in multiple ways, including reducing the amount of time a child is alone, providing peer allies, facilitating the child's integration in the peer group, and augmenting children's social skillfulness and confidence in their personal social agency (ability to achieve proactive social goals, such as initiating dyadic play). Friendship interventions may also ameliorate many of the negative consequences that have been linked with victimization. Forming friendships with classmates may diminish children's loneliness at school. Also, children who have friends at school may feel more enthusiastic about school and less likely to dislike and avoid school. Interventions that aim not only to diminish the incidence of victimization but also to address the personal and relational circumstances that contribute to children's vulnerability to victimization may better address the overall well-being of the child.

Interventions designed to help withdrawn children feel less anxious, interact in a more assertive and proactive prosocial manner, mitigate self-blaming tendencies, and develop close peer friendships should reduce their risk for victimization as well as promote their emotional well-being. Although further investigation of the etiology and intervention needs of aggressive victims is needed, it is reasonable to expect that they may benefit from a combination of the intervention strategies that have been developed for withdrawn and aggressive children. Intervention strategies developed for aggressive children include instruction in nonaggressive social problem-solving techniques and anger control strategies, and retraining hostile attribution tendencies (see Bierman, Greenberg, & CA Conduct Problems Prevention Research Group, 1996; Graham & Juvonen, 1998a; Lochman, Coie, Underwood, & Terry, 1993). Yet, aggressive victims may need more than a simple combination of interventions designed for withdrawn, submissive victims and aggressive children. Because aggressive victims are particularly likely to have experienced abuse within the family from an early age (Schwartz et al., 1997), they may also be in need of more intensive individual and family counseling.

CONCLUSION

Interventions that address victimized children's individual vulnerabilities and augment supportive peer friendships could complement programs that focus on the prevention of victimization at an environmental level. For instance, at the environmental level, classroom rules that prohibit children from excluding others and encourage children to include their peers (see Olweus, 1993a; Paley, 1992; Ross, 1996) may facilitate vulnerable children's use of assertive strategies (perhaps learned through individual-level intervention). Environmental, individual, and relationship-oriented interventions are likely to be complementary because they address the multiple systems that influence peer victimization.

Olweus's (e.g., 1993a) intervention studies have achieved notable success in terminating and preventing victimization among children in school environments. Yet, little progress has been made in implementing interventions that address children's individual and relationship-oriented vulnerability to peer victimization or reduce the negative consequences linked with victimization. It is especially important to address these issues because evidence suggests that consequences of victimization, such as loneliness, school avoidance, and depressive symptoms, endure long after victimization has subsided (Kochenderfer & Ladd, 1996a; Kochenderfer-Ladd & Wardrop, 2001; Olweus, 1993b). We suggest that investigators and practitioners develop comprehensive interventions for children vulnerable to victimization, including components designed to remediate maladaptive individual characteristics (e.g., social withdrawal, submissiveness, self-blaming tendencies) and enhance the social support available to victimized children through peer friendships or other enduring social ties. Such interventions situate victimization in the broader context of related social and emotional difficulties, and aim not only to diminish immediate harm done by victimization but also to mitigate long-lasting social and emotional difficulties and promote victimized children's well-being and adaptive development.

REFERENCES

Asendorpf, J. B. (1990). Beyond social withdrawal: Shyness, unsociability, and peer avoidance. *Human Development, 33,* 250–259.

Asher, S. R. (1993, April). *Inviting children to self-refer.* Paper presented at the Biennial meeting of the Society for Research in Child Development, New Orleans, LA.

Asher, S. R., Parker, J. G., & Walker, D. L. (1996). Distinguishing friendship from acceptance: Implications for intervention and assessment. In W. M. Bukowski & A. F. Newcomb (Eds.), *Cambridge studies in social and emotional development. The company they keep: Friendship in childhood and adolescence* (pp. 366–405). New York: Cambridge University Press.

Bienert, H., & Schneider, B. (1995). Deficit-specific social skills training with peer-nominated aggressive–disruptive and sensitive–isolated preadolescents. *Journal of Clinical Child Psychology, 24,* 287–299.

Bierman, K. L. (1986). Process of change during social skills training with preadolescents and its relation to treatment outcome. *Child Development, 57,* 230–240.

Bierman, K. L., & Furman, W. (1984). The effects of social skills training and peer involvement on the social adjustment of preadolescents. *Child Development, 55,* 151–162.

Bierman, K. L., Greenberg, M. T., & CA Conduct Problems Prevention Research Group. (1996). Social skills training in the Fast Track Program. In R. D. Peters & R. J. McMahon (Eds.), *Banuff international behavioral science series: Vol. 3. Preventing childhood disorders, substance abuse, and delinquency* (pp. 65–89). Thousand Oaks, CA: Sage.

Bjorkqvist, K., Ekman, K., & Lagerspetz, K. (1982). Bullies and victims: Their ego picture, ideal ego picture and normative ego picture. *Scandinavian Journal of Psychology, 23,* 307–313.

Boivin, M., & Hymel, S. (1997). Peer experiences and social self-perceptions: A sequential model. *Developmental Psychology, 33,* 135–145.

Boivin, M., Hymel, S., & Bukowski, W. M. (1995). The roles of social withdrawal, peer rejection, and victimization by peers in predicting loneliness and depressed mood in children. *Development and Psychopathology, 7,* 765–785.

Bowers, L., Smith, P. K., & Binney, V. (1992). Cohesion and power in the families of children involved in bully/victim problems at school. *Journal of Family Therapy, 14*, 371–387.

Bowers, L., Smith, P. K., & Binney, V. (1994). Perceived family relationships of bullies, victims and bully/victims in middle childhood. *Journal of Social and Personal Relationships, 11*, 215–232.

Crick, N. R., & Ladd, G. W. (1990). Children's perceptions of the outcomes of aggressive strategies: Do the ends justify being mean? *Developmental Psychology, 26*, 612–620.

Csapo, M. (1983). Effectiveness of coaching socially withdrawn/isolated children in specific social skills. *Educational Psychology, 3*, 31–42.

Dodge, K. A., & Crick, N. R. (1990). Social information processing bases of aggressive behavior in children. *Personality and Social Psychology Bulletin, 16*, 8–22.

Egan, S. K., Monson, T. C., & Perry, D. G. (1998). Social–cognitive influences on change in aggression over time. *Developmental Psychology, 34*, 996–1006.

Egan, S. K., & Perry, D. G. (1998). Does low self-regard invite victimization? *Developmental Psychology, 34*, 299–309.

Eisenberg, N., Fabes, R. A., & Murphy, B. C. (1995). Relations of shyness and low sociability to regulation and emotionality. *Journal of Personality and Social Psychology, 68*, 505–517.

Finnegan, R. A., Hodges, E. V. E., & Perry, D. G. (1998). Victimization by peers: Associations with children's reports of mother–child interaction. *Journal of Personality and Social Psychology, 75*, 1076–1086.

Gazelle, H., & Ladd, G. W. (2002). *Solitude and interpersonal maladjustment in late childhood: Identifying solitary subgroups that differ in severity of risk.* Manuscript submitted for publication.

Gottman, J. M. (1983). How children become friends. *Monographs of the Society for Research in Child Development, 78* (3, Serial No. 201).

Graham, S., & Juvonen, J. (1998a). A social cognitive perspective on peer aggression and victimization. *Annals of Child Development, 13*, 21–66.

Graham, S., & Juvonen, J. (1998b). Self-blame and peer victimization in middle school: An attributional analysis. *Developmental Psychology, 34*, 587–599.

Harrist, A. W., Zaia, A. F., Bates, J. E., Dodge, K. A., & Pettit, G. S. (1997). Subtypes of social withdrawal in early childhood: Sociometric status and social–cognitive differences across four years. *Child Development, 68*, 278–294.

Hodges, E. V. E., Malone, M. J., & Perry, D. G. (1997). Individual risk and social risk as interacting determinants of victimization in the peer group. *Developmental Psychology, 33*, 1032–1039.

Hodges, E. V. E., & Perry, D. G. (1999). Personal and interpersonal antecedents and consequences of victimization by peers. *Journal of Personality and Social Psychology, 76*, 677–685.

Hudley, C., & Graham, S. (1993). An attributional intervention to reduce peer-directed aggression among African-American boys. *Child Development, 64*, 124–138.

Hymel, S., Rubin, K. H., Rowden, L., & LeMare, L. (1990). Children's peer relationships: Longitudinal prediction of internalizing and externalizing problems from middle to late childhood. *Child Development, 61*, 2004–2021.

Kochenderfer, B. J., & Ladd, G. W. (1996a). Peer victimization: Cause or consequence of school maladjustment? *Child Development, 67*, 1305–1317.

Kochenderfer, B. J., & Ladd, G. W. (1996b). Peer victimization: Manifestations and relations to school adjustment in kindergarten. *Journal of School Psychology, 34*, 267–283.

Kochenderfer-Ladd, B. J., & Ladd, G. W. (1997). Victimized children's responses to peer aggression: Behaviors associated with reduced versus continued victimization. *Development and Psychopathology, 9*, 59–73.

Kochenderfer-Ladd, B. J., & Ladd, G. W. (2001). Variations in peer victimization: Relations to children's maladjustment. In J. Juvonen & S. Graham (Eds.), *Peer harassment in school: The plight of the vulnerable and victimized* (pp. 21–48). New York: Guilford Press.

Kochenderfer-Ladd, B. J., & Wardrop, J. L. (2001). Chronicity and instability of children's peer victimization experiences as predictors of loneliness and social satisfaction trajectories. *Child Development, 72*, 134–151.

Ladd, G. W. (1999). Peer relationships and social competence during early and middle childhood. *Annual Review of Psychology, 50*, 333–359.

Ladd, G. W., & Burgess, K. B. (1999). Charting the relationship trajectories of aggressive, withdrawn, and aggressive/withdrawn children during early grade school. *Child Development, 70*, 910–929.

Ladd, G. W., & Golter, B. S. (1988). Parents' management of preschooler's peer relations: Is it related to children's social competence? *Developmental Psychology, 24*, 109–117.

Ladd, G. W., & Hart, C. H. (1992). Creating informal play opportunities: Are parents' and preschoolers' initiations related to children's competence with peers? *Developmental Psychology, 28*, 1179–1187.

Ladd, G. W., & Kochenderfer-Ladd, B. J. (in press). Identifying victims of peer aggression from early to middle childhood: Analysis of cross-informant data for concordance, estimation of relational adjustment, incidence of victimization, and characteristics of identified victims. *Psychological Assessment*.

Ladd, G. W., Kochenderfer, B. J., & Coleman, C. C. (1997). Classroom peer acceptance, friendship, and victimization: Distinct relational systems that contribute uniquely to children's school adjustment? *Child Development, 68*, 1181–1197.

Ladd, G. W., & Ladd, B. J. (1998). Parenting behaviors and parent–child relationships: Correlates of peer victimization in kindergarten? *Developmental Psychology, 34*, 1450–1458.

Lagerspetz, K., Bjorkqvist, K., Berts, M., & King, E. (1982). Group aggression among school children in three schools. *Scandinavian Journal of Psychology, 23*, 45–52.

Lochman, J. E., Coie, J. D., Underwood, M. K., & Terry, R. (1993). Effectiveness of a social relations intervention program for aggressive and nonaggressive, rejected children. *Journal of Consulting and Clinical Psychology, 61*, 1053–1058.

Malone, M. J., & Perry, D. G. (1995, March). *Features of aggressive and victimized children's friendships and affiliative preferences.* Poster presented at the biennial meeting of the Society for Research in Child Development, Indianapolis, IN.

Morison, P., & Masten, A. (1991). Peer reputation in middle childhood as a predictor of adaptation in adolescence: A seven-year follow-up. *Child Development, 62,* 991–1007.

Olweus, D. (1993a). Bullies on the playground: The role of victimization. In C. H. Hart (Ed.), *Children on playgrounds: Research perspectives and applications* (SUNY Series, Children's Play in Society, pp. 85–128). Albany: SUNY Press.

Olweus, D. (1993b). Victimization by peers: Antecedents and long-term outcomes. In K. H. Rubin & J. B. Asendorpf (Eds.), *Social withdrawal, inhibition, and shyness in childhood* (pp. 315–341). Hillsdale, NJ: Erlbaum.

Paley, V. G. (1992). *You can't say you can't play.* Cambridge, MA: Harvard University Press.

Pellegrini, A. D., Bartini, M., & Brooks, F. (1999). School bullies, victims, and aggressive victims: Factors relating to group affiliation and victimization in early adolescence. *Journal of Educational Psychology, 91,* 216–224.

Perry, D. G., Kusel, S. J., & Perry, L. C. (1988). Victims of peer aggression. *Developmental Psychology, 24,* 807–814.

Perry, D. G., Williard, J. C., & Perry, L. C. (1990). Peers' perceptions of the consequences that victimized children provide aggressors. *Child Development, 6,* 1310–1325.

Pierce, K. A., & Cohen, R. (1995). Aggressors and their victims: Toward a contextual framework for understanding children's aggressor–victim relationships. *Developmental Review, 15,* 292–310.

Rigby, K. (1993). School children's perceptions of their families and parents as a function of peer relations. *Journal of Genetic Psychology, 154,* 501–513.

Ross, D. (1996). *Childhood bullying and teasing: What school personnel, other professionals, and parents can do.* Alexandria, VA: American Counseling Association.

Rubin, K. H. (1985). Socially withdrawn children: An "at risk" population. In B. H. Schneider, K. H. Rubin, & J. E. Ledingham (Eds.), *Peer relationships and social skills in childhood: Issues in assessment and training* (pp. 125–139). New York: Springer-Verlag.

Rubin, K. H. (1993). The Waterloo Longitudinal Project: Correlates and consequences of social withdrawal from childhood to adolescence. In K. H. Rubin & J. B. Asendorpf (Eds.), *Social withdrawal, inhibition, and shyness in childhood* (pp. 291–314). Hillsdale, NJ: Erlbaum.

Rubin, K. H., & Burgess, K. B. (2001). Social withdrawal and anxiety. In M. W. Vasey & M. R. Dadds (Eds.), *The developmental psychopathology of anxiety* (pp. 407–434). Oxford, England: Oxford University Press.

Rubin, K. H., Chen, X., & Hymel, S. (1993). Socioemotional characteristics of withdrawn and aggressive children. *Merrill–Palmer Quarterly, 39,* 518–534.

Rubin, K. H., Chen, X., McDougall, P., Bowker, A., & McKinnon, J. (1995). The

Waterloo Longitudinal Project: Predicting internalizing and externalizing problems in adolescence. *Development and Psychopathology, 7,* 751–764.

Rubin, K. H., & Mills, R. S. L. (1988). The many faces of social isolation in childhood. *Journal of Consulting and Clinical Psychology, 56,* 916–924.

Schwartz, D., Dodge, K. A., & Coie, J. D. (1993). The emergence of chronic peer victimization in boys' play groups. *Child Development, 64,* 1755–1772.

Schwartz, D., Dodge, K. A., Coie, J. D., Hubbard, J. A., Cillessen, A. H. N., Lemerise, E. A., et al. (1998). Social–cognitive and behavioral correlates of aggression and victimization in boys' play groups. *Journal of Abnormal Child Psychology, 26,* 431–440.

Schwartz, D., Dodge, K. A., Pettit, G. S., & Bates, J. E. (1997). The early socialization of aggressive victims of bullying. *Child Development, 68,* 665–675.

Schwartz, D., McFadyen-Ketchum, S. A., Dodge, K. A., Pettit, G. S., & Bates, J. E. (1998). Peer group victimization as a predictor of children's behavior problems at home and in school. *Development and Psychopathology, 10,* 87–99.

Schwartz, D., McFadyen-Ketchum, S., Dodge, K. A., Pettit, G. S., & Bates, J. E. (1999). Early behavior problems as a predictor of later peer group victimization: Moderators and mediators in the pathways of social risk. *Journal of Abnormal Child Psychology, 27,* 191–201.

Smith, P. K., Bowers, L., Binney, V., & Cowie, H. (1993). Relationships of children involved in bully/victim problems at school. In S. Duck (Ed.), *Learning about relationships* (pp. 184–212). Newbury Park, CA: Sage.

Stewart, S. L., & Rubin, K. H. (1995). The social problem-solving skills of anxious–withdrawn children. *Development and Psychopathology, 7,* 323–336.

Strauss, C. C., Forehand, R., Smith, K., & Frame, C. L. (1986). The association between social withdrawal and internalizing problems of children. *Journal of Abnormal Child Psychology, 14,* 525–535.

Trower, P., Gilbert, P., & Sherling, G. (1990). Social anxiety, evolution, and self-presentation: An interdisciplinary perspective. In H. Leitenberg (Ed.), *Handbook of social and evaluation anxiety* (pp. 11–45). New York: Plenum Press.

Troy, M., & Sroufe, L. A. (1987). Victimization among preschoolers: Role of attachment relationship history. *Journal of the American Academy of Child and Adolescent Psychiatry, 26,* 166–172.

4

DATING VIOLENCE EDUCATION: PREVENTION AND EARLY INTERVENTION STRATEGIES

SARAH AVERY-LEAF AND MICHELE CASCARDI

Romantic or dating attachments begin during adolescence, and with many of these relationships comes the onset of dating aggression. Until recently, very little was known about the phenomenon of adolescent dating, and less still about teenage dating violence. Nonetheless, as the past few decades have spotlighted issues surrounding domestic violence (i.e., adult partner violence), methods of primary prevention have begun to target adolescents. In this chapter, we discuss existing prevention and early intervention strategies implemented in secondary school settings, many of which target adolescent dating violence. In the first section, we review research on adolescent dating behaviors and on the prevalence of dating aggression. The following section contains a brief discussion of some of the more politicized, or controversial, issues involved in the study of teenage dating aggression. We also cover research on risk factors for dating violence. In the second half of this chapter we review and synthesize the results of outcome evaluation

We acknowledge the two reviewers of our chapter, Amy Smith Slep, PhD, and Annmarie Cano, PhD, for their helpful feedback.

studies. Conclusions are geared toward educators charged with selecting an antiviolence program for their student populations.

DATING BEHAVIORS AND PREVALENCE OF DATING AGGRESSION

It is difficult to establish a single definition of the phenomenon of *adolescent dating* on which all, or even most, can agree (Dornbusch, 1981). This term can encompass anything from boys and girls "hanging out" with one another within the context of a large, mixed-gender group to a monogamous, committed, sexual relationship. In our own work, we ask students to report on their own dating histories and provide a fairly broad definition of dating for our research participants. For example, we begin our survey by informing participants that

> Students use many different words when they talk about dating, such as "hanging out," "seeing each other," or "hooking up." Some of you may already be dating, while others may not. We want to learn more about your experiences, so answer the survey questions as honestly as you can. There are no right or wrong answers.

We have found that suburban high school students report the onset of dating at about age 12 years, with approximately half of students reporting current involvement with a partner at the time of assessment (Avery-Leaf, Cascardi, O'Leary, & Cano, 1997). Among inner-city middle school students, most reported having their first boyfriend or girlfriend when they were younger than age 9 (Cascardi, 1999). In a sample of 1,276 urban sixth graders (95% African American), more than two thirds reported "going out" with someone currently (Cascardi, 1999). Although these relationships range in intensity (as measured by type and frequency of contact), it is interesting to note that 25%–33% of students in both middle and high schools reported that they will marry their current dating partner. Among middle school students in two cohorts, 66%–87% reported involvement in a current dating relationship at the time of assessment (Cascardi, 1999). Dating at what many adults consider to be an early age does not seem to be an urban phenomenon: A study of nearly 2,000 eighth and ninth graders (mean age 13.9 years) from rural North Carolina reported that 72% of students indicated that they had dated previously (Foshee, Linder, et al., 1996).

Prevalence of Adolescent Dating Violence

Rates of dating aggression vary according to how this variable is defined and what age group is studied. For each type of behavior—verbal aggression, dominance and coercion, physical aggression, and sexual harassment—rates are reviewed where data exist. In general, rates of physical aggression tend to be highest when threats of physical aggression and aggression against objects (e.g., throwing something) are included in the definition (Bookwala, Frieze, Smith, & Ryan, 1992; O'Keefe, 1997). Moreover, rates of all forms of behavior tend to be highest when multiple behavioral questions (e.g., Conflict Tactics Scale [Straus, 1979], which includes psychological and physical aggressive behaviors; O'Keefe, 1997) are used instead of single, global questions (e.g., "Have you ever been hurt physically by your partner?"; Bergman, 1992).

Middle School Students

Behaviors in this age group have only recently been investigated. Data indicate that between 28% and 45% of students have experienced some form of sexual harassment by a peer or group of peers (Cascardi, Avery-Leaf, & O'Brien, 1998; Connolly, McMaster, Craig, & Pepler, 1997). Represented by these data are students from a Canadian urban community of primarily European descent and a U.S. urban community of predominantly African American students. Rates of perpetration of physical aggression against a dating partner vary considerably by region, 5% in urban Canada (Connolly et al., 1997), 21% in rural United States (Foshee et al., 1996), and more than 45% in urban (inner-city) United States (Cascardi et al., 1998).

Across all studies, girls reported higher rates of aggression than boys; however, girls also reported receiving more injuries (Foshee et al., 1996). Only one published study reported rates of sexual aggression, with 1%–5% of students reporting perpetration of sexual aggression (e.g., forced sex by a dating partner) and 7%–15% reporting sexual victimization (Foshee et al., 1996). Foshee and colleagues (1996) reported that psychological aggression (threats, monitoring, insults, and manipulation) occurs with some frequency, with manipulation occurring most often. Girls reported receiving significantly more psychological abuse than boys, although the amount of perpetration of these behaviors for boys and girls was similar, except for manipulation, which was reported more often by the girls.

High School Students

A study by the American Association of University Women (1993) found that 81% of high school youths reported sexual harassment from peers, with similar rates of harassment reported by young men and young women. Rates of verbal and psychological aggression are reported in two thirds to three quarters of dating relationships (Cascardi, Avery-Leaf, O'Leary, & Slep, 1999). Like studies of middle school students, studies of high school students report a large range in the rate of physical aggression in a dating relationship, from 9% to 52% (Cascardi, Avery-Leaf, O'Leary, 1994; Roscoe

& Callahan, 1985). Most estimates tend to cluster either between 10% and 20% (e.g., Henton, Cate, Koval, Lloyd, & Christopher, 1983; Roscoe & Kelsey, 1986) or 30% and 40% (e.g., Malik, Sorenson, Aneshehsel, 1997; O'Keefe, 1997). Moreover, young women consistently report higher rates of inflicting aggression than young men; rates of reported victimization are similar for young men and women. From these data, many researchers conclude that physical aggression occurs in one of three teenagers' dating relationships.

The rate of sexual violence in a multiethnic, economically diverse sample was 15.7% (Bergman, 1992). In contrast to gender patterns for physical aggression, young women reported dramatically higher rates of sexual victimization than did young men; one study found that 17.8% of high school girls reported experiencing forced sexual activity, compared to 0.3% of boys (Molidor & Tolman, 1998). Similarly, Bennett and Fineran (1998) found that 16% of high school girls reported being the victim of sexual violence, whereas only 1% said that they had perpetrated sexual violence. For boys, the rates were 6% and 4%, respectively, for being the victim of sexual violence and perpetrating sexual violence.

College Students

Rates of verbal and psychological aggression among college students are similar to those reported by high school students (e.g., Riggs & O'Leary, 1996). Physical aggression in a dating relationship occurs with notable frequency, with rates ranging from 21.2% (Makepeace, 1981) to 65% (Bookwala et al., 1992). Most estimates are between 21% and 40% (e.g., Arias, Samios, & O'Leary, 1987; Billingham, 1987; Pederson & Thomas, 1992; Riggs & O'Leary, 1996). Again, women typically reported engaging in higher rates of verbal and psychological aggression than did men, although injuries and negative emotional consequences are more severe for the women (e.g., Makepeace, 1986).

The rate of sexual violence among young adults has been well documented. Survey research has indicated that as many as half of all college women report being victims of some form of sexual abuse, and 27% report being victims of rape (15%) or attempted rape (12%; Koss, 1998). Moreover, 25% of the men in Koss's (1998) survey indicated that they had behaved sexually with a woman against her will. Finally, Denmare, Briere, and Lips (1988) found that 22% of undergraduate men reported at least some future likelihood of raping.

Overall, these findings clearly demonstrate that most teenagers begin dating at the middle school level. In these relationships, there is a substantial amount of aggression, including physical and sexual acts of violence. One implication of the early onset of dating violence is that youths may develop frameworks through which to make partner selections and evaluations of their relationships based on the idea that aggression is normative. That is to say, experiencing and observing dating aggression may lead young daters to believe that the violence is an expected, or even inevitable, part of romantic involvement.

CONTROVERSIAL ISSUES IN UNDERSTANDING DATING VIOLENCE

Explanations for partner violence tend to be controversial, highly political, and emotionally charged topics for debate. Such turmoil may be unpleasant at times, or worse, may effectively block crucial dialogue among community members. Despite these difficulties, different perspectives and theories are important to consider for developing education programs to prevent the onset or continuation of dating aggression and must be addressed when discussing issues of dating violence. As the topic is a prerequisite for any implementation of violence prevention in the school settings, we include a discussion of these controversies as a key component of school-based prevention work. Differences of opinion tend to center around gender-related attitudes and beliefs. Below we discuss feminist theory as it pertains to frameworks for program models; issues of gender and reporting styles when collecting data and interpreting research findings; and the role of attitudes about dating violence, which have been the focus of much of the research on this phenomenon.

Feminist Theory

Feminist scholars (Dobash & Dobash, 1979; Yllo, 1993) have highlighted the importance of patriarchal social structure in the etiology of male violence toward female partners. This sociological perspective emphasizes the relationship between gender-based power inequities in the culture at large and male abuses of power and control within intimate relationships. Although changing these inequities in the culture at large with a short-term school-based curriculum may not be possible, a feminist approach targets attitudes and beliefs as the key to preventing partner violence. Specifically, this approach focuses on changing individuals' attitudes toward interpersonal violence, adherence to traditional gender roles, and the behavioral expression of power and control in intimate relationships.

Proponents of the feminist viewpoint advocate consciousness-raising as an essential aspect of prevention and typically recommend women formerly involved in abusive relationships as program implementers. This approach may be viewed as holding men responsible for their violence, but many people view this approach as problematic in that it fails to address female aggression against male partners (Dutton, 1994). Survey research with high school and college dating couples has pointed toward the role of both men and women in the perpetration of physical aggression. These studies have consistently reported that higher percentages of women than men self-reported the perpetration of dating violence in White, African American, and mixed-race samples (Avery-Leaf et al., 1997; Clark, Beckett, Wells, & Dungee-Anderson, 1994; DeMaris, 1990; Foshee et al., 1996; Schwartz, O'Leary, & Kendziora, 1997). However, in terms of the impact of the aggression, men do not report sustaining greater injuries as a result of the aggression (Avery-Leaf et al., 1997).

These findings raise important questions regarding the methods used to assess these rates of aggression, as well as the interpretation of results from these aggression measures. Many feminists maintain that men tend to deny and minimize their own aggression, whereas women do not. Moreover, many argue about the difference in impact and meaning between a woman's aggressive act and that of a man. Most agree that a size and strength differential exists between adult heterosexual partners, but there is less agreement about teenage partners, particularly early adolescents. Most important, when it comes to applying the research findings to the format of an educational program, some feminists would argue for the importance of directing preventive efforts to both men and women in mixed-sex settings. However, many other feminists advocate providing interventions separately to same-sex groups, both to ensure the comfort and safety of participants and to deliver messages appropriate to each gender.

Many feminists object to the use of skills-based programs with mixed-gender audiences. They contend that such programs have "victim-blaming" implications, that is, that a potential message of such programs is that a victim's poor communication, safety skills, anger management skills, and so forth cause partner aggression. Behavioral theorists, on the other hand, advocate skills building as an essential component of dating violence prevention. Here again, this controversy may seriously undermine the success of a program, in that an implementer's belief in the program directly affects the program's impact and potential for success.

Gender

As mentioned above, the issue of gender in understanding the prevalence of teenage dating aggression is complex as well as controversial. Researchers have offered several interpretations of the consistent finding that female adolescents report using physical aggression against a dating partner at higher rates than do male adolescents (Avery-Leaf et al., 1997; Clark et al., 1994; DeMaris, 1990; Foshee et al., 1998; Schwartz et al., 1997). Pederson and Thomas (1992) suggested that boys may underreport their aggressive behavior as a form of denial and girls may overreport their aggressive behavior because of their readiness to accept blame. Others argue that girls may be more willing to report aggressive behaviors because there are fewer social sanctions against their aggressive actions. For boys, there are strong societal messages that "boys do not hit girls." In keeping with this social norm, boys may be more reluctant to report socially sanctioned behavior. Alternatively, girls may indeed be more aggressive, especially when the size difference between boys and girls is small; they may not perceive their actions as harmful if the impact of their action is physically benign.

Some support for this interpretation comes from the work of Harris and colleagues in that aggression from a male is perceived as more serious, harmful, and culpable than that from a female (e.g., Harris & Knight-Bohnhoff, 1996). Foshee (1996) reported that female adolescents are more likely to report perpetrating all forms of physical aggression (mild to severe), whereas male adolescents are more likely to report engaging in sexual aggression (e.g., forced sex). Although the most appropriate interpretation of girls' higher rate of reporting physical aggression is still unclear, the collective findings do not seem to support a feminist perspective in which males unilaterally perpetrate aggression against female partners. Clearly, there appears to be a shift in male and female use of violence over time, with females perpetrating less physical violence in their relationships over time, and males perpetrating relatively more. Unfortunately, the concept of females as perpetrators, particularly girls, is often difficult for many adults—feminists, educators, and parents—to accept.

Another aspect of gender in dating violence perpetration is that of unilateral, as opposed to bilateral, aggression. Here again, it is clear from the research that a model in which there is one (male) abuser and one (female) victim does not characterize most adolescents' experience of dating violence. Numerous studies document that from 43% to 72% of aggression is characterized as mutual combat (e.g., Bookwala et al., 1992; Henton et al., 1983; O'Keefe, Brockopp, & Chew, 1986) in which both partners engage in physical aggression. Moreover, girls are no more likely than boys to report that their aggression was used in self-defense or retaliation (Avery-Leaf et al., 1997; Cascardi, 1999; Makepeace, 1987).

Attitudinal Models

Many theorists posit that partners use aggression against an intimate partner simply because they believe that this method is an acceptable way of resolving conflict. This idea has received much empirical attention; a majority of studies on dating violence include some measure of acceptance of dating aggression as well as various relationship concerns, such as level of conflict, verbal aggression, jealousy, and being a recipient or target of physical aggression by one's partner (e.g., Bookwala et al., 1992; Cano, Avery-Leaf, Cascardi, & O'Leary, 1998; Riggs, 1990). Most researchers have found that such attitudes significantly predict aggressive behaviors (Cano et al.,

1998; O'Keefe, 1997; Riggs & O'Leary, 1996). Although there is general agreement that changing attitudes is a productive aspect of prevention work in this area, the controversies stem from the identification and modification of specific attitudes. For example, popular opinion and feminist theory point to sex role socialization as a key feature of the development of male entitlement beliefs and subsequent violence against a partner (e.g., Birns, Cascardi, & Meyer, 1994). However, research efforts have failed to demonstrate a consistent statistical relationship (Cano et al., 1998; Currie, 1983; Sigelman, Berry, & Wiles, 1984; Thompson, 1991). In contrast, another perspective suggests that both male and female aggression may be motivated by a desire for control, implied by the significant association of coercion and control of a dating partner with dating aggression for male and female college students (Stets & Pirog-Good, 1990). The net effect is often disagreement as to whether sex role factors, as opposed to other attitudinal factors, take precedence in violence prevention efforts.

RISK FACTORS FOR DATING AGGRESSION

Over the past 2 decades, research regarding risk factors for dating and domestic violence has proliferated. Some of the risk factors, particularly those involving knowledge, attitudes, beliefs, and skills, appear amenable to universal prevention programs directed toward all adolescents. Other risk factors, such childhood exposure to violence, suggest selected interventions targeted toward "at-risk" populations. Reviewed below is a list of "causes," or risk factors, for dating violence, integrated with current findings from the research literature.

Community and School Violence

Few studies have examined the role that community violence plays in the prediction of dating violence for youths. Taking both family and community factors into account, Malik and colleagues (1997) found that witnessing or knowing someone involved in a violent altercation resulting in severe injury in the community and also being exposed to female-to-male spousal violence were strong predictors of dating aggression. Similarly, another study reported that exposure to community and school violence was significantly associated with both receiving and inflicting dating violence for both male and female high school students (O'Keefe, 1997).

Parental Violence

Overall, there has been consistent but weak support for the idea that youths who grow up in homes in which they either witness or experience violence are more likely to use violence in their intimate relationships. Although it is true that youths who grow up in violent home environments are at greater risk for relationship violence, it is not the only explanation. Not all youths who come from homes in which there is violence use or tolerate it in their own relationships (Simons, Lin, & Gordon, 1998). The research literature has produced mixed results in regard to the effects of witnessing parental violence. Witnessing parental violence has more consistently been associated with male use of dating aggression than with female use (e.g., Foo & Margolin, 1995; O'Keefe, 1997; Smith & Williams, 1992). Riggs and O'Leary (1996) found that, for girls, witnessing parental aggression was associated with increased acceptance of dating aggression as a means of conflict resolution. In contrast, O'Keefe (1997) found that the relationship between witnessing parental violence and dating aggression was mediated by acceptance of dating aggression for boys. As mentioned earlier, the gender of the violent parent also differs in terms of the effect on teenage dating violence: Malik et al. (1997) found effects on both dating and community aggression of exposure to female-to-male parent spousal violence but not for exposure to male-to-female spousal violence. And a few studies have found no effect of witnessing parent violence (Schwartz et al., 1997; Sigelman et al., 1984).

Child Abuse

Retrospective reports of abuse in childhood and the association of that abuse to current dating aggression have yielded mixed results, with some studies finding a link (e.g., Sigelman et al., 1984) and others reporting no association (e.g., Foo & Margolin, 1995; O'Keefe, 1997). A longitudinal study of 113 families with adolescent boys conducted over 5 years (grades 7–12) investigated the link between parent–child aggression and dating violence (Simons et al., 1998). Results indicated that corporal punishment was significantly associated with dating violence; interestingly, corporal punishment was not predictive of delinquent behaviors, suggesting that corporal punishment specifically "teaches that it is both legitimate and effective to hit those you love" (Simons et al., 1998, p. 475).

Past Behavior

Although violent or aggressive personality characteristics have not been directly studied in dating violence studies of adolescents, use of physical aggression with peers or past dating aggression serves as indirect measures of aggressive personality tendencies. These studies showed that youths who use physical aggression with their peers or show a general tendency toward aggressiveness are also more likely to use aggression with a partner. Consistent support has been found for the link between dating aggression and aggression against a peer for both boys and girls (Riggs & O'Leary, 1996; Riggs, O'Leary,

& Breslin, 1990). However, Bookwala et al. (1992) reported that general use of aggression predicted only male use of dating aggression. This finding was supported in a study of high-risk adolescents who attended an alternative high school: Only male use of peer aggression was significantly associated with young men's use of dating aggression (Chase, Treboux, O'Leary, & Strassberg, 1998). With respect to past aggression in a dating context, it has consistently been shown that use of dating aggression against a previous partner, as well as prior use of verbal aggression, are the strongest predictors of current aggression (Bookwala et al., 1992; Cano et al., 1998).

Sex Roles

The literature is mixed in regard to the importance of sex role socialization. Theoretically, it is argued that typical gender socialization processes prime women for victimization and men for aggression in intimate relationships (e.g., Birns et al., 1994). A few studies have supported the view that women who maintain traditional views about women's roles in society are more likely to be victims of dating aggression, whereas men who adopt traditional beliefs about men's roles are more likely to perpetrate dating aggression (Currie, 1983; Sigelman et al., 1984). To the contrary, some studies have shown no relationship between sex role socialization and dating aggression (Bernard & Bernard, 1983). In another study, female use of dating aggression was predicted by traditional views on women's roles, whereas male use of dating aggression was predicted by nontraditional views of men's roles (Bookwala et al., 1992).

Acceptance of Aggression

The attitudes or beliefs that youths have about how acceptable it is to use aggression is one of the most consistent factors associated with the use of physical aggression in dating relationships for young men (Bookwala et al., 1992; Cano et al., 1998; Cate, Henton, Koval, Christopher, & Lloyd, 1982; Henton et al., 1983; Riggs, 1990; Schwartz et al., 1997). For young women, some studies reported a positive relationship (e.g., Cate et al., 1982), whereas many others showed no relationship (e.g., Bookwala et al., 1992; Schwartz et al., 1997). Studies that reported an association between attitudes and dating aggression for women include measures that tap acceptance of female use of dating aggression (rather than a measure that does not specify gender; e.g., O'Keefe, 1997; Riggs, 1990) and measures that evaluate the acceptance of dating aggression in provocative situations such as humiliation (e.g., Foo & Margolin, 1995). Other research has shown that students who are accepting of verbal aggression and jealousy in hypothetical dating situations are more likely to use them in their actual dating relationships as well (Cascardi, Avery-Leaf, O'Leary, & Slep, 1997; Slep, Cascardi, Avery-Leaf, & O'Leary, 1997).

Verbal Aggression and Jealousy

Verbal aggression, such as insults or spiteful words, predicts the first occurrence of physical aggression among young couples (Murphy & O'Leary, 1989) and is consistently associated with adolescents' use of physical aggression against a dating partner (e.g., Bookwala et al., 1992; Cano et al., 1998). We also know that an adolescent's jealous and controlling behaviors and use of physical aggression predict his or her partner's use of physical aggression (e.g., Cascardi et al., 1997). Bookwala et al. (1992) found an association between dating aggression and jealousy for young women only. Because verbal aggression, jealousy, and attempts to control one's partner often happen before physical aggression is used, it is important to educate students that these actions are warning signs that a relationship is or may become harmful.

Difficulties in Coping

Some theorists suggest that violent acts stem from deficiencies in coping with rejection and negative emotions and that verbal and physical aggression, along with jealous and control tactics, may simply reflect these deficiencies. Although this idea has received some support empirically, it may be a better fit for female aggression than for male aggression. Two studies of high school students conducted by Cano and colleagues (1998) found a relationship among coercion, dominance, and jealous tactics and dating violence. Multivariate analyses indicated that, although past dating violence was a significant predictor of current dating violence for young men and women, self-reported dominance and jealous tactics were significant predictors of female dating violence, and partner dominance and jealous tactics were significant predictors of male violence. Below are other skills, such as anger management and assertiveness, that may be needed to avoid dating aggression.

Conflict and Arguing

The more arguments a couple has, the more likely they are to use relationship violence. Disagreements or conflict in a relationship often sets the stage for relationship violence. In fact, O'Keefe (1997) and Riggs (1990) found that greater relationship conflict was associated with male and female use of dating aggression. The data also inform us that students who used dating aggression to resolve conflicts in past relationships are at heightened risk to continue to use aggression to resolve conflicts in current relationships (e.g., Bookwala et al., 1992; Cano et al., 1998).

Retaliation to "Save Face"

Many students claim that they were provoked into using physical aggression. These provocations include emotions such as jealousy, humiliation, and retaliation. Constructive responses to such provocations generally require an assertive verbal response, which may be beyond the skill level of many adolescents. For example, if a boy sees his girlfriend talking with another boy, he may feel very jealous and react by grabbing or slapping his girlfriend. If a girl thinks her boyfriend has insulted or degraded her, she may respond to this emotional insult by slapping or hitting him. Indeed, studies show that jealousy, anger, and retaliation against emotional harm (such as "saving face") are common reasons for the use of dating aggression (e.g., Follingstad, Hause, Rutledge, & Polek, 1992; O'Keefe, 1997).

Social Deviance

Among a birth cohort of more than 1,000 participants from Dunedin, New Zealand, the two strongest predictors of dating aggression that emerged for both young men and women were violent antisocial behaviors (e.g., firesetting, assault) and substance abuse, reported at age 15 (Moffitt & Caspi, 1999). Moreover, teenage parenting was predictive of aggression as well: For young women, having children before age 21 put them at risk for victimization, whereas for young men, fathering a child before turning 21 increased the likelihood of perpetrating aggression (Moffit & Caspi, 1999).

Summary

Although the extant research on the predictors of dating violence has shown some important factors for identifying those at risk, the relative effects of each factor are not yet clear, nor do we know the additive effects of these factors when they are combined with others. However, across studies, risk factors explain from 40% to 60% of why students use dating aggression (e.g., Cano et al., 1998; O'Keefe, 1997). Verbal aggression and being the recipient of aggression by a partner emerge as consistent predictors of dating aggression (e.g., Cano et al., 1998). Most studies have supported the negative influence of aggressive models in the home or community on dating aggression (e.g., Malik et al., 1997). Moreover, in one study, the negative effects of school and community violence were most evident among youths who witnessed violence in their homes (O'Keefe, 1997).

Taken together, the research reviewed above identifies several factors amenable to change that can and should be targeted by programs aiming to prevent dating violence. In the next section, we review the research documenting the efficacy of school-based dating violence prevention programs. Although there are many domestic violence treatment programs, there are few published evaluations of partner violence prevention programs; thus, knowledge as to the effects of such interventions is limited. Overall, these programs tend to be conceptualized as primary prevention efforts and are aimed at adolescents in high school (despite the fact that many teenagers have already experienced violence in their earliest dating relationships). However, there are also a few more recent evaluations of prevention efforts that target younger (e.g., middle school age) adolescents.

SCHOOL-BASED PARTNER VIOLENCE PREVENTION PROGRAMS

Two evaluations of Levy's (1984) domestic violence prevention program, Skills for Violence Free Relationships, have been undertaken (Jones, 1987; Krajewski, Rybarik, Dosch, & Gilmore, 1996; Levy, 1984). In its entirety, this program is a multisession curriculum for adolescents based on a gender perspective, that is, that beliefs and adherence to traditional sex roles and acceptance of male dominance within a relationship are at the root of partner violence. Although the first study failed to demonstrate change in high school students' attitudes toward the use of violence, it used an extremely limited outcome measure (one that used five global items on a three-point scale of agreement) that may not have been sufficiently sensitive to yield significant pre- to posttest change within the treatment group. The second study (Krajewski et al., 1996) used a survey instrument that had been developed and validated for use with Levy's (1984) 10-session program. The study used a longitudinal design that assessed knowledge and attitudes at three time points (pre-, post-, and 5-month follow-up). Initial effects were found on both attitudes and knowledge, but these effects were not maintained at follow-up.

In another longitudinal study, the 10-session STAR (Southside Teens About Respect) curriculum was evaluated with a cohort of urban African American students over 2 years (Schewe, 2000). Of the 333 students in the original sample, 118 completed all of the dependent measures at all four time points. The curriculum was one component of a comprehensive, community-based intervention involving a media campaign, a hotline, parent and teacher training, and the training of peer advocates. Results of the study comparing students who received 2 years of the curriculum to students who received 1 year to those who never participated in the curriculum indicated that the school-based interventions had clear effects on students' conflict behavior, self-ratings of relationship skills, and help-seeking behavior. Although not statistically significant, violence supportive attitudes and attitudes justifying violence in relationships also showed trends in the right direction. Analyses of the data from each year suggest that students increase their resolve to seek help following abuse after just one year of the curriculum. Therefore, information on help-seeking behavior could be reduced in the second year of the curriculum.

Given the findings that students receiving the intervention in 2 consecutive years benefited considerably more than students who did not receive the intervention or received the intervention only 1 year, staff should consider expanding the program to include 3 or more consecutive years. Finally, given the data indicating that students are beginning to date and experience violence in their dating relationships at an early age, interventions should probably begin at grade 4, 5, or 6.

An evaluation of a 1-day violence prevention program implemented in Canadian high schools also focused on attitudes toward and knowledge of domestic violence (Jaffe, Suderman, Reitzel, & Killip, 1992). This program was not based on a health-oriented curriculum but consisted instead of a presentation by several speakers from the community (including police and domestic violence agency personnel). Students received either a full-day or half-day program, but results were reported for all students receiving a program, and thus it is not clear whether there were differences based on program length. Overall, results indicated significant improvements for both young men and women in attitude, knowledge, and "behavioral intent" (i.e., what respondents said they would do in hypothetical conflict situations). However, for some of the male students, a backlash effect was found in which attitude significantly worsened (i.e., acceptance of violence increased). This finding may suggest the use of gender-neutral materials rather than those based on a gender model of domestic violence (in which males are perpetrators and females are victims), so as to avoid defensiveness from male participants.

More recently, Hilton and colleagues investigated the backlash that arose in the Jaffe et al. (1992) study (Hilton, Harris, Rice, Krans, & Lavigne, 1998). To test the theory that the backlash was linked to victim or perpetrator status, Hilton and colleagues offered an antiviolence education program to 350 Canadian 11th graders who completed surveys measuring knowledge and attitudes as well as asking about their own experiences of inflicting or receiving aggression in a dating relationship. Although in this study a large-scale assembly (consisting of presentations by police officers and former abuse victims) offered to 2,500 students showed no effects, another intervention (consisting of 3 hours of small-group workshops led by a variety of presenters, including a sexual assault counselor, a men's counselor, a psychologist, and a police officer) was successful in changing attitudes and improving knowledge, with no backlash observed. Moreover, victim or perpetrator status was not found to be related to benefits derived from the program or to attendance. The authors concluded that the workshops were superior to the "single-event mass training" (Hilton et al., 1998, p. 737) and speculated that the workshops allowed for key features such as "repeating information, practicing skills, monitoring attendance, and rewarding participation" (p. 737).

A significant change in Canadian high school students' attitudes after a two- or four-session dating violence intervention (which consisted of two didactic sessions on dating violence and two supplemental activities) was reported in another evaluation (Lavoie, Vezina, Piche, & Boivin, 1995). However, the nature of the attitude scale was not reported, nor was there a control group. Another evaluation (Kaufman, Kantor, & Jasinski, 1995) compared one New England high school receiving a multilevel treatment (5-session curriculum for freshman health students; focus groups; community interaction) with a similar high school from a nearby district. Results indicated that male students' attitudes and knowledge improved as a result of the program, and reports of peer aggression decreased.

A large-scale evaluation of a dating violence program for middle school students used the Safe Dates curriculum and community intervention (Foshee et al., 1998). Foshee and colleagues implemented a 10-session program, which included a theater production and poster contest, and community services such as a hotline, support groups for teenagers, and parent materials. Primarily composed of White students, 14 middle schools in a rural southern U.S. state participated in the evaluation, and data were collected from 1,700 eighth and ninth graders. Results indicated that there were significant decreases 1 month after the program in psychological aggression, with decreases in sexual aggression exhibiting "suggestive trends" (p. 48). Moreover, students in the treatment condition endorsed more prosocial dating norms and reported that they used more positive communication skills after the program than did those in the control schools. Although no reductions in physical aggression were noted, it is unclear whether this reflects weak program effects or the limitations of measuring changes in behaviors 1 month after the program. A longer term follow-up study is needed to clarify this issue.

Our own curriculum, the Building Relationships in Greater Harmony Together (BRIGHT) program (Cascardi & Avery-Leaf, 1998) has undergone a series of evaluations in two types of settings: suburban high schools and urban middle schools (see following discussion for details). The BRIGHT program treats dating aggression as a multidetermined phenomenon (i.e., it has social and psychological causes). The program is sensitive to gender inequities while providing a psychoeducational, skills-based approach focusing on attitude change and skill enhancement, recognizing that both males and females may be victims or perpetrators within a dating relationship. In two pilot studies of the BRIGHT program, one conducted at an ethnically diverse high school and the second at a predominantly White high school, students who received the program perceived dating violence as significantly less justified after receiving the program; control students did not demonstrate attitude change. We then conducted a larger study in six multiethnic high schools in Suffolk County, New York. Results indicated that students who received the program (as compared to control groups) showed significant gains in knowledge and were significantly less accepting of attitudes that support dating violence. Recipients of the program reported higher intentions to seek help if they were involved in a harmful relationship in the future.

We recently completed an evaluation of the BRIGHT program in several large, inner-city middle schools consisting largely of African American students (Cascardi et al., 1999). More than 15,500 seventh and eighth graders participated in the study. Five middle schools were assigned to one of three conditions: single program dose, double dose (students received the program in spring and the following fall), and control (survey only). Although the single dose did seem to be effective in producing gains in knowledge and help-seeking intentions as well as decreases in intent to use aggression, the double dose showed greater improvements in behavioral intentions. Moreover, the double dose showed attitude changes not seen in the single-dose conditions. Unfortunately, knowledge and help-seeking intention effects disappeared after the double dose. The help-seeking intention effect is discouraging; students may have perceived their immediate environment as unhelpful, resulting in lower intentions to seek help. Alternatively, it is also possible that students perceived themselves as less likely to be involved in an aggressive dating relationship and therefore were less likely to perceive a need for help. Evidence suggests that a single dose of the BRIGHT program decreases the frequency with which verbal aggression and jealous and control tactics are used against a partner, as with the Safe Dates study. Moreover, additional evidence suggests that boys who received a single dose reported significantly less peer aggression and sexual harassment than those who had not.

One of the few program evaluations conducted in a multiethnic middle school setting sampled 440 sixth, seventh, and eighth graders in a small Florida city (Macgowan, 1997). (The sample was from a total of 740; only those who attended at least four of five sessions and completed at least 19 of 22 items on the pre- and posttests were retained.) The 5-session program focused on helping students recognize healthy as well as abusive relationship dynamics, with one session specifically devoted to skills. Overall, students receiving the program demonstrated significantly greater gains on 6 of the 22 survey items as compared to the control group immediately postintervention. The gains were primarily on items measuring knowledge and attitudes about nonphysical violence.

Taken together, these studies demonstrate that prevention programs tend to be effective at changing the acceptance of aggression, which is a strong correlate of aggressive behavior (Cano et al., 1998). Behavior change has not been consistently shown, and differential effects by gender appear to be fairly common. In general, however, program evaluation findings indicate promising effects on attitudes, knowledge, and beliefs associated with partner violence. This outcome is an important accomplishment, as it surely bodes well for the future relationships of these young participants, despite the lack of documentation of longer term outcomes.

Additionally, the immediate program effects on violence have not been clearly demonstrated. Here it is important to bear in mind that, although these programs are conceptualized as primary prevention efforts (i.e., stopping problem behaviors from occurring in the first place), they are often experienced by teenagers as secondary interventions, because many adolescents experience partner aggression in their very earliest intimate relationships. Thus, the difficulty in demonstrating program success in decreasing violent behaviors lies in part in the variation among participants in their past experiences with violence (and with dating in general). However, one might argue that the very fact of bringing the topic of domestic violence into the classroom, combined with the various changes in policy and services for victims of violence, argues well for the reduction of intimate partner violence in the future. Further research using alternate interventions and longer term follow-ups will be necessary to help identify the important characteristics of effective interventions.

PROGRAM SELECTION

In this section we discuss two broad criteria that may be used to choose a dating violence prevention program: program beneficiaries and aspects of program delivery. With respect to beneficiaries, there are clearly advantages as well as drawbacks to a general, inclusive approach to prevention that targets an entire school population versus a more specific focus on at-risk groups. There are obvious benefits to generating changes in school climate by a more global strategy, but there are certainly compelling reasons for providing more intensive services to those at higher risk for violence. What does seem clear, however, is that certain programs are more appropriate for certain populations, and program selection must be made with intended targets in mind. Some programs are designed for implementation by school personnel or other providers working with youths, whereas others are implemented by specialists who interact with students only in the context of the program. Again, each approach features distinct pros and cons.

Focus on General vs. At-Risk Populations

Although it is arguable that a focus on students identified as being at higher risk to engage in dating aggression makes sense to target limited resources, we advocate targeting the whole population of adolescents. There are several compelling advantages to this approach. First, and perhaps foremost, a global approach allows preventive efforts to reach those not yet engaging in aggressive behaviors, including many potential perpetrators who may not be identified as being at risk. Moreover, implementing programs across the entire group eliminates the issue of stigma and may provide a window of opportunity to treat high-risk individuals who are unlikely or unwilling to seek or participate in treatment otherwise. Last, as mentioned earlier, "casting the widest net" allows the greatest possibility for environmental change, such as peer group norms. For adolescents, this is a powerful way to affect established norms and introduce a climate of nonacceptance for aggression and abuse.

Focus on Gender

One of the most important, as well as controversial, issues pertaining to school-based partner violence prevention lies in the theory on which the program is based. Some programs frame partner violence in gender terms, focusing on males as perpetrators and females as victims, while others emphasize that both males and females can be victims or perpetrators. Several of the evaluations published investigate programs based on this feminist model (Jaffe et al., 1992; Jones, 1987; Krajewski et al., 1996; Lavoie et al., 1995; Levy, 1984). These studies either failed to demonstrate change in high school students' attitudes toward the use of violence or showed a backlash effect (increased acceptance of violence) for some of the male students (Jaffe et al., 1992). These findings may suggest that gender-neutral materials should be chosen rather than those based on a model of domestic violence in which males are described as perpetrators and females as victims.

Another issue has to do with the decision to administer the intervention separately to young men or women or to target mixed-gender groups. There are costs and benefits to both kinds of sessions. Because the research literature does not demonstrate that one method is more effective than the other, it is probably best to select the grouping that seems most appropriate for a particular school or community. Some of the advantages of same-gender sessions are that they allow students to express themselves without fear, shame, or embarrassment and may be more likely to increase self-disclosures. Same-gender groups may decrease male defensiveness if they feel that the program characterizes males as perpetrators and females as victims. Mixed-gender programs also have some advantages: They allow young men to learn what young women think and vice versa. They also allow for healthy exchange (with proper facilitation) between young men and women about gender stereotypes and double standards regarding dating behavior and acceptance of aggression in relationships. A sequential approach, in which students initially meet in same-gender groups and then in mixed-gender groups, may be a compromise approach.

Focus on Adult vs. Adolescent Violence

Many domestic violence agencies use personal and often in-person testimony of a formerly battered woman as the focus of school-based prevention efforts. However, studies across various topic areas (e.g., dental hygiene, drunk driving, cigarette smoking) have consistently demonstrated that scare tactics (i.e., showing gruesome pictures of car accidents to prevent drunk driving) simply do not work. In our experience, interventions are most effective when students perceive that the message is directly relevant to some aspect of their own experience.

Exclusive Focus on Serious Aggression vs. Less Severe Tactics

Many programs focus on more serious forms of violence. Although this focus seems compelling from a public health perspective, an argument may also be made for targeting more subtle forms of aggression. That is, the "lesser" forms are strongly associated with more severe aggressive behaviors. For example, verbal aggression is one of the most consistently reported predictors of physical aggression (Murphy & O'Leary, 1989). Moreover, verbal aggression is far more prevalent than physical aggression, and thus program participants may perceive that the program message is more relevant to their own experience and may be more likely to "buy into" the program. Another problem with targeting severe aggression behaviors is that they may be more entrenched and difficult to change. For the few students engaged in these extreme behaviors, a more intensive and individually tailored intervention may be needed. All prevention educators should either be equipped to handle student disclosures or have a ready list of up-to-date referral resources that they can assist the student in contacting.

Different behaviors targeted for prevention will necessitate different intervention strategies. For example, stressing some of the more extreme aggressive behaviors calls for an emphasis on safety and may generate intense emotional reactions from those who are involved in violent situations. Alternatively, a focus on more normative levels of conflict allows for the teaching and practicing of communication skills as well as anger management strategies. These latter approaches are more universally applicable to students and may be more appropriate lessons for the general classroom.

Optimal Time Allocations

Program lengths vary from a day or less to a semester or a year, and actual classroom time devoted to the program varies as well. Program length will also vary according to the instructional goals. For example, skills-based programs need to be longer to allow time to practice; programs that emphasize increasing awareness of the problem of domestic or dating violence may be only one class session or one half-day assembly.

Despite agreement as to the importance of preventing intimate partner violence, surprisingly little time has been devoted to these efforts in the classroom. Programs range in length from 2.5 hours (Lavoie et al., 1995) to 10 or more classroom sessions (Foshee et al., 1998; Krajewski et al., 1996), still a relatively low "dose." Furthermore, only two studies specifically reported making comparisons between a longer and a shorter intervention (Jaffe et al., 1992; Lavoie et al., 1995). In the Jaffe et al. (1992) study, students received either a full-day or a half-day program, but results were reported for all students receiving a program, and thus it is not clear whether there were differences based on dose. The other study's results were complicated by the fact that the groups differed before the program began, and both groups showed changes after receiving the program (Lavoie et al., 1995). What this means is that it is still not clear whether longer programs would show stronger, or more lasting, effects on students' use of aggression and aggression-related behaviors.

Another unresolved issue has to do with the effects of violence prevention programs over time. As these programs are cumbersome and extremely costly to evaluate, most do not include a long-term follow-up assessment. In the only two evaluations reviewed that used a longitudinal design, results are mixed. One study reported initial effects on both knowledge and attitudes, but these disappeared at the 5-month follow-up (Krajewski et al., 1996). Among middle school students, modest effects on violent behaviors washed out at the 1-month follow-up, but students retained gains in awareness and some of the skills measured (Foshee, 1996). In our own work, attitude gains washed out after 3 months, but gains in knowledge and intentions to seek help were retained at the follow-up (Cascardi et al., 1997).

Selection of Program Implementers

Perhaps the most important key to successful programs is the competence of the facilitator or implementer. Dating violence is an emotionally sensitive issue, and some teachers may not be sufficiently prepared to effectively manage student reactions to this topic. Although many programs are available in manual form (and thus almost anyone can obtain and use the program), research points to the importance of specialized training in program implementation. A recent study demonstrated that student response is significantly linked to teachers' knowledge of and teaching performance of a dating violence prevention program (DeFronzo et al., 1999). Moreover, teachers who receive training are significantly more motivated to implement such programs and feel more comfortable with and knowledgeable about the material (Avery-Leaf & Cascardi, 1999).

Several pros and cons are associated with choosing a schoolteacher to implement a program as opposed to an "outside" person (e.g., a domestic violence professional or a battered woman's advocate). The advantage of using a teacher is that he or she is likely to be a skilled educator with polished pedagogical as well as classroom management skills. Moreover, teachers have an ongoing relationship with their students and can incorporate a program on dating violence into the existing academic curriculum. A teacher can continue to implement the program with new classes at no additional cost to the school. However, the effectiveness of a teacher as a program implementer will depend on the nature of his or her relationship with students and his or her ability to maintain consistent and constructive communication patterns in the classroom. Also, classroom teachers who operate as program implementers will have to maintain a list of community resources so they can refer students who self-disclose problems with abuse. Alternatively, there are advantages to using an outside advocate. Domestic violence experts probably have a larger knowledge base than teachers and an emotional sensitivity toward students who self-disclose during class. Furthermore, an advocate may be better able to educate students about community resources and provide effective referrals for those involved in dating violence.

Optimal Settings for Program Implementation

Most programs are classroom-based so as to reach the maximum number of students from a range of levels and experiences. This strategy is particularly important when the students most at risk are those least likely to volunteer to participate in an extracurricular program. However, there are also advantages to using a small group approach in any of a variety of settings (e.g., guidance, correctional, mental health, after school, church youth groups).

As most evaluations of dating violence prevention program have been conducted in school settings, more is known regarding the effectiveness of school-based programs than those used in other contexts. However, rather than pursue the question of whether school or community efforts are superior, it may be more fruitful to focus on how best to combine prevention strategies in the two arenas.

RECOMMENDATIONS FOR PROGRAM SELECTION

Despite a paucity of research and methodological flaws, we can offer a few recommendations for program selection. On a practical level, it is important to target the population as a whole rather than working with subgroups of students. Not only will this approach allow for those not yet engaging in negative behaviors to be treated (a preventive approach), but it will also provide schools with the ability to treat high-risk individuals who are unlikely (or unwilling) to seek treatment. In school settings there are several effective ways to implement prevention programs with the entire population—for example, integrate the program into a mandated course or into orientation for incoming students.

Moreover, training school personnel to administer the prevention program is not only cost-effective but also an excellent way to ensure that program messages get reinforced over time. When program implementers interact with students regularly, there are unlimited opportunities for program content to be revisited. Also effective is the ongoing modeling of effective communication and other prosocial skills on the part of program implementers.

It is clear that partner violence prevention programs need to adopt a gender-neutral focus, particularly if one is targeting mixed-gender groups. This is crucial to avoid resistance to the program message by defensive individuals. Furthermore, it is recommended that school-based programs also include a skills component and use a group format for maximum efficiency and cost effectiveness. Mental health professionals often add skill-building approaches to help people develop and maintain healthy, nonviolent relationships over the life span. Specifically, social skills such as communication and conflict resolution are believed to decrease conflict escalation and use of aggression. Anger management techniques may ameliorate problems with emotional control and impulsivity. Moreover, it is essential to introduce skills training early, as these skills take practice and can reduce conflict both within and outside of the dating context.

It is also clearly fruitful to focus on attitude change, as this has been proved to be a consistently successful program objective. Social psychologists have long established that in the short term, attitude change is relatively easy to accomplish and can be done efficiently and effectively in a group setting such as a classroom. Changing attitudes that condone aggression is an important part of promoting respectful relationship behaviors as well as enabling adolescents to accurately evaluate whether relationships are healthy or harmful.

Another recommendation is to include booster sessions in the program, so as to retain the changes evident immediately postprogram. Last, including a peer counseling component is important, as we know that teenage victims seek help from friends far more often than from professionals (Watson, Cascardi, Avery-Leaf, & O'Leary, 2001). See Exhibit 4.1 for a summary of recommendations.

Educators, clinicians and, more recently, legislators agree that early interventions to help teenagers learn healthy ways of interacting and

EXHIBIT 4.1
Recommendations for Programming

- Target the whole population.
- Train existing personnel to administer the program.
- Maintain a gender-neutral focus, especially in mixed-gender classrooms.
- Begin skills training early.
- Target attitude change.
- Provide booster sessions after program is completed.
- Include peer counseling.

recognize hurtful relationship dynamics are needed at the secondary school level for all students. Many states have mandated that dating violence curricula be implemented as a graduation requirement. These policies speak to the need to integrate the current findings on adolescent dating violence and to use the collective knowledge as a basis for intervention and for making recommendations to educators and policymakers.

REFERENCES

American Association of University Women Educational Foundation. (1993). *Hostile hallways: The AAUW survey on sexual harassment in America's schools.* Washington, DC: Author.

Arias, I., Samios, M., & O'Leary, K. D. (1987). Prevalence and correlates of physical aggression during courtship. *Journal of Interpersonal Violence, 2,* 82–90.

Avery-Leaf, S., & Cascardi, M. (1999). *Small Business Innovation Research Program, Phase I Final Report.* Unpublished manuscript.

Avery-Leaf, S., Cascardi, M., O'Leary, K. D., & Cano, A. (1997). Efficacy of a dating violence prevention program on attitudes justifying aggression. *Journal of Adolescent Health, 21,* 11–17.

Bandura, A. (1977). *Social learning theory.* Englewood Cliffs, NJ: Prentice-Hall.

Bennett, L., & Fineran, S. (1998). Sexual and severe physical violence among high school students: Power beliefs, gender, and relationship. *American Journal of Orthopsychiatry, 68*(4), 645–652.

Bergman, L. (1992). Dating violence among high school students. *Social Work, 37,* 21–27.

Bernard, M. L., & Bernard, J. L. (1983). Violent intimacy: The family as a model for love relationships. *Family Relations, 32,* 283–286.

Billingham, R. E. (1987). Courtship violence: The patterns of conflict resolution strategies across seven levels of emotional commitment. *Family Relations, 36,* 283–289.

Birns, B., Cascardi, M., & Meyer, S. (1994). Gender roles and wife abuse: A developmental perspective. *American Journal of Orthopsychiatry, 64,* 50–59.

Bookwala, J., Frieze, I. H., Smith, C., & Ryan, K. (1992). Predictors of dating violence: A multivariate analysis. *Violence and Victims, 7,* 297–311.

Cano, A., Avery-Leaf, S., Cascardi, M., & O'Leary, K. D. (1998). Dating violence in two high school samples: Discriminating variables. *Journal of Primary Prevention, 18,* 431–446.

Cascardi, M. (1999). *Third semiannual progress report.* Centers for Disease Control and Prevention. Atlanta, GA.

Cascardi, M., & Avery-Leaf, S. (1998). *Building relationships in greater harmony together (BRIGHT) program.* Glen Ridge, NJ: DVPP, Inc.

Cascardi, M., Avery-Leaf, S., & O'Brien, M. K. (1998). *Dating violence among middle school students in an low income urban community.* Paper presented at the 727 grantee meeting, Centers for Disease Control and Prevention, Atlanta, GA.

Cascardi, M., Avery-Leaf, S., & O'Leary, K. D. (1994, August). *Building a gender sensitive model to explain male and female use of dating violence: Preliminary results.* Paper presented at the 102nd annual meeting of the American Psychological Association, Los Angeles, CA.

Cascardi, M., Avery-Leaf, S., O'Leary, K. D., & Slep, A. (1997). *Can dating violence be prevented? Effect of a dating violence prevention program on attitudes and behavior.* Paper presented at the 5th biannual meeting of the International Family Violence Conference, Durham, NH.

Cascardi, M., Avery-Leaf, S., O'Leary, K. D., & Slep, A. S. (1999). Factor structure and convergent validity of the Conflict Tactics Scale in high school students. *Psychological Assessment, 11*(4), 546–555.

Cate, R. M., Henton, J. M., Koval, J., Christopher, R. S., & Lloyd, S. (1982). Premarital abuse: A social psychological perspective. *Journal of Family Issues, 3,* 79–90.

Chase, K. A., Treboux, D., O'Leary, K. D., & Strassberg, Z. (1998). Specificity of dating aggression and its justification among high-risk adolescents. *Journal of Abnormal Child Psychology, 26*(6), 467–473.

Clark, M. L., Beckett, J., Wells, S. M., & Dungee-Anderson, D. (1994). Courtship violence among African-American college students. *Journal of Black Psychology, 20*(3), 264–281.

Connolly, J. A., McMaster, L., Craig, W., & Pepler, D. (1997). Dating, puberty, and sexualized aggression in early adolescence. In A. Slep (Chair), *Dating violence: Predictors and consequences in normative and at-risk populations.* Symposium conducted at the annual meeting of the Association for the Advancement of Behavior Therapy, Miami, FL.

Currie, D. W. (1983). A Toronto model. *Social Work With Groups, 6,* 179–188.

DeFronzo, R. A., O'Brian, M. K., & Cascardi, M. (1999, July). *The classroom implementation of a teen dating violence prevention project.* Paper presented at the 6th International Family Violence Research Conference, Durham, NH.

Demare, D., Briere, J., & Lips, H. M. (1988). Violent pornography and self-reported likelihood of sexual aggression. *Journal of Research in Personality, 22*(2), 140–153.

DeMaris, A. (1990). The dynamics of general transfer in courtship violence: A biracial exploration. *Journal of Marriage and the Family, 52,* 219–231.

Dobash, R. E., & Dobash, R. P. (1979). *Violence against wives: A case against the patriarchy.* New York: Free Press.

Dornbusch, S. M. (1981). Sexual development, age, and dating: A comparison of biological and social influences upon one set of behaviors. *Child Development, 52*(1), 179–185.

Dutton, D. G. (1994). The origin and structure of the abusive personality. *Journal of Personality Disorders, 8*(3), 181–191.

Follingstad, D. R., Hause, E. S., Rutledge, L. L., & Polek, D. S. (1992). Effects of battered women's early responses on later abuse patterns. *Violence and Victims*, 7(2), 109–128.

Foo, L., & Margolin, G. (1995). A multivariate investigation of dating aggression. *Journal of Family Violence*, 10, 351–377.

Foshee, V. A. (1996). Gender differences in adolescent dating abuse prevalence, types and injuries. *Health Education Research*, 11, 275–286.

Foshee, V. A., Bauman, K. E., Ximena, B. A., Helms, R. W., Koch, G. G., & Linder, G. F. (1998). An evaluation of Safe Dates: An adolescent dating violence prevention program. *American Journal of Public Health*, 88, 45–50.

Foshee, V. A., Linder, G. F., Bauman, K. E., Langwick, S. A., Arriaga, X. B., Heath, J. L., et al. (1996). The Safe Dates project: Theoretical basis, evaluation design, and selected baseline findings. *American Journal of Preventive Medicine*, 12(Suppl. 5), 39–46.

Harris, M. B., & Knight-Bohnhoff, K. (1996). Gender and aggression I: Perceptions of aggression. *Sex Roles*, 112, 1–25.

Henton, J., Cate, R., Koval, J., Lloyd, S., & Christopher, S. (1983). Romance and violence in dating relationships. *Journal of Family Issues*, 4, 467–482.

Hilton, N. Z., Harris, G. T., Rice, M. E., Krans, T. S., & Lavigne, S. E. (1998). Antiviolence education in high schools. *Journal of Interpersonal Violence*, 13(6), 726–742.

Jaffe, P. G., Suderman, M., Reitzel, D., & Killip, S. M. (1992). An evaluation of a secondary school primary prevention program on violence in intimate relationships. *Violence and Victims*, 7, 129–146.

Jones, L. E. (1987). *School curriculum project evaluation report*. Minnesota Coalition for Battered Women.

Jonson-Reid, M., & Bivens, L. (1999). Foster youth and dating violence. *Journal of Interpersonal Violence*, 14(12), 1249–1262.

Kaufman, K. G., Kantor, & Jasinski, J. (1995, July). *Prevention of dating violence: Evaluation of a multidimensional model*. Paper presented at the 4th International Family Violence Research Conference, Durham, NH.

Koss, M. P. (1998). Hidden rape: Sexual aggression and victimization in a national sample of students in higher education. In M. E. Odem & J. Clay-Warner (Eds.), *Confronting rape and sexual assault* (pp. 51–69). Wilmington, DE: SR Books/Scholarly Resources Inc.

Krajewski, S. S., Rybarik, M. F., Dosch, M. F., & Gilmore, G. D. (1996). Results of a curriculum intervention with seventh graders regarding violence in relationships. *Journal of Family Violence*, 11(2), 93–112.

Lavoie, F., Vezina, L., Piche, C., & Boivin, M. (1995). Evaluation of a prevention program for violence in teen dating relationships. *Journal of Interpersonal Violence*, 10(4), 516–524.

Levy, B. (1984). *Skills for violence-free relationships*. Santa Monica: Southern California Coalition on Battered Women.

Macgowan, M. J. (1997). An evaluation of a dating violence prevention program for middle school students. *Violence and Victims, 12,* 223–235.

Makepeace, J. M. (1981). Courtship violence among college students. *Family Relations, 30,* 97–102.

Makepeace, J. M. (1986). Gender differences in courtship violence victimization. *Family Relations, 35,* 383–388.

Makepeace, J. M. (1987). Social factor and victim–offender differences in courtship violence. *Family Relations, 36,* 87–91.

Malik, S., Sorenson, S. B., & Aneshehsel, C. S. (1997). Community and dating violence among adolescents: Perpetration and victimization. *Journal of Adolescent Health, 21,* 291–302.

Moffit, T. E., & Caspi, A. (1999). *Findings about partner violence from the Dunedin multidisciplinary health and development study* (National Institute of Justice Research in Brief). Washington, DC: U.S. Department of Justice.

Molidor, C., & Tolman, R. M. (1998). Gender and contextual factors in adolescent dating violence. *Violence Against Women, 4*(2), 180–194.

Murphy, C. M., & O'Leary, K. D. (1989). Psychological aggression predicts physical aggression in early marriage. *Journal of Consulting and Clinical Psychology, 57,* 579–582.

O'Keefe, M. (1997). Predictors of dating violence among high school students. *Journal of Interpersonal Violence, 12,* 546–568.

O'Keefe, M., Brockopp, K., & Chew, E. (1986). Teen dating violence. *Social Work, 30,* 463–468.

O'Keefe, M., & Treister, L. (1998). Victims of dating violence among high school students: Are the predictors different for males and females? *Violence Against Women, 4*(2), 195–223.

Pederson, P., & Thomas, C. D. (1992). Prevalence and correlates of dating violence in a Canadian university sample. *Canadian Journal of Behavioral Science, 24,* 490–501.

Riggs, D. S. (1990). *Test of a theoretical model of self-reported courtship aggression.* Unpublished doctoral dissertation, University of Stony Brook, Stony Brook, NY.

Riggs, D. S., & O'Leary, K. D. (1996). Aggression between heterosexual dating partners: An examination of a causal model of courtship aggression. *Journal of Interpersonal Violence, 11,* 519–540.

Riggs, D. S., O'Leary, K. D., & Breslin, B. F. (1990). Multiple correlates of physical aggression in dating couples. *Journal of Interpersonal Violence, 5,* 61–73.

Roscoe, B., & Callahan, J. E. (1985). Adolescents self-report of violence in families and dating relations. *Adolescence, 79,* 545–553.

Roscoe, B., & Kelsey, T. (1986). Dating violence among high school students. *Psychology, 23,* 53–59.

Schewe, P. A. (2000, May). *Southside Teens About Respect (STAR): An intervention to promote healthy relationships and prevent teen dating violence.* Paper presented at the National Sexual Violence Prevention Conference, Dallas, TX.

Schwartz, M., O'Leary, S. G., & Kendziora, K. T. (1997). Dating aggression among high school students. *Violence and Victims, 12*, 295–305.

Sigelman, C. K., Berry, C. J., & Wiles, K. A. (1984). Violence in college students' dating relationships. *Journal of Applied Social Psychology, 5*(6), 530–548.

Simons, R. L., Lin, Kuei-Hsiu, & Gordon, L. C. (1998). Socialization in the family of origin and male dating violence: A prospective study. *Journal of Marriage and the Family, 60*(2), 467–478.

Slep, A., Cascardi, M., Avery-Leaf, S., & O'Leary, K. D. (1997). *An attitudinal and behavioral model of physical aggression in high school dating relationships.* Paper presented at the 5th International Family Violence Research Conference, Durham, NH.

Smith, J. P., & Williams, J. G. (1992). From abusive household to dating violence. *Journal of Family Violence, 10*, 153–165.

Stets, J. E. & Pirog-Good, M. A. (1990). Interpersonal control and courtship aggression. *Journal of Personal and Social Relationships, 7*, 371–394.

Straus, M. A. (1979). Measuring intrafamily conflict and aggression: The Conflict Tactics Scale (CTS). *Journal of Marriage and the Family, 41*, 75–88.

Thompson, E. H. (1991). The maleness of violence in dating relationships: An appraisal of stereotypes. *Sex Roles, 24*, 261–278.

Watson, J., Cascardi, M., Avery-Leaf, S., O'Leary, K. D. (2001). High school students' responses and reactions to dating aggression. *Violence & Victims, 16* (3), 339–348.

Yllo, K. (1993). Through a feminist lens. In R. J. Gelles & D. R. Loseke (Eds.), *Current controversies in family violence.* Newbury Park, CA: Sage.

5

GUIDELINES FOR DEVELOPING RAPE PREVENTION AND RISK REDUCTION INTERVENTIONS

PAUL A. SCHEWE

CONSTRUCTS TARGETED IN EDUCATIONAL RAPE PREVENTION PROGRAMMING

Constructs that are commonly the focus of many rape prevention programs include correcting rape myths, increasing empathy for rape victims, emphasizing negative consequences for rapists, increasing rape awareness, teaching self-defense, increasing assertiveness skills, and teaching students to avoid high-risk situations. This portion of the chapter will review research associated with each construct and will provide recommendations for addressing these constructs in educational rape prevention programs.

This manuscript was originally prepared for the Illinois Coalition Against Sexual Assault. Special thanks go to Alan Berkowitz, John Foubert, Mary Heppner, Kim Lonsway, Hugh Potter, Stephanie Riger, and Sarah Ullman for their comments on an earlier draft of this chapter. The purpose of this chapter is to provide a set of guidelines that rape prevention educators can use in selecting or developing curricula for use in middle and high schools. In preparation for writing this manuscript, 33 empirical evaluations of rape prevention programs from 1984 to 2000 were reviewed. A brief summary of the programs reviewed can be found in Appendix A.

Rape Myths

A review of recent literature reveals that rape myth acceptance is the most common construct addressed in rape prevention programming. A variety of irrational beliefs are associated with rape and sexual offending (Burt, 1980; Hildebran & Pithers, 1989; Jenkins-Hall, 1989; Malamuth, 1989; Muehlenhard & Linton, 1987; Murphy, 1990), making rape myths an ideal target for prevention programming. For example, Pithers, Kashima, Cumming, Beal, and Buell (1988) analyzed the case records of 64 incarcerated rapists and found that cognitive distortions justifying rape (i.e., rape myths) were the second most frequent immediate precursor to rape (anger was the first).

In published evaluations of rape prevention programs over the past 15 years, rape myths were frequently targeted in successful intervention programs and were rarely targeted in unsuccessful programs. One bias in these studies is the fact that "rape myth acceptance" scales are the most commonly used outcome measures. It therefore makes sense that programs that target commonly held rape myths would perform better on the outcome measures (Lonsway, 1996). Nonetheless, given the strong theoretical link between rape myth acceptance and actual sexual offending, and the positive results of programs that attempt to change rape myth acceptance among young men and women, correcting rape myths should continue to be a primary target of any rape prevention program.

Effective interventions targeting rape myths have ranged from as minimal as the presentation of brief written material (Malamuth & Check, 1984) to as thorough as a 2-hour workshop targeting only empathy and rape myths (Lee, 1987). One warning is that a presentation of false beliefs about rape should not be confused with the presentation of factual information alone. Factual information such as legal definitions of rape, descriptions of victims and offenders, description of rape trauma syndrome, and information about local resources for survivors has been found to have no effect on students' attitudes about rape nor their empathy for victims of rape (Borden, Karr, & Caldwell-Colbert, 1988; Lenihan, Rawlins, Eberly, Buckley, & Masters, 1992; Schewe & O'Donohue, 1993b).

One common method for presenting rape myths to students is to give them a short true–false quiz covering various myths and facts about rape. After the quiz is completed, the answers to the questions can be discussed, and the facilitator can provide additional pieces of information to further explain and clarify the myths and facts. One danger, however, that educators need to avoid is sending the unintended message that "You're stupid for believing these myths, so I'm going to correct your dumb beliefs." Furthermore, the last thing that educators want during a presentation is to get into a debate with participants about the accuracy of the statistics. An alternative approach is to explore why we believe certain things about rape. It is important for the presenter to include him- or herself by using "we" language, because people all have had rape myths inside their heads, and this can help overcome the finger-pointing tone of many "myth–fact" presentations (K. A. Lonsway, American Bar Foundation, personal communication, July 7, 1999).

Also, by exploring why people believe some of these myths (e.g., media messages, outdated gender roles and stereotypes), educators can take advantage of teenagers' propensity to fight the establishment. Developmentally, teenagers are attempting to establish their independence. One way they express this is by doing things that run counter to the norms of the larger society. For example, the more that adults are shocked and disapproving of body piercing, the more body parts teenagers have pierced. Antismoking campaigns have used this developmental stage to their advantage by telling teenagers that the "big tobacco companies" are conning youths into believing that smoking is glamorous or pleasurable. Teenagers can then rebel against tobacco companies by not smoking. In rape prevention, educators can demonstrate to teenagers how society is telling them to adopt traditional gender roles, that men and women cannot work together to develop mutually satisfying relationships, and that teenagers will inevitably use violence in their relationships just like previous generations. Teenagers can then rebel against societal attitudes, myths, and media messages by working to develop healthy relationships.

Victim Empathy

Victim empathy is a cognitive–emotional recognition of a rape victim's trauma (Hildebran & Pithers, 1989). Programs that target victim empathy attempt to help students understand the experiences of a rape victim and involve both an understanding of the victim's experience of the actual rape and the aftermath of rape (shame, guilt, depression, pregnancy, and social sanctions—what has been called the "second assault"; Williams & Holmes, 1981). The idea behind these interventions is that students who understand the horrible experience of rape would never inflict that type of pain on anyone and would be more likely to help and believe a person who reports that he or she has been raped.

Examination of the evaluation literature reveals strong support for including victim empathy in rape prevention programs. In the 10 programs identified in the literature that targeted victim empathy, 8 reported clear positive effects. Notably, the only program to report clear long-term (more than 7 months) positive effects of an intervention included victim empathy as a key component of the program (Foubert, 2000; Foubert & McEwen, 1998). The two exceptions provide useful information for developers of prevention curricula. In Berg's study of 54 college men, she found that men who were asked to empathize with a female rape victim reported a greater likelihood of sexual aggression than did men who were asked to empathize with an adolescent male who was victimized by another adolescent male (Berg,

Lonsway, & Fitzgerald, 1999). In a similar study, Ellis, O'Sullivan, and Sowards (1992) found that when mixed-gender groups of undergraduates were asked to consider a situation in which a close friend told them that she was raped, women became more rejecting of rape myths, but men became less rejecting of them. Review of the other empathy programs revealed that having males empathize with other male victims of rape was a key part of many of those more successful programs.

Typical victim empathy interventions involve having participants listen to survivors' stories of rape and the aftermath of rape, engage in written exercises describing a victim's experiences, or imagine themselves as a victim of rape. In describing the experiences of a rape victim, care must be taken to avoid fueling deviant fantasies about rape. Whenever male participants are in the audience, empathy-inducing exercises should absolutely include at least one scenario in which the victim is male. To reflect the reality of male rape, the perpetrator should also be male and should have a heterosexual orientation.

Out of concern that such interventions might encourage homophobia, Foubert (2000) included a homophobia scale in his evaluation and found no change in homophobia among male participants following the intervention. Foubert's intervention included a videotape describing a male police officer being raped by two men. At the conclusion of the video, peer educators indicated that the video depicted an act of violence, not sex, and that the next part of the program would draw parallels between the male police officer's experiences and that of female rape survivors.

Victim empathy interventions are very intense. If done carefully, they have great potential to create positive change. If done poorly, they have serious potential for harm.

Negative Consequences for Perpetrators

Perceived rewards, costs, and low probability of punishment can be viewed as contributory factors of rape (Bandura, 1973; Ellis, 1989; Jenkins-Hall, 1989; Scully & Marolla, 1985). Decision-making theory asserts that people weigh the costs and benefits of certain actions, along with the probabilities of potential outcomes, when deciding which course of action to take. This assertion is based on the view that, in general, humans are self-interested and hedonistic and will make decisions that maximize personal gain. Breslin, Riggs, O'Leary, and Arias (1988) found that male undergraduates who committed acts of dating violence anticipated fewer negative consequences than did nonaggressive students. Scully and Marolla (1985) used information from interviews with 114 incarcerated rapists to suggest that most rapists viewed rape as a rewarding, low-risk act. Further evidence that the decision to rape is a controlled, purposeful decision comes from an analysis of the situations in which rapes occur. Rape generally occurs in situations in which the probability of being prosecuted is low, which indicates that rapists are not operating under conditions of uncontrollable hostility or sexual desire but on the contrary are purposefully deciding to rape because of the expected outcome of the behavior.

Decision theories suggest that information that changes men's perceptions of rape such that they begin to view it as (a) less rewarding, both in the short- and long-term, than consensual sex; (b) more costly than consensual sex (i.e., in terms of imprisonment, guilt, loss of job); and (c) more likely to lead to negative consequences (i.e., high probability of getting caught or feeling guilt) might be beneficial in preventing attempted rape. However, of the rape prevention programs evaluated in the literature, only three addressed the negative consequences of raping for men (Intons-Peterson, Roskos-Ewoldsen, Thomas, Shirley, & Blut, 1989; Schewe & O'Donohue, 1996; Schewe & Shizas, 2000). Of these three studies, two evidenced positive outcomes, and the third, a combination of outcome expectancies and victim empathy, was less effective than a program targeting rape-supportive cognitions.

Given the strong theoretical support and mixed empirical support for interventions focusing on the negative consequences that raping holds for perpetrators, educators may want to consider adding this type of information to their curricula. Age and gender of the audience certainly become considerations here, however. Discussing the pros and cons of developing a consenting sexual relationship and contrasting these with the negative consequences of forced sexual activity is not an intervention that should be provided to young students (elementary and middle school students). Also, this type of intervention may be best reserved for an all-male audience, as the information is not as relevant to a female audience.

In a video produced by Schewe and O'Donohue (1996), male actors portray and discuss the negative consequences they suffered as a result of their attempts to force sexual activity. Another possible intervention involves having students complete a list of all short-term and long-term consequences of consenting and nonconsenting sex. Lecture and discussion could then emphasize the negative consequences of raping (e.g., guilt, fear, worry about getting caught, negative response of the victim, possible loss of freedom, loss of family support, peer disapproval) and the positive consequences of putting the extra time and effort into developing a consensual sexual relationship (self-respect, respect and approval from others, reward of an appreciative partner). Such an intervention, perhaps combined with efforts to improve communication or increase healthy relationship skills, might lead directly to less rape and increased prosocial sexual interactions.

The "bystander approach" to rape prevention is another potentially powerful tool for influencing students' perceptions of the likelihood of experiencing negative consequences as a result of using force in sexual relationships. By teaching students how they can intervene to prevent rape and assist survivors of rape, students should begin to perceive rape as a risky behavior (high likelihood of getting caught) with a high likelihood of negative consequences such as peer disapproval (A. Berkowitz, Independent Consultant, personal communication, June 15, 1999).

Knowledge and Rape Awareness Programs

The type of information covered in this class of interventions includes the definitions of rape, legal terms, statistics regarding the prevalence of rape, ways that society condones and perpetuates rape, descriptions of typical perpetrators or victims, descriptions of the rape trauma syndrome, gender roles, gender differences, and information on local resources for victims of rape. These programs seem to operate on the premise that the more students understand and know about rape, the less likely it is that they will become victims or perpetrators. However, perhaps the clearest message that comes from the evaluation of literature is that these programs rarely work. The success these programs do report often is based on increases in knowledge or changes in attitudes among female participants, with little or no change among male participants, the population for whom change is most essential (Schewe & O'Donohue, 1993a).

Although programs primarily targeting knowledge or rape awareness seem to have little or no direct effect in changing attitudes or behavior, this type of information may be an important part of prevention programs in that it establishes relevance and motivation among participants (Gray, Lesser, Quinn, & Bounds, 1990; Petty & Cacioppo, 1986; Schewe & Shizas, 2000). Therefore, when designing interventions, educators should briefly discuss rape definitions and the local prevalence of rape but then focus on constructs more closely associated with attitude and behavior change.

When statistics are used, they will be more effective when they refer to local rather than regional figures (Gray et al., 1990). For example, "one out of four women at this school or in this town" will have more of an impact than "one out of four women in the United States" The key to effectively using statistics and factual information is to understand that increasing knowledge is not a goal but rather a means to an end. When designing curricula, use statistics to establish personal relevancy for the audience. That way, when students ask why they should bother to learn about sexual assault, the answer easily becomes "because sexual assault effects nearly everyone at some point in their lives, and you will want to know what to do to stop yourself from committing rape, to avoid being raped, or to assist a friend who has been raped."

High-Risk Situations

Early research identifying high-risk situations for sexual assault such as using alcohol, hitchhiking, attending parties, frequenting fraternities, dating in isolated locations, and being involved with older teenage men (Muehlen-hard & Linton, 1987; Ullman, 1997) suggests that educating women to avoid these high-risk situations could be an important part of efforts to reduce the incidence of rape among program participants. The staff of one program addressing this construct found that they were able to successfully increase women's perceptions of their vulnerability to rape and increase their intentions to avoid "risk-taking" behaviors (Gray et al., 1990). Hanson and Gidycz's (1993) risk reduction program was successful in decreasing women's involvement in situational factors associated with rape and in decreasing victimization among women who did not have a history of sexual victimization.

To help students make safe decisions, young women need to be taught about dangers such as dating older men, date rape drugs, alcohol, isolated locations. They need to be taught to date in groups, to stay in public areas, and to find recreational activities that do not involve drugs or alcohol. They need to know that it is possible for rape to occur within a trusting, loving relationship; therefore, it is important to attend to these situational risk factors even when they are with a long-time acquaintance or boyfriend.

There are two major cautions for educators attempting to incorporate information regarding high-risk situations into their curricula. One caution is that these programs should not be used for male or mixed-gender audiences. In presenting information about high risk situations, women in the audience may learn that date rape occurs very frequently, that most rapes go unreported to police, and that they should avoid alcohol and isolated dating locations. Men in the same audience may learn that rape is a common experience (i.e., "normal"); that if they do commit rape, the chances of being caught are very slim; and that if they get a woman intoxicated and take her to an isolated location, their chances of being caught are even slimmer. Given the differences in the information that men and women need concerning rape, it is important that more programs are developed exclusively for each gender, and programs that attempt to target both sexes should carefully select information to present.

A second caution is that information regarding high-risk situations might unintentionally increase victim blaming. Educators implementing such programs have the difficult job of teaching women about situations in which sexual assault is more likely to occur, while at the same time instilling the belief that rape is never the victims' fault, regardless of her prior behavior.

Self-Defense Strategies

Teaching women self-defense strategies seems to be an effective tool in helping students avoid rape. A evaluation of a model mugging course found that 46 of 48 women assaulted after taking the course fought back sufficiently to avoid harm (Peri, 1991). Other studies have cited beneficial psychological consequences for women taking self-defense classes as compared with a no-treatment control group (Cohen, Kidder, & Harvey, 1978).

Furthermore, there is strong evidence concerning the types of strategies that are effective in deterring an attacker. Researchers have found that women who fought back forcefully and used multiple self-defense strategies were more likely to avoid rape; that women who screamed or fled when confronted with weapons experienced less severe sexual abuse; and that increased physical injury was associated with pleading, crying, reasoning, and the women's use of drugs or alcohol (Bart & O'Brien, 1984; Ullman & Knight, 1993; see also chapter 6). Two programs that included a discussion of self-defense strategies (Hanson & Gidycz, 1993; Women Against Rape, 1980) were effective in decreasing the incidence of victimization, increasing confidence in the use of self-defense strategies, or increasing willingness to confront a perpetrator.

Particularly when program staff address female audiences, they should discuss effective rape avoidance strategies (e.g., fleeing, yelling, using physical force) or offer actual instruction in self-defense techniques. When they discuss effective rape avoidance strategies, it is important that they include some of the social barriers that may prevent women from using effective defense strategies. For example, students might be too embarrassed to yell or scream, may be afraid of losing a friend if they fight back, or may be so shocked that someone they trust is attacking them that they are unable to react.

The one danger that must be avoided in these types of interventions is the subtle, unintentional message that women who do not attempt to resist rape are somewhat responsible for the outcome of the attack. The danger of this message being conveyed can be reduced by stressing that the decision whether to resist a specific attacker in a particular situation is a very personal one, and the only person responsible for the attack is the one who initiated it.

Communication, Assertiveness, and Limit Setting

Miscommunication has been implicated as a cause of date rape for many years. Results of one study involving prison inmates suggested that rapists are particularly poor at interpreting negative cues from women on first dates when compared to violent nonrapists and nonviolent nonrapists (Lipton, McDonel, & McFall, 1987). Men may interpret women's behavior more sexually than do women, and this misunderstanding can lead to sexual offending in several ways (Muehlenhard & Linton, 1987). For example, a man is more likely to interpret behaviors such as kissing and cuddling as preliminaries to intercourse. If the woman resists the man's advances, he might assume that she really wants sex but is merely offering token resistance so as not to appear promiscuous (Check & Malamuth, 1983). Even if he believes her when she says "no," he might feel "led on" by her behavior, and many people believe that leading on a man justifies rape (Muehlenhard & Linton, 1987). Furthermore, misunderstandings might increase a man's anger toward the woman, and anger has been found to be the most common immediate precursor to rape (Groth, 1979; Pithers et al., 1988).

Muehlenhard and Andrews (1985) studied men's reactions to a woman's stating directly that she did not want to do anything more than kiss. The researchers found that this direct form of limit setting decreased men's ratings of how much the woman wanted to have sex, it decreased men's ratings of how likely they would be to try sexual behaviors beyond kissing, it decreased men's ratings of how much the woman led the man on, and it decreased men's ratings of how justified the man was to engage in petting after the woman said "no" (Muehlenhard & Andrews, 1985).

The construct of "communication skills" has been included along with other interventions in at least three rape prevention programs that have been evaluated and published in the scientific literature. Each program has indicated some level of success in changing knowledge and attitudes, although communication skills were not evaluated specifically as an outcome measure (Foubert & McEwen, 1998; Gilbert, Heesacker, & Gannon, 1991; Proto-Campise, Belknap, & Wooldredge, 1998).

Teaching communication skills (e.g., accurately interpreting information, asking for clarification, clearly expressing limits, using "I" statements to express feelings) holds great potential for improving rape prevention programs because all people can benefit from better communication skills. However, because good measures for evaluating the effectiveness of communication training have not been used, evaluation data do little to inform the use of communication training in rape prevention programs, nor do they offer guidance for educators seeking to design such programs. As in the teaching of self-defense skills, the subtle message that women who do not communicate clearly may be somewhat responsible for being raped must be avoided. Stressing that the only person responsible for the attack is the one who initiated it can reduce this danger.

OTHER CONSIDERATIONS

Several variables can affect the outcome of rape intervention programs, including the amount of confrontation in the program, the gender and race of presenters and audience, and the number of sessions in the program. In this section I examine a few of these variables.

Lessons Learned From the Literature on Persuasion

Researchers have shown that prevention programs should be tailored to the specific audience being addressed and that citing rape statistics derived from the local community has a greater impact on attitude change than citing statistics from national surveys (Gray et al., 1990). Attitude change research has suggested that the presenter should be an expert in the field and that he or she should be likeable and similar to the audience (Brehm & Kassin, 1990). The research further suggested that a longer presentation is better than a shorter one, provided it does not contain weak or redundant arguments. The presenter should take a strong stand against sexual assault and repeat the strongest arguments once or twice (Brehm & Kassin, 1990).

Confrontation

The one study that specifically examined a "confrontational" format in a rape prevention program found that confrontation resulted in a greater tolerance for rape among men (Fischer, 1986). Heppner, Good, et al. (1995) found that one third of the men in their study reacted to a prevention program in a bored or negative manner. In a subsequent study, she and her colleagues worked to reduce male defensiveness by letting men know that they are leaders in their schools, telling them they can be part of the solution, and by praising men for getting training (Heppner, Neville, Smith, Kivlighan, & Bershuny, 1999). Other rape educators, in an attempt to be as nonconfrontational as possible, have adopted the bystander approach of teaching students how to help survivors of sexual assault. The true goal of these rape prevention programs, changing participants' attitudes and beliefs about rape, is left unstated. The only rape prevention program to document positive changes that were largely maintained at a 7-month follow-up used this approach to attitude change (Foubert, 2000).

Gender of Audience

As noted, some of the information included in rape prevention programs is more appropriate for one gender or the other. Many authors have cited strong arguments for addressing single-gender audiences in rape prevention programs (Berkowitz, 1992; Lonsway, 1996; Schewe & O'Donohue, 1993a), and a few have specifically addressed a program's impact on single-gender versus mixed-gender classrooms. Kline (1993) found greater positive changes for male participants in a single-gender group as compared to male participants in a mixed-gender group. Furthermore, both male and female participants in the single-gender groups reported a more positive group experience than those in the mixed-gender groups. Similarly, Earle (1996) found that presenting a rape prevention program to all-male groups in a peer education format was more effective than mixed-gender groups led by administrators.

When possible, single-gender curricula should be developed. However, because of practical constraints (schools often are not willing or able to split up classrooms), mixed-gender curricula should be developed that avoid blaming men, blaming victims, or unintentionally teaching men how to rape and get away with it.

Gender of Presenters

Educators and researchers hold a variety of beliefs about the gender of the presenter as it relates to the audience. Some believe that male presenters will have the greatest impact on male audiences and that female presenters will have the greatest impact on female audiences. Others believe exactly the opposite. Still others believe that a male–female team of presenters works best for all audiences because of the team's ability to model healthy male–female relationships. Unfortunately, only one published study has specifically addressed the gender of the presenters in their experimental design. Jones and Muehlenhard (1990) found that the gender of presenters (male, female, or male–female team) had no impact on the outcome of the prevention program to a mixed-gender audience.

Age of Audience

It is important to know where the audience is developmentally with regards to dating and sexuality. With younger students, frank discussions about sex, rape, and dating may not be appropriate, and parents and school administrators may frown on such presentations. With younger students, a focus on increasing healthy relationship skills (e.g., communication skills, anger management skills) may be better than a more direct presentation targeting rape-related beliefs and attitudes. Another developmentally appropriate way to address younger audiences is to focus on sexual harassment (teasing, name calling, gender discrimination) rather than sexual assault (A. Berkowitz, Independent Consultant, personal communication, June 15, 1999). Many of the interventions used in rape prevention programs can be easily modified to address sexual harassment, which is an easier topic to address in mixed-gender audiences because males and females are more equally likely to be victims and perpetrators, especially at younger ages.

Race and Ethnicity of the Audience

Heppner and colleagues' 1999 study is the only one by the time of this writing that has tested the effects of including culturally relevant material in a prevention program. Their study compared the effects of a "color-blind" intervention to one that subtly but purposefully integrated African American content and process into the intervention. The results indicated that "Black students in the culturally relevant treatment condition were more cognitively engaged in the intervention than their peers in the traditional treatment condition" (p. 16). "Cultural relevance" involved having an African American group facilitator, including incidence and prevalence figures for both African American and White populations, targeting race-related rape myths and facts, and including culture-specific information concerning the recovery process of African American and White women.

"Dead-Man" Rule

In a psychotherapy class in graduate school, I remember being told by the instructor, "Never tell a client to do what a dead man can do." For example, telling a substance-abusing client to not drink, to avoid going to bars, to stay away from his old drinking buddies, and to avoid stressful situations violates the "dead-man" rule. All of the instructions listed above are things that a dead man could do. The point of the dead-man rule is that we should always attempt to increase desirable behaviors and not only focus on decreasing negative behaviors. This rule can be applied to rape prevention programming as well. Educators should avoid focusing only on decreasing negative behavior (don't drink alcohol, don't objectify women, don't go out alone, don't perpetuate sexist stereotypes) and instead provide plenty of instruction aimed at increasing positive behaviors (do date in groups, do respect women, do communicate your feelings and beliefs, do intervene to prevent rape and assist survivors).

Presentation Methods

To maximize learning, programs should include several presentation methods. Students' memory for information will be enhanced when they hear it, see it, write it, read it, speak it, and do it. In the Heppner, Humphrey, Hillenbrand-Gunn, and DeBord (1995) study, which compared a standard video and lecture presentation to an interactive drama in which the audience actively engaged in rewriting the script for the actors to re-enact, they found that students in the interactive drama condition were more motivated to hear the message, more able to recognize consent and coercion, and more likely to demonstrate behavioral changes. Generalizing from this study and from the literature on persuasion and attitude change, one can conclude that interactive presentations will generally be more effective than didactic lectures.

Presenters should do the following: try engaging students in discussions that draw on their own experiences; have students engage in role-plays to practice skills that they have learned or to help them understand the perspective of another person; assign written exercises to help cement memories and reinforce what was learned; assign homework that involves parents, thus giving parents the opportunity to reinforce at home what their child has learned at school; and try using videotaped presentations that capture students' attention. In several interventions, videos alone were as effective as alternate treatments or video plus discussion and were more effective than discussion alone (Anderson et al., 1998; Harrison, Downes, & Williams, 1991; Mann, Hecht, & Valentine, 1988). Youths today are extremely video-oriented. Videos have the advantage of presenting consistent information using professional actors in a format that is designed to capture students' attention. In my own studies, an amateur video was effective in changing the attitudes of high-risk men (Schewe & O'Donohue, 1996), and a videotaped talk show addressing date rape was more effective in changing rape-supportive beliefs among college men than a peer-mediated rape prevention curricula (Schewe & Shizas, 2000).

The cognitive dissonance literature suggests that changing behavior can be an effective way of changing attitudes. Rape prevention programming can take advantage of this knowledge by having students engage in activities that are the opposite of supporting rape. Such activities might include participating in anti-rape discussions, making anti-rape posters or artwork, performing in a dramatic presentation, or convincing another person not to use force in sexual relations. The cognitive dissonance literature suggests that students who engage in anti-rape activities should show a positive shift in their attitudes concerning rape.

An example of an exercise that exploits cognitive dissonance is as follows: At the end of a rape prevention program, the presenter hands students a piece of paper with the following two sentences on it, along with spaces for up to 10 responses. "Joe is a man who feels that he can force sexual activity on women whenever he wants to. Write a list of arguments that you would use to convince Joe not to rape women." By convincing Joe not to rape women, students' attitudes against rape should be strengthened. Also, by writing down the information that they just learned, students will be more likely to remember the material.

Number of Sessions

Practical limitations often allow only a single session, and almost all of the programs reviewed for this manuscript were single-session interventions. However, as a general rule, more sessions will be better than fewer sessions. In Heppner and colleagues' 1999 evaluation of a three-session rape prevention program, the strongest predictor of whether a male student would change and stay changed over a 5-month period was how many of the sessions he attended. Some curricula developers have overcome some of the practical barriers to multiple sessions by designing their curricula to meet state guidelines for health education. For example, the Safe-T for Teens program has replaced the existing health education classes in several middle schools with its own 30-hour curricula that emphasizes healthy relationship skills and sexual abuse prevention.

Theoretical Orientation

My review of the rape prevention research has revealed no clear distinctions between theoretical orientations with regard to the success of rape prevention programs. However, it does seem that theory-based interventions were more effective than nontheoretically based interventions. "Rape awareness" programs are one example of an intervention that lacks a theoretical framework, unless of course the authors are willing to argue that a lack of awareness of rape causes rape. When developing rape prevention curricula, it is extremely important to have a clear belief about the causes and risk factors for rape and to develop a curriculum with this belief in mind.

One Example of a Prevention Model

Although research has not positively identified any factors that are either necessary or sufficient to cause rape, certain factors logically are more likely to be necessary preconditions. The theoretical model that I am proposing is based on factors that may play a necessary role in acquaintance rape. On the basis of this model, the prototypical, or modal, date rapist is one who (a) lacks empathy for victims of rape, (b) believes in a variety of cognitive distortions justifying rape (rape myths), and (c) believes that it is in his own best interest to rape while in a situation he perceives as conducive to rape. This model is described more fully below. I hypothesize that addressing these core issues of victim empathy, rape myths, and the negative consequences of raping in a program designed to prevent rape will result in more attitude and behavior change than will a prevention program that addresses only one of these issues.

Schewe and O'Donohue (1993a) reviewed several of the major contemporary psychological explanations of the etiology of rape, including deviant sexual arousal (Abel, Blanchard, & Becker, 1978), social skills or perception problems (Lipton, McDonel, & McFall, 1987), belief in rape myths (Burt, 1980), psychopathic deviance (Armentrout & Hauer, 1978), and internal affective motivations (Groth, 1979). It is interesting to see how each of the theories reviewed may be interrelated with a lack of victim empathy, rape myths, or the cognitive distortion that the benefits of raping might outweigh the costs. For example, deviant sexual arousal (arousal to aggression or victim resistance or pain) might act to increase the perceived benefits that one might receive from raping.

Problems with perceiving negative cues from women might also contribute to a decision to rape (McFall, 1990). Failing to perceive negative cues from women could lead a man to overestimate the benefits and underestimate the costs of proceeding with sexual advances. Several rape myths such as the belief that women want to be raped, that relationships between men and women are naturally adversarial, and that women are responsible for their own rape can be considered consistent with victim empathy. Other rape myths (e.g., women who are hitchhiking, drunk, or dressed provocatively get what they deserve; being "led on" justifies rape) contribute more directly to a belief that rape is justified. Psychopathic deviance and internal affective motivations can both be clearly linked to victim empathy. Indeed, lack of empathy may be a trait similar to traits found in antisocial individuals (American Psychiatric Association, 1989), or it may be a state brought on by temporary anger toward women or toward the victim (Groth, 1979).

In one test of this model (Schewe & Shizas, 2000), a rape prevention program targeting rape myths, victim empathy, and the negative consequences of raping was more effective in changing men's scores on Burt's (1980) Rape Myth Acceptance scales and Malamuth's (1989) Attraction to Sexual Aggression scale than was a well-established, peer-mediated rape prevention program.

Limitations of This Literature Review

One limitation of this review is that it was based only on reports of rape prevention evaluations that have been published in scientific journals. One bias in these journals is that studies with negative outcomes are less likely to be published. For rape advocates developing curricula, the lessons that can be learned from unsuccessful programs are at least as important, and may be more important, than the lessons learned from programs documenting success.

One important qualifier of this review is that the programs evaluated focused on the *primary prevention* of rape (preventing new instances of rape) and not *secondary prevention* (preventing re-victimization or targeting at-risk populations) or *tertiary prevention* (reducing the pain and suffering of survivors or treating or punishing perpetrators). Because of this focus on primary prevention, several important constructs such as "what a person should do if she or he has been raped" or "important community resources" were generally not included in these programs. However, because some individuals in any audience will have already experienced sexual assault, these constructs should certainly be integrated into any educational program addressing rape, sexual harassment, dating violence, or child abuse.

Another limitation is that the "success" of programs is rather loosely defined and, for the purposes this review, I relied primarily on the individual authors' definitions of success. The following are some examples that illustrate this problem. Consider the program that is successful in increasing participants' knowledge on a 20-item true–false quiz compared to a program that documents changes in knowledge, attitudes, empathy for rape victims, and self-reported likelihood of raping. Saying that both programs are "successful" is overly simplistic. Or consider the program that reports overall positive changes but further examination reveals that all of the change can be accounted for by the female participants in the mixed-gender audience. Or what if all of the positive changes came only from the male participants in the audience? Are these programs successful?

Time is another problem. Most programs were evaluated immediately pre- and postintervention. Most of the programs that included a longer term follow-up found a decrease from the initial positive effects. So what about programs that compared attitudes before and several weeks after treatment and found no positive effects? Although the authors may have concluded that these programs were not effective, are they really less effective than a program that reports immediate initial improvements with no longer term follow-up?

A final consideration regarding success is that most evaluations used a different set of outcome measures. Although many programs used Burt's Rape Myth Acceptance scales, many programs did not, which makes comparisons across studies tenuous at best. Furthermore, at least one of Burt's scales has some serious problems with reliability and validity (Schewe & O'Donohue, 1998). The best studies are those that evaluate multiple interventions within the same study, use a wide variety of outcome measures, and include a long-term follow-up evaluation of treatment effects. However, limiting the review to such studies would reduce the number of reviewed articles to nearly zero.

SUMMARY

Although our knowledge of how to prevent rape is still in its infancy, the number of people dedicated to eradicating rape and improving the quality of rape prevention programs continues to expand. Following is a list of lessons that have been learned from the hard work of educators and researchers. With the help of future research and experience, this list will continue to grow.

- The discussion of rape myths is a common component of many successful programs.
- "Victim empathy" interventions should include at least one scenario in which the victim is male.
- Few programs have targeted the negative consequences of rape for perpetrators, although this component seems to have great promise.
- Increasing rape awareness should not be the only goal of a prevention program.
- Improving communication skills is a worthy goal, but the effectiveness of attempting to teach communication skills in a rape prevention program has yet to be demonstrated.

- Teaching students to reduce their risk of being raped by avoiding high-risk situations is an intervention best suited for a female audience, and caution is needed to avoid victim blaming.
- Teaching women self-defense strategies seems to be an effective tool in helping students avoid rape.
- Presentations should be tailored to the particular audience's age, gender, and race.
- Programs for younger students can focus on building healthy relationships and decreasing sexual harassment.
- Single-gender audiences are preferable to mixed-gender audiences.
- Local statistics will have a greater impact on audiences than national statistics.
- Programs should avoid confrontation, blaming men, or blaming victims.
- Programs should focus on increasing healthy behaviors, not just decreasing negative behaviors.
- Several presentation methods should be used. Students should be actively involved in antirape activities. Programs can benefit from supplementation with videos.
- Students should be provided with multiple sessions whenever possible.
- Theory-based rape prevention programs are generally more effective. Presenters should articulate their beliefs about the causes of rape and keep them in mind as they develop curricula.

Prevention educators should be constantly trying to improve their curricula. Even if a program demonstrates initial positive effects, it is likely that these effects will begin to fade after a few weeks or months. By always working to increase the quality of the curricula and by increasing the number of sessions, educators will greatly increase the likelihood that a program will have lasting effects.

Rape Prevention Articles Included in the Review of Outcome Evaluation Research, 1984–1999, by Date of Publication

Author, year	Sample	Constructs addressed	Format	Outcome measures	Research design	Results
Malamuth & Check, 1984	70 male and 73 female college students	Rape myths	Brief written debriefing following exposure to sexual violence	Rape myth measure	Pre–post, no control group	Positive changes following debriefing
Fischer, 1986	716 college students	Human sexuality and sexual aggression	Lecture Unspecified "confrontational" format	Rape-related beliefs and attitude surveys	Pre–post, alternate treatments, and control group	"Confrontation" resulted in greater tolerance for rape among men; lecture resulted in positive changes
Lee, 1987	24 male college students	Rape myths, empathy	2-hour lecture/discussion	ATR	Pre–post only, no control group	Positive changes following the workshop
Borden et al., 1988	25 male and 25 female college students	Legal terms, descriptions, rape trauma syndrome, resources	45-minute lecture	ATR, RES	Pre- and 4-week posttreatment, no-treatment control group	No changes
Mann et al., 1988	36 male and 56 female college students	Assertiveness, sexual attitudes, gender scripts	Video and discussion Video only Discussion only	Rape attitudes	Pre–post, alternate treatment groups	Positive changes for video, with or without discussion, no change for discussion-only group
Intons-Peterson et al., 1989	105 male college students	Myths, facts, stats, and consequences of rape	Video following exposure to sexual violence	RMA, Likelihood	Pre–post 2-week follow-up, treatment and placebo control groups	Positive changes for treatment group at posttest and follow-up

Study	Sample	Content	Format	Measures	Design	Results
Johnson & Russ, 1989	80 male and 80 female college students	Historical mistreatment of women	Written speeches	Likelihood, perceptions of victim responsibility and enjoyment	Pre–post, no control group	Positive changes, more so for men
Nelson & Torgler, 1990	25 male and 64 female college students	Not described	Video Written material	ATW, Forcible Rape Scale	Pre–post, alternate treatments, and placebo control group	No differences between placebo and treatment groups
Jones & Muehlenhard, 1990	588 male and female college students	Society is to blame for rape, or men are to blame for rape	Lecture with male, female, or male and female copresenters	Attitude measures	Post only, treatment and control groups	Successful at changing attitudes, but less so for men. No effect of presenters' gender or lecture focus
Gilbert et al., 1991	75 male college students	Communication, rape myths, relationship issues, negative consequences of raping, empathy	Lecture and Discussion	RMA, AIV, ASB, Likelihood	Pre–post, treatment and control group	Positive changes among men in the treatment group
Harrison et al., 1991	45 male and 51 female college students	Sex in advertising, portrayal of unwanted sexual advances	Video alone or with discussion	ATR	Pre–post, alternate treatments	Positive changes among men regardless of discussion
Feltey et al., 1991	188 high school students	Gender role socialization	45-minute lecture	Judgments about the acceptability of sexual coercion	Pre and 6-week post, no control group	Men were less tolerant of sexual coercion after the program

APPENDIX A (Continued)

Author, year	Sample	Constructs addressed	Format	Outcome measures	Research design	Results
Fonow et al., 1992	582 college students	Rape myths	Live or videotaped workshop	RMA, AIV, ASB and the Rape Blame Scale	Pre–post, alternate treatments, and a no-treatment control group	Positive attitude change
Ellis et al., 1992	51 male and 100 female college students	Contemplated exposure to a rape survivor, empathy	Discussion	Myths and Facts about Rape, AIV, ASB	Post only, no control group	Women became more rejecting of rape myths, men became less rejecting.
Lenihan et al., 1992	318 male and 503 female college students	Impact of rape, statistics, definitions, characteristics of offenders, resources	Lecture, video, personal testimony	RMA, AIV, ASB	Pre–post, treatment, and a no-treatment control group	Positive changes among women, no changes among men
Berg, 1993	54 male college students	Empathy and rape myths	1.5-hour workshop, two audiotapes	RMA, AIV, ASB, RES, Likelihood	Pre–post, alternate treatments	No change in empathy or rape attitudes, men asked to empathize with female victim reported greater likelihood of sexual aggression
Schewe & O'Donohue, 1993b	55 "high-risk" male college students	Empathy Rape facts intervention	Two treatment videos, behavioral exercise	Likelihood, RES, AIV, ASB, Arousal Conformity	Pre–post, alternate treatments, and a no-treatment control group	Rape facts not sufficient to produce change. Some support for empathy

Study	Sample	Content	Format	Measures	Design	Results
Holcomb et al., 1993	331 male and female college students	How and when consent takes place, how men and women can prevent date rape	Lecture and discussion 35 minutes	DRAS	Post only, treatment and a no-treatment control group	Immediate positive gains, greater gains for men
Hanson & Gidycz, 1993	360 female college students	Rape myths and facts, protective behavior, high-risk situations	Lecture and discussion and videos	SES, dating behavior, sexual communication, rape awareness	Pre–post, treatment, and a no-treatment control group	Increased awareness, decreased risk behavior, no change in communication, decrease in victimization among women without a history of sexual abuse
Dallager & Rosen, 1993	47 male and 98 female college students	Human sexuality, oppression and abuse	Lecture	RMA, AIV	Pre–post, treatment, and a no-treatment control group	Decrease in RMA scores, no change in AIV scores
Lenihan & Rawlins, 1994	636 college fraternity and sorority members	Myths and facts, leadership, alcohol, legal and social responsibility	Lecture and discussion by administrator	RMA, AIV, ASB, SC	Pre and 6-week post, no control group	No change in scores at 6-week follow-up
Frazier et al., 1994	117 college sorority and 75 fraternity members	Consent, campus resources	Interactive drama, 2 hours	Attitudes toward sex and dating, gender	Pre–post and follow-up, treatment, and a no-treatment control group	Minimal changes at posttest disappear at 1-month follow-up
Heppner, Good, et al., 1995	257 male and female college students	Prevalence and impact of rape	Lecture, video, Q&A, 1 hour	ASB, RMA	Pre–post and follow-up, no control group	Positive immediate gains mostly lost at 2-month follow-up

Author, year	Sample	Constructs addressed	Format	Outcome measures	Research design	Results
Heppner, Humphrey, et al., 1995	258 male and female college students	Consent, myths and facts, gender socialization, campus resources, empathy	Didactic-video Interactive drama	RMA, CCC	Pre–post and 2 follow-ups, alternate treatments, and a no-treatment control group	Immediate positive gains from both interventions decay at 5-month follow-up
Schewe & O'Donohue, 1996	74 "high-risk" male college students	Rape-supportive cognitions Empathy and outcome expectancies	Video, behavioral exercise, 1 hour	ASA, RMA, AIV, ASB, Conformity	Pre–post, alternate treatments, and a no-treatment control group	Rape-supportive cognitions better than combined empathy and outcome expectancies
Earle, 1996	347 male college students	Rape attitudes	Peer-led, all male interactive format Administrator led, coed, small-group discussion Administrator led, coed, lecture	ATR, ATW	Pre–post, alternative treatments, and a no-treatment control group	The all-male interactive peer-led format was most effective in improving post-tx scores relative to control group
Foubert & Mariott, 1997	114 college fraternity men	How to help a sexual assault survivor, empathy, communication, societal norms	Video, lecture and discussion, 1 hour	RMA	Pre–post and follow-up, treatment and a no-treatment control group	Positive changes at posttest rebound somewhat at 2-month follow-up
Lonsway et al., 1998	59 male and 111 female college students	Leadership training in rape education	A semester-long course	IRMA, adversarial heterosexual beliefs, ATF	Pre–post, placebo control group (Human Sexuality class), 2-year follow-up	Positive changes in CARE students compared to control maintained at follow-up

Study	Sample	Content	Format	Measures	Design	Results
Proto-Campise et al., 1998	429 high school students	Rape myths, warning signs, communication, media influence, definitions, statistics, and community resources	Lecture and discussion, 1 hour	24 True–false items	Pre–post, treatment and control groups	Treatment participants showed a significant increase in knowledge on the posttest
Foubert & McEwen, 1998	155 college fraternity men	How to help a sexual assault survivor, empathy, communication, societal norms	Video, peer mediated lecture/discussion, 1 hour	RMA, Likelihood	Pre–post and follow-up, treatment and control groups	Positive changes at posttest maintained at 7-month follow-up
Anderson et al., 1998	215 college students	Rape myths	Interactive talk show and discussion Video and discussion	RMA, ATR–R	Pre–post, 7-week follow-up, alternative treatments, and a no-treatment control group	Immediate positive gains rebounded at 7-week follow-up. Interactive format no more effective than video
Heppner et al., 1999	119 college men	Myths and facts, empathy, consent, and how to help a survivor	"Color blind" or culturally relevant (African American) Both interventions entailed three 90-minute sessions including a video, discussion, interactive drama, panel discussion with survivors, and role-playing	RMA, SIARA, SES Likelihood, SVAWS–SV	Pre–post, 5-month follow-up, alternate treatments, and no treatment control group	Black students were more cognitively engaged in the culturally relevant condition. Overall, 1/3 of students' scores improved then rebounded, 1/3 steadily improved, and 1/3 steadily deteriorated.

APPENDIX A (Continued)

Author, year	Sample	Constructs addressed	Format	Outcome measures	Research design	Results
Schewe & Shizas, 2000	255 college men	Victim empathy, rape myths, outcome expectancies Rape awareness Talk show (placebo)	Rape prevention video Peer-mediated lecture and discussion Videotaped talk show	ASA, ASB, RMA	Pre–post, alternate treatments, placebo, and a no-treatment control group	The peer-mediated rape awareness program was equivalent to no-treatment. Positive changes for the talk show and video intervention. Video had greater effect on "high-risk" men.

Note. AIV = Acceptance of Interpersonal Violence Scale (Burt, 1980); ASA = Attraction to Sexual Aggression (Malamuth, 1989); ASB = Adversarial Sexual Beliefs (Burt, 1980); ATF= Attitudes Toward Feminism Scale (Fassinger, 1985); ATR = Attitudes Toward Rape (Feild, 1978); ATW = Attitudes Toward Women (Nelson, 1988); CCC = The Comprehension of Consent/Coercion Measure (Heppner, Humphrey, et al., 1995); Conformity = The Rape Conformity Assessment (Schewe & O'Donohue, 1998); DRAS = Date Rape Attitude Scale (Holcomb et al., 1993); IRMA = Illinois Rape Myth Acceptance Scale (Payne et al., 1999); Likelihood = Likelihood of Raping Index (Malamuth, Haber, & Feshbach, 1980); RES = Rape Empathy Scale (Deitz et al., 1982); RMA = Rape Myth Acceptance Scale (Burt, 1980); SC = The Sexual Conservatism Scale (Burt, 1980); SES = Sexual Experiences Survey (Koss & Gidycz, 1985); SIARA = The Scale for the Identification of Acquaintance Rape Attitudes (Humphrey, 1996); SVAWS–SV = Sexual Violence Subscale of the Severity of Violence Against Women Scale (Marshall, 1992).

130 *PAUL A. SCHEWE*

REFERENCES

Abel, G. G., Blanchard, E. B., & Becker, J. V. (1978). An integrated treatment program for rapists. In R. T. Rada (Ed.), *Clinical aspects of the rapist*. New York: Grune & Stratton.

American Psychiatric Association. (1989). *Treatments of psychiatric disorders*. Washington, DC: Author.

Anderson, L. A., Stoelb, M. P., Duggan, P., Heiger, B., Kling, K. H., & Payne, J. P. (1998). The effectiveness of two types of rape prevention programs in changing the rape-supportive attitudes of college students. *Journal of College Student Development, 39*, 131–142.

Armentrout, J., & Hauer, A. (1978). MMPIs of rapists of adults, rapists if children, and non-rapist sex offenders. *Journal of Clinical Psychology, 34*(2), 330–332.

Bandura, A. (1973). *Aggression: A social learning analysis*. Englewood Cliffs, NJ: Prentice-Hall.

Bandura, A. (1977). *Social learning theory*. Englewood Cliffs, NJ: Prentice-Hall.

Bart, P. B., & O'Brien, P. B. (1984). *Stopping rape: Successful survival strategies*. Elmsford, NY: Pergamon.

Berg, D. R. (1993). *The use of rape-specific empathy induction in rape education for college men: A theoretical and practical examination*. Unpublished master's thesis, University of Illinois, Urbana–Champaign.

Berg, D. R., Lonsway, K. A., & Fitzgerald, L. F. (1999). Rape prevention education for men: The effectiveness of empathy-induction techniques. *Journal of College Student Development. 40*(3), 219–234.

Berkowitz, A. (1992). College men as perpetrators of acquaintance rape and sexual assault: A review of recent research. *Journal of American College Health, 40*, 175–181.

Borden, L. A., Karr, S. K., & Caldwell-Colbert, A. (1988). Effects of a university rape prevention program on attitudes and empathy toward rape. *Journal of College Student Development, 29*(2), 132–136.

Brehm, S. S., & Kassin, S. M. (1990). *Social psychology*. Boston: Houghton-Mifflin.

Breslin, F. C., Riggs, D. S., O'Leary, K. D., & Arias, I. (1988). *The impact of interpersonal violence on dating violence: A social learning analysis*. Unpublished manuscript.

Burt, M. (1980). Cultural myths and supports for rape. *Journal of Personality and Social Psychology, 38*(2), 217–230.

Check, J. V. P., & Malamuth, N. M. (1983). Sex role stereotyping and reactions to depictions of stranger versus acquaintance rape. *Journal of Personality and Social Psychology, 45*, 344–356.

Cohen, E. S., Kidder, L., & Harvey, J. (1978). Crime prevention versus victimization: The psychology of two different reactions. *Victimology, 3*, 285–296.

Dallager, C., & Rosen, L. A. (1993). Effects of a human sexuality course on attitudes rape and violence. *Journal of Sex Education and Therapy, 19*, 193–199.

Deitz, S., Blackwell, K., Daley, P., & Bentley, B. (1982). Measurement of empathy toward rape victims and rapists. *Journal of Personality and Social Psychology, 43,* 372–383.

Earle, J. P. (1996). Acquaintance rape workshops: Their effectiveness in changing the attitudes of first year college men. *NASPA Journal, 34,* 2–18.

Ellis, L. (1989). *Theories of rape: Inquiries into the causes of sexual aggression.* New York: Hemisphere.

Ellis, A. L., O'Sullivan, C., & Sowards, B. (1992). The impact of contemplated exposure to a survivor of rape on attitudes toward rape. *Journal of Applied Social Psychology, 22,* 889–895.

Fassigner, R. E. (1985). *Development of the attitudes toward feminism scale.* Unpublished manuscript, Ohio State University, Columbus, OH.

Feild, H. S. (1978). Attitudes toward rape: A comparative analysis of police, rapists, crisis counselors, and citizens. *Journal of Personality and Social Psychology, 36*(2), 156–179.

Feltey, K. M., Ainslie, J. J., & Geib, A. (1991). Sexual coercion attitudes among high school students: The influence of gender and rape education. *Youth & Society, 23,* 229–250.

Fischer, G. J. (1986). College student attitudes toward forcible date rape: Changes after taking a human sexuality course. *Journal of Sex Education and Therapy, 12,* 42–46.

Fonow, M., Richardson, L., & Wemmerus, V. (1992). Feminist rape education: Does it work? *Gender & Society, 6*(1), 108–121.

Foubert, J. D. (1998). *The men's program: How to successfully lower men's likelihood of raping.* Holmes Beach, FL: Learning Publications.

Foubert, J. D. (2000). The longitudinal effects of a rape prevention program on fraternity men's attitudes, behavioral intent, and behavior. *Journal of American College Health, 48,* 158–163.

Foubert, J. D., & Marriott, K. A. (1997). Effects of a sexual assault peer education program on men's belief in rape myths. *Sex Roles, 36,* 259–268.

Foubert, J. D., & McEwen, M. K. (1998). An all-male rape prevention peer education program: Decreasing fraternity men's behavioral intent to rape. *Journal of College Student Development, 39*(6), 548–555.

Frazier, P., Valtinson, G., & Candell, S. (1994). Evaluation of a coeducational interactive rape prevention program. *Journal of Counseling & Development, 73,* 153–158.

Gilbert, B., Heesacker, M., & Gannon, L. (1991). Changing the sexual aggression-supportive attitudes of men: A psychoeducational intervention. *Journal of Counseling Psychology, 38*(2), 197–203.

Gray, M., Lesser, D., Quinn, E., & Bounds, C. (1990). Effects of rape education on perception of vulnerability and on reducing risk-taking behavior. *Journal of College Student Development, 31*(2), 217–223.

Groth, A. N. (1979). *Men who rape: The psychology of the offender.* New York: Plenum Press.

Hanson, K. A., & Gidycz, C. A. (1993). Evaluation of a sexual assault prevention program. *Journal of Consulting and Clinical Psychology, 61,* 1046–1052.

Harrison, P. J., Downes, J., & Williams, M. (1991). Date and acquaintance rape: Perceptions and attitude change strategies. *Journal of College Student Development, 32*(2), 131–139.

Heppner, M. J., Good, G., Hillenbrand-Gunn, T., Hawkins, A., Hacquard, L., Nichols, R., et al. (1995). Examining sex differences in altering attitudes about rape: A test of the elaboration likelihood model. *Journal of Counseling & Development, 73,* 640–647.

Heppner, M. J., Humphrey, C. F., Hillenbrand-Gunn, T. L., & DeBord, K. A. (1995). The differential effects of rape prevention programming on attitudes, behavior, and knowledge. *Journal of Counseling Psychology, 42,* 508–518.

Heppner, M. J., Neville, H. A., Smith K., Kivlighan, D. M., & Bershuny, B. S. (1999). Examining immediate and long-term efficacy of rape prevention programming with racially diverse college men. *Journal of Counseling Psychology, 46*(1), 16–26.

Hildebran, D., & Pithers, W. (1989). Enhancing offender empathy for sexual-abuse victims. In D. Laws (Ed.), *Relapse prevention with sex offenders* (pp. 236–243). New York: Guilford Press.

Holcomb, D., Sarvela, P., Sondag, K. A., & Holcomb, L. (1993). An evaluation of a mixed-gender date rape prevention workshop. *College Health, 41,* 159–164.

Humphrey, C. F. (1996). *Scale for the identification of acquaintance rape attitudes (SIARA).* Unpublished manuscript, University of Missouri-Columbia.

Intons-Peterson, M. J., Roskos-Ewoldsen, B., Thomas, L., Shirley, M., & Blut, K. (1989). Will educational materials reduce negative effects of exposure to sexual violence? *Journal of Social and Clinical Psychology, 8,* 256–275.

Jenkins-Hall, K. D. (1989). The decision matrix. In D. R. Laws (Ed.), *Relapse prevention with sex offenders* (pp. 159–166). New York: Guilford Press.

Johnson, J. D., & Russ, I. (1989). Effects of salience of consciousness-raising information on perceptions of acquaintance versus stranger rape. *Journal of Applied Social Psychology, 19,* 1182–1197.

Jones, J., & Muehlenhard, C. (1990, November). *Using education to prevent rape on college campuses.* Paper presented at the annual meeting of the Society for the Scientific Study of Sex, Minneapolis, MN.

Kline, R. J. (1993). The effects of a structured-group rape-prevention program on selected male personality correlates of abuse toward women. *Dissertation Abstracts International.*

Koss, M. (1988). Hidden rape: Sexual aggression and victimization in a national sample of students in higher education. In A. Burgess (Ed.), *Rape and sexual assault II* (pp. 3–25). New York: Garland.

Koss, M. P. & Gidycz, C. A. (1985). Sexual Experiences Survey: Reliability and validity. *Journal of Consulting & Clinical Psychology, 53*(3), 422–423.

Lee, L. (1987). Rape prevention: Experimental training for men. *Journal of Counseling and Development, 66,* 100–101.

Lenihan, G., & Rawlins, M. (1994). Rape supportive attitudes among Greek students before and after a date rape prevention program. *Journal of College Student Development, 35,* 450–455.

Lenihan, G., Rawlins, M., Eberly, C. G., Buckley, B., & Masters, B. (1992). Gender differences in rape supportive attitudes before and after a date rape education intervention. *Journal of College Student Development, 33,* 331–338.

Lipton, D. N., McDonel, E. C., & McFall, R. M. (1987). Heterosocial perception in rapists. *Journal of Consulting and Clinical Psychology, 55,* 17–21.

Lonsway, K. A. (1996). Preventing acquaintance rape through education: What do we know. *Psychology of Women Quarterly, 20,* 229–265.

Lonsway, K. A., Klaw, E., Berg, D., Waldo, C., Kothari, C., Mazurek, C., et al. (1998). Beyond "no means no": Outcomes of an intensive program to train peer facilitators for campus acquaintance rape education. *Journal of Interpersonal Violence, 13,* 73–92.

Malamuth, N. M. (1989). The attraction to sexual aggression scale: Part one. *Journal of Sex Research, 26*(1), 26–49.

Malamuth, N. M., & Check, J. V. P. (1984). Debriefing effectiveness following exposure to pornographic rape depictions. *Journal of Sex Research, 20,* 1–13.

Malamuth, N. M., Haber, S., & Feshbach, S. (1980). Testing hypotheses regarding rape: Exposure to sexual violence, sex differences, and the "normality" of rapists. *Journal of Research in Personality, 14*(1), 121–137.

Mann, C. A., Hecht, M. L., & Valentine, K. B. (1988). Performance in a social context: Date rape versus date right. *Central States Speech Journal, 3/4,* 269–280.

Marshall, L. L. (1992). Development of the violence against women scale. *Journal of Family Violence, 7,* 103–120.

McFall, R. M. (1990). The enhancement of social skills: An information-processing analysis. In W. Marshall, D. R. Laws, & H. E. Barbaree (Eds.), *Handbook of sexual assault* (pp. 311–330). New York: Plenum Press.

Muehlenhard, C. L., & Andrews, S. (1985, November). *Sexual aggression in dating situations: Do factors that cause men to regard it as more justifiable also make it more probable?* Paper presented at the annual meeting of the Association for the Advancement of Behavior Therapy, Washington, DC.

Muehlenhard, C. L., & Linton, M. A. (1987). Date rape and sexual aggression in dating situations: Incidence and risk factors. *Journal of Counseling Psychology, 34,* 186–196.

Murphy, W. D. (1990). Assessment and modification of cognitive distortions in sex offenders. In W. L. Marshall, D. R. Laws, & H. E. Barbaree (Eds.), *Handbook of sexual assault* (pp. 331–342). New York: Plenum Press.

Nelson, M. C. (1988). Reliability, validity, and cross-cultural comparisons for the simplified Attitudes Toward Women Scale. *Sex Roles, 18*(5–6), 289–296.

Nelson, E. S., & Torgler, C. C. (1990). A comparison of strategies for changing college students' attitudes toward acquaintance rape. *Journal of Humanistic Education and Development, 29,* 69–85.

Payne, D. L., Lonsway, K. A., & Fitzgerald, L. F. (1999). Rape myth acceptance: Exploration of its structure and its measurement using the Illinois Rape Myth Acceptance Scale. *Journal of Research in Personality, 33*(1), 27–68.

Peri, C. (1991, March). Below the belt: Women in the martial arts. *Newsletter of the National Women's Martial Arts Federations,* 6–14.

Petty, R., & Cacioppo, J. (1986). *Communication and persuasion: Central and peripheral routes to attitude change.* New York: Springer-Verlag.

Pithers, W. D., Kashima, K., Cumming, G. F., Beal, L. S., & Buell, M. (1988). Relapse prevention of sexual aggression. In R. Prentky & V. Quinsey (Eds.), *Human sexual aggression: Current perspectives* (pp. 244–260). New York: New York Academy of Sciences.

Proto-Campise, L., Belknap, J., & Wooldredge, J. (1998). High school students' adherence to rape myths and the effectiveness of high school rape-awareness programs. *Violence Against Women, 4,* 308–328.

Scarce, M. (1995). *Men can stop rape: A rape education curriculum guide for men.* Unpublished manuscript, Ohio State University, Columbus.

Schewe, P. A., & O'Donohue, W. T. (1993a). Rape prevention: Methodological problems and new directions. *Clinical Psychology Review, 13,* 667–682.

Schewe, P. A., & O'Donohue, W. T. (1993b). Sexual abuse prevention with high risk males: The roles of victim empathy and rape myths. *Violence and Victims, 8*(4), 339–351.

Schewe, P. A., & O'Donohue, W. T. (1996). Rape prevention with high risk males: Short-term outcome of two interventions. *Archives of Sexual Behavior, 25*(5), 455–471.

Schewe, P. A., & O'Donohue, W. T. (1998). Psychometrics of the Rape Conformity Assessment and other measures: Implications for rape prevention. *Sexual Abuse, 10*(2), 97–112.

Schewe, P. A., & Shizas, N. (2000, May). *Rape prevention with college age males: Short-term outcomes of a videotaped intervention vs. a peer-mediated group discussion.* Paper presented at the National Sexual Violence Prevention Conference, Dallas, TX.

Scully, D., & Marolla, J. (1985). "Riding the bull at Gilley's": Convicted rapists describe the rewards of rape. *Social Problems, 32*(3), 251–263.

Ullman, S. E. (1997). Review and critique of empirical studies of rape avoidance. *Criminal Justice and Behavior, 24*(2), 177–204.

Ullman, S. E., & Knight, R. A. (1993). The efficacy of women's resistance strategies in rape situations. *Psychology of Women Quarterly, 17,* 23–38.

6

RAPE AVOIDANCE: SELF-PROTECTION STRATEGIES FOR WOMEN

SARAH E. ULLMAN

Research on rape avoidance strategies has documented how women may effectively resist sexual assault and rape. Data show that a variety of resistance strategies may be helpful to women in avoiding completion of rape and that the level of offender violence is the most important determinant of victim injury. In this chapter, I discuss the contextual characteristics of the assault, including victim–offender relationship, alcohol use, and social situation, as they affect the outcomes of rape attacks. I discuss social-psychological barriers to resisting sexual attacks, particularly by acquaintances. I review this area of research and recommend ways to enhance women's ability to avoid rape until the broader goal of primary prevention of rape can be effected in society. I suggest how to incorporate several key components (self-defense training, education about risk reduction strategies, and information

I am grateful to the following people for providing invaluable insights and suggestions for revisions on an earlier version of this chapter: Sarah Avery-Leaf, Karen Bachar, Leanne Brecklin, Kim Breitenbecher, Chris Gidycz, Mary Heppner, Kim Lonsway, Martha McCaughey, and Paul Schewe.

about social-psychological barriers) into risk reduction programs targeted to women in educational and community settings.

BACKGROUND

Rape is endemic to American society: Community prevalence studies have shown that 14% to 25% of adult women have experienced rape (Kilpatrick, Edmunds, & Seymour, 1992; Koss, 1993; Russell, 1984). Young women (e.g., ages 16–19 years) constitute a subgroup at particularly high risk for sexual assault (Bachman, 1994), making interventions targeted to this age group most important. Recent reviews have suggested that society needs to focus "rape prevention" programs on men to reduce sexual aggression and "risk reduction" programs on women to teach effective resistance strategies (Bachar & Koss, 2000; Rozee & Koss, 2001). Although many rape prevention programs exist and some have been evaluated, most of these studies have focused on changing attitudes such as rape myths or increasing women's self-efficacy (see Brecklin & Forde, 2001; Breitenbecher, 2000; Flores & Hartlaub, 1998; Gidycz, Dowdall, & Marioni, in press; Lonsway, 1996; Schewe & O'Donohue, 1993; Yeater & O'Donohue, 1999, for reviews). These studies are based on the rationale that changing rape-supportive attitudes may help to reduce the occurrence of rape.

However, few empirical data demonstrate that these programs are effective in changing rape-related attitudes over long periods of time (Heppner, Humphrey, Hillenbrand-Gunn, & DeBord, 1995; Heppner, Neville, Smith, Kivlighan, & Gershuny, 1999). It is currently unknown whether attitude change actually reduces the occurrence of rape (see Schewe, chapter 5, this volume, for a review and discussion of constructs targeted by educational rape prevention programs). For example, a recent meta-analysis of studies of rape intervention programs for college students found little change in rape myth attitudes as the follow-up time of assessment increased (Brecklin & Forde, 2001). In addition, programs targeting both genders were less effective than programs targeting only one gender. Finally, unpublished studies of programs (e.g., doctoral dissertations) showed less effectiveness than studies of programs that were published in scientific journals, suggesting a possible bias toward publication of significant results. In one of the few published studies to date assessing future victimization risk, Hanson and Gidycz (1993) found a decrease in rates of sexual assault victimization over a 9-week period in college women without a prior history of sexual assault who were exposed to a risk reduction program that included discussion of self-defense strategies and risky dating behaviors. However, two subsequent evaluations of sexual assault education prevention programs found no reduction in sexual assault risk at follow-up, regardless of sexual assault history (Breitenbecher & Gidycz, 1998; Breitenbecher & Scarce, 1999).

Because women's vulnerability to rape is heavily determined by situational factors that increase their proximity to motivated offenders, focusing on women's personality characteristics or backgrounds also may not effectively reduce rape (Koss, Dinero, Seibel, & Cox, 1988). On the basis of a review of rape prevention education programs, Lonsway (1996) concluded that sexuality education is not adequate for changing rape-related attitudes if it does not explicitly address sexual violence (see also Lonsway et al., 1998) and that programs seem to be more effective if they discuss women's roles and status in society. Some researchers have argued that risk reduction programs should focus more on teaching women self-defense, given that few studies show that changing attitudes reduces rape (Koss, Goodman, et al., 1994). In addition, most studies have shown that victims cannot be distinguished from nonvictims on attitudinal variables such as sex role beliefs, rape myth acceptance, acceptance of interpersonal violence, and adversarial sexual beliefs (Amick & Calhoun, 1987; Koss, 1985; Koss & Dinero, 1989).

Many researchers have expressed valid concerns that interventions targeting women that either teach self-defense or simply educate women about effective resistance strategies to rape hold women responsible for rape prevention (see, e.g., Yeater & O'Donohue, 1999). However, as long as men continue to rape, women and girls should at a minimum be provided with information and training on effective methods of self-protection. They also need access to knowledge about situations and behaviors that may increase their risk, just as the general public needs access to information about protection from other public health threats such as HIV infection. This type of education can be done without holding women responsible or blaming them for their own victimization, and it may empower women, particularly if educators include information about gender role socialization and social psychological barriers to self-protection (both discussed in this chapter).

GOALS OF THIS CHAPTER

The primary goal of this chapter is to review recent research on rape avoidance strategies (e.g., behavioral responses that may thwart rape attempts), highlight risky situational factors, and examine the interaction between avoidance strategies and situational factors. Review of these data shows the importance of developing multifactor theoretical models to predict avoidance of completed rape and physical injuries. The second goal is to demonstrate how information about resistance strategies and risky situational variables can be used in risk reduction programs. Although more research is needed, there are clearly some guidelines that can be given based on the empirical literature to enhance women's ability to escape potential rape situations and reduce the severity of sexual abuse and physical injuries if attacked. This goal is important because completed rapes are associated with greater psychological and physical health consequences than attempted rapes, including posttraumatic stress disorder (PTSD), anxiety, depression, suicidal ideation and suicide attempts, risk of sexually transmitted diseases, and acute and chronic physical health problems (Kilpatrick et al., 1985; Koss, Heise, & Russo, 1994; Siegel, Golding, Stein, Burnam, & Sorenson, 1990). I cover several topics, including: (a) women's use of verbal and physical resistance strategies; (b) characteristics of rape situations and risky contexts including alcohol use, victim–offender relationship, rapist types, and weapon use; (c) formal self-defense training for women; and (d) social-psychological barriers to resistance.

Although much of the literature on resistance strategies (e.g., verbal and physical responses to attack) is focused on rape by strangers and acquaintances, data have suggested that rapes by intimate partners are as violent as those by strangers (Koss et al., 1988; Stermac, DuMont, & Dunn, 1998) and that they are related to the same degree of psychological symptoms, such as anxiety and depression (Koss et al., 1988; Ullman & Siegel, 1993). In addition, it is argued that risk reduction programs targeting women need to include both self-defense training and risk reduction education, so that women may be able to avoid potential rape situations and thwart rape attempts should they occur. These risk reduction programs may be presented in the context of education about gender role socialization and the relative status of women, as some research suggested that decreases in rape supportive attitudes are more likely in programs that include this information (Lonsway, 1996). Traditional gender roles encourage women and girls to be psychologically and physically passive in their interactions with men, which may put them at risk for sexual victimization. In a prospective study of college women, Greene and Navarro (1998) found that low assertiveness in sexual situations predicted subsequent victimization.

Women are socialized to accept various rape-supportive beliefs and to blame themselves for their victimization (Morokoff, 1983; Walker & Browne, 1985). Social-psychological barriers, such as embarrassment and fear of stigmatization by peers, may result from female sex role socialization, including the encouragement of women to put others' needs above their own. These barriers may reduce women's ability to perceive dangerous situations and to escape sexually aggressive men and therefore may also need to be addressed (Nurius, 2000).

RAPE AVOIDANCE:
SITUATION, RAPIST, AND VICTIM FACTORS

Several factors within rape situations have been studied in relation to the likelihood of avoiding a completed rape. These factors include whether there was a social situation surrounding the assault, prerape behavior by victims and offenders, victim–offender relationship, alcohol use by offenders and victims, and other assault characteristics such as weapon presence, assault location, time of day, and environmental intervention (e.g., whether there were other people present who might have intervened or otherwise deterred the assailant from continuing an attack). In a review of the literature, Ullman (1997) examined evidence regarding the relationship of each factor with rape and physical injury outcomes and concluded that multivariate models are needed to examine their interrelations in predicting these assault outcomes. Clearly, some of these factors are interrelated. For instance, stranger attacks are more likely to occur outdoors, at night, and with weapons than are attacks by known offenders. But more specifically, we need to know how victim resistance, offender verbal threats, and physical violence can predict assault outcomes for women within specific assault situations (Ullman & Knight, 1993).

Resistance Strategies

In a review of the literature on rape avoidance, forceful resistance strategies of fighting, fleeing, and screaming used by women were all effective across several studies in avoiding rape and physical injury (Ullman, 1997). In addition, lack of resistance and nonforceful verbal strategies of pleading, begging, and reasoning with the offender were ineffective. Other factors generally associated with avoiding completed rape include outdoor attacks, attacks at night, and those where environmental interventions occur (see Ullman, 1997, for a review and critique of rape avoidance studies). Forceful strategies seem to be effective even in attacks with offenders carrying weapons and in dangerous assault situations (e.g., in attacks with violence, at night) and against both known and stranger assailants. Thus far, research has indicated that forceful physical resistance in particular enhances avoidance of completed rape even in assaults with weapons, regardless of rapist type and offender use of violence (Ullman, 1997).

Despite this positive news, there has been continued concern and belief that physically fighting an attacker may result in physical injury by increasing the offender's use of violence (Prentky, Burgess, & Carter, 1986). Most studies demonstrating positive correlations between women's use of fighting and their physical injury have failed to take into account whether the women were being attacked physically at the time they resisted and the possibility that this prior physical violence by the offender was the determinant of victim injury (see Ullman, 1997). The sequence of offender violence and victim resistance in relation to assault outcomes must be assessed because results are misleading when simple correlations of resistance with assault outcome are performed regardless of when the resistance occurred during the attack (see Ullman, 1997). Specifically, positive correlations of forceful fighting by victims with physical injury seem to be spurious, resulting from the fact that victims are already being more violently attacked in these situations before they resist (Ullman, 1997). When the sequence of attack–resistance–injury is taken into account, studies have shown that fighting back leads to less rape completion and *no* increase or decrease in physical injury (Quinsey & Upfold, 1985; Ullman, 1998; Ullman & Knight, 1992). Clearly, these different results have implications for the rape avoidance advice given to women, who must weigh the options and potential consequences of resistance in deciding how to respond to an attack. The most important implication of this research is that women should be encouraged (if they are able and so choose) to resist rape with the forceful strategies of fleeing, screaming, and fighting known to be associated with decreased rape completion.

Victim–Offender Relationship, Context, and Rape Outcome

Evidence concerning the "association" or "relationship" of victim–offender relationship to rape avoidance is mixed, although comparisons of stranger rapes to all types of known offender attacks grouped together show more rape avoidance in response to strangers (Ullman, 1997). Not surprisingly, gang rapes seem to be more violent (Gidycz & Koss, 1990), and it is more difficult for women to avoid completed rape in these cases (Ullman, 1999) than in single offender cases. Alcohol use by offenders and victims as well as unplanned, spontaneous social situations surrounding the assault (e.g., bars, parties) are associated with rape completion (Abbey, Ross, McDuffie, & McAuslan, 1996; Parks & Miller, 1997; Ullman & Brecklin, 2000; Ullman, Karabatsos, & Koss, 1999a, 1999b). The effects of resistance used in these circumstances have not been evaluated, although evidence has suggested that resistance may be less effective in isolated, indoor locations with intimate perpetrators when no environmental intervention occurs (Ullman, 1997). Because rape situations vary on many dimensions, it is important to identify clusters of characteristics that commonly co-occur and the effects of different types of victim resistance in those attacks. In the next sections I discuss several situational and behavioral factors associated with sexual assault attack outcomes that have been the focus of research attention.

Alcohol Use by Perpetrators and Victims

One of the more studied risk factors associated with severe outcomes (e.g., rape, physical injuries) during sexual assaults is alcohol use; it is clearly present in up to one half to two thirds of sexual assaults (Abbey, 1991; Pernanen, 1991). A lifetime history of heavy drinking by men and women is associated with an increased risk of lifetime involvement in sexual aggression (Berkowitz, 1992; Calhoun, Bernat, Clum, & Frame, 1997) and sexual victimization (Burnam et al., 1988; Kilpatrick, Acierno, Resnick, Saunders,

& Best, 1997; Koss & Dinero, 1989; Testa & Livingston, 2000), respectively, which suggests that interventions to reduce drinking-related assaults should address abusive drinking in general. Yet the role of alcohol in actual rape attacks is unclear. Alcohol's presence does not necessarily mean that it is a causal factor in rapes or in the resulting injuries experienced by victims. For instance, alcohol use during assault is correlated with other factors that are also associated with the rape outcome, such as social situations in which victim and offender are only slightly acquainted with each other (e.g., parties, bars). It may be these risky social contexts, not drinking itself, that confers sexual assault risk. It seems more likely that alcohol use may interact with risky situations to increase victimization risk. Research on both college and community samples has indicated that both victim and offender alcohol use are associated with more completed rapes and that victim resistance may be less likely in attacks involving alcohol (Abbey & Ross, 1992; Harrington & Leitenberg, 1994; Ullman, Karabatsos, & Koss, 1999b; Ullman & Knight, 1993). Although alcohol use by victims clearly makes it less likely that they can effectively resist rapes on a behavioral level, other social-psychological barriers to resistance have been identified such as fear of rejection by the man or one's peers, embarrassment, and perceiving that one is too intoxicated to escape even if one resists (Norris, Nurius, & Dimeff, 1996; Testa & Parks, 1996).

Current research findings on the relationship of alcohol and outcomes of sexual assaults are inconsistent. Several studies have examined alcohol's role in rape outcomes more specifically and are reviewed here. Offender alcohol use has been thought to potentially lead to disinhibition of violence that may then contribute to more severe assault outcomes (e.g., completed rape, physical injuries), which is based on experimental evidence demonstrating that alcohol is associated with aggression in laboratory settings (see Bushman & Cooper, 1990, and Hull & Bond, 1986, for reviews). Furthermore, several field studies showed offender alcohol use is associated with victim physical injury in sexual assaults (Coker, Walls, & Johnson, 1998; Johnson, Gibson, & Linden, 1978; Martin & Bachman, 1998). In a national sample of college women, Ullman et al. (1999b) found that preassault alcohol use (i.e., drinking before the attack) by the victim and the offender were each related to more severe sexual victimization but that alcohol did not interact synergistically with other factors, such as offender aggression, to predict more severe outcomes. In fact, offender violence was actually related to more severe sexual victimization in attacks *without* offender alcohol use, which is consistent with recent National Crime Victimization Survey data showing more completed rape in cases without offender drinking (Martin & Bachman, 1998).

Other recent data have suggested that alcohol and violence (e.g., physical aggression) may be independent strategies offenders use to complete rapes (Cleveland, Koss, & Lyons, 1999) and that each is more predictive of physical injury in the absence of the other (Ullman & Brecklin, 2000). This finding makes sense because if an offender is drunk, the victim may fear that he is out of control and will become more violent, and therefore she may decide not to resist. Alternatively, if an offender gets the victim drunk, he may impair her ability to resist (Harrington & Leitenberg, 1994), whereas without alcohol he may need to use more violence to complete rape. Another analysis of self-reported data from college men showed *no* evidence that offender drinking prior to attack per se leads to more physical aggression against victims and a higher likelihood of rape completion (Ullman et al., 1999a).

Alcohol is more common in assaults by acquaintances and in spontaneous, unplanned social situations (Abbey et al., 1996; Brecklin & Ullman, 2001; Ullman & Brecklin, 2000). However, in one study, alcohol did not interact with the social situation or how well victims knew their attackers in predicting the rape outcome, except that unplanned social situations were related to more severe sexual victimization when offenders were *not* drinking (Ullman et al., 1999b).

Clearly, alcohol is associated with the outcomes of sexual assaults; however, more studies are needed to evaluate the exact nature of alcohol's role in the physical injury outcome of rapes, not just the completed rape outcome examined in most current studies. Alcohol abuse prevention efforts are clearly integral to prevention of sexual assault. More research is needed on the role of alcohol in different assault contexts to integrate specific information about alcohol's role into prevention programs. Two tentative conclusions can be drawn from these findings about alcohol and rape. First, it cannot be assumed that drinking before assault causes offenders to become more violent and complete rape more. Sex offender researchers have argued that alcohol is unlikely to cause someone to commit rape who is not otherwise predisposed to sexual aggression (Seto & Barbaree, 1995). Second, it cannot be assumed that a woman's drinking in and of itself increases sexual victimization risk. It seems to put women at greater risk of completed rape, possibly because of situational, behavioral, and social-psychological factors that are not yet completely understood. Educators addressing drinking as a risk factor for sexual assault must be cautious to avoid implying that drinking is a sole explanation for rape and that refraining from drinking will stop sexual assault. Drinking alcohol should be addressed as one of many situational and behavioral risk factors associated with rape.

Victim–Offender Relationship, Resistance, and Outcome

Research results are inconsistent about whether resistance is more or less effective in response to strangers or known men. In general, women seem more likely to avoid stranger rapes (Bart & O'Brien, 1985; Ruback & Ivie, 1988; Ullman & Knight, 1991), probably because they are more willing to resist these attackers. Most research has shown much less use of resistance overall by women in response to attacks by perpetrators they know (Amick & Calhoun, 1987; Finkelhor & Yllo, 1985; Ullman & Siegel, 1993), yet equal efficacy of resistance (for avoiding rape completion) when effective forceful strategies are used (Ullman & Siegel, 1993). The fact that women are less predisposed to resist attacks by known men makes them much more vulnerable to completed rape, particularly by intimate partners. Although Koss (1985) found that all victims were equally likely to use physical resistance in rapes in a college population, other studies have shown less physical resistance to intimates than to strangers and acquaintances (Amir, 1971; Bart & O'Brien, 1985; Ullman & Siegel, 1993).

A significant proportion of domestic violence situations also involve sexual assaults (Walker, 1984), which may be repeated within an intimate relationship and are obviously much more difficult for victims to avoid. Many women in marital relationships report not resisting assaults by their husbands because they felt it was their duty to submit, knew it would make the husband more violent if they resisted, wanted to protect their children, and knew from past experience that resistance was useless as they did not feel psychologically and physically trained to fight (Finkelhor & Yllo, 1985). Clearly prevention of rape in intimate relationships may require dealing with chronically violent men who repeatedly assault their partners in marriage or in cohabiting or dating relationships (Levy, 1991; Walker, 1984). Obviously, resistance within intimate relationships is a complicated and difficult issue for women that needs further research. On the basis of interviews with female survivors of sexual violence, some researchers have argued that the only way to effectively end sexual assault in relationships is to end the relationship (Kelly, 1988). That is, freeing oneself from a violent relationship may be a common strategy for avoiding both physical and sexual assaults by intimate partners when the offender will not cease their violent behavior. In summary, research suggests that forceful resistance strategies can enhance women's ability to avoid completed rape by known and stranger assailants.

Rapist Type

Few studies have examined how resistance may vary in efficacy depending on the type of rapist. This issue is of concern if certain types of rapists (e.g., sadists) are more likely to respond to victim resistance with increased physical violence, as some researchers have warned (Prentky et al., 1986). The only study of an empirically validated rapist typology indicated no differences in effectiveness of different resistance strategies on rape and physical injury outcomes according to rapist type (Ullman & Knight, 1995). Although this finding requires replication, it suggests that concerns that sadistic rapists or other specific rapist types (e.g., pervasively angry, opportunistic, nonsadistic sexual, vindictive) will cause more injury to victims who forcefully resist attack are unfounded (Prentky et al., 1986). The best predictor of victim injury is the level of offender violence used during the attack, an observable behavior not requiring women to determine the type of rapist to decide whether to resist. Although more research is needed to replicate these findings regarding resistance to different rapist types, there is no empirical evidence suggesting that women need to assess the type of rapist attacking them before deciding how to respond, a concern raised most recently by Yeater and O'Donohue (1999) in their review of sexual assault prevention programs. To summarize, educators should not discourage women to resist rape because of fears that offenders will respond with increased violence; available evidence has not supported such fears.

Weapons

Weapons are another crucial situational element that has been studied in relation to sexual assault. Offenders who display weapons to their victims are more likely to complete rape (Bart & O'Brien, 1985; Becker, Skinner, Abel, Howell, & Bruce, 1982; Lizotte, 1986; Quinsey & Upfold, 1985). Evidence is mixed regarding the relationship of weapons to victim physical injury (Block & Skogan, 1986; Griffin & Griffin, 1981; Skogan & Block, 1983). Weapon-related assaults are also associated with an increased risk of PTSD in rape victims (Kilpatrick, Saunders, Amick-McMullan, & Best, 1989). However, most rapes are perpetrated without weapons, particularly rapes by known assailants. In a study of National Crime Victimization Survey (NCVS) data from 1992 to 1994, only 11% of rape incidents involved weapons (Bachman, 1998). Even when weapons are used, physical injury tends to be minor; the completed rape itself is often the most serious outcome for victims (Ullman, 1997).

Fortunately, victim resistance seems to be as effective for avoiding rape by an armed assailant as it is for an unarmed assailant (Ullman, 1997). More important, some data have suggested that armed resistance may be one of the most effective ways to avoid rape completion (Kleck & Sayles, 1990; Quigley, 1989), although it has not been specifically shown if this is true in cases where offenders also have weapons. However, few women are likely to have weapons ready for use in contexts involving men they know and trust, who are largely responsible for sexual assaults (Koss et al., 1988; Russell, 1984). Rapists may use weapons to inhibit victim resistance as opposed to causing gratuitous injuries. Nonlethal weapons of convenience (e.g., sticks, stones) are more likely to be used to injure victims than lethal weapons (Ullman & Knight, 1993), which could be due to less victim resistance to lethal weapons (Ullman, 1997). More research is needed to clarify the role of different types of weapons in rapes and how different types of resistance strategies may vary in effectiveness in response to offenders with different weapons. Similarly, research on women who do resist rape with weapons would be helpful, even though resistance with weapons is quite uncommon in rapes. Until larger samples of sexual assaults with different types of weapons can be analyzed in detail, specific recommendations about how to address the role of different types of weapons in risk reduction efforts cannot be provided. However, women can be informed that it is possible to successfully avoid rape even by an offender bearing a weapon (by using forceful resistance). In addition, data have suggested if they are able to resist rape with a weapon themselves, women are likely to avoid completed rape (Kleck & Sayles, 1990; Quigley, 1989).

Risky Situations and Contexts

Risky contexts are important to understand to effectively avoid rape. Lifestyle or "routine activities" theories of victimization may explain risk of stranger sexual assault (Meier & Miethe, 1993). According to these theories, victimization can happen because of a convergence of risky situations, suitable targets, motivated offenders, and absence of capable guardians (see Miethe & Meier, 1994). For instance, these theories traditionally have been useful in explaining the risk of violent victimization by strangers, which is typically associated with engaging in activities outdoors, at night, with delinquent peers (Lauritsen, Laub, & Sampson, 1992). However, different models may be needed for sexual victimization by acquaintances and intimates, as these attacks often occur indoors, in isolated locations, and may be part of a series of attacks by the same perpetrator. Factors associated with risk of acquaintance rape specifically include women initiating dates, men paying for dates, use of alcohol or drugs by one or both parties, and a woman going to a man's residence (Koss, 1985; Muehlenhard & Linton, 1987). A recent prospective study of college women indicated that prior victimization, alcohol use, multiple sexual partners, poor psychological adjustment, and insecurity about relationships with men were risk factors for sexual victimization (Greene & Navarro, 1998).

Parks and Miller's (1997) research on bar-related victimization is timely in addressing a highly risky alcohol-related context in which sexual assault risk may be magnified by situational and social cognitive factors. Interestingly, their study of women who drink at bars showed that exposure to the bar environment itself increased risk of severe victimization, whereas intoxication in the bar setting did not predict more severe victimization (Parks & Zetes-Zanatta, 1999). This result suggests that the mere presence of women in a bar setting, and not necessarily their heavy drinking behavior, may put them at risk for sexual victimization. These findings are consistent with experimental research that has demonstrated that women who drink in bars are viewed as legitimate targets of sexual aggression and judged to be more responsible for their assaults than victims who do not drink in bars (Abbey et al., 1996; Norris & Cubbins, 1992). Men may view women in bars as legitimate targets of physical and sexual aggression, however, regardless of their drinking behavior in the bar.

Research on fraternities and gang rape may also help to understand the contexts that facilitate individual sexual assault and gang rape (Sanday, 1990). Current empirical work is unable to answer whether fraternity members or college athletes are more likely to commit sexual aggression either alone or in groups (see Koss & Cleveland, 1996), but more research is needed on both of these potentially high-risk populations. One recent longitudinal evaluation of a rape prevention program with fraternity men indicated a 7-month decline in rape myth acceptance and self-reported likelihood of committing rape, but *no* decline in sexually coercive behavior was shown (Foubert, 2000).

Because relationships involve private contexts, strategies that girls and women in socially sanctioned relationships with boys and men or on dates use to avoid sexual assault are much harder to determine. As Yeater and O'Donohue (1999) noted, one cannot advocate that all women shun all men to avoid rape. However, just as risk of violence in general for a woman is highest from her intimate partner, sexual assault risk is high from intimate partners as well. Knowing that one has the right to refuse sexual advances no matter what one's relationship to a man is important for women, but the culture must support women's sexual integrity.

Just as women have become more capable of leaving abusive men in recent decades as a result of increased educational and occupational opportunities, they are less willing to put up with sexual assault, evidenced by increased enrollment in self-defense training and greater willingness to label rape as a crime and their own forced sexual experiences as rapes (Warshaw, 1988). Although rape reporting and prosecution remain low, with less than one quarter of 1992–1994 NCVS rape victimization incidents reported to police and less than 6% resulting in arrest (Bachman, 1998), this does not mean that women's consciousness of what rape is and their right to be free of it has not changed in recent decades.

Women's empowerment and consequent ability to avoid victimization are of course likely to differ dramatically across class, race, sexual orientation, and disability lines. Wyatt's (1992) community-based research indicated that African American women cited riskiness of their living circumstances as a contributor to their sexual assaults. Inclusive intervention efforts with women need to address the varying needs of subgroups who may face a variety of contexts and concomitant victimization risks. Clearly different contexts (e.g., places, groups, relationships) may affect sexual assault risk, but much more research is needed to understand how these specific contexts affect risk and the impact of behaviors on attack outcomes within these contexts. Most rape research has addressed macrolevel or microlevel correlates of rape risk; multilevel analyses are needed to develop effective risk reduction strategies.

Self-Defense

Although no empirical longitudinal studies of the efficacy of self-defense training exist, anecdotal data have suggested that this type of training enhances women's ability to thwart future assaults (Cummings, 1992; Peri, 1991). Clearly, this training has beneficial psychological effects of increased confidence, assertiveness, perceived control over life, and self-efficacy, as well as increased mastery of actual physical skills (Cohn, Kidder, & Harvey, 1978; Finkenberg, 1990; Kidder, Boell, & Moyer, 1983; Madden, 1995; McDaniel, 1993; Quinsey, Marion, Upfold, & Popple, 1986). In a controlled experimental study, Ozer and Bandura (1990) found that women trained in physical self-defense skills had enhanced efficacy and coping and decreased perceived vulnerability to assault. These women also reported increased freedom of action and decreased avoidant behaviors.

McCaughey (1997) argued persuasively that self-defense training empowers women and girls to overcome passive female gender role socialization that encourages them to be detached from their bodies and to perceive themselves as too weak to protect themselves from men's violence. This socialization may also underlie the well-documented fear of sexual assault in women in contemporary American society that leads women to restrict their behavior to avoid rape (Gordon & Riger, 1989; Warr, 1985). Self-defense educators report that they first must help women to overcome their fear of hurting the attacker, their aversion to using violence, and feelings that they do not deserve to protect themselves. These social-psychological factors are part of the inability of many women to see themselves as active agents capable of protecting themselves and thwarting attacks. Mastery of physical self-defense techniques is critical to overcoming these barriers and feeling efficacious (McCaughey, 1997). McCaughey also noted that child sexual abuse survivors have an especially difficult time, according to self-defense instructors she interviewed, in defending themselves and overcoming these barriers, which may account for their greater revictimization as adults and the ineffectiveness of current rape prevention programs for previously victimized women (Hanson & Gidycz, 1993).

In summary, more research should be focused on evaluating self-defense training, particularly its role in women's avoidance of rape. Rape intervention programs need to provide access to self-defense training for women who wish to learn how to defend themselves, given the clear data showing that forceful verbal and physical resistance enhance rape avoidance.

Social-Psychological Barriers

Norris et al.'s (1996) research identified social-psychological barriers in dating situations that may need to be addressed for high school and college women to enable them to resist date rape, including embarrassment and fear of peer group rejection for resisting sexual aggression by men. Again, these barriers may also be rooted in gender role socialization that encourages women to put the needs of others, especially men, above their own needs. Society holds women responsible for rape and puts women in a double bind by blaming them for men's sexually aggressive behavior (Morokoff, 1983; Walker & Browne, 1985). Thus, women deny rape by failing to self-label as rape victims, and they internalize self-blame for an experience that made them feel victimized but for which the costs of acknowledgment may be too high (Koss, 1985). In a recent review, Nurius (2000) documented social cognitive processes involved in perceiving potential sexual victimization threat from acquaintances. Nurius presented research showing that women reported low perceived personal risk for sexual aggression from an acquaintance and thus a low level of preparedness to prevent or protect against this threat. She argued that to develop effective resistance efforts, more research is needed on factors shaping risk perceptions and how these factors influence women's risk reduction and self-protection.

Research has shown that concerns about rejection by men, embarrassment at how others might negatively judge their resistance, and fears of being stigmatized by friends or peers affect women's decisions about how to respond to acquaintance sexual aggression (Cook, 1995; Norris et al., 1996). Some of the fears of negative reactions from others are well-founded, as recent research has shown that women experience a range of negative social reactions from others (e.g., blame, stigma, controlling responses, egocentric responses, disbelief) when disclosing sexual assaults (Ullman, 1996, 2000). Nurius (2000) argued that social concerns may override women's ability to see they are in danger and to act on their perceptions in acquaintance sexual assault situations. Additionally, alcohol may focus women on positive aspects of a social situation, like having fun and meeting men, instead of potential danger cues indicating imminent assaults.

In a recent study of college women's experiences of acquaintance sexual assault, Nurius, Norris, Young, Graham, and Gaylord (2000) reported that women were more likely to respond assertively to a man's sexual aggression when he used physical force, when she was concerned about injury, when she was not concerned about preserving the relationship, and when she felt angry and confident. Conversely, women used diplomatic responses when the man used verbal coercion, when she was self-conscious of her responses, and when she felt more sad and less angry. These correlational results suggest that interventions need to address women's emotional responses to sexual assault situations. In addition, this study implies that increasing women's confidence may play a key role in increasing their ability and willingness to actively resist sexual aggression, a finding echoed by the self-defense literature (McCaughey, 1997).

Breitenbecher and Scarce (2001) recently evaluated whether incorporating an educational component about social-psychological barriers into their prevention program might lead to a reduced risk of sexual victimization in 94 college women. The treatment group received a 90-minute educational program that included information about sexual assault prevalence, rape myths, sex role socialization, and rape as an act of power. The additional component was a skills-building exercise of sexual communication designed to teach women effective verbal and behavioral responses to sexual assault after imagining the emotions and cognitions they would expect in such a situation. At 7-months posttest, the treatment group showed no reduction in sexual assault risk compared with a control group of women. Furthermore, other outcome variables including knowledge about sexual assault, dating behaviors, sexual communication, and perception of risk were not affected by program participation. The authors suggested that low statistical power may have been a problem, but also that one-shot interventions may be inadequate to reduce victimization. In addition, the program did not include actual physical training in resistance or self-defense to sexual assault, which the authors suggested might be necessary to reduce victimization risk.

In summary, clearly social psychological barriers may affect women's ability to avoid sexual victimization and may need to be addressed in risk reduction efforts. More research is needed to determine whether efforts to reduce these barriers in women can lower their risk of being attacked and help them to avoid completed rapes once an assault has begun. Educating women about these barriers may help them become more aware of and less influenced by internal barriers to their own self-protection.

IMPLICATIONS

Research and Practice

Research and practice in the area of rape prevention must build on available evidence that clearly has indicated that situational characteristics and behaviors individuals engaged in are important for understanding the risk of being attacked, severity of injuries, and level of sexual assault sustained by victims. Alcohol is a potent risk factor commonly present in sexual assaults that must be targeted to address this crime, but the role of alcohol in a variety of contexts needs further attention in research and in developing and evaluating the effectiveness of intervention programs. Gidycz et al.'s (1999) recent longitudinal study of college women showed that alcohol use predicted adolescent and subsequent sexual victimization, indicating the potential importance of drinking in general as a risk factor for being victimized and of drinking at the time of the assault as a risk factor for sustaining more severe rape and injury outcomes discussed earlier in this review.

In addition to alcohol use, men's choice to use violence against women to accomplish sexual activity is just as important and probably more important a target for intervention attempts. Self-reported willingness to rape if they would not get caught is as high as 35% in the college male population (Malamuth, Sockloskie, Koss, & Tanaka, 1991). Men's use of physical violence is strongly related to the severity of physical injuries and sexual abuse sustained by victims (Ullman, 1997). This information is important because of the immediate and long-term health consequences for women of sustaining more violent completed rapes, including acute injuries, PTSD, and chronic health problems (Golding, 1994). Costs to society and to individual women are high for the crime of rape (Cohen & Miller, 1998), making prevention of this important public health problem critically important.

Much more research is needed to understand effective rape avoidance in different situational contexts such as bars, in isolated places and dating situations, and within intimate relationships. Although it is true that data about the effectiveness of rape resistance strategies cannot be generalized to all rape situations, empirical data clearly have shown that forceful resistance strategies (e.g., fighting, fleeing, screaming) do increase avoidance of rape without increasing risk of physical injuries across several studies for attacks by strangers and known assailants (Ullman, 1997). This conclusion does not mean that formal longitudinal studies of self-defense strategies are unnecessary; such studies are needed and have yet to be conducted (Yeater & O'Donohue, 1999). More research on rape avoidance more generally is needed as well. Even with data showing the efficacy of resistance to rape, self-defense alone will not stop rape.

Prevention and Risk Reduction Programs

Most rape prevention programs do not focus on teaching women in depth about risky situations, effective resistance strategies, and actual self-defense, which this review of research has shown to be important for avoiding completed rape and injury. Few evaluations of rape prevention programs have examined whether participants' future risk of victimization or perpetration actually is reduced. Without evaluations that assess this outcome, it is unclear whether existing rape prevention programs actually work. The few programs reviewed here that have assessed this outcome have mostly failed to demonstrate reduced victimization. Two programs that showed some efficacy in reducing future victimization over brief follow-up periods did not show this effect for all women (e.g., women with a history of previous victimization; Hanson & Gidycz, 1993) or still showed high revictimization rates among program participants (Marx, Calhoun, Wilson, & Meyerson, 2001). Furthermore, other studies have failed to replicate these results (Breitenbecher & Gidycz, 1998; Breitenbecher & Scarce, 1999). These aforementioned programs have included a variety of components including education about rape prevalence, rape myths and attitudes, characteristics of victims and offenders, how to label sexually coercive behavior, risky situations, safe dating behaviors, how to resist rape, effects of rape on women, and local resources for victims (see Gidycz et al., in press, for a review). Even when evaluations show positive effects, it is impossible to know which components of these programs may be producing changes in participants.

More programs need to be designed and evaluated to determine which components are most important for reducing victimization. Providing information about risky situations and behaviors, including resistance, is likely to be important and has been included in some of these programs, yet their overall lack of efficacy in reducing future victimization may mean that actual self-defense training is needed and that giving women information alone is not enough.

Most risk reduction programs try to keep women from ever being attacked (e.g., through behavioral restriction), but it is important to recognize that many women are being attacked and that they can be empowered to thwart these attacks (McCaughey, 1997). Although society and even feminists may feel uncomfortable teaching women how to defend themselves physically, it is critical that we no longer avoid this form of intervention (see McCaughey, 1997, for a discussion of the politics of rape prevention programming and funding under the 1994 Violence Against Women Act). Effective rape resistance strategies of screaming, fighting, and fleeing must be taught to women through oral presentations as well as physical self-defense classes. These classes should be evaluated to assess their effectiveness in helping women avoid rape and enhancing women's well-being overall. High school and college campus rape prevention programs should make self-defense classes available for women, and community programs should be funded to provide self-defense training to women in the general population. Although this type of risk reduction effort will not stop rapists from possibly choosing weaker targets for attack, it is one way to reduce the probability of more completed rapes and for society to support women's efforts to defend themselves. Interventions with women can also address social-psychological barriers such as embarrassment and fear of social rejection by peers (Norris et al., 1996) as well as beliefs they are unable to resist rape or not worthy of being free from sexual assault (McCaughey, 1997). Evaluations of rape intervention programs targeted to women must evaluate these components (e.g., self-defense training, educational components concerning risk reduction, and social-psychological barriers). Studies should include long-term follow-up assessments to determine whether favorable attitude change persists, given the problem of attitudinal rebounding over time (see Heppner et al., 1995; Heppner et al., 1999) and whether risk of actual victimization is effectively reduced.

Risk reduction programs may need to be tailored to women with different victimization histories, such as child sexual assault survivors and women victimized as adolescents (Gidycz, personal communication, November 1999). An evaluation found that a risk reduction program that focused on discussion of self-defense strategies and risky dating behaviors was successful at decreasing subsequent sexual victimization but not with previously victimized women (Hanson & Gidycz, 1993). A subsequent multisite evaluation of a risk reduction program showed that women victimized during a 2-month follow-up interval had a reduced risk of sexual revictimization at a 6-month follow-up, suggesting that once having experienced a sexual assault, women who had the program were better able to use it (Gidycz et al., 2001). Another study of 66 college women with a history of sexual victimization expanded on a risk reduction program of Hanson and Gidycz (1993) and found no differences in overall rates of sexual assault revictimization between program participants and a control group after 2 months but found lower rates of completed rape for program participants (Marx et al., 2001). Research also has indicated that there may be changes in women, such as decreased self-competence after an assault in adolescence, which are related to later revictimization (Marioni, Loh, Gidycz, Dowdall, & Pashdag, 1999). Such changes could be targeted in intervention programs with previously victimized women and may be particularly affected by self-defense training (Ozer & Bandura, 1990). Something about being victimized leads to higher risk of subsequent rape that future research must identify to develop intervention programs tailored to these women's needs.

I do not wish to imply that women are responsible for rape prevention. This idea has always been the pitfall of interventions aimed at women. However, as McCaughey (1997) argued, there is a difference between advocating a prevention approach that restricts women's freedom (e.g., telling them not to go out at night, not to drink alcohol) and supporting a prevention approach that enhances women's freedom (e.g., providing information about risk, teaching self-defense skills). The failure to provide information about effective resistance strategies that are based on research and training in self-defense techniques allows men to continue to complete more rapes of more women, which are clearly associated with more serious psychological and physical health consequences (Golding, 1999). Rapists have readily reported that they plan their attacks and look for easy targets but are thwarted by women who act assertively and make it difficult to complete rape by resisting (Bart & O'Brien, 1985). Sexually aggressive men expect women to submit and may be surprised when this action does not occur. Just as Western culture is changing its expectations about women's roles in the workforce and other public spheres, women are simultaneously demanding to be free of violence. Educators can help women to identify barriers to their own self-assertion, such as feelings that they are not worthy of self-protection, and help women define men's sexual aggression as wrong and the responsibility of men, not women.

Developmentally appropriate primary prevention programs targeting boys and men must be developed and evaluated to reduce sexual aggression. Rape prevention programs can be integrated with other antiviolence prevention programming and must focus on generalized aggression and sex role socialization (Bachar & Koss, 2000). However, given that effective rape prevention with boys and men has yet to be identified and implemented, more intervention efforts are also necessary with women. Even though research has demonstrated this efficacy, currently few risk reduction programs focus on teaching women formal self-defense or even about risky situations and effective resistance strategies. In light of the current pervasiveness of sexual assault in our society, "while the ethical burden to prevent rape does not lie with us [women] but with rapists and a society which upholds them, we will be waiting a very long time if we wait for men to decide not to rape" (Marcus, 1992, p. 400).

REFERENCES

Abbey, A. (1991). Acquaintance rape and alcohol consumption on college campuses: How are they linked? *American Journal of College Health, 39,* 165–170.

Abbey, A., & Ross, L. T. (1992, August). *The role of alcohol in understanding misperception and sexual assault.* Paper presented at the annual meeting of the American Psychological Association, San Francisco, CA.

Abbey, A., Ross, L. T., McDuffie, D., & McAuslan, P. (1996). Alcohol and dating risk factors for sexual assault among college women. *Psychology of Women Quarterly, 20,* 147–169.

Amick, A. E., & Calhoun, K. S. (1987). Resistance to sexual aggression: Personality, attitudinal, and situational factors. *Archives of Sexual Behavior, 16,* 153–163.

Amir, M. (1971). *Patterns in forcible rape.* Chicago: University of Chicago Press.

Bachar, K. J., & Koss, M. P. (2000). From prevalence to prevention: Closing the gap between what we know about rape and what we do. In C. M. Renzetti, R. K. Bergen, & J. L. Edelson (Eds.), *Sourcebook on violence against women* (pp. 117–142). Thousand Oaks, CA: Sage.

Bachman, R. (1994). *Violence against women* (NCJ Report No. 145325). Washington, DC: U.S. Government Printing Office.

Bachman, R. (1998). The factors related to rape reporting behavior and arrest: New evidence from the National Crime Victimization Survey. *Criminal Justice and Behavior, 25,* 8–29.

Bart, P. B., & O'Brien, P. (1985). *Stopping rape: Successful survival strategies.* New York: Pergamon.

Becker, J. V., Skinner, L. J., Abel, G. G., Howell, J., & Bruce, K. (1982). The effects of sexual assault on rape and attempted rape victims. *Victimology, 7,* 106–113.

Berkowitz, A. (1992). College men as perpetrators of acquaintance rape and sexual assault: A review of recent research. *Journal of American College Health, 40,* 175–181.

Block, R., & Skogan, W. C. (1986). Resistance and nonfatal outcomes in stranger-to stranger predatory crime. *Violence and Victims, 4,* 241–253.

Brecklin, L. R., & Forde, D. R. (2001). A meta-analysis of rape education programs. *Violence and Victims, 16,* 303–321.

Brecklin, L. R., & Ullman, S. E. (2001). The role of offender alcohol use in rape attacks: An analysis of National Crime Survey data. *Journal of Interpersonal Violence, 16,* 3–21.

Breitenbecher, K. H. (2000). Sexual assault on college campuses: Is an ounce of prevention enough? *Applied and Preventive Psychology, 9,* 23–52.

Breitenbecher, K. H., & Gidycz, C. A. (1998). An empirical evaluation of a program designed to reduce the risk of multiple sexual victimization. *Journal of Interpersonal Violence, 13,* 472–488.

Breitenbecher, K. H., & Scarce, M. (1999). A longitudinal evaluation of the effectiveness of a sexual assault education program. *Journal of Interpersonal Violence, 14,* 459–478.

Breitenbecher, K. H., & Scarce, M. (2001). An evaluation of the effectiveness of a sexual assault education program focusing on psychological barriers to resistance. *Journal of Interpersonal Violence, 16,* 387–407.

Burnam, M. A., Stein, J. A., Golding, J. M., Siegel, J. M., Sorenson, S. B., Forsythe, A. B., et al. (1988). Sexual assault and mental disorders in a community sample. *Journal of Consulting and Clinical Psychology, 56,* 843–850.

Bushman, B. J., & Cooper, H. M. (1990). Effects of alcohol on human aggression: An integrative research review. *Psychological Bulletin, 107,* 341–354.

Calhoun, K. S., Bernat, J. A., Clum, G. A., & Frame, C. L. (1997). Sexual coercion and attraction to sexual aggression in a community sample of young men. *Journal of Interpersonal Violence, 12,* 392–405.

Cleveland, H. H., Koss, M. P., & Lyons, J. (1999). Rape tactics from the survivors' perspective. *Journal of Interpersonal Violence, 14,* 532–547.

Cohen, M. A., & Miller, T. R. (1998). The cost of mental health care for victims of crime. *Journal of Interpersonal Violence, 13,* 93–110.

Cohn, E., Kidder, L., & Harvey, J. (1978). Crime prevention vs. victimization prevention: The psychology of two different reactions. *Victimology, 3,* 285–296.

Coker, A. C., Walls, L. G., & Johnson, J. E. (1998). Risk factors for traumatic physical injury during sexual assaults for male and female victims. *Journal of Interpersonal Violence, 13,* 605–620.

Cook, S. L. (1995). Acceptance and expectation of sexual aggression in college students. *Psychology of Women Quarterly, 19,* 181–194.

Cummings, N. (1992). Self-defense training for college women. *American Journal of College Health, 40,* 183–188.

Finkelhor, D., & Yllo, K. (1985). *License to rape: Sexual abuse of wives.* New York: Free Press.

Finkenberg, M. E. (1990). Effect of participation in Tae Kwon Do on college women's self concept. *Perceptual and Motor Skills, 71,* 891–894.

Flores, S. A., & Hartlaub, M. G. (1998). Reducing rape myth acceptance in male college students: A meta-analysis of intervention studies. *Journal of College Student Development, 39,* 438–448.

Foubert, J. D. (2000). The longitudinal effects of a rape-prevention program on fraternity men's attitudes, behavioral intent, and behavior. *Journal of American College Health, 48,* 158–163.

Gidycz, C. A., Dowdall, C. L., & Marioni, N. L. (in press). Interventions to prevent rape and sexual assault. In J. Petrak & B. Hedge (Eds.), *The trauma of adult sexual assault: Treatment, prevention, and policy.* New York: Wiley.

Gidycz, C. A., Lynn, S. J., Rich, C. L., Marioni, N. L., Loh, C., & Blackwell, L. M., et al. (2001). The evaluation of a sexual assault risk reduction program: A multi-site investigation. *Journal of Consulting and Clinical Psychology, 69,* 1073–1078.

Gidycz, C. A., & Koss, M. P. (1990). A comparison of group and individual sexual assault victims. *Psychology of Women Quarterly, 14,* 325–342.

Gidycz, C. A., Lynn, S. J., Marioni, N. L., Dowdall, C. L., Loh, C., Pashdag, J., et al. (1999, November). *A prospective and longitudinal analysis of sexual victimization and revictimization.* Poster presented at the annual meeting of the International Society of Traumatic Stress Studies, Miami, FL.

Golding, J. M. (1994). Sexual assault history and physical health in randomly selected Los Angeles women. *Health Psychology, 13,* 130–138.

Golding, J. M. (1999). Sexual-assault history and long-term physical health problems: Evidence from clinical and population epidemiology. *Current Directions in Psychological Science, 8,* 191–194.

Gordon, M. T., & Riger, S. (1989). *The female fear.* New York: Free Press.

Greene, D. M., & Navarro, R. L. (1998). Situation-specific assertiveness in the epidemiology of sexual victimization among university women: A prospective path analysis. *Psychology of Women Quarterly, 22,* 589–604.

Griffin, B. S., & Griffin, C. T. (1981). Victims in rape confrontation. *Victimology, 6,* 59–75.

Hanson, K. A., & Gidycz, C. A. (1993). Evaluation of a sexual assault prevention program. *Journal of Consulting and Clinical Psychology, 61,* 1046–1052.

Harrington, N. T., & Leitenberg, H. (1994). Relationship between alcohol consumption and victim behaviors immediately preceding sexual aggression by an acquaintance. *Violence and Victims, 9,* 315–324.

Heppner, M. J., Humphrey, C. F., Hillenbrand-Gunn, T. L., & DeBord, K. A. (1995). The differential effects of rape prevention programming on attitudes, behavior, and knowledge. *Journal of Counseling Psychology, 42,* 508–518.

Heppner, M. J., Neville, H. A., Smith, K., Kivlighan, D. M., & Gershuny, B. S. (1999). Examining immediate and long-term efficacy of rape prevention programming with racially diverse college men. *Journal of Counseling Psychology, 46,* 16–26.

Hull, J. G., & Bond, C. F. (1986). Social and behavioral consequences of alcohol consumption and expectancy: A meta-analysis. *Psychological Bulletin, 99,* 347–360.

Johnson, S. D., Gibson, L., & Linden, R. (1978). Alcohol and rape in Winnipeg, 1966–1975. *Journal of Studies on Alcohol, 39*, 1887–1894.

Kelly, L. (1988). *Surviving sexual violence.* England: Polity Press.

Kidder, L. H., Boell, J. L., & Moyer, M. M. (1983). Rights consciousness and victimization prevention: Personal defense and assertiveness training. *Journal of Social Issues, 39*, 155–170.

Kilpatrick, D. G., Acierno, R., Resnick, H. S., Saunders, B. E., & Best, C. L. (1997). A 2-year longitudinal study of the relationships between violent assault and substance use in women. *Journal of Consulting and Clinical Psychology, 65*, 834–847.

Kilpatrick, D. G., Best, C. L., Veronen, L. J., Amick, A. E., Villeponteaux, L. A., & Ruff, G. A. (1985). Mental health correlates of criminal victimization: A random community survey. *Journal of Consulting and Clinical Psychology, 53*, 866–873.

Kilpatrick, D. G., Edmunds, C. N., & Seymour, A. K. (1992). *Rape in America: A report to the nation.* Arlington, VA: National Victim Center.

Kilpatrick, D. G., Saunders, B. E., Amick-McMullan, A., & Best, C. L. (1989). Victim and crime factors associated with the development of crime-related posttraumatic stress disorder. *Behavior Therapy, 20*, 199–214.

Kleck, G., & Sayles, S. (1990). Rape and resistance. *Social Problems, 37*, 149–162.

Koss, M. P. (1985). The hidden rape victim: Personality, attitudinal, and situational characteristics. *Psychology of Women Quarterly, 9*, 192–212.

Koss, M. P. (1993). Detecting the scope of rape: A review of prevalence research methods. *Journal of Interpersonal Violence, 8*, 198–222.

Koss, M. P., & Cleveland, H. H. (1996). Athletic participation, fraternity membership, and date rape. *Violence Against Women, 2*, 180–190.

Koss, M. P., & Dinero, T. E. (1989). Discriminant analysis of risk factors for sexual victimization among a national sample of college women. *Journal of Consulting and Clinical Psychology, 57*, 242–250.

Koss, M. P., Dinero, T. E., Seibel, C. A., & Cox, S. L. (1988). Stranger and acquaintance rape: Are there differences in the victim's experience? *Psychology of Women Quarterly, 12*, 1–24.

Koss, M. P., Goodman, L. A., Browne, A., Fitzgerald, L. F., Keita, G. P., & Russo, N. F. (1994). *No safe haven: Male violence against women at home, at work, and in the community.* Washington, DC: American Psychological Association.

Koss, M. P., Heise, L., & Russo, N. F. (1994). The global health burden of rape. *Psychology of Women Quarterly, 18*, 509–537.

Lauritsen, J. L., Laub, J. H., & Sampson, R. J. (1992). Conventional and delinquent activities: Implications for the prevention of violent victimization among adolescents. *Violence and Victims, 7*, 91–108.

Levy, B. (1991). *Dating violence: Young women in danger.* Seattle, WA: Seal Press.

Lizotte, A. J. (1986). Determinants of completing rape and assault. *Journal of Quantitative Criminology, 2*, 203–217.

Lonsway, K. A. (1996). Preventing acquaintance rape through education: What do we know? *Psychology of Women Quarterly, 20,* 229–265.

Lonsway, K. A., Klaw, E. L., Berg, D. R., Waldo, C. R., Kothari, C., Mazurek, C. J., et al. (1998). Beyond "no means no": Outcomes of an intensive program to train peer facilitators for campus acquaintance rape prevention. *Journal of Interpersonal Violence, 13,* 73–92.

Madden, M. E. (1995). Perceived vulnerability and control of martial arts and physical fitness students. *Perceptual and Motor Skills, 80,* 899–910.

Malamuth, N. M., Sockloskie, R. J., Koss, M. P., & Tanaka, J. S. (1991). Characteristics of sexual aggressors against women: Testing a model using a national sample of college students. *Journal of Consulting and Clinical Psychology, 59,* 670–681.

Marcus, S. (1992). Fighting bodies, fighting words: A theory and politics of rape prevention. In J. Butler & J.W. Scott (Eds.), *Feminists theorize the political* (pp. 385–402). New York: Routledge.

Marioni, N. L., Loh, C., Gidycz, C. A., Dowdall, C. L., & Pashdag, J. A. (1999, August). *Role of self-blame in predicting sexual revictimization.* Paper presented at the annual meeting of the American Psychological Association, Boston, MA.

Martin, S. E., & Bachman, R. (1998). The contribution of alcohol to the likelihood of completion and severity of injury in rape incidents. *Violence Against Women, 4,* 694–712.

Marx, B. P., Calhoun, K. S., Wilson, A. E., & Meyerson, L. A. (2001). Sexual revictimization prevention: An outcome evaluation. *Journal of Consulting and Clinical Psychology, 69,* 25–32.

McCaughey, M. (1997). *Real knockouts: The physical feminism of women's self-defense.* New York: New York University Press.

McDaniel, P. (1993). Self-defense training and women's fear of crime. *Women's Studies International Forum, 16,* 37–45.

Meier, R. F., & Miethe, T. D. (1993). Understanding theories of criminal victimization. In M. Tonry (Ed.), *Crime and justice: A review of research* (Vol. 17, pp. 459–499). Chicago: University of Chicago Press.

Miethe, T. D., & Meier, R. F. (1994). *Crime and its social context: Toward an integrated theory of offenders, victims, and situations.* Albany: SUNY Press.

Morokoff, P. (1983). Toward the elimination of rape: A conceptualization of sexual aggression against women. In A. P. Goldstein (Ed.), *Prevention and control of aggression* (pp. 101–144). New York: Pergamon.

Muehlenhard, C. L., & Linton, M. A. (1987). Date rape and sexual aggression in dating situations: Incidence and risk factors. *Journal of Counseling Psychology, 34,* 186–196.

Norris, J., & Cubbins, L. A. (1992). Dating, drinking, and rape: Effects of victim's and assailant's alcohol consumption on judgments of their behavior and traits. *Psychology of Women Quarterly, 16,* 179–191.

Norris, J., Nurius, P. S., & Dimeff, L. A. (1996). Through her eyes: Factors affecting women's perception of and resistance to acquaintance sexual aggression threat. *Psychology of Women Quarterly, 20,* 123–145.

Nurius, P. S. (2000). Risk perception for acquaintance sexual aggression: A social–cognitive perspective. *Aggression and Violent Behavior, 5,* 63–78.

Nurius, P. S., Norris, J., Young, D. S., Graham, T. L., & Gaylord, J. (2000). Interpreting and defensively responding to threats: Examining appraisals and coping with acquaintance sexual aggression. *Violence and Victims, 15,* 187–208.

Ozer, E. M., & Bandura, A. (1990). Mechanisms governing empowerment effects: A self-efficacy analysis. *Journal of Personality and Social Psychology, 58,* 472–486.

Parks, K. A., & Miller, B. A. (1997). Bar victimization of women. *Psychology of Women Quarterly, 21,* 509–525.

Parks, K. A., & Zetes-Zanatta, L. M. (1999). Women's bar-related victimization: Refining and testing a conceptual model. *Aggressive Behavior, 25,* 349–364.

Peri, C. (1991, March). Below the belt: Women in the martial arts. *Newsletter of the National Women's Martial Arts Federation,* 6–14.

Pernanen, K. (1991). *Alcohol and human violence.* New York: Guilford Press.

Prentky, R. A., Burgess, A. W., & Carter, D. (1986). Victim response by rapist type: An empirical and clinical analysis. *Journal of Interpersonal Violence, 1,* 688–695.

Quigley, P. (1989). *Armed and female.* New York: St. Martin's Press.

Quinsey, V. L., Marion, G., Upfold, D., & Popple, K. T. (1986). Issues in teaching physical methods of resisting rape. *Sexual Coercion and Assault, 1,* 125–130.

Quinsey, V. L., & Upfold, D. (1985). Rape completion and victim injury as a function of female resistance strategy. *Canadian Journal of Behavioral Science, 17,* 40–50.

Rozee, P. D., & Koss, M. P. (2001). Rape: A century of resistance. *Psychology of Women Quarterly, 25,* 295–311.

Ruback, R. B., & Ivie, D. L. (1988). Prior relationship, resistance, and injury in rapes: An analysis of crisis center records. *Violence and Victims, 3,* 99–111.

Russell, D. E. H. (1984). *Sexual exploitation: Rape, child sexual abuse, and workplace harassment.* Beverly Hills, CA: Sage.

Sanday, P. R. (1990). *Fraternity gang rape: Sex, brotherhood, and privilege on campus.* New York: New York University Press.

Schewe, P., & O'Donohue, W. (1993). Rape prevention: Methodological problems and new directions. *Clinical Psychology Review, 13,* 667–682.

Seto, M. C., & Barbaree, H. E. (1995). The role of alcohol in sexual aggression. *Clinical Psychology Review, 15,* 545–566.

Siegel, J. M., Golding, J. M., Stein, J. A., Burnam, M. A., & Sorenson, S. B. (1990). Reactions to sexual assault: A community study. *Journal of Interpersonal Violence, 5,* 229–246.

Skogan, W., & Block, R. (1983). Resistance and injury in non-fatal assaultive violence. *Victimology, 8,* 215–226.

Stermac, L., DuMont, J., & Dunn, S. (1998). Violence in known-assailant sexual assaults. *Journal of Interpersonal Violence, 13,* 398–412.

Testa, M., & Livingston, J. A. (2000). Alcohol and sexual aggression: Reciprocal relationships over time in a sample of high-risk women. *Journal of Interpersonal Violence, 15,* 413–427.

Testa, M., & Parks, K. A. (1996). The role of women's alcohol consumption in sexual victimization. *Aggression and Violent Behavior: A Review Journal, 1,* 217–234.

Ullman, S. E. (1996). Social reactions, coping strategies, and self-blame attributions in adjustment to sexual assault. *Psychology of Women Quarterly, 20,* 505–526.

Ullman, S. E. (1997). Review and critique of empirical studies of rape avoidance. *Criminal Justice and Behavior, 24,* 177–204.

Ullman, S. E. (1998). Does offender violence escalate when rape victims fight back? *Journal of Interpersonal Violence, 13,* 179–192.

Ullman, S. E. (1999). A comparison of gang and individual rape incidents. *Violence and Victims, 14,* 123–134.

Ullman, S. E. (2000). Psychometric characteristics of the Social Reactions Questionnaire: A measure of reactions to sexual assault victims. *Psychology of Women Quarterly, 24,* 169–183.

Ullman, S. E., & Brecklin, L. R. (2000). Alcohol and adult sexual assault in a national sample of women. *Journal of Substance Abuse, 12,* 1–16.

Ullman, S. E., Karabatsos, G., & Koss, M. P. (1999a). Alcohol and sexual aggression in a national sample of college men. *Psychology of Women Quarterly, 23,* 673–689.

Ullman, S. E., Karabatsos, G., & Koss, M. P. (1999b). Alcohol and sexual assault in a national sample of college women. *Journal of Interpersonal Violence, 14,* 603–625.

Ullman, S. E., & Knight, R. A. (1991). A multivariate model for predicting rape and physical injury outcomes during sexual assaults. *Journal of Consulting and Clinical Psychology, 59,* 724–731.

Ullman, S. E., & Knight, R. A. (1992). Fighting back: Women's resistance to rape. *Journal of Interpersonal Violence, 7,* 31–43.

Ullman, S. E., & Knight, R. A. (1993). The efficacy of women's resistance strategies in rape situations. *Psychology of Women Quarterly, 17,* 23–38.

Ullman, S. E., & Knight, R. A. (1995). Women's resistance strategies to different rapist types. *Criminal Justice and Behavior, 22,* 263–283.

Ullman, S. E., & Siegel, J. M. (1993). Victim–offender relationship and sexual assault. *Violence and Victims, 8,* 121–134.

Walker, L. E. (1984). *The battered woman syndrome.* New York: Springer.

Walker, L. E., & Browne, A. (1985). Gender and victimization by intimates. *Journal of Personality, 53,* 179–195.

Warr, M. (1985). Fear of rape among urban women. *Social Problems, 32,* 238–250.

Warshaw, R. (1988). *I never called it rape.* New York: Harper & Row.

Wyatt, G. E. (1992). The sociocultural context of African American and White American women's rape. *Journal of Social Issues, 48,* 77–91.

Yeater, E. A., & O'Donohue, W. (1999). Sexual assault prevention programs: Current issues, future directions, and the potential efficacy of interventions with women. *Clinical Psychology Review, 19,* 739–771.

7

FOSTERING MEN'S RESPONSIBILITY FOR PREVENTING SEXUAL ASSAULT

ALAN D. BERKOWITZ

Men must take responsibility for preventing sexual assault, because most assaults are perpetrated by men against women, children, and other men. Even though only a minority of men may commit sexual assault, all men can have an influence on the culture and environment that allows other men to be perpetrators. Thus, effective sexual assault prevention requires that men look at their own potential for violence as well as take a stand against the violence of other men. This chapter provides an overview of the issues involved in men taking responsibility for sexual assault prevention, suggests a philosophy and pedagogy for rape prevention, provides a developmental model for prevention programs, makes recommendations for advancing the field, and reviews promising interventions and strategies. The chapter's primary focus is the prevention of sexual assault perpetrated by men

The author thanks Michael Kimmel, Deborah Mahlsdedt, and Paul Schewe for their thoughtful comments on an earlier version of this manuscript. The portion of this chapter titled "Essential Program Elements," including Exhibit 7.2, is adapted from A. Berkowitz, "Critical Elements of Sexual-Assault Prevention and Risk Reduction Programs for Men and Women" in C. Kilmartin, *Sexual Assault in Context* (2001) by permission of Learning Publications, Holmes Beach, FL.

against women (or young men and young women) who know each other in college or high school settings.

Scholars and researchers who study the male gender role have noted that masculinity is often defined in opposition to femininity, which is devalued or seen as less desirable (Kilmartin, 2000; Levant & Pollack, 1995; Pleck, 1981). Teaching boys and men to devalue or objectify women and girls may facilitate behavior in which men and boys overlook, disrespect, harass, or abuse girls and women. These ways of treating women may in turn create discomfort among men whose values conflict with the male socialization process. Whether or not men choose to act out these negative potentials, all men struggle with the conflicts and issues created by a definition of self that devalues women and limits what is acceptable behavior for men. Thus, sexual assault prevention should help men explore how they are taught to be men, the conflicts and discomfort associated with trying to live up to the male role, and how they may intentionally or unintentionally enable the coercive sexual behavior of other men. As I have noted elsewhere, "It is the experience of masculinity itself—how men think of themselves as men— that creates the psychological and cultural environment that leads men to rape . . . this environment is perpetuated through men's relationships with and expectations of each other" (Berkowitz, 1994c, p. 1). Capraro (1994) made a similar assertion:

> Our understanding of the specific act of rape should be embedded in our understanding of masculinity. Rape is not an isolated behavior, but a behavior linked in men's lives to larger systems of attitudes, values and modalities or conduct that constitute masculinity. In this model, rape prevention work begins with men and with men's questioning of prevailing assumptions about masculinity and their rethinking of what it means to be a man. I am extremely skeptical of any rape prevention work that proposes solutions to the problem of rape but leaves masculinity, as we know today, largely intact. (p. 22)

Asking men to make a shift may not be as difficult as it may seem for several reasons. First, men already feel uncomfortable with their socialization as men and the pressure to live up to a masculine ideal. Researchers have conceptualized the difficulty of trying to live up to inherently contradictory gender role expectations as "gender role conflict," and an extensive research literature has documented that most men do experience role conflict as well as its negative psychological consequences (Mahalik, 1999; Sharpe & Heppner, 1991). Second, while male peer support and pressure increase the likelihood of sexual assault (Berkowitz, 1992; Muehlenhard & Linton, 1987; Schwartz & DeKeseredy, 1997), recent research has suggested that men overestimate the extent to which their peers endorse gender stereotypes about sexual attitudes and behavior (Berkowitz, 2000a). Thus, the peer pressures men feel may in part be based on misperceptions of other men's attitudes and behavior. Finally, the research literature has shown that rape proclivity is strongly associated with *hypermasculinity*, or the tendency to overconform to perceived male gender role expectations (Berkowitz, Burkhart, & Bourg, 1994). These findings converge in the hypothesis that sexual assault prevention for men should have an explicit gender focus (Kilmartin, 2001) and that interventions that reveal men's true feelings about male gender role expectations could (a) help reduce the pressures men feel to be sexually active in ways that lead to sexual assault and (b) encourage men to express their discomfort with other men's coercive behavior, thus potentially inhibiting such behavior.

This approach to prevention is not recommended for all men. Men who have a history of previous sexual assaults have not benefited from educationally oriented sexual assault prevention programs (Gilbert, Heesacker, & Gannon, 1991) and may need more intensive treatment within clinical or judicial systems, or both.

TERMINOLOGY: SEXUAL ASSAULT PREVENTION, RISK REDUCTION, AND DETERRENCE

Professionals have struggled to develop adequate terminology to describe men's and women's roles in preventing sexual assault in intimate relationships. Responsibility for prevention can be defined by who takes the initiative with respect to sexual intimacy, with the assumption that it is responsibility of the person initiating to ensure that the intimacy is mutual, uncoerced, and consenting (Berkowitz, 1994b). Because sexual activity is often initiated by men, and because almost all sexual assaults are perpetrated by men against women, children, or other men, the term *prevention* in this chapter is used primarily to describe programs directed to male audiences.

Programs for potential victims can help reduce the risk of sexual assault by empowering participants to engage in actions that decrease the likelihood of victimization, although this risk may not be totally eliminated (see Ullman, chapter 6, this volume). The terms *empowerment, risk reduction*, and *deterrence* have been used in the literature to describe programs that teach women actions that can reduce the potential risk of assault, increase protective factors and skills for self-defense, and foster social activism to end violence against women. Risk reduction and deterrence strategies can also be considered a form of prevention because they can prevent individuals from becoming victims. Because most victims of sexual assaults are women, risk reduction, safety enhancement, and empowerment programs should primarily be directed toward women. However, because a smaller percentage of men may also be victimized, programs with male audiences should acknowledge and be sensitive to issues of male victimization. The critical elements of effective risk reduction–deterrence–prevention programs for women have been outlined by Berkowitz (2001) and are provided in the discussion that follows.

WHY ALL-MALE PROGRAMS?

A consensus is emerging among researchers that sexual assault prevention is most effective when conducted in separate-gender groups. This conclusion was found in six reviews of the evaluation literature on sexual assault prevention programs, with all of them recommending all-male programs as the preferred prevention strategy for men (Brecklin & Forde, 2001; Breitenbecher, 2000; Gidycz, Dowdall, & Marioni, 2002; Lonsway, 1996; Schewe, chapter 5, this volume; Yeater & O'Donohue, 1999). These researchers have based their conclusions on several factors, including (a) the different strategies and goals for men's and women's programs and the danger of inconsistent messages when both groups are combined (Gidycz et al., 2002; Schewe, chapter 5, this volume; Yeater & O'Donohue, 1999); (b) outcome studies indicating that mixed-gender programs are less effective than separate-gender programs (Berkowitz 1994b; Brecklin & Forde, 2001; Lonsway, 1996); and (c) the testimony of participants in all-male workshops.

With respect to conflicting strategies and messages, Gidycz and colleagues (2002) concluded that

> The goals for men and women's programs diverge in a number of respects making it difficult to structure the content for mixed-sex programs. Although a number of mixed-sex programs have focused on rape-myth acceptance and sex role attitudes and thus, assessed these variables post-intervention as measures of program efficacy, the literature does not support a link between these types of attitudes and the experience of being a victim for women (see Koss & Dinero, 1989). Thus, while challenging these attitudes seems to be an appropriate goal for men, we believe that programs for women need to help them identify and cope with characteristics of sexually aggressive men and situations that are particularly risky.

Schewe (chapter 5, this volume) notes that it might be inappropriate to share risk reduction messages with men because it could provide potential rapists with information about what makes women vulnerable to rape.

Evaluation studies also have suggested that single-gender programs are more effective. These conclusions are consistent across a wide range of studies using different methodologies and experimental designs. For example, in Lonsway's review (1996), all three programs provided to all-female audiences had a positive impact, as did most of the studies conducted with all-male audiences. Similarly, Earle (1996) compared two coeducational programs with an all-male program developed by Berkowitz (1994b) and found the latter to be more beneficial for men. In contrast to single-gender programs, evaluations of programs provided to coeducational groups are less clear regarding their benefits for both men and women. Thus, of the 25 studies reviewed for this chapter, only 5 demonstrated an equal impact on men and women (Fonow, Richardson, & Wemmerus, 1992; Frazier, Valtinson, & Candell, 1994; Malamuth & Check, 1984; Mann, Hecht, & Valentine, 1988; Rosenthal, Heesacker, & Neimeyer, 1995), four others reported a negative impact on all or some of the men (Earle, 1996; Ellis, O'Sullivan, & Sowards, 1992; Fisher, 1986; Heppner, Good, et al., 1995), and five additional studies found that men (Earle, 1996; Harrison, Downes, & Williams, 1991; Heppner, Humphrey, Hillenbrand-Gunn, & DeBord, 1995; Holcomb, Sarvela, Sondag, Hatton, & Holcomb, 1993) or women (Lenihan & Rawlins, 1994) benefited more than the other gender. Similarly, in three comprehensive high school studies reviewed by the National Research Council (Crowell & Burgess, 1996), young men and young women benefited equally in only one study, and a small group of young men showed change in the undesired direction in another. Thus, a review of existing evaluation studies and literature reviews indicates that separate-gender programs are more effective than are coeducational program formats.

This conclusion is supported by a recent study in which Brecklin and Forde (2001) conducted the most comprehensive analysis of rape prevention program evaluations as of this writing. In a meta-analysis of 43 evaluation studies, they determined that both men and women experienced more beneficial change in single-gender groups than in mixed-gender groups.

Male workshop participants articulated several benefits from all-male discussions in participant evaluations of an all-male rape prevention program developed by Berkowitz (1994b). Reasons given in favor of all-male programs included the following:

- Men are more comfortable, less defensive, and more honest in all-male groups.
- Men are less likely to talk openly and participate in the presence of women.
- Mixed-gender discussions can become polarized.
- Single-gender groups reveal a diversity of opinions among men that may not be expressed if women are present.
- Men feel safe disagreeing or putting pressure on each other in all-male groups.
- Focusing on risk reduction in mixed-gender groups can result in men assigning responsibility for the assault to women.

In evaluations of this workshop over a 10-year period, a majority of men attending stated that it should be kept all male. A selection of typical evaluation comments is provided in Exhibit 7.1. It is noteworthy that many of the attitudes men express in favor of all-male workshops (e.g., viewing gender

EXHIBIT 7.1
Evaluation Comments Favoring All-Male Workshops

- I liked the all-male atmosphere.
- The workshop provided an opportunity to express feelings and frustrations freely.
- Keep it all males.
- Men won't speak freely or openly with women around.
- The conversation would not be honest or as frank. It would be too hard to speak with women present.
- It's easier to talk with an all-guy crowd.
- It's hard to be open about women when women are around.
- If the program were coeducational, it would become a "battle of the sexes."
- Men would worry about women taking what they say the wrong way if there were women in the room.
- I wouldn't want to make victims who were present uncomfortable.

Note. From *Unpublished Program Evaluations, Hobart College Rape Prevention Program for Men* (pp. 1–3), by A. D. Berkowitz and J. Earle, 1995, Geneva, NY: Hobart College. Copyright 1995 by Hobart College. Reprinted with permission.

dialogue as adversarial or feeling comfortable in expressing men's complaints about women) are attitudes and beliefs that need to be changed if men are to take responsibility for rape prevention. The purpose of providing such an opportunity is to bring these beliefs and attitudes into the open so that they can be challenged and transformed. Fear of embarrassment, "political correctness," or judgment might inhibit men from expressing these feelings in the presence of women. Furthermore, the opportunity to have an open, honest dialogue with other men also serves to contradict men's socialization and experience of sharing intimate feelings only with women.

Men's preference for single-gender discussions parallels the development of women's consciousness-raising groups early in the history of the women's movement. It is interesting to note that most men will indicate a preference for a coeducational workshop prior to participation in an all-male workshop but will change their minds after having the experience of an open, honest discussion with other men.

Given that all-male workshops are the intervention of choice for working with men, what is the best format for such programs? What are the areas that should be addressed or at least mentioned in sexual assault prevention programs?

PROGRAM FORMAT

A variety of program formats have been discussed in the literature, including lectures, viewing of videos or movies, structured discussions, panels of victims, and interactive discussions following a video or presentation of scenarios. The literature has suggested that the quality and interactive nature of the discussion may be more important than the format in which the material is presented (Breitenbecher, 2000). Davis (2000) defined this dimension as "program process":

> Program process issues are aimed at making the content palatable to the learner, effectively engaging the learner, reducing defensiveness, and facilitating thoughtful evaluation of the information being presented. That is, process strategies should be geared towards enhancing the "learnability" of the intended outcomes. (p. 83)

Heppner, Humphrey, et al. (1995) demonstrated, for example, that an interactive, nonblaming program format resulted in a deeper level of processing among participants than did a lecture format. Earle (1996) compared lecture, structured presentation, and interactive discussion formats and found that the interactive discussion was most effective in changing men's attitudes about rape. Flores and Hartlaub (1998) compared human sexuality courses, workshops, video presentations, and other formats and found that they all were equally effective in reducing rape myth acceptance. In contrast, sexual assault prevention programs focusing on factual information alone have been found ineffective in producing desired changes, as have those that adopt a blaming or confrontational approach toward men (Schewe, chapter 5, this volume). Lonsway (1996), after conducting a comprehensive overview of the evaluation literature, concluded that "programs with the greatest effectiveness involve interactive participation such as role-playing and peer counseling . . . participant interaction is an element common to many rape prevention programs and one that is generally reported to co-occur with desirable attitude change" (p. 247). Thus, the quality of the discussion in a workshop experience seems to be one of the most important factors in producing change among male (or female) participants. This is consistent with findings from the drug prevention, sexual assault prevention, and child abuse prevention fields and is consistent across a wide variety of studies with different methodologies, samples, and intervention strategies:

> In general, any intervention that provides for active participation is more effective than one that requires only passive participation. For example, interactive theater with audience participation is a more powerful intervention than a presentation without discussion or audience participation. An interactive theater presentation with audience discussion followed by discussion in small groups is an ideal way to combine large and smaller program formats. Creating intensive programs which foster interaction, discussion and reflection require that we focus on process as well as content, and replace rigid structure with flexibility. (Berkowitz, 2001, p. 77)

ESSENTIAL PROGRAM ELEMENTS

Several workshops for men have been developed since the early 1990s, when Berkowitz (1992), Birnbaum and Weinburg (1991), Corcoran (1992), and Kivel (1992) articulated the need for a male role in the prevention of sexual assault and violence. Since then, several programs and curricula have been developed that focus on men's responsibility for preventing sexual assault, including workshops by Berkowitz (1994b), Katz (1995), Schewe and O'Donohue (1996), Foubert and colleagues (Foubert, 2000; Foubert & Marriott, 1997; Foubert & McEwen, 1998), Mahlstedt and Corcoran (1999), and Men Can Stop Rape (MCSR, 2000). These programs are designed to encourage open, honest discussion in all-male audiences and tend to focus on one or more of the following themes: developing empathy for victims; learning how to achieve mutual, uncoerced consent in intimate relationships; teaching skills for intervening with other men to prevent sexual assault or interrupt sexism; and understanding the cultural and socialization issues that contribute to the problem. Information on these programs is provided in Appendix A.

These sexual assault prevention programs share several common assumptions:

- Men should take primary responsibility for preventing sexual assault.
- The best approach to working with men is to view them as prevention partners rather than blaming them for the problem of rape and sexual assault.
- Workshops are most effective when conducted by peer educators in small, all-male groups.
- Discussions should be interactive and encourage honest sharing of feelings, ideas, and beliefs.
- Opportunities should be created to discuss and critique prevailing understandings and (mis)perceptions of men's experience.

In addition to these underlying assumptions, each program emphasizes one or more of the program elements listed below. (The components of men's prevention programs that follow are adapted from Berkowitz [2001], which provides an overview of effective program elements for all-male, all-female, and coeducational workshops. See Exhibit 7.2 for more information.)

In practice, it may not be possible to incorporate all of these elements in a particular program, and in fact it may be possible to develop a highly effective program that is based on only a few. When possible, however, it is important to cover all or most of these at least briefly in the context of an interactive workshop format. Thus, the suggested program components should serve as guidelines rather than requirements. These guidelines can also be used as a training outline for peer educators and staff who will be

EXHIBIT 7.2
Critical Elements of Sexual Assault Prevention Programs for Men

1. Emphasize men's responsibility for preventing sexual assault.
2. Emphasize that sexual activity is a choice.
3. Provide information about the definitions and severity of the problem.
4. Inform participants about relevant local laws and policies.
5. Explore characteristics of risky situations.
6. Understand consent and how to be sure that both parties are fully consenting.
7. Address the role of alcohol and other drugs.
8. Distinguish issues of miscommunication from abuse of power or coercion.
9. Understand the range of coercive behaviors that men are socialized to employ.
10. Explore relevant aspects of male gender socialization and the role of sexism in facilitating sexual assaults.
11. Challenge rape myths and reduce victim blaming.
12. Challenge myths and assumptions regarding the role of sexuality and sexual activity in men's lives.
13. Address men's false fear of false accusation.
14. Reduce enabling behavior and increase bystander interventions among men.
15. Increase empathy for victims and understanding of the impact of rape.
16. Educate about heterosexist or ethnocentric assumptions about sexuality and sex.
17. Acknowledge male victimization.
18. Provide information about local resources and services.
19. Explore opportunities for men to take social action to raise other men's awareness about the problem of sexual assault.

Note. Adapted from A. Berkowitz, "Critical Elements of Sexual-Assault Prevention and Risk Reduction Programs for Men and Women" in C. Kilmartin, *Sexual Assault in Context* (2001) by permission of Learning Publications, Holmes Beach, FL.

facilitating programs. In general, individuals involved in providing a program should be familiar with relevant research and information for each program element. Familiarity with these elements will ensure that facilitators have been exposed to the wide range of issues that pertain to sexual assault.

1. *Emphasize men's responsibility for preventing sexual assault.* Men's denial of the problem of sexual assault because of the assumption that sexual assault is a "women's problem" and the failure of most men to intervene with other men are two barriers to effective prevention for men. Thus, men's programming should clearly outline men's responsibility for prevention and help participants understand how men are hurt by sexual assault, not only indirectly through relationships with victims but also directly in terms of how it hurts men and men's relationships with each other. As noted earlier, men should be enlisted as partners in the prevention of sexual assault rather than being blamed or accused of causing the problem.

2. *Emphasize that sexual activity is a choice and that all people, at any time, are free to choose whether or not to be sexually active and how.* There is a danger of reinforcing the assumption that all or most men are sexually active. For example, studies of college students indicated that men routinely overestimate the amount of sexual activity of their peers, thus creating increased pressure to be sexually active (Berkowitz, 1993, 2000a; Morgan 1997). In one study, more than two thirds of men reported experiencing unwanted sex because of perceived pressure from male peers (Muehlenard & Cook, 1988). Data from several secondary school settings have indicated that high school men overestimate their peers' sexual activity even more dramatically (Berkowitz, 2000b; B. Bruce, 1999). It is thus important that the choice to not be sexually active is emphasized and that myths about the presumed sexual activity of older and younger men are debunked.

3. *Provide information about the legal definitions and severity of the problem of sexual assault.* When possible, this information should be specific to your school, campus, or community (Gray, Lesser, Quinn, & Bounds, 1990).

4. *Inform participants about relevant local laws and policies.* This includes school or campus policies for colleges and universities, as well as local and state policies. When confronted with information on sexual assault, men may focus on legal details and definitions as a way of avoiding the interpersonal, moral, and emotional aspects of the issue. Thus, a focus on statistics and information should be minimized to allow time for discussion and interaction, and overly legalistic and formalistic discussions should be avoided. It is useful to remind participants that if they learn ways to ensure that all sexual intimacy is mutual and consenting, concern with the law and definitions will become unnecessary.

5. *Explore characteristics of risky situations.* Ambiguity about sexual intent, unresponsiveness on the part of the other person, and unverified assumptions about what the other person wants are examples of situations that are problematic or risky.

6. *Understand consent and how to be sure that both parties are fully consenting.* According to Berkowitz (1994b), consent requires that both parties are fully conscious, have equal ability to act, are positive and sincere in their desires, and have clearly communicated their intent. A consent model avoids technical and legalistic discussions regarding whether or not a rape occurred and helps men focus on what they can do to minimize

their risk of perpetrating a sexual assault. An excellent way to promote discussion about risky situations and explore the conditions of consenting intimacy is through the discussion of realistic scenarios that can occur on campus or in a community. These scenarios can explore gender differences in the misperception of sexual intent (Abbey, 1982, 1987) and foster discussion about whether both parties were consenting in a particular situation.

7. *Address the role of alcohol and other drugs.* This should be done from the perspective of both victim and perpetrator (including the use of "date rape" drugs). It is extremely important to discuss the effects of alcohol consumption and how alcohol can facilitate assault both physiologically and cognitively (Abbey, McAuslan, & Ross, 1998; Abbey, Zawacki, & McAuslan, 2000). Abbey, Ross, and McDuffie (1994) have identified five effects of alcohol on men that may be implicated in a sexual assault perpetrated by a male on a female:

   - It encourages the expression of traditional gender role beliefs about sexual behavior.
   - It triggers alcohol expectancies associated with male sexuality and aggression.
   - It engages stereotypes about the sexual availability of women who drink alcohol.
   - It increases the likelihood that men will misperceive women's friendly cues as a sign of sexual interest.
   - Inebriation is viewed as a justification for men to commit sexual assault.

8. *Distinguish issues of miscommunication from abuse of power or coercion.* Although poor communication is a risk factor for sexual assault, all sexual assault results from the imposition of one person's wishes on another. Strategies for improving communication assume that both parties have equal power, which is not the case in situations leading to sexual assault (Corcoran, 1992). Thus, although communication strategies may be emphasized and can form the basis for a workshop on healthy relationships, they should not be the main focus of sexual assault prevention programs. There is evidence, however, that teaching women assertive communication may be an effective risk reduction strategy (Muehlenhard & Andrews, 1985).

9. *Understand the range of coercive behaviors that men are socialized to employ.* Coercive behaviors should be presented in the context of a continuum ranging from verbal pressure to im-

plied threats of force, actual force, or rape. The Sexual Experiences Survey (Koss & Gidycz, 1987) is an excellent survey instrument for documenting the range of coercive behaviors that constitute unwanted intimacy. Presentation of physically violent rapes or of situations in which lack of permission is clearly evident may allow men to disown the possibility that they could also be perpetrators in a more ambiguous situation. Instead, men must learn that there are more subtle forms of coercion and influence that operate in interpersonal relationships and learn the skills necessary to ensure that equality of choice and action is the basis of all intimate relationships. In some cases, men may act in ways that are experienced as coercive by the other person without realizing that this is the case. Thus, the full range of coercive situations, from subtle to overt, and from verbal to physical, and from intentional to unintentional should be discussed and represented in examples. Understanding the dynamics of coercive behavior and the possibility of unintentional coercion are critical issues for men.

10. *Explore relevant aspects of male gender socialization and the role of sexism in facilitating sexual assault.* Many of the traditional behaviors and roles that men are socialized into can increase the likelihood of sexual assault (Berkowitz, Burkhart, & Bourg, 1994; Kilmartin, 2001). These gender roles are taught to all men and therefore we are all influenced by them. Educational programs should thus include discussion of the relationship between gender role socialization, gender role stereotyping, and sexual assault.

11. *Challenge rape myths and reduce victim blaming.* Myths about victims and perpetrators that serve to justify or condone sexual assault must be discussed and critiqued. Lonsway and Fitzgerald (1994) and Ward (1995) have provided an extensive discussion of rape myths and their role in victim blaming. Preliminary studies reviewed by Berkowitz (2000a) have suggested that men overestimate the extent to which other men adhere to these rape myths.

12. *Challenge myths and assumptions regarding the role of sexuality and sexual activity in men's lives.* Frequent heterosexual sex is equated with masculinity in many men's upbringing, whether or not this is actually true in men's lives (Levant & Pollack, 1995; Pleck, 1981). Pressures men feel to be sexually active and to live up to male myths of sexual activity and prowess are thus important to deconstruct and critique. As noted earlier, these myths perpetuate false perceptions of other men's

sexual activity, with most men overestimating the sexual activity of friends and peers (Berkowitz, 2000a).

13. *Address men's false fear of false accusation.* Men's (false) fear of false accusation provides an opportunity to explore strategies for achieving consent and the ways in which men can be unintentionally coercive. False accusations do occur but they are extremely rare, accounting for only 2% of all rape charges, a false accusation rate which is similar to that for other crimes (U.S. Department of Criminal Justice, 1989). This misperception is fostered by the media, which may provide prominent coverage to occasional instances of false accusations while devoting less attention to frequently occurring rapes. In workshop discussions, men frequently overestimate the rate of false reports, believing that most men are unfairly accused. Most men, however, are willing to acknowledge on reflection that a man may think he has permission when he actually does not. This discussion allows men to understand how a woman could have been assaulted even though the man she accuses claims to be innocent.

14. *Reduce enabling behaviors and increase bystander interventions among men.* Programs for men must move beyond a focus on individual responsibility to emphasize men's responsibility to each other to intervene and challenge inappropriate comments, actions, or behavior. Research that is based on social norms theory (Berkowitz, 2000a; S. Bruce, 2000; Kilmartin et al., 1999) has documented that most men are in fact uncomfortable with the behavior of the minority of men who exploit or objectify women. Prevention programs should therefore help men move from passive silence (which may be misinterpreted as support) to active opposition and intervention when inappropriate behavior is witnessed. An overview of the literature on bystander behavior and its application to sexual assault prevention for men is found in Berkowitz (2000a). This issue can be addressed in workshops by providing and discussing statistics about true norms of discomfort among men and by analyzing scenarios in which men stand by and do not confront behavior that makes them feel uncomfortable.

15. *Increase empathy for victims and understanding of the impact of rape.* Most men are capable of empathy and will be inhibited from acting in coercive ways when the full effects and trauma of sexual assault are understood. This information can be provided by victim stories and testimony, in skits and vignettes, or by the personal sharing of men who have been secondary victims. (Note that I discuss several philosophical and meth-

odological issues in victim empathy approaches later in this chapter.)

16. *Educate about heterosexist or ethnocentric assumptions about sexuality and sex.* Sexual assault can occur between individuals of any race or sexual orientation. It is thus important to provide information or examples that dispel myths about the identity of perpetrators and victims. One technique for doing this is to provide a scenario that uses names for the perpetrator and victim that could be male or female (e.g., Chris and Pat). A discussion about participant assumptions regarding Chris and Pat's gender and race can be illuminating.

17. *Acknowledge male victimization.* Men may have particular difficulty acknowledging that a male can be the victim of unwanted sex. It is thus important to carefully define and provide statistics on male victimization and explore men's discomfort discussing this issue. Michael Scarce (1997), victim advocate and educator, has written an excellent book on issues facing male victims.

18. *Provide information about local community resources and services.* Participants should be made aware of the local community services for victims, such as rape crisis centers, the availability of rape kits/exams, victim support and advocacy services, and activities and programs for men.

19. *Explore opportunities for men to take social action to raise other men's awareness about the problem of sexual assault.* Workshop participants should be encouraged to become involved in political and social efforts to end violence against women. This could include participating (as appropriate) in a local Take Back the Night Event, sponsoring a White Ribbon Campaign (Kilmartin, 1996), establishing a chapter of Men Against Violence (Hong, 2000), or taking part in efforts to call attention to the problem of sexual assault. Information on programs that provide men an opportunity to engage in social activism and foster societal change with respect to sexual assault are provided in Appendix B.

AN INTEGRATED DEVELOPMENTAL MODEL OF RAPE PREVENTION FOR MEN

Individual men and communities of men may differ in their recognition of the problem of intimate violence against women and in their willingness to take responsibility for ending it. Are there certain approaches that are more appropriate with particular groups of men or individual campuses? Because sexual assault prevention can be conceptualized as a developmental process of change, different interventions are recommended for men at earlier and later stages in the change process.

There are two useful frameworks for looking at men's responsibility for sexual assault prevention from a developmental perspective. One addresses bystander behavior. If men live in a culture that encourages or condones violence against women, individual men may vary along a bystander continuum from passive indifference to commitment to intervene. Research on bystander behavior has identified five stages in this process: noticing the event, interpreting it as a problem, feeling responsible for a solution, possessing the necessary skills to act, and intervention (Latane & Darley, 1970). Berkowitz (1998, 2000a) has suggested that the stages of the bystander model can provide an organizing framework for sexual assault prevention efforts.

Men's willingness to take responsibility for preventing sexual assault can also be conceptualized in terms of a "stages of change" model. The stages of change theory outlines an individual's readiness for change in stages and proposes interventions to create movement from one stage to another. It has led to the development of "motivational interviewing," which has been used successfully in therapeutic interventions for drug abusers (Miller & Rollnick, 1991). Five stages are posited within stages of change theory: precontemplation, contemplation, preparation, action, and maintenance.

Both the bystander behavior and the stages of change models attempt to match interventions with the individual's ability to take responsibility for change. In Table 7.1, the stages within each model are matched with questions or goals that can be addressed with men regarding their relationship to the problem of sexual assault. These questions are designed to introduce cognitive dissonance about beliefs and assumptions prevalent at each stage and provide information that will foster a shift to the next stage.

The different approaches to working with men described here (empathy induction, conditions of consent, and bystander interventions) map nicely onto the proposed developmental model. Thus, an empathy induction approach might be most effective in situations where there is little awareness or recognition of the problem. Although empathy induction approaches do not challenge or attempt to change men's socialization and identity as men, they begin the process by encouraging men to acknowledge and take the problem of rape seriously. Teaching men the conditions of consent introduces the need for men to change personal behavior by providing skills that can be used to prevent individual men from perpetrating sexual assault. The consent model requires that men question their assumptions and beliefs about intimacy, consent, and perceptions of intent and consider the fact that men can be wrong about what sexual partners want. Thus, it requires a deeper level of change than empathy induction

TABLE 7.1
A Developmental Model of Sexual Assault Prevention Interventions for Men

Stage of bystander behavior or change	Questions or concerns for men
1. Notice the event (Precontemplation)	Is sexual assault a problem on this campus? How is sexual assault defined? Is it possible for a man to sexually assault someone and not realize it?
2. Interpret it as a problem (Contemplation)	How does sexual assault hurt men? How does sexual assault hurt women? Are men falsely afraid of false accusations? How are men hurt by other men's behavior?
3. Feel responsible for a solution (Preparation)	How can I be sure that the desire for intimacy is mutual? What are the different ways that men can be unintentionally coercive? What can men do to change other men?
4. Possess the skills to act and intervene (Action)	Learn conversational skills. Take active steps to reduce risk factors for sexual assault. Learn to intervene in other men's behavior.
5. Maintenance	What responses from women and other men serve to reinforce and promote changes in men's attitudes and behavior?

approaches. The bystander model moves beyond individual change by framing sexual assault prevention as a social problem that requires that men intervene in other men's behavior (Corcoran & Mahlstedt, 1998; Funk & Berkowitz, 2000; Mahlstedt & Corcoran, 1999). Both the conditions of consent and bystander approaches implicitly ask men to re-examine the socialization and cultural conditioning of men and promote alternate ways of being a man.

Thus, rather than the different approaches to working with men being viewed as mutually exclusive, they can be conceptualized as stages along a continuum of change. Intervention strategies can be designed that begin at the level of awareness of most men in the population of concern and then followed with sequenced activities that attempt to move participants into later stages. When there is time, this staging can be incorporated into individual workshop interventions, or it can provide a framework for designing and sequencing activities over a longer period of time, such as an academic year. Thus, each approach to rape prevention may be appropriate as a sexual assault prevention strategy in a given environment, with appropriately sequenced interventions moving men through the stages of change and bystander behavior models.

FUTURE DIRECTIONS FOR THE FIELD

Progress as of this writing in developing rape prevention programs for men and in evaluating their effectiveness has been slowed by conceptual and methodological limitations (Burkhart, Bourg, & Berkowitz, 1994, Schewe & O'Donohue, 1993). Thus, in this final section I make recommendations for addressing several methodological limitations and for improving the effectiveness of prevention programs.

Research and Measurement Issues

Several researchers have pointed out the need for more sensitive and contemporary measures of behavior, particularly measures of empathy and other measures of program outcome, and for comparative evaluation of prevention programs.

Empathy Induction

Empathy induction programs use a variety of formats, presenting participants with stories of female victims, male victims, or both female and male victims. Ten published studies using this approach were reviewed by Schewe (chapter 5, this volume). In the two unsuccessful interventions (and in an 11th study Schewe did not review conducted by Berg, Lonsway, and Fitzgerald in 1999), men were asked to empathize with a female victim only. The other eight programs, which included both male and female victims, were successful in producing attitude change.

It is interesting to speculate about why the three programs with only female victims were unsuccessful in changing men's attitudes. Perhaps asking men to empathize with female victims is unsuccessful if other questions and concerns of men are not addressed first. Thus, it may be necessary to first empathize with men's concerns and misunderstandings about sexual assault before asking these same men to be sympathetic to women's experience as victims.

A victim empathy approach developed by Foubert (Foubert, 2000; Foubert & Marriott, 1997; Foubert & McEwen, 1998) has successfully changed men's attitudes using a video of a male survivor of rape telling his story. Davis (1999) and Scarce (1999) expressed concerns about this approach, noting the absence of female voices and the danger of appealing to traditional masculinity through a focus on men's helping persona.

In light of the current research and concerns about workshops with only male or female victim perspectives, it seems prudent to incorporate the perspectives of both male and female victims in programs designed to enhance victim empathy.

Outcome Measures

Several researchers have suggested that instruments used to evaluate program effectiveness are outdated or lacking in focus. For example, Lonsway and Fitzgerald (1994), in an extensive review of the literature on rape myths, identified problems in conceptual clarity and definitional consistency, domain articulation, psychometric adequacy, and theoretical power. These problems led them to develop a new instrument that addresses these difficulties, the Illinois Rape Myth Acceptance Scale (Payne, Lonsway, & Fitzgerald, 1999). Another new scale has been developed by Lanier and Elliot (1997). Berg, Lonsway, and Fitzgerald (1999) identified similar problems in their review of instruments measuring empathy, noting that the measures commonly used to assess empathy focus on a generic sense of empathy, which may not capture the more rape-specific form of empathy that empathy induction programs attempt to foster in men. They proposed that measures of empathy should be developed that are more specific to the experience of rape. Thus, future evaluations of sexual assault prevention programs should make use of these newer attitude scales and attempt to conceptualize empathy in a way that is more specific to the problem of rape.

Although one of the strongest influences on men's behavior is other men, outcome variables have seldom focused on measures relevant to men's experience of each other. This is despite considerable evidence from studies reported by Berkowitz (2000a) suggesting that men misperceive other men's degree of sexual activity, adherence to rape myths, willingness to use coercion to gain sex, and level of discomfort with language which objectifies and degrades women. Berkowitz (2000a) suggested that these misperceptions encourage men to keep their true feelings hidden from other men and encourage passive bystander behavior. Measures should therefore be developed that assess perceptions men have of each other that can be used to evaluate future program effectiveness. It is possible that changes on these dimensions of men's experience may need to occur before actual reductions in the rates of perpetration take place.

Finally, it is also important to develop specific outcome measures that are appropriate to the goals of risk reduction and deterrence programs for women. In existing research, most outcome measures have been gender neutral despite the fact that gender-specific programs have been shown to be more desirable and effective. Thus, outcome measures must be developed that are gender specific and that evaluate the different program outcomes that are sought for each gender.[1]

Comparative Evaluations

Breitenbecher (2000) reviewed 15 studies that compared the relative effectiveness of two or more program formats. She found that different treatments tended to have equal effectiveness and concluded that "the literature suggests that some intervention is better than no intervention, and that different interventions are most often equal in terms of effectiveness" (p. 31). This finding supports the conclusion that program process (Davis, 2000), or how the program is delivered, may be more important than program content, or what material is presented.

Program Design and Implementation

In addition to the issues presented earlier in this chapter, several areas of program design and implementation remain problematic. These areas include developing methods for fostering interactive discussion, developing collaborative partnerships with women, addressing the needs of subpopulations of men, and developing environmental approaches to sexual assault prevention that can create a comprehensive environment of change.

Fostering Interactive Discussions

As noted earlier, the evaluation literature has highlighted the importance of interactive discussions that emphasize program process in addition to content. Davis (2000) reviewed three program process dimensions that are important to constructing a safe learning environment: all-male workshops, facilitators the audience can identify with (e.g., peer educators), and small interactive discussion groups. To ensure that programs provide safe and effective learning environments for men, program facilitators need to be trained in process and facilitation skills in addition to being provided with information and materials. Experiences with Hobart College's rape prevention program (described in Appendix A) suggest that facilitator training should provide male facilitators with the opportunity to explore personal issues and challenges; create safety to allow intimate feelings and perceptions to be shared; and teach men that it is possible to have open, honest discussion in all-male groups. Such training discussions are transforming, resulting in facilitators changing their views about gender, intimacy, and sexual assault (Mahlstedt & Corcoran, 1999; Simon, Paris, & Ramsay, 1994). This training experience provides male facilitators with the ability to create similar conditions in workshops with peers.

Working With Female Colleagues

Men involved in providing rape prevention programs for men have a responsibility to work closely and collaboratively with female colleagues, soliciting their views, input, and support. Although it is important for men to take responsibility for rape prevention, women have developed and led several highly effective programs. Hong (2000) and Mahlstedt and Corcoran (1999) have explored in depth the issues and pedagogy involved in women training men. At Hobart College, female colleagues, staff, student leaders, and rape crisis center staff were given the opportunity to view the men's rape prevention program each year, providing the opportunity for valuable feedback and dialogue. It is important to develop such relationships before initiating prevention programming for men to ensure that there is compatibility of goals and methods, to avoid sending mixed or competing messages, and to prevent competition for scarce resources. Men's programs should also incorporate a social activism component that explicitly supports and contributes to victim advocacy and service agencies.

A workshop for men and women led by a coeducational team would be a perfect follow-up to a single-gender workshop. This experience would allow both genders to listen to each others' perspectives after addressing the issue separately and allow facilitators to model collaboration and respect between women and men.

Subpopulations of Men

Tailoring rape prevention programs for men to the characteristics of particular male groups is an important strategy. The literature on successful prevention programs has suggested that relevance is a critical component of program success (Berkowitz, 1997, 2001). The Mentors in Violence Prevention program (Katz, 1995) was developed for working with athletes, and both The Men's Program (Foubert, 1998) and the Fraternity Violence Education Project (Mahlstedt & Corcoran, 1999) have primarily been used with fraternity members. However, very few studies have looked at ethnic issues in sexual assault prevention for men. Heppner, Neville, Smith, Kivlighan, and Gershuny (1999) conducted the only study assessing the differential impact of programs on men from different racial backgrounds. They found that generic race-neutral programs were effective for White men but not for men of color and that programs with a copresenter of color and relevant ethnic content were effective for both groups. In another study, no difference was found in the rates of sexual aggression among Asian American and White men, but differences were found between the groups in the relative influence of individualistic and collectivistic determinants of aggressive behavior (Hall, Sue, Narang, & Lilly, 2000). These results strongly suggest the importance of developing programs that are either tailored to the needs of a particular group or conducted in a way that is inclusive and welcoming of all backgrounds. A critical oversight is the lack of research examining the needs of gay and bisexual men with respect to rape prevention programming.

Creating a Comprehensive Environment of Change

Researchers who have reviewed and critiqued the evaluation literature have noted that attitudinal changes that result from sexual assault prevention programs are of short duration (Brecklin & Forde, 2001; Gidycz et al., 2002; Lonsway, 1996; Schewe, chapter 5, this volume). These improvements in men's attitudes tend to "rebound" after a period of time, that is, after a few months, the initial changes disappear. This phenomenon is often seen as an indication of program failure. However, given the prevalence and intensity of attitudes men have learned over a lifetime, one can also view the temporary changes produced by an intervention of approximately an hour as a success. Perhaps it is unrealistic to expect longer lasting changes to come about from a single, short intervention. For example, there is some evidence that the rebound effect can be eliminated for some men when interventions are longer and take place over time (Heppner et al., 1999).

Anderson et al. (1998) suggested that a variety of interventions should be offered throughout an individual's college experience, with later interventions serving as "boosters" for earlier ones. Sequenced programs could be combined with environmental interventions such as social norms marketing campaigns to correct misperceptions relating to sexual assault (Berkowitz, 2000a). Similar techniques have been effectively used in the drug prevention field (Berkowitz, 1997, 2000a). Thus, interventions that are sequenced, synergistic, and mutually reinforcing are likely to be more effective than single, isolated ones that do not contain common messages or refer to each other. These interventions can be directed at individuals who are at risk for perpetuating an assault, to groups of men who live or associate with each other, and to the larger campus community. What is important is that all sexual assault prevention efforts be viewed comprehensively and integrated with each other to create common and reinforcing messages.

Environmental interventions that have been successfully used on other campuses include the White Ribbon Campaign, a week of men's activism to prevent violence against women first developed in Canada (Kilmartin, 1996); appropriate participation in Take Back the Night Marches; formation of Men Against Violence chapters (Hong, 2000); and social norms media campaigns to correct men's misperception of other men's attitudes and behaviors (Berkowitz, 2000a; S. Bruce, 2000; Kilmartin et al., 1999).

A case example of a sequenced, integrated intervention was developed by Alan Berkowitz and Rocco Capraro at Hobart College over a period of 10 years. During first-year orientation, a brief program introduced new students to the problems of sexual assault. In the beginning of the fall semester, all first-year men were required to attend the Rape Prevention Program for Men (Berkowitz, 1994b). A parallel workshop focusing on risk reduction and deterrence was offered to first-year women at the same time. Each program contained references to the opposite gender program. Similar workshops were offered throughout the year to upper-class men in fraternities and on athletic teams and as part of resident adviser training. This was followed by a winter symposium extending over a period of weeks titled "Men and Masculinity," which addressed issues of contemporary importance to men through a combination of all-campus lectures open to men and women and more focused, interactive discussions and workshops for men only (Capraro & Berkowitz,

1986–1990). In the spring, a White Ribbon Campaign was conducted the week before Take Back the Night to raise men's awareness of the problem of violence against women and reduce backlash from men who felt defensive as a result of the march. During the march, men gathered to look at the Clothesline Project and then met in small groups with trained facilitators to discuss what participants could do to prevent intimate violence against women. At the conclusion of the Take Back the Night March, the men joined the female marchers to listen to several speeches and personal testimonials in the form of speak-outs by women. A debriefing was held after the speak-outs to provide men with the opportunity to reflect on and share reactions to what they heard. This format modeled men's accountability to women in sexual assault prevention work, the need for men and women to work collaboratively, and the need for men and women to have separate spaces to do gender work.

CONCLUSION

Almost 2 decades of research and program development have resulted in dramatic gains in the creation of interventions that address men's responsibility for preventing sexual assault. Insights developed from the women's movement and feminist studies in particular have led to new understandings of men's experience and the development of new strategies for working with men. The most promising interventions provide men the opportunity to drop the "tough" guise of masculinity and engage in open, honest discussion about their feelings, attitudes, and behaviors in a nonblaming environment. The process of honest dialogue about sexual assault prevention in a safe environment of men contradicts many aspects of men's socialization and fosters actions that can inhibit or prevent sexual assault.

I have presented a theoretical and programmatic rationale for working in all-male groups to prevent sexual assault, reviewed critical program elements and effective strategies, proposed an integrative developmental model for working with men, and made recommendations for the future. I hope that new research will refine further an understanding of what is effective with men and why it is effective and also lead to the development of new and better programs to help eliminate sexual assault and rape.

END NOTE

[1]Editor's note: Schewe, in collaboration with Berkowitz, Heppner, Lonsway, and 30 prevention educators from the Illinois Coalition Against Sexual Assault, is currently in the process of developing such a measure.

APPENDIX A
MODEL RAPE PREVENTION PROGRAMS FOR MEN

This appendix provides information on programs designed exclusively for men that have published protocols and outlines that can be easily replicated on college campuses and in secondary schools. Although all these programs were developed for use with a college-age audience, they can be adapted for younger men by incorporating issues such as sexual harassment (which may be more relevant and appropriate for younger audiences than an exclusive focus on rape prevention). The programs are presented in the order that they were developed, from oldest to most recent.

Rape Prevention Program for Men

Developer: Alan D. Berkowitz, Independent Consultant, Trumansburg, NY; 607-387-3789; *alan@fltg.net*

Berkowitz (1994b) was among the first to develop a protocol and program focusing on men's responsibility for preventing sexual assault. The Rape Prevention Program for Men (RPPM) was developed at Hobart College in 1987 and has been offered as a required workshop for all first-year men each year since. It attempts to bring men's discomfort with the opportunistic and coercive sexual behavior of some men out in the open so that discomfort with such behavior can be shared and acted on. It also teaches guidelines for consenting sexual intimacy. *Consent* is defined as a situation in which both parties are fully conscious, equally free to act, and have positively and clearly communicated their intent (Berkowitz, 1994a). The workshop encourages men to share their "frustrations at being a male on campus," as well as issues such as men's (false) fear of false accusation, intimate situations in which attribution of responsibility is unclear to men, and developing empathy for sexual assault victims. The original form of the workshop used a video that portrayed events leading up to and after a sexual assault. The video has since been replaced by scenarios that portray an intimate encounter between a male and female, men's discomfort with other men's language and behavior, and men's experience of pressure to be sexually active from other men (sample workshop scenarios can be obtained from the author).

This program was evaluated in a study by Earle (1996) that compared three program formats with a nontreatment (control) group. The RPPM is single gender and conducted in small groups by trained peer facilitators with a focus on discussion and interaction. It was compared with two coeducational programs presented by professional staff. One used an interactive, small group discussion format, and the other was a large group lecture. Of the three interventions, only the RPPM produced positive changes in rape myth acceptance and attitudes toward women in comparison with the control group.

The RPPM was also evaluated in a study by Davis (1997, 2000), in which it was compared with another small group, interactive rape prevention program with a focus on issues of male socialization. Both programs reduced rape-supportive attitudes and increased men's understanding of the difference between consent and coercion in a posttest administered immediately after the workshop, although these improvements were no longer present 6 weeks later.

Mentors in Violence Prevention Program

Developer: Center for the Study of Sport in Society, Northeastern University; 617-373-4025; *www.sportinsociety.org*

The Mentors in Violence Prevention (MVP) program trains student-athletes to exercise leadership among peers by teaching skills to intervene when other men speak or act inappropriately toward women. MVP was originally developed by Jackson Katz (1995) and is a program of the Center for the Study of Sport in Society at Northeastern University. The MVP model involves three sessions each year with each participating college team. A fourth session is scheduled for athletes who are interested in presenting programs to younger audiences. The main focus of the workshop is the "MVP Playbook," a series of party and residence hall scenarios portraying actual or potential sexual assaults, inappropriate language, and bystander behavior. The goal of MVP is to teach men to take responsibility for sexual assault prevention by intervening in other men's behavior. In addition to programs for male college and high school students, the MVP model can be used with nonathletes and has been adopted by the Marine Corps for use with its soldiers. MVP is currently being evaluated to determine its effectiveness.

Date Rape Prevention: A Video Intervention for College Students

Developer: Northwest Media; 800-777-6636; *www.northwestmedia.com/health/daterape.html*

This 45-minute videotaped program contains three segments that cover rape myths, victim empathy, and the negative consequences of committing rape. The first segment portrays college students with a variety of viewpoints discussing a publicized rape that occurred on their campus. The purpose of this segment is to provide the audience with more accurate information to replace widely held rape-supportive beliefs. The second segment presents several victims of rape as they tell about their abuse. The purpose of this segment is to help the male audience empathize with the pain that rape survivors feel both during and after being raped. The final segment portrays several men who have sexually coerced or raped women. The purpose of this segment is to highlight the negative consequences that raping holds for men. Program segments are described in more detail in Schewe and O'Donohue (1996), the authors of the program. The segments can stand alone, be incorporated into previously existing workshops, or used in sequence.

This video was evaluated in a study comparing it to a peer-facilitated discussion of sexual assault, a placebo intervention, and a control group. Of the four conditions, only the video and the placebo were effective in changing posttreatment scores on scales assessing rape myth and attitude toward sexual assault, while only the video was effective in changing scores for "high-risk" males. Thus, it may show some promise as an effective tool for working with men who have high rape proclivity.

The Men's Program

Developer: John D. Foubert, Office of the Dean of Students, University of Virginia; 804-924-3736; NOMORE@*virginia.edu*

The Men's Program is designed to build empathy in men for female rape survivors. It is presented in a lecture format, with discussion of a video developed by the Seattle Police Department describing the rape of a male police officer by two other men. The program is designed to help men understand what it might feel like to be raped to develop empathy for female victims. It assumes that men will be able transfer the empathy generated by the workshop to female victims and draws from research suggesting that victim empathy approaches are less effective when female victims are portrayed (Schewe, chapter 5, this volume). An excellent manual has been developed for those interested in training peer educators who can offer the program (Foubert, 1998), and the author has cited studies that the workshop has produced reductions in rape-supportive attitudes in several studies (Foubert, 2000; Foubert & Marriott, 1997; Foubert & McEwen, 1998).

This program has generated controversy for several reasons. Davis (1999) reviewed the evaluation studies of the workshop and concluded that "the results of these studies raise concerns about the confidence with which several claims are made based on tenuous findings and important methodological limitations" (p. 756). These include the fact that in two of the three studies, changes in the experimental group were also observed in the control group (Foubert & Marriott, 1997; Foubert & McEwen, 1998), undermining the author's claim of program effectiveness. Davis (1999) and Scarce (1999) also objected to the absence of women's voices in the workshop and its appeal to traditional models of masculinity (i.e., men's helper persona). In addition, Scarce argued that the workshop may stimulate men's latent homophobia by portraying the rape of a man by a man. Finally, the author's claim that the program can "successfully lower men's likelihood of raping" (which is featured prominently on the cover of the workshop manual) actually refers to a reduction in men's self-reported intent of raping, which was not associated with a reduction in actual levels of coercive behavior in a 7-month follow-up.

Despite these criticisms, The Men's Program is theoretically based and is one of the most thoroughly evaluated rape prevention programs for men. The video comes with an excellent manual and supporting materials.

Fraternity Violence Education Project

Developer: Deborah Mahlstedt, Department of Psychology, West Chester University, West Chester, PA; 610-436-3525; contact *dmahlstedt@wcpa.edu*

The FVEP provides fraternity leaders with an intensive exposure to issues of violence against women. During a one-semester course, participants are exposed to an extensive feminist analysis of male violence and power and receive training to present skits to fraternity members about male violence and sexual harassment. The workshops are offered over the course of the second semester, followed by a final term paper evaluating the year-long experience. The program, described in Mahlstedt and Corcoran (1999), has a manual with an excellent outline of the training curriculum, workshop skits and exercises, and a video titled "Men's Work" (Mahlstedt, 1999). The FVEP manual and video portray changes male facilitators experience over time as traditional values and gender definitions are examined and revised. A major focus of FVEP has been to qualitatively evaluate how men change and process material when exposed to a feminist analysis of male violence, privilege, and patriarchy. The program has not been evaluated quantitatively.

The video follows a group of fraternity brothers enrolled in FVEP over the course of their 1-year training period. In an all-male, peer-led seminar, they explore the causes of violence against women, examine their own attitudes and behavior, and begin speaking to other men on campus about men's responsibility to stop violence against women. The video provides a framework for college-age men to understand the causes of violence against women and what men can do to stop it. It examines difficult issues such as sexual objectification, peer pressure, and male privilege, and it presents positive role models for young men, challenging them to take responsibility to stop violence against women.

The video can be used in a variety of ways. In a large group format it provides an introduction to the issue of sexual assault and inspires young men to take action. In small group workshop settings, it can be used to involve men in more in-depth discussions about the causes and ways to prevent violence against women. Finally, in mixed-sex classroom settings, the video can be used to educate students about the issue and show women and men how men can take responsibility to end violence against women. The video is organized into five segments that each focus on a causal element—such as sexual objectification, male institutional power, hypermasculinity, and alcohol, and each section ends with a discussion question.

Speaking With Men About Sexism and Sexual Violence Trainer's Manual

Developer: Men Can Stop Rape, P.O. Box 5144, Washington, DC 20037-7144; 202-265-6530; *info@mrpp.org* or *http://www.mencanstoprape.org*

Men Can Stop Rape (MCSR) of Washington, DC, is a nonprofit organization that works to prevent rape and other forms of male violence through community education, consulting, research, and public action (see description in Appendix B). MCSR sponsors activities to empower male youths and the institutions that serve them to work as allies with women in preventing rape and other forms of men's violence. MCSR sponsors training weekends in which men and women are taught to facilitate a sexual assault prevention workshop developed by MCSR. The training manual is available separately. The manual covers facts, myths, and causes of sexual assault; describes ways for men to interrupt sexism and intervene in problematic behavior of men; discusses process issues in facilitating a workshop for men; and provides a workshop outline. The manual is thorough and comprehensive and is an excellent resource for rape prevention educators. This program has not yet been evaluated.

Note. From *Speaking with men about sexism and sexual violence: Training packet.* Copyright 2000 by Men Can Stop Rape. Reprinted with permission.

APPENDIX B
RESOURCES FOR SOCIAL ACTION
TO PREVENT SEXUAL ASSAULT

Men Against Violence

A campus-based program developed at Louisiana State University focusing on men's responsibility for ending all forms of men's violence. Contact 225-388-5718; *www.geeocities.com/MAVatLSU*

Men Can Stop Rape

Men Can Stop Rape, formerly The Men's Rape Prevention Project, based in Washington, DC, empowers male youths and the institutions that serve them to work as allies with women in preventing rape and other forms of men's violence. It sponsors variety of programs and activities in the metropolitan Washington area, an email newsletter, and national workshops and trainings. An excellent web site contains links to men's antiviolence organizations nationally and globally, along with relevant resources and publications. Contact P.O. Box 5144, Washington, DC 20037-7144; 202-265-6530; *info@mrpp.org* or *http://www.mencanstoprape.org*

Take Back the Night

Almost all college campuses and communities have an annual Take Back the Night march during which women walk in solidarity to protest violence against women and create safety. The roles of male participants vary across communities. In some cases, men participate as equals, and in others men's involvement is restricted. The best way for men to support Take Back the Night efforts is to develop parallel activities that foster men's responsibility for preventing sexual assault, educate men about the goals and purposes of Take Back the Night, and reduce backlash against it. Participation in Take Back the Night should be limited to what is comfortable for women organizers and participants. Contact your campus sexual assault prevention coordinator or local rape crisis center for information about this event in your community.

White Ribbon Campaign

A public education campaign to help educate men to take action to stop violence against women. Those interested in hosting a White Ribbon Campaign should get a copy of *Make a Difference: The White Ribbon Week Student Action Kit*. Contact 800-328-2228; *www.whiteribbon.ca*

REFERENCES

Abbey, A. (1982). Sex differences in attributions for friendly behavior: Do males misperceive females' friendliness? *Journal of Personality and Social Psychology, 42*, 830–838.

Abbey, A. (1987). Misperceptions of friendly behavior as sexual interest: A survey of naturally occurring incidences. *Psychology of Women Quarterly, 11*, 173–194.

Abbey, A., McAuslan, P., & Ross, L. T. (1998). Sexual assault perpetration by college men: The role of misperceptions of sexual intent, and sexual beliefs and experiences. *Journal of Social and Clinical Psychology, 17*, 167–195.

Abbey, A., Ross, L. T., & McDuffie, D. (1994). Alcohol's role in sexual assault. In R. R. Watson (Ed.), *Addictive behaviors in women* (pp. 92–123). Totowa, NY: Humana Press.

Abbey, A., Zawacki, M. A., & McAuslan, P. (2000). Alcohol's effects on sexual perception. *Journal of Studies on Alcohol, 61*, 688–697.

Anderson, L., Stoelb, M. P., Duggan, P., Hieger, B., Kling, K. H., & Payne, J. P. (1998). The effectiveness of two types of rape prevention programs in changing the rape-supportive attitudes of college students. *Journal of College Student Development, 39*, 131–142.

Berg, D. R., Lonsway, K. A., & Fitzgerald, L. F. (1999). Rape prevention education for men: The effectiveness of empathy-induction techniques. *Journal of College Student Development, 40,* 219–234.

Berkowitz, A. D. (1992). College men as perpetrators of acquaintance rape and sexual assault. *Journal of American College Health, 40,* 175–181.

Berkowitz, A. D. (1993, October). *Innovative approaches to behavioral health and social justice issues on campus.* Paper presented at the Annual Conference of the Association of College and University College Counseling Center Directors, Keystone, CO.

Berkowitz, A. D. (1994a). Acquaintance rape prevention workshop outline for facilitators. In A. Berkowitz (Ed.), *Men and rape: Theory, research, and prevention programs in higher education* (pp. 83–86). San Francisco, CA: Jossey-Bass.

Berkowitz, A. D. (1994b). A model acquaintance rape prevention program for men. In A. Berkowitz (Ed.), *Men and rape: Theory, research, and prevention programs in higher education* (pp. 35–42). San Francisco, CA: Jossey-Bass.

Berkowitz, A. D. (1994c). Introduction. In A. Berkowitz (Ed.), *Men and rape: Theory, research, and prevention programs in higher education* (pp. 1–2). San Francisco, CA: Jossey-Bass.

Berkowitz, A. D. (1997). From reactive to proactive prevention: Promoting an ecology of health on campus. In P. C. Rivers & E. Shore (Eds.), *A handbook on substance abuse for college and university personnel* (pp. 119–140). Westport, CT: Greenwood Press.

Berkowitz, A. D. (1998). How we can prevent sexual harassment and sexual assault. *Educators' Guide to Controlling Sexual Harassment, 6*(1), 1–4.

Berkowitz, A. D. (2000a). *Applications of social norms theory to other health and social justice issues.* Manuscript submitted for publication.

Berkowitz, A. D. (2000b). [Perception of alcohol use and sexual activity among high school students]. Unpublished data.

Berkowitz, A. D. (2001). Critical elements of sexual assault prevention and risk reduction programs. In C. Kilmartin (Ed.), *Sexual assault in context: teaching college men about gender* (pp. 75–96). Holmes Beach, FL: Learning Publications.

Berkowitz, A. D., Burkhart, B. R., & Bourg, S. E. (1994). Research on men and rape. In A. Berkowitz (Ed.), *Men and rape: Theory, research, and prevention programs in higher education* (pp. 67–71). San Francisco, CA: Jossey-Bass.

Berkowitz, A. D., & Earle, J. (1995). Unpublished program evaluations, Hobart College Rape Prevention Program for Men. Geneva, NY: Hobart College.

Birnbaum, M., & Weinberg, J. (1991). Men unlearning rape. *Changing Men, 22,* 23–24.

Brecklin, L. R., & Forde, D. R. (2001). A meta-analysis of rape education programs. *Violence and Victims, 16,* 303–321.

Breitenbecher, K. H. (2000). Sexual assault on college campuses: Is an ounce of prevention enough? *Applied and Preventive Psychology, 9,* 23–52.

Bruce, B. (1999). [Workshop evaluations]. Unpublished data. Santa Fe, NM: Santa Fe Rape Crisis Center.

Bruce, S. (2000). *"A man ..." sexual assault education for men: A sociocultural approach* (James Madison University Year One Report). Harrisonburg, VA: James Madison University Health Education Department. Available from *www.jms.edu/health/ctr/aMan*.

Burkhart, B. R., Bourg, S. E., & Berkowitz, A. D. (1994). Research on men and rape: Methodological problems and future directions. In A. Berkowitz (Ed.), *Men and rape: Theory, research, and prevention programs in higher education* (pp. 67–72). San Francisco, CA: Jossey-Bass.

Capraro, R. L. (1994). Disconnected lives: Men, masculinity, and rape prevention. In A. Berkowitz (Ed.), *Men and rape: Theory, research, and prevention programs in higher education* (pp. 21–34). San Francisco, CA: Jossey-Bass.

Capraro, R. L., & Berkowitz, A. D. (1986–1990). *Men and masculinity: A symposium at Hobart College* [Symposium Schedules, Office of the Dean]. Geneva, NY: Hobart College.

Corcoran, C. (1992). From victim control to social change: A feminist perspective on campus rape and prevention programs. In J. Chrisler & D. Howard (Eds.), *New directions in feminist psychology* (pp. 130–140). New York: Springer Verlag.

Corcoran, C., & Mahlstedt, D. (1998). Preventing sexual assault on campus: A feminist perspective. In C. Forden, A. Hunter, & B. Birns (Eds.), *A psychology of women reader: Common and diverse experiences* (pp. 291–299). Needham Heights, MA: Allyn & Bacon.

Crowell, N. A., & Burgess, A. W. (1996). *Understanding violence against women.* Washington, DC: National Academy Press.

Davis, T. L. (1997). *The effectiveness of a sex role socialization focused date rape prevention program in reducing rape supportive attitudes in college fraternity men.* Unpublished master's thesis, University of Iowa, Ames.

Davis, T. L. (1999). The men's program: How to successfully lower men's likelihood of raping. *Journal of College Student Development, 40,* 755–757.

Davis, T. L. (2000). Programming for men to reduce sexual violence. In D. Liddel & J. Lund (Eds.), *Powerful programs for student learning: Approaches that make a difference* (New Directions for Student Services, pp. 79–89). San Francisco, CA: Jossey-Bass.

Earle, J. P. (1996). Acquaintance rape workshops: Their effectiveness in changing the attitudes of first year men. *NASPA Journal, 34*(1), 2–16.

Ellis, A. L., O'Sullivan, C. S., & Sowards, B. A. (1992). The impact of contemplated exposure to a survivor of rape on attitudes towards rape. *Journal of Applied Social Psychology, 22,* 889–895.

Fischer, G. J. (1986). College student attitudes towards forcible date rape: Changes after taking a human sexuality course. *Journal of Sex Education and Therapy, 12,* 42–46.

Flores, S. A., & Hartlaub, M. G. (1998). Reducing rape-myth acceptance in male college students: A meta-analysis of intervention studies. *Journal of College Student Development, 39,* 438–444.

Fonow, M. M., Richardson, L., & Wemmerus, V. A. (1992). Feminist rape education: Does it work? *Gender and Society, 6,* 108–121.

Foubert, J. D. (1998). *The men's program: How to successfully lower men's likelihood of raping.* Holmes Beach, FL: Learning Press.

Foubert, J. D. (2000). The longitudinal effect of a rape-prevention program on fraternity men's attitudes, behavioral intent, and behavior. *Journal of American College Health, 48,* 158–163.

Foubert, J. D., & Marriott, K. A. (1997). Effects of a sexual assault peer education program on men's beliefs in rape myths. *Sex Roles, 36*(3/4), 259–268.

Foubert, J. D., & McEwen, M. K. (1998). An all-male rape prevention peer education program: Decreasing fraternity men's behavioral intent to rape. *Journal of College Student Development, 39*(6), 548–556.

Frazier, P., Valtinson, G., & Candell, S. (1994). Evaluation of a coeducational interactive rape prevention program. *Journal of Counseling and Development, 731,* 153–158.

Funk, R. E., & Berkowitz, A. D. (2000, May). *Preventing sexual violence: A simple matter of justice.* Paper presented at the CDC National Sexual Violence Prevention Conference, Dallas, TX.

Gidycz, C. A., Dowdall, C. L., & Marioni, N. L. (2002). Interventions to prevent rape and sexual assault. In J. Petrak & B. Hedge (Eds.), *The trauma of adult sexual assault: treatment, prevention, and policy* (pp. 235–260). New York: Wiley.

Gilbert, B. J., Heesacker, M., & Gannon, L. J. (1991). Changing men's sexual aggression–supportive attitudes: A psychoeducational intervention. *Journal of Counseling Psychology, 38,* 197–203.

Gray, M., Lesser, D., Quinn, E., & Bounds, C. (1990). Effects of rape education on perception of vulnerability and on reducing risk-taking behavior. *Journal of College Student Development, 31*(2), 217–223.

Hall, G. C. N., Sue, S., Narang, D. S., & Lilly, R. S. (2000). Culture-specific models of men's sexual aggression: Intra- and interpersonal determinants. *Cultural Diversity and Ethnic Minority Psychology, 6*(3), 252–267.

Harrison, P. J., Downes, J., & Williams, M. D. (1991). Date and acquaintance rape: Perceptions and attitude change strategies. *Journal of College Student Development, 32,* 131–139.

Heppner, M. J., Good, G. E., Hillenbrand-Gunn, T. L., Hawkins, A. K., Hacquard, L. L., Nichols, R. K., et al. (1995). Examining sex differences in altering attitudes about rape: A test of the elaboration likelihood model. *Journal of Counseling and Development, 73,* 640–647.

Heppner, M. J., Humphrey, C. F., Hillenbrand-Gunn, T. L., & DeBord, K. A. (1995). The differential effects of rape prevention programming on attitudes, behavior, and knowledge. *Journal of Counseling Psychology, 42,* 508–518.

Heppner, M. J., Neville, H. A., Smith K., Kivlighan, D. M., & Gershuny, B. S. (1999). Examining immediate and long-term efficacy of rape prevention programming with racially diverse college men. *Journal of Counseling Psychology, 46*(1), 16–26.

Holcomb, D. R., Sarvela, P. D., Sondag, K. A., Hatton, E. W., & Holcomb, L. C. (1993). Evaluation of a mixed-gender date rape prevention workshop. *Journal of American College Health, 41,* 159–164.

Hong, L. (2000). Towards a transformed approach to prevention: Breaking the link between masculinity and violence. *Journal of American College Health, 48,* 269–279.

Katz, J. (1995). Reconstructing masculinity in the locker room: The mentors in violence prevention project. *Harvard Educational Review, 65*(2), 163–174.

Kilmartin, C. T. (1996). The White Ribbon Campaign: Men working together to end men's violence against women. *Journal of College Student Development, 37,* 347–348.

Kilmartin, C. T. (2000). *The masculine self.* Boston: McGraw-Hill.

Kilmartin, C. T. (2001). *Sexual assault in context: Teaching college men about gender.* Holmes Beach, FL: Learning Publications.

Kilmartin, C. T., Conway, A., Friedberg, A., McQuiod, T., Tschan, P., & Norbet, T. (1999). *Using the social norms model to encourage male college students to challenge rape-supportive attitudes in male peers.* Paper presented at the Virginia Psychological Association Spring Conference, Virginia Beach.

Kivel, P. (1992). *Men's work: How to stop the violence that tears our lives apart.* Center City, MN: Hazeldon.

Koss, M. P., & Dinero, T. E. (1989). Discriminant analysis of risk factors for sexual victimization among a national sample of college women. *Journal of Consulting and Clinical Psychology, 57,* 242–250.

Koss, M. P., & Gidycz, C. A. (1987). Sexual experiences survey: Reliability and validity. *Journal of Consulting and Clinical Psychology, 53,* 422–423.

Lanier, C. A., & Elliot, M. N. (1997). A new instrument for the evaluation of a date rape prevention program. *Journal of College Student Development, 38*(6), 673–676.

Latane, B., & Darley, J. M. (1970). *The unresponsive bystander: Why doesn't he help?* New York: Appleton-Century-Crofts.

Lenihan, G., & Rawlins, M. (1994). Rape supportive attitudes among Greek students before and after a date rape prevention program. *Journal of College Student Development, 35,* 450–455.

Levant, R. F., & Pollack, W. S. (1995). *The new psychology of men.* New York: Basic Books.

Lonsway, K. A. (1996). Preventing acquaintance rape through education: What do we know? *Psychology of Women Quarterly, 20,* 229–265.

Lonsway, K. A., & Fitzgerald, L. F. (1994). Rape myths: A review. *Psychology of Women Quarterly, 18,* 133–164.

Mahalik, J. R. (1999). Incorporating a gender role strain perspective in assessing and treating men's cognitive distortions. *Professional Psychology: Research and Practice, 30*(4), 333–340.

Mahlstedt, D. (1998). *Getting started: A dating violence peer education program for men.*

Fraternity Violence Education Project. West Chester, PA: West Chester University.

Mahlstedt, D. (1999). *Men's work: Fraternity brothers stopping violence against women*. Insight Media: New York.

Mahlstedt, D., & Corcoran, C. (1999). Preventing dating violence. In C. Crawford, S. David, & J. Sebrechts (Eds.), *Coming into her own* (pp. 311–327). San Francisco, CA: Jossey Bass.

Malamuth, N. M., & Check, J. V. P. (1984). Debriefing effectiveness following exposure to pornographic rape depictions. *Journal of Sex Research, 20*, 1–13.

Mann, C. A., Hecht, M. L., & Valentine, K. B. (1988). Performance in a social context: Date rape versus date right. *Central States Speech Journal, 3/4*, 269–280.

Men Can Stop Rape. (2000). *Speaking with men about sexism and sexual violence: Training packet*. Washington, DC: Author.

Miller, W. R., & Rollnick, S. (1991). *Motivational interviewing: Preparing people for change*. New York: Guilford Press.

Morgan, S. (1997, April). *How much sex? How much alcohol? A study of perceived norms*. Paper presented at the Annual Meeting of the Eastern Sociological Society, Baltimore, MD.

Muehlenhard, C. L., & Andrews, S. L. (1985, November). *Sexual aggression in dating situations: Do factors that cause men to regard it as more justifiable also make it more probable?* Paper presented at the annual meeting of the Association for the Advancement of Behavior Therapy, Washington, DC.

Muehlenhard, C. L., & Cook, S. W. (1988). Men's reports of unwanted sexual activity. *Sex Research, 24*, 58–72.

Muehlenhard, C. L., & Linton, M. A. (1987). Date rape and sexual aggression in dating situations: Incidence and risk factors. *Journal of Counseling Psychology, 34*(2), 186–196.

Payne, D. L., Lonsway, K. A., & Fitzgerald, L. F. (1999). Rape myth acceptance: Exploration of its structure and its measurement using the Illinois Rape Myth Acceptance Scale. *Journal of Research in Personality, 33*, 27–68.

Pleck, J. H. (1981). *The myth of masculinity*. Cambridge, MA: MIT Press.

Rosenthal, E. H., Heesacker, M., & Neimeyer, G. J. (1995). Changing the rape-supportive attitudes of traditional and non-traditional male and female college students. *Journal of Counseling Psychology, 42*, 1–7.

Scarce, M. (1997). *Male on male rape: The hidden toll of stigma and shame*. New York: Insight.

Scarce, M. (1999). The ends do not justify the means: A call for the abandonment of the men's program model of rape education for men. *Outspoken: Official Newsletter of the North American Coalition Against Sexual Violence, 3*(4), 3–4.

Schewe, P. A., & O'Donohue, W. T. (1993). Rape prevention: Methodological problems and new directions. *Clinical Psychology Review, 13*, 667–682.

Schewe, P. A. & O'Donohue, W. T. (1996). Rape prevention with high risk males:

Short-term outcome of two interventions. *Archives of Sexual Behavior, 25*(5), 455–471.

Schwartz, M. D., & DeKeseredy, W. S. (1997). *Sexual assault on campus: The role of male peer support.* Thousand Oaks, CA: Sage Publications.

Sharpe, M. J., & Heppner, P. P. (1991). Gender role, gender role-conflict, and psychological well-being in men. *Journal of Counseling Psychology, 38*(3), 323–330.

Simon, A. K., Paris, J., & Ramsay, C. A. (1994). Student perspectives on facilitating rape prevention programs. In A. Berkowitz (Ed.), *Men and rape: Theory, research, and prevention programs in higher education* (pp. 43–50). San Francisco, CA: Jossey-Bass.

U.S. Department of Criminal Justice. (1989). *Crime in the United States: Uniform crime reports for the United States.* Washington, DC: U.S. Government Printing Office.

Ward, C. A. (1995). *Attitudes toward rape: Feminist and social psychological perspectives.* London: Sage Publications.

Yeater, E. A., & O'Donohue, W. O. (1999). Sexual assault prevention programs: Current issues, future directions, and the potential efficacy of interventions with women. *Clinical Psychology Review, 19*(7), 739–771.

8

RECENT THERAPEUTIC ADVANCES IN THE PREVENTION OF DOMESTIC VIOLENCE

SABINA M. LOW, NATALIE D. MONARCH, SCOTT HARTMAN, AND HOWARD MARKMAN

Domestic violence is a growing national concern and social health issue in the United States given the pervasiveness of violence among couples. Identification of risk factors for domestic violence and the empirical evaluation of prevention efforts are critical when one considers that domestic violence is the most common cause of nonfatal injury to women in the United States (Kyriacou et al., 1999). It has been estimated that at least 2 million wives are severely assaulted by their husbands each year (Straus & Gelles, 1990). Rates of aggression among couples before marriage are also high. One study that examined courtship aggression among couples who marry found that 31% of men and 44% of women reported instances of aggression in the year before marriage (O'Leary et al., 1989). Another attempt at measuring rates of premarital aggression estimated that 36% of the couples had

Information for individuals or clinicians on PREP workshops and training is available by calling 303-759-9931.

at least one episode of husband-to-wife premarital aggression (McLaughlin, Leanord, & Senchak, 1992).

Studies that look at perpetrators of violence in relationships present a different picture depending on the source of the statistics. Invariably, when clinical "victim" populations are used, women are more likely to be the victims of violence. A recent survey on violence and threats of violence against women in America found that men assaulted female partners roughly three times more than female partners assaulted men (Goodyear-Smith & Laidlaw, 1999). On the other hand, epidemiological research has suggested that men and women are just as likely to perpetrate violence toward their partners (Malone, Tyree, & O'Leary, 1980; Stets & Straus, 1990; Straus & Gelles, 1986). The same holds true for premarital aggression (see O'Leary et al., 1989) and for patients presenting at emergency rooms who are surveyed for violence (Ernst, Nick, Weiss, Houry, & Mills, 1997).

However, several caveats are in order when interpreting prevalence data. First, rates of aggression are not equivalent for severe physical aggression (see O'Leary, 1999), and physical aggression by men is more likely to result in emergency room visits (Randall, 1990) and more injuries (Cascardi, Langhinrichsen, & Vivian, 1992; Foshee, 1996; Stets & Straus, 1990) than is physical aggression by women. Violence directed against women is also more likely to result in negative emotional consequences, such as lowered self-esteem and depression (Holtzworth-Munroe, Smutzler, Bates, & Sandin, 1997). Accumulating evidence suggests that women are more likely to be killed by their partners (Kellerman & Mercy, 1992; Randall, 1990). Thus, although both partners may engage in violent behaviors, women are clearly more at risk for physical injury and emotional distress than are men.

Household poll data released from the U.S Department of Justice, collected between 1993 and 1998, has suggested that domestic abuse rates may be decreasing. Specifically, the survey found that women abused by men they live with fell from 1.1 million in 1993 to roughly 900,000 in 1998 (Hedges, 2000). Also among the findings was a 74% decrease in murders of a wife or domestic partner by Black men between 1976 and 1998. The number of murders by White men of a spouse or domestic partner also fell by 44% during this time. Despite the decrease in domestic abuse rates, many of the risk factors for becoming a victim of domestic violence remain unchanged. For instance, the poll found that cohabitation places women at greater risk for attack. Some reasons offered for the decrease in domestic abuse rates include a better criminal justice system and a stronger economy in some urban areas, which are indirectly associated with rates of domestic violence. Of course, these data must be viewed with some caution, given that women often do not report abuse out of fear that their children will be removed. Instead, many women seek help in outside agencies and shelters or do not seek help at all (Hedges, 2000).

A plethora of theories exist regarding what causes and maintains the high incidence of domestic violence. Myriad risk factors also have been examined, including sociodemographic characteristics, cultural institutions, individual psychopathology, and relationship characteristics. For the purposes of this chapter, we examine sociodemographic characteristics that place men and women at risk for violence, risk factors in the relationship context and physiological risk factors as observed in the marital dyad, and how they can inform prevention and intervention programs. We then explore some primary and secondary intervention programs that have empirically demonstrated effectiveness in reducing levels of domestic violence. Finally, we discuss future directions and recommendations for prevention programs.

SOCIODEMOGRAPHIC CHARACTERISTICS LINKED TO DOMESTIC VIOLENCE

The development of intervention and prevention programs necessitate an understanding of risk factors across sociodemographic, relational, and physiobiological domains. Knowledge of such risk factors is important because prevention programs will be most effective when they address how such factors affect the lives of couples experiencing violence. For example, if one partner is dealing with alcoholism, the benefits of intervention are maximized to the extent that alcohol issues are concurrently addressed or addressed prior to teaching couples new skills. Also, knowledge of age as a risk factor and its developmental trend can be assets in implementing intervention or prevention programs. Spousal abuse rates reach a peak in the late teenage years and decrease with age, with the most marked decreases occurring from the 20s to the 30s (O'Leary, 1999). As abuse rates change across the life span, so do the circumstances (e.g., socioeconomic status [SES], job instability) and the consequences of abuse (e.g., impact on children, level of psychological abuse). The developmental trajectory of spousal abuse and the risk factors and correlates of abuse for a given age range must be understood to effectively implement and assess intervention programs.

SES

SES has long been recognized as a risk factor for aggression. Contrary to earlier reports of domestic violence occurring more often at both ends of the socioeconomic scale (i.e., both lower and upper class), it is now well established that spousal aggression is more common among couples from working- and middle-class socioeconomic backgrounds, compared with those who are more affluent (Gelles, 1974; McLaughlin, Leanord, & Senchak, 1992). Unstable employment and unemployment, as well as lower levels of education for the male partner, have been associated with increased risk of injury to the female partner (Kyriacou et al., 1999). There is also some evidence that women who have more years of education than their partner are more likely to be victims of violence (Goodyear-Smith & Laidlaw, 1999; Kyriacou et al., 1999). This finding may also be an artifact of accumulating evidence that shows that women are at increased risk for violence when they have more status or power (in this case education) than their partner (see Babcock, Waltz, Jacobson, & Gottman, 1993; Malik & Lindahl, 1998). It may be that men who find their female partners' high status or power threatening on some levels resort to violence instead of implementing more prosocial strategies for achieving power and control.

Age

Age is also related to increased incidents of domestic violence. An inverse relationship between age and incidence of violence has consistently been found with longitudinal data (see Gelles, 1974; O'Leary, 1999; Suitor, Pillemer, & Straus, 1990), with the highest rates of violence among those ages 18 to 29 years (Bachman & Pillemer, 1992). More specifically, according to one report, more than 20% of men between ages 18 and 25 and 16.9% of men between ages 26 and 35 committed at least one act of domestic violence in the past year (National Research Council Institute of Medicine, 1998). A large-scale study of men's reports of husband–wife violence by O'Leary (1999) supported the age by prevalence of aggression interaction, with a decrease from 37% to 2% across the age span of 20–70 years. Evidence also suggests that aggression declines with marriage. When following 272 engaged couples (mean age for men and women being 25.3 and 23.6 years, respectively) through 30 months into the marriage, O'Leary et al. (1989) found that aggression rates dropped from 44% to 32% for women (as perpetrators) and from 31% to 25% for men. In this study, the physical aggression almost never involved weapons and was most commonly in the form of pushing, grabbing, and shoving.

Other research, however, has suggested that age does not seem to differentiate abused from nonabused women in clinical samples (Stark & Flitcraft, 1987). As of this writing, no sound empirical explanation exists for the significantly higher rates of domestic violence among younger couples. It may be that the correlates of younger couples, such as alcohol use and job instability, combine to place them at greater risk. The relationship between age and domestic violence mirrors that of marital research, which has suggested that marital distress and destructive conflict tend to emerge early in marriage, with the most rapid declines in marriage occurring during the first 10 years of marriage (Glenn, 1998). It also reflects the developmental course of physical aggression in general, with a peak of aggression in men occurring in the late teenage years, and most criminal behavior tapering off around age 30

(Wilson & Hernstein, 1985). Clearly, this finding justifies the need for directing prevention efforts at premarital and newlywed couples.

It is also important not to assume that the reduction of one form of violence means the absence of an abusive environment. Usually when there is one form of extreme violence between partners, there are less violent forms of abuse, such as emotional and verbal abuse. Consequently, high levels of emotional abuse can remain even after physical violence has diminished (Jacobson, Gottman, Gortner, Berns, & Shortt, 1996).

Cohabitation

Living together before marriage has also been associated with increased rates of premarital violence compared with couples who live apart before marriage (McLaughlin et al., 1992; Stets & Straus, 1990; Yllo & Straus, 1981), possibly because the proximity of living in a shared environment is more conducive to violent behavior. It is also likely that living together before marriage is more common among couples with less family support, lower incomes, and more job instability—all risk factors for violence.

Race

Race has also emerged as a risk factor for premarital violence, although results have been more mixed in this area. The majority of research examining race has not accounted for important cultural variables when interpreting results. Several studies have found higher rates of premarital violence among Black couples (Makepeace, 1987; O'Keefe, Brockopp, & Chew, 1986), even after controlling for SES (McLaughlin et al., 1992); others have found no differences across race after controlling for SES (see Holtzworth-Munroe, Smutzler, Bates, & Sandin, 1997). Because many of the demographic factors mentioned thus far (i.e., SES, age, cohabitation, and race) are interrelated, it will be important to disentangle the direct and indirect predictors of marital violence.

Social Support

The finding that integration into a network of family and friends, and active association with other social groups and communities, buffer against marital distress and marital violence is not new (Straus, Gelles, & Steinmetz, 1980). In general, data have suggested that social support is an important protective factor against marital violence and, conversely, that social isolation is a predisposing risk factor for victimization (National Research Council Institute of Medicine, 1998). Whether social isolation precedes or results from violence in the home is less clear.

Social isolation can be a risk factor not just for victims but also for potential perpetrators and for the couple as a unit. For example, it has been documented that perpetrators of abuse tend to be less socially connected than matched control groups (Bogyo, 1998). On the other hand, perpetrators of abuse may be part of a specialized social network (e.g., fraternities) that promotes alcohol use, as well as beliefs that support the use of force or intimidation against women (Koss & Gaines, 1993). Additionally, social support systems for couples may be a powerful determinant in marital outcomes. Greater overlap between spouses' social networks has been associated with greater marital adjustment (Julien & Markman, 1991), as well as with relationship stability (Cotton, Cunningham, & Antill, 1993).

Gender Stereotyping and Inequality

Finally, a relationship has been found between adherence to traditional gender socialization practices and domestic violence. Sexual inequality and the male-dominated organization of society has long been theorized to be an enabling structure for domestic violence (Koss & Gaines, 1993; Straus, 1980). From this perspective, pervasive, underlying cultural values dictate gender equality, and violence against women will continue as long as true egalitarian relationships are not valued in society. The association between egalitarian relationships and violence is evident in countries with pronounced gender stereotyping and patriarchal hierarchies. For example, one survey of Nicaraguan women estimated the percentage of women experiencing violence at about 50% (Ellsberg, Caldera, Herrera, Winkvist, & Kullgren, 1999). In general, lack of resources for women—in the form of governmental and nongovernmental health agencies—along with culturally rigid gender prescriptions, combine to muffle the needs of these victims of violence. Thus, violence prevention efforts have worldwide implications.

Indeed, some preventive avenues are currently being explored internationally. One program in Israel (Steiner, 1999) targets high-risk preteenage and adolescent girls who are in distress, often because of exposure to marital violence in their homes. This program combines both feminist and family systems-oriented therapy as a means to diffuse potentially harmful cultural prescriptions.

Alcohol Use

Problem drinking behavior is another salient risk factor for partner aggression (Leanord & Senchak, 1996; Pan, Neidig, & O'Leary, 1994). Interestingly, rates of alcohol use and aggression toward partners follow the same trend over time (i.e., both decrease with age and reach a peak around ages 18–24; McMurran, 1999; O'Leary, 1999). Because alcoholism and problem drinking are both major risk factors for physical violence between partners, it is likely to be a concomitant issue for couples seeking treatment. It is important to address both alcohol and violence problems, because the elimination of problem drinking does not eliminate violent behavior between partners (Stith, Crossman, & Bischof, 1991).

Family History of Violence

An early history of exposure to marital violence is a major risk factor for engaging in partner violence (Hotaling & Sugarman, 1986; McMurran, 1999), as is being a victim of abuse as a child (Dutton, 1998a; Holtzworth-Munroe, Smutzler, Bates, & Sandin, 1997; Oriel & Fleming, 1998). The association between a history of family violence and being abusive in a later relationship is especially strong for men (Hotaling & Sugarman, 1986; Straus, 1980). These studies highlight the intergenerational transmission of violence and the importance of the family in shaping and perpetuating maladaptive cognitions that support the use of violence.

Associations Among Risk Factors

Taken together, although many of the sociodemographic risk factors are interconnected, it is hard to confirm their unique contributions to marital violence. In particular, the associations among SES, ethnicity, cohabitation, and marital violence are less than clear and are likely to vary by age and by the stage of the relationship, as well as by level of and intensity of violence. For example, one study found that wife's level of education, husband's race, and cohabitation are significant predictors of premarital aggression but only for moderate levels of aggression (McLaughlin et al., 1992).

RELATIONSHIP RISK FACTORS
FOR DOMESTIC VIOLENCE

Earlier we mentioned that knowledge of sociodemographic risk factors is important in identifying at-risk populations and in determining the appropriate intervention. That is, knowledge of risk factors may help identify couples at risk for violence, but this knowledge is of little use in determining the behaviors one would want to target in an intervention program. More dynamic behavioral predictors of domestic violence—which also occur in advance of the targeted violence—may be more amenable to intervention. From a cognitive–behavioral perspective, marital violence is often thought of as the extreme end on a continuum of negative behaviors that can occur within marital relationships (O'Leary, 1993). That is, marital violence can be seen as an extreme form of marital distress, which is not to imply that marital distress causes marital violence. The marital distress—

marital violence association can be bidirectional, and many distressed relationships never turn violent (O'Leary, 1999).

Relationship Distress and Communication

Reports of violence by couples are one of the strongest predictors of the future stability of the marriage. More specifically, work by Rogge and Bradbury (1999) revealed that reports of violence or aggression were the strongest predictor of divorce in the first 4 years of marriage, while the quality of communication was the best predictor of marital satisfaction. When "psychological" aggression was taken into account, there was an increased ability to predict divorce, showing the significance of factors such as psychological abuse that may be precursors to more serious violence. Longitudinal studies have shown that destructive marital conflict and negative communication are the leading risk factors for future marital distress (e.g., Gottman, 1994; Markman & Hahlweg, 1993). Specific destructive patterns of communication include the demand–withdraw pattern, escalation, invalidation, withdrawal, and negative interpretations (Markman, Stanley, & Blumberg, 2001).

Researchers have also suggested that marital aggression might be caused by couples' failure to use proactive coping mechanisms in resolving marital conflicts (Markman & Kraft, 1989). In fact, studies have demonstrated that violent individuals tend to lack problem-solving and conflict resolution skills (Holtzworth-Munroe & Anglin, 1991; Riggs, O'Leary, & Breslin, 1990). This lack of effective conflict resolution within marriages, because of one or both partners, might lead to negative escalation, ultimately resulting in physical violence (Holtzworth-Munroe, Beatty, & Anglin, 1995; Holtzworth-Munroe, Smutzler, Bates, & Sandin, 1997).

Thus, the targeted skills in programs designed to prevent divorce (e.g., communication skills training, cognitive restructuring) may have implications for the prevention of marital violence. This holds true to the extent to which marital distress leads to violence over time. These findings point out not only the advantage of screening for violence among couples planning for marriage but also the importance of targeting destructive communication patterns and violence when determining couples' needs and levels of risk for marital dissolution.

Power Relations and Domestic Violence

Because almost all violent couples are distressed, but not all distressed couples are violent, it has been scientifically important to identify characteristics that discriminate between violent and distressed but nonviolent couples. Even though communication deficits and destructive conflict are characteristic of distressed couples, only recently have investigators examined the dynamics among couples experiencing marital violence and started testing theories that have been provided.

One area that has recently been examined in a research setting is the association between domestic violence and power relations in marriage. Equal distributions of power (e.g., education, job status, income) have been associated with less marital distress and lower risk of violence and with greater ability to prevent conflict from escalating (Goodyear-Smith & Laidlaw, 1999). When there is an unequal distribution of power in the relationship, and the husband has relatively less power than his wife, the risk for marital violence increases (Babcock, Waltz, Jacobson, & Gottman, 1993). In light of such findings, it has been suggested that domestic violence is an attempt at regaining or compensating for a lack of power in the relationship. More specifically, men who lack power through economic resources or feel that other resources are unavailable or ineffective in bringing about change may resort to violence in their relationships as a way of exerting power. When one considers income and education level as types of power, it is not surprising to find a relationship between increased risk for violence in relationships in which women have a relatively higher income or level of education than their male partner. There is also evidence that in already distressed relationships, imbalances in status and decision-making power are associated with higher incidences of violence (Babcock et al., 1993).

Taken together, these findings are consistent with research indicating that many abusive men are actually quite fearful, jealous, and easily threatened (Dutton, 1998a), and any threats to their own power may elicit angry reactions. Thus, violence in domestic relationships is probably best conceptualized as an interaction between individual temperaments or personalities and the power balance in the relationship.

Demand–Withdraw Pattern

To disentangle the relationship between marital distress, marital violence, and power, Babcock et al. (1993) examined power discrepancies in maritally distressed but nonviolent couples and in maritally violent couples. For these analyses, the first aspects of power considered were power bases, or a person's education level, income, and occupation status. Second, power processes such as communication patterns were examined. One pattern of communication common among couples seeking therapy is the demand–withdraw interaction, in which the "demander" puts pressure on the partner through criticism or complaints, and the "withdrawer" (usually the man in nonclinical populations) retreats through defensiveness or avoidance (Christensen & Heavy, 1990). Finally, power outcomes were considered, defined by who has the final say in making decisions.

Findings revealed that husbands' and wives' poor communication skills, husbands' low decision-making power, and high levels of the husband demand–wife withdraw patterns were all associated with increased violence against the wife. Furthermore, the husband demand–wife withdraw pattern discriminated the domestically violent from distressed but nonviolent couples. The finding that violent couples show elevated levels of husband demand–wife withdraw is in contrast to the more common pattern among couples receiving therapy, in which the wife typically demands and the husband withdraws. It may be that men in violent relationships may be using physical aggression to compensate for the lack of power associated with the demander role. However, it may also be that the demander is an aggressive role, especially in cases in which the other partner chooses to withdraw because of protection or diffusion of conflict. In short, it is difficult to assume that the demander always has less power in the relationship, particularly when the demander may be seeking a specific response, such as withdrawal. Although verbal skills did not distinguish the violent couples from nonviolent but distressed couples, when both partners have poor communication skills the frequency of violence is likely to increase. Specifically, when both partners in a violent relationship lack good communication skills, violence is likely to increase as husband decision-making power decreases, and the husband demand–wife withdrawal pattern increases (Babcock et al., 1993). Hence, the relationship between poor communication skills and violence is complex and is moderated by other power processes.

OBSERVED INTERACTIONS OF VIOLENT COUPLES

Whereas a global communication deficit may characterize domestically violent couples, it cannot distinguish violent from nonviolent couples. As a construct, global communication deficits offer little practical utility for treatment and intervention efforts. It is much easier to target a specific behavior, like the demand–withdraw pattern, when designing prevention and intervention programs for domestically violent couples.

To better understand specific behavior interactions, it is helpful to move beyond self-report data of how one communicates or responds to the partner and observe the dynamics between spouses (Markman & Notarius, 1987). Most research examining interactions and communication patterns among maritally violent couples overrelies on self-report data. Very few researchers have systematically observed the interaction patterns of domestically violent couples despite the potential wealth of useful information for preventing and treating domestic violence. Those researchers who have used observational methods of studying interactions among domestic violence couples have found that physically aggressive husbands are more negative than the maritally distressed but nonviolent husbands (Burman, John, & Margolin, 1992). Another pattern of communication found to characterize maritally distressed couples is a tendency to reciprocate or continue negative behaviors. Contrary to the stereotypical portrait of the passive female victim, there is some evidence that women in physically violent relationships are more likely to reciprocate negative behavior than are women in nonviolent relationships (Burman et al., 1992).

To better understand the interpersonal dynamics of physically abusive husbands and their wives, Cordova, Jacobson, Gottman, Rushe, and Cox (1993) observed the communication patterns of domestically violent couples, distressed but nonviolent couples, and happily married couples. By matching the violent couples and the distressed but nonviolent couples on marital satisfaction, they were able to disentangle the effects of marital distress and physical violence. Results from this study found that violent husbands had a higher proportion of aversive behavior (i.e., negative verbal remarks) than did nonviolent husbands. Patterns of negative reciprocity also distinguished violent from nonviolent and happily married couples, with violent couples demonstrating more negative reciprocity during the interaction. Across all three groups, women were just as likely as men to perpetuate the negativity. Other observational studies of nonviolent arguments in research laboratories have provided support for the notion that women in violent relationships are not simply passive receivers during interactions, suggesting that there is something unique to be learned about abusive couples that cannot be obtained by studying violent individuals (Burman et al., 1992; Margolin, John, & Gleberman, 1988).

Research examining the interactions of violent couples improves the understanding of dynamics between individuals that may initiate and perpetuate negativity and violence and helps identify the dynamics of violent couples for the purposes of intervention programs. However, these data are less helpful in explaining violent spouses who are also violent in relationships outside the marriage. Many researchers have attempted to expand the scientific understanding of batterers by classifying violent husbands based on interviews, personality variables, and police records (Ceasar, 1988; Gondolf, 1988; Hamberger & Hastings, 1986). On the basis of this research, three types of batterers have emerged: family only, dysphoric–borderline, and generally violent–antisocial batterers (Holtzworth-Munroe & Stuart, 1994). Family-only batterers display the least amount of violence both in and outside of the home and exhibit little or no psychopathology. Dysphoric–borderline batterers engage in moderate to severe violence that is usually directed toward the wife but also show some violence outside the home. This group is characterized by borderline personality characteristics and is prone to alcohol abuse. The violent–antisocial batterers engage in the highest levels of violence both within and outside the home and are likely to have some antisocial personality disorder traits or alcohol abuse problems (Holtzworth-Munroe, Meehan, Herron, Rehman, & Stuart, 2000). There is some preliminary evidence of a fourth subtype, characterized by low-level antisocial behavior, because characteristics are intermediate to those in the family-only and violent–antisocial batterers (Holtzworth-Munroe et al., 2000).

CLASSIFYING BATTERERS BY PHYSIOLOGICAL MARKERS

There is general consensus that batterers can be classified according to whether their violent behavior extends outside of the marriage (Dutton, 1998b; Gondolf, 1988; Gottman et al., 1995; La Taillade, Waltz, Jacobson, & Gottman, 1992). One factor that may distinguish these two types of batterers is heart rate reactivity, a physiological measure that has been linked to criminality, sensation-seeking, and hostility (Farrington, 1987, 1997; Kagan, 1994; Raine, 1993). To see if physiological reactivity was a distinguishing characteristic of these two hypothetical types of batterers, Gottman et al. (1995) looked at male batters who lowered or increased their heart rates during a marital discussion about areas of conflict. Their study found that men who lowered their heart rates were generally violent outside the marriage toward friends, coworkers, and strangers, compared with men who raised their heart rates. Men with lowered heart rates were also more belligerent and contemptuous, were more likely to have witnessed physical violence between their parents, and were more prone to psychopathology than the other violent men. However, within the marriage, frequency of violence was not associated with heart rate activity.

Jacobson and Gottman (1998) have labeled the group that lowered their heart rate the "cobras" because, like the cobras who sit and focus on their prey before making the attack, these men are calming themselves down internally and focusing their attention on their target before acting. During a heated conversation, these men appear to be in a hostile rage, but internally they are calming themselves down, gathering their internal resources to make an attack. The group that had an increased heart rate during the interaction was labeled "pit bulls" because, like pit bulls, their level of aggression and anger builds until an attack is made.

HOW RESEARCH CAN INFORM PREVENTION EFFORTS

Research on predictors of marital violence and, specifically, observational studies of the interactions between spouses in a violent marriage, have highlighted specific behaviors and destructive communication patterns that can be targeted in prevention programs. Because marital violence is thought of as the extreme end of a continuum of negative behaviors that occur within marital relationships, it is important for prevention purposes to target the negative behaviors couples engage in prior to the onset of violence. Research has supported the association among marital aggression, poor problem-solving abilities, and ineffective conflict resolution skills, which can lead to an escalation of violence (Holtzworth-Munroe & Anglin, 1991; Holtzworth-Munroe, Beaty, & Anglin, 1995; Markman & Kraft, 1989). Using this cognitive–behavioral model of relationship violence, an effective way of approaching the prevention of marital violence would be to focus on teaching couples skills designed to prevent the escalation of marital conflict. Ideally the issue of communication and conflict management can be addressed among couples prior to the onset of violence in their marriages. Such primary prevention is intended to promote couples' current well-being and prevent the development of future dysfunctional behavior (Cowen, 1983).

PREVENTION AND RELATIONSHIP ENHANCEMENT PROGRAM

An empirically evaluated primary prevention program that focuses on enhancing couples' communication and conflict resolution skills is the Prevention and Relationship Enhancement Program (PREP; Markman, Stanley, & Blumberg, 2001). PREP is designed for couples who are planning marriage, with the principle aim of helping couples gain skills that inoculate the marriage from future distress. PREP is a research-based program that delineates the risk factors distinguishing distressed from nondistressed marriages. More specifically, PREP is based on evidence that poor communication, negative reciprocity, and deficits in conflict management among distressed couples leads to the relationship dissatisfaction. PREP is a 12-hour program that teaches couples communication skills designed to promote focused and noncritical discussions, problem-solving skills, and self-regulation of affect (Markman, Floyd, Stanley, & Storaasli, 1988).

The main focus of PREP is to help couples learn to deal with conflict effectively using a variety of communication skills. To promote more effective discussions between spouses, PREP teaches couples the speaker–listener technique. Couples using the speaker–listener technique designate one partner as the speaker and the other as the listener. The speaker has the floor, and his or her job is to discuss an issue from his or her own point of view. The listener's job is to listen to the speaker without interrupting and then to paraphrase the speaker's words. This dialogue continues until the speaker feels that his or her opinion has been heard. The listener then takes on the role of the speaker, and vice versa. Use of the speaker–listener technique slows conflictual discussions to prevent the escalation of conflict. Furthermore, use of the speaker–listener technique allows both partners to feel heard—an essential element for decreasing negative escalation.

In addition to the speaker–listener technique, couples are taught ground rules to protect these discussions from escalation. Some of the rules include speaking from one's own perspective rather than assuming what their partner is thinking and concentrating on the problem issue before moving onto problem solution. The PREP program also teaches couples how to use time-outs when discussions get too heated to prevent the escalation of conflict. In essence, partners are taught several skills that enable them to temporarily end a conflict discussion if it is starting to escalate.

Couples using the skills taught in PREP workshops have reported greater satisfaction with conflict discussions, greater relationship satisfaction, and lower levels of conflict escalation. Follow-up research has also shown that PREP is effective in lowering problem intensity, in helping couples to engage in less negative communication patterns, and in lowering negative escalation as much as 4 years after participation in the program (Markman, Renick, Floyd, Stanley, & Clements, 1993). In fact, couples receiving PREP training were less likely to engage in physical aggression up to 4 years after learning the PREP skills. Thus, PREP addresses many of the behavioral predictors of marital violence.

However, it is unclear whether a primary prevention program focused on conflict management would reach those couples most at risk for marital violence (Holtzworth-Munroe et al., 1995). Furthermore, PREP alone does not address the sociodemographic variables associated with the presence of marital violence, including a family history of violence, violence in previous relationships, and substance abuse.

Research examining the relationship between risk factors and preventive outcomes has shown that the onset of marital violence among newlyweds without a past history of aggression is unlikely (Coie et al., 1993). Furthermore, although enhancing affect management is useful for couples at risk for experiencing violence, the level of anger among violent partners, the degree of fear among abused partners, and the presence of power differentials suggest that anger management, and husband violence in general, should be addressed before beginning communication and problem-solving training (Jacobson et al., 1994).

It is important to address concerns surrounding the safety of working with couples when there is risk for or current violence in the relationship. That is, is it ever appropriate and effective to work with couples who are experiencing violence in their relationship? PREP is not a treatment program for domestic violence, although its focus on helping couples communicate better and use more positive problem-solving strategies, as well as informing couples about the use and misuse of power and control, has been linked to the prevention of violence in the first place. Specifically, over a 5-year period, couples who participated in PREP premaritally had one fourth the number of aggressive incidents compared to control couples (Markman, Renick, Floyd, Stanley, & Clements, 1993). Other researchers have demonstrated the benefits of doing conjoint therapy with some violent couples (O'Leary, 1999). For example, Heyman and Neidig (1997) found that conjoint therapy with violent couples is not only safe but also can result in decreased physical aggression between spouses. PREP makes it clear to couples that safety is the primary concern, and concerns for safety should drive the treatment strategy.

We believe that there are various forms of domestic violence and various intervention strategies that uphold our concern for safety. The distinction lies in cases in which there is male battering (Type A) versus couples in which there is some aggression but no intimidation or ongoing threat to the woman (Type B). In the case of battering, an individually oriented domestic violence program could be most appropriate, whereas Type B couples might benefit most from joint work to target mutually escalating and angry arguments. In short, PREP could be a useful strategy for preventing more serious levels of violence for couples with low levels of low-intensity aggression. Caution should be exercised in choosing any treatment strategy, and those who work with couples should be aware of the legal guidelines surrounding domestic violence, as well as local resources that may maximize the safety of the individual.

STOP ANGER AND VIOLENCE ESCALATION

As alluded to earlier, interpersonal violence between spouses can occur before or after engagement and can be conceptualized as the culmination of long-standing problems in the relationship that often continue after the relationship is over. These relationships are marked by increasingly frequent and intense conflict, as well as by a reduction of more positive interactions between partners. For this reason, efforts aimed at preventing marital violence before it occurs must involve the reduction of causal risk factors such as negative communication patterns and the bolstering of protective factors such as healthy commitment and the development of a broader support network. This approach is in accordance with current practice in prevention science (Coie et al., 1993). Thus, for the most part, primary prevention of marital violence is practically synonymous with prevention of divorce efforts like PREP (Markman, Stanley, & Blumberg, 2001) and fall under the rubric of premarital intervention generally (for an overview of premarital intervention, see Hartman, Whitton, Markman, & Stanley, in press). Thus, there remains a paucity of primary prevention programs explicitly targeting marital violence, compared with the numerous secondary prevention programs and treatment protocols aimed at helping couples at-risk for violence (i.e., based on demographics, high levels of distress, history of family violence) or for couples already experiencing violence, respectively.

Whereas primary prevention in psychology is proactive, in that it seeks to build adaptive strengths in normal populations to ward off maladaptive problems (Albee & Gullotta, 1997), secondary prevention is more selective because it targets those identified as at-risk for developing certain kinds of psychopathology. Thus, a secondary prevention program dealing with marital violence would target those who are already showing some of the causes, or markers, of violence and administer an educational or skills-building program to these couples. One example is the Stop Anger and Violence Escalation (SAVE) program developed by Peter Neidig, which is based on his previous treatment program for couples in the military already experiencing physical aggression (the Domestic Conflict Containment Program; Neidig, 1985, 1989a, 1989b; Neidig & Friedman, 1984).

SAVE (Neidig, 1989c, 1989d) is a 4-hour workshop targeting couples in the military considered to be at high risk for experiencing marital violence (e.g., unsubstantiated reports of violence, levels of violence not severe enough to meet the criteria for nonvoluntary referral to treatment). SAVE is a structured educational program that provides couples with an understanding of the consequences of physical aggression in relationships, reduces their tolerance for acceptance of such behavior, and acquaints couples with the risk factors for conflict escalation. It should be noted that the risk factors mentioned earlier are quite severe. Other risk factors that might be less potent, but nevertheless predictive of marital violence, are psychological abuse, being younger, having a lower income, and having an alcohol problem (Pan, Neidig, & O'Leary, 1994). Conceivably, SAVE may be adapted for use with couples exhibiting these latter characteristics as well. SAVE has been used with thousands of couples since 1989.

PREP/SAVE PROGRAM

A natural adaptation of SAVE was undertaken by Holtzworth-Munroe and colleagues (Holtzworth-Munroe, Markman, et al., 1995) in which the PREP program (Markman, Stanley, & Blumberg, 1994) was combined with SAVE and administered to engaged and newly married couples. This PREP/SAVE program incorporates both the conflict management and skills-building approach of PREP and the more informational content of SAVE that heightens awareness specifically about risk for domestic violence. Efficacy of this hybrid model is currently being evaluated with couples at military bases in Colorado. As part of a community efficacy study, first-time domestic violence offenders go through the PREP/SAVE program if they are not deemed imminently dangerous (Silliman, Stanley, Coffin, Markman, & Jordan, 2002). Clearly, it represents an encouraging step toward conceptualizing marital violence as an outcome that can and should be addressed via prevention efforts and not merely with treatment efforts.

PHYSICAL AGGRESSION COUPLES TREATMENT

Another similar effort to PREP and SAVE is Physical Aggression Couples Treatment (PACT; Heyman & Neidig, 1997), an empirically tested program for couples experiencing violence in their relationship. Unlike PREP and SAVE, PACT targets violent couples, and as such, is best conceived of as tertiary prevention. Like PREP and SAVE, PACT focuses on the prevention of anger and conflict and on improvement of couples' communication skills to prevent future violence. PACT has three basic stages: (a) the reduction of violence and anger management; (b) the improvement of relationship factors such as communication, jealousy, and power; and (c) educating couples about alternatives to violence. As a joint program, PACT has demonstrated that there are advantages over gender-specific forms of treatment. Specifically, because both couples are encouraged to explore their role in the conflict, PACT participants are often less defensive, and reports of aggression are typically more accurate with both partners present. Furthermore, it is easier to work on relationship factors when both partners are present and can agree on certain practices (e.g., calling a time-out).

Finally, there is empirical support that those who participated in PACT had lower levels of mild and severe aggression at posttreatment, and PACT couples were higher on marital adjustment and had more positive feelings toward their spouse. Couples also experienced a significant reduction in the number of dominance and isolation behaviors and on maladaptive beliefs that support the use of physical aggression. One-year follow-up results indicated that the reduction in husbands' physical aggression was significantly lower, and marital adjustment was still significantly better than pretreatment ratings.

FUTURE DIRECTIONS

Domestic violence is a startling epidemic, with roughly 1.6 million women being the victims of physical assaults by their husbands each year (Straus & Gelles, 1990). The mental and emotional repercussions stemming from domestic violence are severe and need to be addressed. Given the body of research on relationship distress and marital aggression, clinicians must increasingly focus on the specific demographic, relationship, and physiological risk factors associated with domestic violence. This chapter has discussed evidence of how PREP has had positive effects in the prevention of domestic violence. Because there are always concerns about generalizing from couples who come in to research centers to the broader community, PREP is being implemented and evaluated across diverse samples and settings. For instance, military samples and couples in Germany and Australia are being examined to test the impact of the intervention.

We have also emphasized the importance of secondary prevention programs that are best suited for individuals and couples identified as being at risk for domestic violence. One such secondary prevention program is SAVE, which focuses on educating at-risk couples about the predictors and consequences of domestic violence. However, SAVE is lacking a component focused on teaching couples skills to address these predictors of violence. Therefore, the development of PREP/SAVE program is promising in its focus on identifying couples at risk for domestic violence and then educating these couples on the risks and consequences of violence, as well as teaching them skills they can use to prevent the onset and escalation of violence.

Research on risk factors can inform the format of violence prevention programs. For example, on the basis of findings regarding social support as a buffer against domestic violence, primary and secondary prevention efforts regarding marital violence might include opportunities for couples to congregate regularly. Many services delivered to individual couples can be applied in a group format, providing the added benefits of support and modeling. For instance, booster sessions that allow couples to brush up on their conflict resolution skills have been considered but not implemented in a group format. Beyond providing couples with the opportunity to practice valuable skills, booster sessions involving participants from the original sessions might provide couples with a sense of belonging to small cohort, or social network. Perhaps this aspect of program delivery should be further analyzed in research. Certainly, exposure to "veteran couples" who act as mentors for newlyweds has been an effective component of many church-based marriage preparation programs (see McManus, 1996). In this latter case, affiliation with a larger religious community and more involved interaction with other experienced couples is almost a "double protection" against some of the factors associated with relationship distress.

Clinicians interested in prevention should consider not only the relevance of their program content to the clinical problem in question but also how they can effectively reach the populations most in need of these services (i.e., marketing research-based programs). Those interested in reaching couples at risk for violence via prevention efforts might attend to suggestions already made regarding the design and implementation of more generic premarital intervention programs (Silliman & Schumm, 1999; Williams, Riley, Risch, & Van Dyke, 1999). More specifically, researchers exploring marketing strategies to attract certain populations, like marriage education participants (e.g., Morris, Cooper, & Gross, 1999), have emphasized consideration of the "five Ps": price, product, place, people, and promotion. We have already addressed the product in this chapter, stressing the need for clinicians to tailor their interventions specifically to issues of couples at risk for violence. For example, programs that go beyond the routine emphasis on constructive communication skills (e.g., listening, empathy) or negotiation strategies and inform at-risk couples about escalation patterns and the impact of stress and power dynamics on relationship functioning, might be especially relevant.

What about other aspects of the intervention delivery, such as place or setting in which it is delivered and the price of the program? Given the relative preponderance of violence among low-income families, having such prevention programs available at community-oriented organizations makes sense. Some research-based prevention efforts transmit information about warning signs of abuse to local communities and mental health centers so that it can filter down to those seeking services (see Perez & Rasmussen, 1997). Furthermore, the media are often convenient and relatively inexpensive channels with which to reach a large audience, or promote these principles. Finally, but perhaps most importantly, clinicians planning on working with couples should make safety the first priority, and although we know that conjoint strategies work for some aggressive couples, individual work is a necessity for other types of interpersonal violence (e.g., battering, ongoing intimidation). Couples should be provided with information regarding available resources and treatment options in the community that best suit their needs.

Clearly there is a great deal more that needs to be done in preventing domestic violence. In particular, there is a need for empirical investigations of prevention programs and follow-up investigations. Ideally, more experimental investigations will use control groups, because most prevention studies thus far have been quasiexperimental. Our hope is that, as researchers and clinicians are made more aware of the prevalence of domestic violence and the risk factors associated with this phenomenon, there will be a decline in the devastation of couples and families in the United States.

REFERENCES

Albee, G. W., & Gullotta, T. P. (1997). Primary prevention's evolution. In G. W. Albee & T. P. Gullotta (Eds.), *Primary prevention works: Vol. 6. Issues in children's and families' lives* (pp. 3–22). Thousand Oaks, CA: Sage.

Babcock, J., Waltz, J., Jacobson, N., & Gottman, J. M. (1993). *Journal of Consulting and Clinical Psychology, 61*, 40–50.

Bachman, R., & Pillemer, K. A. (1992). Epidemiology and family violence involving adults. In R. T. Ammerman & M. Hersen (Eds.), *Assessment of family violence: A clinical and legal sourcebook. Wiley series on personality processes* (pp. 108–120). New York: John Wiley & Sons.

Bogyo, G. R. (1998). Social isolation and community connectedness among adjudicated spousal assaulters in northern British Columbia, Canada. *Dissertation Abstracts International: Section B: The Sciences and Engineering, 59*(5-B): 2412.

Burman, B., John, R., & Margolin, G. (1992). Observed patterns of conflict in violent, nonviolent, and nondistressed couples. *Behavioral Assessment, 14*, 15–37.

Cascardi, M., Langhinrichsen, J., & Vivian, D. (1992). Marital aggression: Impact, injury, and health correlates for husbands and wives. *Archives of Internal Medicine, 152*, 1178–1184.

Ceasar, P. L. (1988). Exposure to violence in families of origin among wife abusers and martially nonviolent men. *Violence and Victims, 3,* 49–64.

Christensen, A., & Heavy, C. L. (1990). Gender and social structure in the demand/withdraw pattern of marital conflict. *Journal of Personality and Social Psychology, 59,* 73–81.

Coie, J. D., Watt, N. F., West, S. G., Hawkins, J. D., Asarnow, J. R., Markman, H. J., et al. (1993). The science of prevention: A conceptual framework and some directions for a national research program. *American Psychologist, 48,* 1013–1022.

Cordova, J. V., Jacobson, N. S., Gottman, J. M., Rushe, R., & Cox, G. (1993). Negative reciprocity and communication in couples with a violent husband. *Journal of Abnormal Psychology, 102,* 559–564.

Cotton, S., Cunningham, J., & Antill, J. (1993). Network structure, network support, and the marital satisfaction of husbands and wives. *Australian Journal of Psychology, 45,* 176–181.

Cowen, E. L. (1983). Primary prevention in mental health: Past, presents, and future. In R. D. Felner, L. A. Jason, J. N. Moritsugu, & S. S. Farber (Eds.), *Preventive psychology: Theory, research, and practice.* New York: Pergamon Press.

Dutton, D. G. (1998a). *The abusive personality: Violence and control in intimate relationships.* New York: Guilford Press.

Dutton, D. G. (1998b). *The domestic assault of women.* Boston: Allyn & Bacon.

Ellsberg, M., Caldera, T., Herrera, A., Winkvist, A., & Kullgren, G. (1999). Domestic violence and emotional distress among Nicaraguan women: Results from a population-based study. *American Psychologist, 54,* 30–36.

Ernst, A., Nick, T., Weiss, S., Houry, D., & Mills, T. (1997). Domestic violence in an inner city ED. *Annals of Emergency Medicine, 30,* 190–197.

Farrington, D. P. (1987). Implications of biological findings for criminological research. In S. A. Mednick, R. E. Moffitt, & S. A. Stack (Eds.), *The causes of crime: New biological approaches* (pp. 93–113). New York: Cambridge University Press.

Farrington, D. P. (1997). The relationship between low resting heart rate and violence. In A. Raine, P. Brennan, D. Farrington, & S. Mednick (Eds.), *Biosocial bases of behavior, NATO ASI series. Series A: Life sciences* (pp. 1–20). New York: Plenum Press.

Foshee, V. A. (1996). Gender differences in adolescent dating abuse prevalence, types, and injury. *Health Education Research: Theory and Practice, 11,* 275–286.

Gelles, R. J. (1974). *The violent home: A study of physical aggression between husbands and wives.* Newbury Park, CA: Sage.

Glenn, N. D. (1998). The course of marital success and failure in five American 10-year marriage cohorts. *Journal of Marriage and the Family, 60,* 569–576.

Gondolf, E. W. (1988). Who are those guys? Toward a typology of batterers. *Violence and Victims, 3,* 187–203.

Goodyear-Smith, F., & Laidlaw, T. M. (1999). Aggressive acts and assaults in intimate relationships: Towards an understanding of the literature. *Behavioral Sciences and the Law, 17,* 285–304.

Gottman, J. M. (1994). *Why marriages succeed or fail.* New York: Simon & Schuster.

Gottman, J. M., Jacobson, N. S., Rushe, R. H., Shortt, J. W., Babcock, J., La Taillade, J. J., et al. (1995). The relationship between heart rate reactivity, emotionally aggressive behavior, and general violence in batterers. *Journal of Family Psychology, 9,* 227–248.

Hamberger, L. K., & Hastings, J. E. (1986). Personality correlates of men who abuse their partners: A cross-validation study. *Journal of Family Violence, 4,* 323–341.

Hartman, S. G., Whitton, S. W., Markman, H. J., & Stanley, S. M. (in press). Premarital intervention. In E. Craighead (Ed.), *Encyclopedia of psychology and neuroscience.* New York: Wiley.

Hedges, M. (2000, May 18). Study: Domestic abuse down. *Daily Camera* [Boulder, CO], pp. 1A, 9A.

Heyman, R. E., & Neidig, P. H. (1997). Physical aggression couples treatment. In K. Halford & H. J. Markman (Eds.), *Clinical handbook of marriage and couples intervention* (pp. 589–617). New York: Wiley.

Holtzworth-Munroe, A., & Anglin, K. (1991). The competency of responses given by maritally violent versus nonviolent men to problematic marital situations. *Clinical Psychology Review, 12,* 605–617.

Holtzworth-Munroe, A., Beatty, S. B., & Anglin, K. (1995). The assessment and treatment of marital violence: An introduction for the marital therapist. In N. S. Jacobson & A. S. Gurman (Eds.), *Clinical handbook of couple therapy* (2nd ed., pp. 317–339). New York: Guilford Press.

Holtzworth-Munroe, A., Markman, H. J., O'Leary, K. D., Neidig, P., Leber, D., Heyman, R. E., et al. (1995). The need for marital violence prevention efforts: A behavioral–cognitive secondary prevention program for engaged and newly married couples. *Applied and Preventive Psychology, 4,* 77–88.

Holtzworth-Munroe, A., Meehan, J. C., Herron, K., Rehman, U., & Stuart, G. L. (2000). Testing the Holtzworth-Munroe and Stuart Batterer Typology. *Journal of Clinical and Consulting Psychology, 68,* 1000–1019.

Holtzworth-Munroe, A., Smutzler, N., Bates, L., & Sandin, E. (1997). Husband violence: Basic facts and clinical implications. In W. K. Halford & H. J. Markman (Eds.), *Clinical handbook of marriage and couples interventions* (pp. 129–156). New York: Wiley.

Holtzworth-Munroe, A., & Stuart, G. L. (1994). Typologies of batterers: Three subtypes and the differences among them. *Psychological Bulletin, 116,* 476–497.

Hotaling, G. T., & Sugarman, D. B. (1986). An analysis of risk markers in husband to wife violence: The current state of knowledge. *Violence and Victims, 1,* 101–124.

Jacobson, N. S., & Gottman, J. M. (1998). *When men batter women.* New York: Simon & Schuster.

Jacobson, N. S., Gottman, J. M., Gortner, E., Berns, S., & Shortt, J. (1996). Psychological factors in the longitudinal course of battering: When do the couples split up? When does the abuse decrease? *Violence and Victims, 11,* 371–392.

Jacobson, N. S., Gottman, J. M., Waltz, J., Rushe, R., Babcock, J., & Holtzworth-Munroe, A. (1994). Affect, verbal content, and psychophysiology in the arguments of couples with a violent husband. *Journal of Consulting and Clinical Psychology, 62,* 982–988.

Julien, D., & Markman, H. J. (1991). Social support and social networks as determinants of individual and marital outcomes. *Journal of Social and Personal Relationships, 8,* 549–568.

Kagan, J. (1994). *Galen's prophecy: Temperament in human nature.* New York: Basic Books.

Kellerman, A. L., & Mercy, J. A. (1992). Men, women, and murder: Gender specific differences in rates of fatal violence and victimization. *Journal of Trauma, 33,* 1–5.

Koss, M. P., & Gaines, J. A. (1993). The prediction of sexual aggression by alcohol use, athletic participation, and fraternity affiliation. *Journal of Interpersonal Violence, 8,* 94–106.

Kyriacou, D. N., Deirdre, A., Taliaferro, E., Stone, S., Tubb, T., Linden, J., et al. (1999). Risk factors for injury to women from domestic violence. *New England Journal of Medicine, 341,* 1892–1898.

La Taillade, J. J., Waltz, J., Jacobson, N. S., & Gottman, J. M. (1992, November). *Marital versus other interpersonal violence: An examination of differences and correlates.* Poster session presented at the meeting of the Association for the Advancement of Behavior Therapy, Boston.

Leanord, K. E., & Senchak, M. (1996). Prospective prediction of husband marital aggression within newlywed couples. *Journal of Abnormal Psychology, 105,* 369–380.

Makepeace, J. M. (1987). Social factors and victim–offender differences in courtship violence. *Family Relations, 36,* 87–91.

Malik, N. M., & Lindahl, K. M. (1998). Aggression and dominance: The roles of power and culture in domestic violence. *Clinical Psychology: Science and Practice, 5,* 409–423.

Malone, J., Tyree, A., & O'Leary, K. D. (1980). Generalization and containment: Different effects of aggressive histories for wives and husbands. *Journal of Marriage and the Family, 51,* 687–697.

Margolin, G., John, R. S., & Gleberman, L. (1988). Affective responses to conflictual discussion in violent and nonviolent couples. *Journal of Consulting and Clinical Psychology, 56,* 24–33.

Markman, H. J., Floyd, F., Stanley, S. M., & Storaasli, R. (1988). The prevention of marital distress: A longitudinal investigation. *Journal of Consulting and Clinical Psychology, 56,* 210–217.

Markman, H. J., & Hahlweg, K. (1993). The prediction and prevention of marital distress: An international perspective. *Clinical Psychology Review, 13,* 29–43.

Markman, H. J., & Kraft, S. A. (1989). Men and women in marriage: Dealing with gender differences in marital therapy. *Behavior Therapist, 12,* 51–56.

Markman, H. J., & Notarius, C. I. (1987). Coding marital and family interaction: Current status. In T. Jacob (Ed.), *Family interaction and psychopathology: Theories, methods, and findings. Applied clinical psychology* (pp. 329–390). New York: Plenum Press.

Markman, H. J., Renick, M. J., Floyd, F. J., Stanley, S. M., & Clements, M. (1993). Preventing marital distress through communication and conflict management training: A 4- and 5-year follow-up. *Journal of Consulting and Clinical Psychology, 61,* 70–77.

Markman, H. J., Stanley, S. M., & Blumberg, S. (1994). *Fighting for your marriage: Positive steps for a loving and lasting relationship.* San Francisco, CA: Jossey-Bass.

Markman, H. J., Stanley, S., & Blumberg, S. L. (2001). *Fighting for your marriage: Positive steps for preventing divorce and preserving a lasting love.* San Francisco, CA: Jossey-Bass.

McLaughlin, I. G., Leanord, K. E., & Senchak, M. (1992). Prevalence and distribution of premarital aggression among couples applying for a marriage license. *Journal of Family Violence, 7,* 309–319.

McManus, M. J. (1996). The marriage-saving movement. *The American Enterprise, 7,* 28–35.

McMurran, M. (1999). Alcohol and violence. *Child Abuse Review, 8,* 219–230.

Morris, M. L., Cooper, C., & Gross, K. H. (1999). Marketing factors influencing the overall satisfaction of marriage education participants. *Family Relations, 48,* 251–261.

National Research Council Institute of Medicine. (1998). In R. Chalk & P. A. King (Eds.), *Violence in families: Assessing prevention and treatment programs.* Washington, DC: National Academy Press.

Neidig, P. H. (1985). *The Domestic Conflict Containment Program workbook.* Atlanta, GA: Behavioral Science Associates.

Neidig, P. H. (1989a). *Anger control instructor's guide.* Atlanta, GA: Behavioral Science Associates.

Neidig, P. H. (1989b). *Anger control participant's workbook.* Atlanta, GA: Behavioral Science Associates.

Neidig, P. H. (1989c). *Stop Anger and Violence Escalation (SAVE) instructor's guide.* Atlanta, GA: Behavioral Science Associates.

Neidig, P. H. (1989d). *Stop Anger and Violence Escalation (SAVE) participant's workbook.* Atlanta, GA: Behavioral Science Associates.

Neidig, P. H., & Friedman, D. H. (1984). *Spouse abuse: A treatment program for couples.* Champaign, IL: Research Press.

O'Keefe, N., Brockopp, K., & Chew, E. (1986). Teen dating violence. *Social Work, 31,* 465–468.

O'Leary, K. D. (1993). Through a psychological lens: Personality traits, personality disorders, and levels of violence. In R. J. Gelles & D. R. Loseke (Eds.), *Current controversies on family violence*. Newbury Park, CA: Sage.

O'Leary, K. D. (1999). Developmental and affective issues in assessing and treating partner aggression. *Clinical Psychology: Science and Practice, 6,* 400–414.

O'Leary, K. D., Barling, J., Arias, I., Rosenbaum, A., Malone, J., & Tyree, A. (1989). Prevalence and stability of physical aggression between spouses. *Journal of Consulting and Clinical Psychology, 57,* 263–268.

Oriel, K. A., & Fleming, M. F. (1998). Screening men for partner violence in a primary care setting: A new strategy for detecting domestic violence. *Journal of Family Practice, 46,* 493–498.

Pan, H. S., Neidig, P. H., & O'Leary, K. D. (1994). Predicting mild to severe husband-to-wife physical aggression. *Journal of Consulting and Clinical Psychology, 62,* 975–981.

Perez, P. J., & Rasmussen, K. (1997). An ounce of prevention: A model for working with couples at risk for battering. *Contemporary Family Therapy: An International Journal, 19,* 229–251.

Raine, A. (1993). *The psychopathology of crime: Criminal behavior as a clinical disorder.* San Diego, CA: Academic Press.

Randall, T. (1990). Domestic violence intervention calls for more than treating injuries. *Journal of the American Medical Association, 264,* 939–940.

Riggs, D. S., O'Leary, K. D., & Breslin, F. C. (1990). Multiple correlates of physical aggression in dating couples. *Journal of Interpersonal Violence, 5,* 61–73.

Rogge, M. R., & Bradbury, T. N. (1999). Recent advances in the prediction of marital outcomes. In R. Berger & M. Hannah (Eds.), *Preventive approaches in couples therapy* (pp. 331–360). Philadelphia: Brunner/Mazel.

Silliman, B., & Schumm, W. R. (1999). Improving practice in marriage preparation. *Journal of Sex and Marital Therapy, 25,* 25–43.

Silliman, B., Stanley, S. M., Coffin, W., Markman, H. J., & Jordan, P. L. (2002). Preventive interventions for couples. In H. A. Liddle, D. A. Santisteban, R. F. Levant, & J. H. Bray (Eds.), *Family psychology: Science-based interventions* (pp. 123–146). Washington, DC: American Psychological Association.

Stark, E., & Flitcraft, A. (1987). Personal power and institutional victimization: Treating the dual trauma of woman battering. In F. Ochberg (Ed.), *Post traumatic therapy* (pp. 115–151). New York: Brunner/Mazel.

Steiner, Y. (1999). Psychology and domestic violence around the world. *American Psychologist, 54,* 21–29.

Stets, J. E., & Straus, M. A. (1990). Gender differences in reporting marital violence and its medical and psychological consequences. In M. A. Straus & R. J. Gelles (Eds.), *Physical violence in American families: Risk factors and adaptations to violence in 8,145 families* (pp. 151–165). New Brunswick, NJ: Transaction.

Stith, S. M., Crossman, R. K., & Bischof, G. P. (1991). Alcoholism and marital violence: A comparative study of men in alcohol treatment programs and batterer treatment programs. *Alcoholism Treatment Quarterly, 8,* 3–20.

Straus, M. A. (1980). Sexual inequality and wife beating. In M. A. Straus & G. T. Hotaling (Eds.), *The social causes of husband–wife violence*. Minneapolis: University of Minnesota Press.

Straus, M. A., & Gelles, R. J. (1986). Societal changes in family violence from 1975 to 1985 as revealed by two national surveys. *Journal of Marriage and the Family, 48*, 465–479.

Straus, M. A., & Gelles, R. J. (1990). *Physical violence in American families*. New Brunswick, NJ: Transaction Books.

Straus, M. A., Gelles, R. J., & Steinmetz, S. K. (1980). *Behind closed doors: Violence in the American family*. Newbury Park: Sage.

Suitor, J., Pillemer, K., & Straus, M. A. (1990). Marital violence in a life course perspective. In M. A. Straus & R. J. Gelles (Eds.), *Physical violence in American families: Risk factors and adaptations to violence in 8,145 families* (pp. 305–317). New Brunswick, NJ: Transaction.

Williams, L. M., Riley, L. A., Risch, G. S., & Van Dyke, D. T. (1999). An empirical approach to designing marriage preparation programs. *The American Journal of Family Therapy*.

Wilson, J. Q., & Hernstein, R. J. (1985). *Crime and human nature*. New York: Simon & Schuster.

Yllo, K., & Straus, M. A. (1981). Interpersonal violence among married and cohabiting couples. *Family Relations, 30*, 339–347.

9

VIOLENCE AND THE ELDERLY POPULATION: ISSUES FOR PREVENTION

DEBORAH HENDERSON, JEFFREY A. BUCHANAN,
AND JANE E. FISHER

Mistreatment of elderly people is not a new problem. Since the introduction of the phrase *granny battering* in Baker's (1975) article in *Modern Geriatrics*, however, elder abuse has been conceptualized in a variety of ways. Once viewed as an issue associated with aging, elder abuse is now viewed as an issue of family violence and a crime.

The incidence of elder abuse is unclear due to differing definitions and other barriers to identification such as isolation of victims and reluctance among various professionals to report abuse. It is estimated, however, that between 4% and 6% of the elderly population has been or is currently being abused (Ansello, 1996). This figure is alarming when one considers that nearly a quarter of the population was older than age 65 in 2000 (McDonald & Abrahams, 1990). Considering such estimates, it is clear that mental health professionals must begin to understand why abuse in this population is occurring so that we may take steps to prevent it. This is not an easy task, however, given the lack of consensus as to what constitutes elder abuse.

Most definitions of elder abuse include the following categories of mistreatment: physical abuse, psychological or verbal abuse, financial abuse or exploitation, and neglect. Although there tends to be general agreement regarding these broad categories, there is much less agreement regarding what kinds of behaviors should be included within each category. In general, however, it can be stated that *physical abuse* of an elderly person includes such acts as striking, pushing, or otherwise causing physical harm; *psychological or verbal abuse* includes such acts as threatening the elderly person, humiliating him or her, enforcing isolation, or repeated name calling; *financial abuse or exploitation* includes such acts as misusing the elderly person's money or taking control of possessions or property without permission or rights to do so; *neglect* of an elderly person includes such acts as refusing medical assistance, food, or required medications; failing to provide adequate care such as bathing; or (in the case of self-neglect) failing to perform adequate daily care activities such as grooming or eating (Penhale, 1993; Wolf, 1996).

Lack of consensus in defining elder abuse has been problematic in several ways, including creating confusion in discriminating between what is "normal" family conflict and what is abuse, difficulties in comparing findings across studies regarding possible causes or consequences of abuse, difficulties in determining what an effective course of treatment for the abused victim or the abuser should include, and difficulties in communicating research findings to the public. It is beyond the scope of this chapter to resolve these difficulties, however.

We acknowledge that the current state of research and policy in the area of elder abuse is less than ideal; in this chapter we attempt to summarize what we do know about this problem. Specifically, we discuss popular theoretical explanations for the causes of elder abuse, describe the characteristics that tend to be associated with an increased probability of abuse, identify some of the barriers to identification, and describe some effective prevention strategies.

In this chapter we discuss elder abuse within a context of family violence. Although there is likely considerable disagreement as to what constitutes a violent act (i.e., violence could denote an act involving physical force alone or could imply the violation of one's rights), we limit our discussion to the areas of physical mistreatment and psychological or verbal mistreatment for two reasons. First, there is greater consensus regarding whether physical and psychological mistreatment ought to be considered abusive than there is regarding either self-neglect or other neglect and financial exploitation. Second, it has been suggested that physical mistreatment and psychological or verbal mistreatment may be more functionally similar to each other than they are to other forms of elder mistreatment (Wolf, 1996; Wolf & Pillemer, 1989). If this is indeed the case, then it is reasonable to discuss issues related to these two areas together and separately from issues related to financial abuse and neglect.

THEORETICAL EXPLANATIONS FOR ELDER ABUSE

Theoretical models are important for several reasons. At a minimum, they allow for focusing efforts on identifying causal variables. Identifying these causal pathways is important because it allows for the generation of strategies for intervention or prevention (Haynes, 1992). A sound theoretical model, however, will do more than this; it will make predictions that can be tested empirically. Unfortunately, theory building has encountered many obstacles in the field of elder abuse research. Among these obstacles are the differing definitions of elder abuse, the inability to randomly assign research participants (i.e., elder victims and abusers) to groups for testing, findings that are incomparable across studies because of different criteria for what constitutes abuse and different outcome measures, and the covert nature of elder abuse.

For these and other reasons (e.g., the likelihood that abuse arises from multiple causal pathways), the causes and effects of elder abuse have not been adequately studied. Nevertheless, from a review of the literature it is clear that a handful of theories predominate. These are briefly reviewed here.

Transgenerational Violence

The theory of transgenerational violence holds that abuse is a learned behavior and that victims of child abuse are themselves more likely to become abusers than are individuals who were not victims (Kosberg, 1988; Janz, 1990). This increased likelihood has been termed the *cycle of violence*. According to this theory, perpetrators have learned that behaving aggressively is an effective or acceptable way to respond to frustrating situations. Although there are some data to support this theory with regard to spousal abuse (Hotaling & Sugarman, 1990) and child abuse (Straus, Gelles, & Steinmetz, 1980), there are as yet no convincing data that would support the extension of the transgenerational violence theory to elder abuse (Biggs, Kingston, & Phillipson, 1995).

Social Exchange Theory

Social exchange theory assumes that social interactions involve the exchange of rewards and punishments (Finkelhor, 1983; Phillips, 1989). According to this theory, rewards are achieved by receiving resources (e.g., money, support), services, or positive sentiments, whereas punishments include the receipt of negative sentiments or the withdrawal or loss of resources. This theory suggests that, when relationships are unbalanced with regard to the exchange of rewards and punishments (i.e., when one person delivers more rewards than he or she receives in return), an imbalance of power occurs that leads to abusive behavior. Interestingly, the social exchange theory predicts that abuse will occur regardless of the direction in which the imbalance occurs; that is, either the elderly victim or the caregiver may be in the "powerless" position. This theory has received support from the descriptive literature, which clearly has shown that dependency of the abuser on the victim is a risk factor for elder abuse (Wolf, Strugnell, & Godkin, 1982).

Excessive Demands

The excessive demands or "exhausted caregiver" theory proposes that the stress of providing care to an elderly person increases the risk that the caregiver will behave abusively (Curry & Stone, 1995). Although some critics claim that this theory relieves the perpetrator of accountability (Pillemer & Finkelhor, 1989; Tomita, 1990), others claim that excess stress does in fact occur in caregivers of elderly people and, therefore, prevention efforts should be focused on relieving this stress for the benefit of the elderly victim (Eastman, 1984; Grafstrom, Nordberg, & Winblad, 1992). This theory has become quite popular among mental health practitioners and the public, possibly because it lends itself so easily to intervention strategies. Not coincidentally, many services (e.g., Meals on Wheels, home care) supported by various governmental funding agencies are directed at decreasing the burden of caring for an elderly person.

External Stress

The external stress theory suggests that individuals who are experiencing excess stress not directly related to caregiving may be more likely to abuse an elderly care recipient than individuals who are not experiencing these external pressures (Block & Sinnot, 1979; Hudson, 1986). External stressors that may contribute to the probability of engaging in abuse behavior for these caregivers include job stress, marital stress, and financial pressures. Like the excessive demand theory, the external stress theory appears to shift accountability away from the perpetrator. However, it also suggests some interesting intervention strategies—job training, marital counseling, and stress management training to name a few. Given that elder abuse is likely caused by a multitude of factors, a theory that suggests such novel intervention approaches may be well worth investigating further.

Ageism

Ageism refers to attitudes toward elderly people that are characterized by a lack of valuing. Such prejudicial attitudes, it has been suggested, may lead to abusive behavior, as the needs or rights of elderly people are seen as less important than the needs or rights of other people, particularly the caregiver (Fulmer, 1989). In Western culture, in particular, elderly people tend to be regarded with less respect than younger people, perhaps because they are no longer viewed as "carrying their own weight" in a culture that is built around individual achievement. Taking care of an elderly relative in this climate may be viewed more with resentment than with tenderness, thus making abuse a more likely occurrence.

RISK FACTORS ASSOCIATED WITH ELDER ABUSE

Because of the necessarily correlational nature of studies on elder abuse, risk factors (rather than causal factors) for elder abuse are the focus of much attention. Risk factors include those characteristics of the victim, the perpetrator, or the environment that, when present, increase the probability that elder abuse will occur. The number of risk factors that have been associated with elder abuse is large, but most risk factors assume that there is some type of caregiving arrangement in place. Identifying the presence of these risk factors is critical if prevention or intervention is to be initiated. We identify some of the most common risk factors for elder abuse here. For a more comprehensive review, please see Johnson (1991) and Kosberg (1988).

Risk Factors for the Victim

Following are summaries of some of the most common risk factors for elder abuse victims.

Gender

Until fairly recently, it was accepted that most victims of elder abuse were women (O'Malley, 1987; Wolf, Strugnell, & Godkin, 1982). One explanation given for this gender factor was that there are proportionately more elderly women than there are elderly men, and therefore it is more likely that an abused elderly person would be female. Another possible explanation was that women tend to be physically weaker and more passive, thus leaving them more vulnerable to physical mistreatment. However, Tatara (1993) has reported that there in fact are more male than female victims and suggested that it is possible men are being "paid back" for previous abuses that they themselves inflicted, or that they are more likely to make inappropriate choices (e.g., gambling or drinking) that affect their ability to interact effectively with their caregivers. Although it is unclear whether men or women are more likely to be abused, it is clear that both men and women are abused and that both should be considered potential victims of elder abuse.

Age

As elderly people age, the probability that they will be abused increases (Whittaker, 1993). Age is associated with more health problems and therefore greater impairment, which may make the elderly person more reliant on and therefore more vulnerable to the abuser (who may be experiencing excessive stress). It has been clearly documented that the risk of abuse increases with physical or mental impairment (Block & Sinnot, 1979). This increase is especially the case for individuals with a diagnosis of dementia, who tend to exhibit aggressive behaviors during caregiving tasks with some frequency (O'Malley, Everitt, O'Malley, & Campion, 1983). Caregivers may not understand this behavior as being a consequence of a medical condition and instead personalize the behavior, viewing it as uncooperativeness or retaliatory in nature (Garcia & Kosberg, 1993; Kosberg & Cairl, 1986). Alternatively, some caregivers state that, even though they do understand that the elderly person's behavior is caused by an impairment and is not intentional, they still justify their own abusive behavior as resulting from anger toward the elderly person's behavior (Garcia & Kosberg, 1993).

Substance Abuse

Elderly people who abuse substances are at greater risk for being abused than those who do not (Kosberg, 1988). This may be because the elderly substance abuser is more likely to live in a situation that is less stable (e.g., financially, emotionally) than nonabusers, or perhaps because he or she may be less aware that the caregiving being received is inadequate or harmful. Other possibilities include provocative behavior on the part of the elderly individual; very often, individuals addicted to drugs or alcohol behave in erratic, insensitive, or otherwise ineffective ways. It is possible that such behavior, directed toward a caregiver, may function to increase the probability of abusive behavior, along with other relevant factors.

Psychological Problems

Psychological or emotional factors that have been identified as risk factors for abuse include depression, anxiety, a tendency to blame oneself for problems, a tendency to excuse the behavior of family members, and apathy. Individuals possessing these characteristics may be likely to deny or take the blame for abuse, fail to take action to protect themselves from abuse, or isolate themselves from others; isolation itself a risk factor for abuse. That is, elderly people who are isolated from social contact are in a position that limits the possibility that an abusive situation will be identified as such by individuals outside of the system (Grafstrom, Nordberg, & Winblad, 1992).

Risk Factors for the Perpetrator

Perpetrators of elder abuse are typically younger than age 60 and are living with or close to the elderly victim in a caregiving role (Quinn & Tomita, 1986). Abusers tend more often to be female than male, as caregiving tends to fall to the daughters of elderly people rather than to their sons.

Psychological Problems

Although psychopathology has been identified as a risk factor associated with elder abuse, it has not been shown that any particular diagnoses make a person more likely to engage in abusive behavior (Tomita, 1990). However, it has been suggested (Kosberg, 1988) that psychological problems may make it more difficult for caregivers to interact effectively with elderly care recipients; that is, a caregiver may have difficulty controlling anger or frustration and take these feelings out on the elderly victim. It is also possible that caregivers experiencing psychological problems may have unrealistic expectations with regard to the elderly person's abilities and the caregiving situation.

Substance Abuse

Like psychological problems, substance abuse has been documented as a risk factor that interferes with the ability to regulate one's behavior toward an elderly care recipient. Indeed, substance abuse is one of the better documented risk factors (Fulmer, 1989; Godkin, Wolf, & Pillemer, 1989; O'Malley, Segel, & Perez, 1979; Pillemer & Wolf, 1989). The increased risk associated with substance abuse may be caused by the cost of maintaining an alcohol or drug habit; that is, this cost may be an additional stressor. In addition, servicing this habit may take priority over providing for the needs of the elderly victim. Certainly, alcohol or drug use may impair judgment and lessen inhibitions, and this may result in increased incidences of abuse, intentional or not.

Inadequate Caregiving Skills

Caregivers tend most often to be family members of the elderly care recipient. As such, they tend to lack formal training in caregiving skills, an issue that can be particularly problematic when the care recipient is experiencing either physical or mental impairment or exhibits problem behavior such as aggressiveness (common in patients with dementia). Lacking these skills, caregivers may misinterpret the elderly person's behavior as being retaliatory or stubborn and may become angry or frustrated. These care-givers are unlikely to know the most effective way to gain control over the care recipient's behavior and may resort to aggressive means of gaining this control.

Stress

Caregivers who are experiencing excess stress, either from external sources or from the caregiving itself, are at greater risk for engaging in abusive behavior than those who are able to manage their stress effectively (Brody, 1985; Hudson, 1986). Unfortunately, those family members placed in the role of caregiver for an elderly relative often experience this caregiving task as an additional burden to an already stressful life; occupational stress, parenting, marital issues, health problems, and financial pressures are some of the other stressors that caregivers may be experiencing. For example, Wolf and Pillemer (1989) found that 34% of a sample of caregivers in abuse cases reported long-term financial problems, 24% reported a recent financial diffi-culty, 32% reported a recent change in living arrangements, 26% reported a long-term medical complaint, 24% reported a recent medical complaint, and 15% reported a recent divorce. Also, the more dependent the care recipient is in terms of physical, emotional, and financial needs, the more stressful the caregiving role becomes (Ansello, King, & Taler, 1986).

One stressor that should not be ignored is the possibility that care-givers may themselves be an elderly person and experiencing dementia or a cognitive impairment. Giordano and Giordano (1983), Steinmetz (1983), and Ryden (1988) have documented that aggressive behavior on the parts of both the caregiver and the care recipient are associated with cognitive impairments.

Dependence

Dependence, typically financial, of the caregiver on the care recipient has been associated with an increased probability of physical and psychologi-cal abuse (Pillemer, 1985; Wolf & Pillemer, 1989). It has been generally assumed that it is the dependency of the victim, not the abuser, that deter-mines the vulnerability of the older person to abuse. However, it seems that this is more often true in cases of neglect, in which caregiving is seen as an unwanted obligation. When caregivers depend on an elderly care recipient for financial or emotional support, they tend to report more feelings of anger, impotence, and frustration (Curry & Stone, 1995). These feelings may lead to an increased probability of abuse.

Contextual Risk Factors

Certain environments contribute more to the probability of elder abuse than others. Although these environmental, or contextual, factors do not exist separately from risk factors associated with the victim and the abuser, it is worthwhile to note them to aid in identifying which situations are more likely to lead to elder abuse. Caregiving environments that are more likely to lead to an abusive relationship are those that include financial difficulties, a history of family violence or family conflict, a scarcity of social support, and overcrowded living arrangements.

Financial Difficulties

Caregiving very often involves an increase in financial burden; caring for an elderly person who may require expensive medications or who has other special needs (such as constant supervision) can place pressure on an already strained situation. This is especially true when the caregiver has children in the household, a low-paying job, or both. In this situation, both the caregiver and the care recipient (and other members of the household) may become frustrated, anxious, depressed, and resentful. To make matters worse, caregiving for an elderly person is a task that typically becomes more demanding over time, both financially and in terms of other resources. Therefore, feelings of hopelessness may arise as caregivers and care recipients alike see no end in sight. Such feelings on the part of either or both person may result in provocative or abusive behavior.

Family Conflict

Family conflict, current or past, seems to lead to an increased probability of violence toward elderly people. In families in which there is a history of harsh discipline or child abuse, adult children may carry over their childhood experiences into the caregiving situation. That is, they may "correct" the elderly care recipient aggressively or "pay back" the elderly person by treating him or her harshly. It is also the case that family conflicts that exist between children and their parents do not disappear simply because one (or both) of them are now elderly (Blenkner, 1965). Old conflicts (e.g., power struggles, personality differences) are likely to show up in the caregiving relationship, albeit with the positions of power often reversed. Family members who have not learned to communicate effectively with one another are likely to continue to communicate ineffectively, perhaps violently.

Inadequate Social Support

The support of family, friends, and others (e.g., a community service agency) can be of great importance in decreasing the burden of caregiving and the stress of coping with a multitude of pressures (Pillemer, 1986). This is true whether the support is directed toward the caregiver, the care recipient, or both. When caregivers have no one to turn to, they experience a decrease in the frequency with which they engage in pleasant activities; an increase in the stress associated with caregiving; a decrease in control over how their time is structured; a decrease in privacy; an increase in financial burden; and an increase in depression, anger, and related symptoms. When the care recipient is isolated from social support, he or she will typically experience more depression and more health problems, leading to an increased demand on the caregiver (Gottlieb, 1991), and there is a lesser probability that abuse will be identified.

Overcrowded Living Arrangements

Overcrowded living arrangements are associated with conflict in many settings (Kosberg, 1988; Pillemer, 1985). In the caregiving setting, this situation often translates into tension and hostility by the caregiver, some of which is likely to be directed toward the elderly person. When caregivers experience a lack of privacy and a sense of "invasion," they are more likely to blame the elderly person verbally and possibly to punish them physically. The elderly victim in this situation may experience a great deal of stress and anxiety; often, elderly people are reluctant to move in with their relatives for this reason or because they, too, experience the close living quarters as invasive.

BARRIERS TO IDENTIFICATION AND REPORTING

Despite the available information about the risk factors for elder abuse, many barriers exist to identifying an abusive situation and, once it has been identified, to reporting the abuse to the appropriate agency. Therefore, it is not enough simply to know what the risk factors are; it is necessary to identify the barriers to identification and reporting so that solutions may be developed and implemented. These barriers can be grouped into three broad categories: societal or cultural barriers, victim barriers, and clinician barriers.

Societal or Cultural Barriers

The privacy of family life is held as a high priority in the United States and other countries. When conflict arises within a family, it is often considered a private matter best handled within the context of the family unit itself; outside interference is commonly viewed with repugnance. Family members are reluctant to seek outside assistance, and observers (e.g., the family physician, friends of the family) are reluctant to intrude. In addition, the family is oftentimes viewed by society as it would exist in its ideal form; that is, as a nurturing and safe environment. Unfortunately, this is too often not the case, and adhering to this view may lead observers to interpret evidence of abuse as evidence of some other event (e.g., accidents or natural results of aging) or to overlook it entirely. Victims and caregivers themselves may fail to seek assistance even when they believe that it might be helpful because doing so would be an admission that the family is not as harmonious as it "should be." That is, seeking assistance would be an admission of failure. Compounding this problem is the lack of clarity regarding what ought to be considered abuse and what ought to be considered normal family conflict (Browne, 1989). Without benchmarks, observers may be more willing to err on the side of family privacy.

Ageism, too, is a barrier to the identification of an abusive situation. As the rights of elderly people are considered less important than the rights of other, "more productive," members of society, the value placed on their treatment decreases. They may be viewed as receiving the quality of treatment they deserve, which is based on their ability to contribute to society or the family system. As Fulmer (1989) noted, ageist attitudes might even lead observers to believe that the victim deserved the abuse.

Ageist attitudes may even be reflected in public policy. Compared to child abuse, elder abuse receives far less funding from the government. For example, on the average each state spends approximately $45.00 per child resident for child protective services, as compared with $3.80 per elderly resident for elder protective services. In addition, despite increases in reported elder abuse, funding for elder abuse decreased from 6.6% of state budgets in 1981 to 4.0% in 1989 (Goldstein, 1996).

Victim Barriers

Elderly people tend to be isolated to a greater degree than are younger, more active members of society. This isolation is one of the crucial barriers to detection of elder abuse (Wolf & Pillemer, 1989). Isolation may be a consequence of poor health, lack of transportation, lack of a social network, or a preference on the part of the elderly person or may be imposed on the elderly person by his or her caregiver. Regardless of the causes for isolation, however, the isolated elderly person has far fewer opportunities either to seek help or to be identified as in need of help. This situation is of concern because, as Wolf and Pillemer have suggested, victims of elder abuse tend to be more isolated than are nonvictims.

One of the most common and frustrating barriers to the detection and reporting of elder abuse is the reluctance of the victim to acknowledge the abuse. There are several reasons for this reluctance, including victims' fears of reprisal from their abuser if they reveal that abuse has occurred. Alternatively, victims may fear that their abuser (usually a son or daughter) will get into trouble, and so they will try to avoid this, even at the risk of their own lives. Victims may fear that if they report the abuse they will be sent to a nursing home or other environment that they perceive as worse than their current environment, or fear that they will get into trouble (or will not be helped) because they contributed to an incident that resulted in the abuse.

Elderly victims are often embarrassed of their situation; that is, embarrassed that they were unable to control the situation or that they have raised children who could behave in such a manner or who could possibly not love them. The embarrassment may extend to the belief that they or their family will lose social status if the abuse is revealed. Victims may even take the blame for their abuser's behavior, reasoning that if they had been a better parent the abuse would not have occurred (Steinmetz, 1983).

Victims may also be reluctant to report abuse if their abuser is pleading with them or threatening them not to (e.g., "If you loved me, you wouldn't do it," or "If you do it, I will leave, and you won't be able to take care of yourself"). Victims may also think that they will not be believed if they tell someone that they are being abused; they may also be uncertain whether what is being done to them could really be called "abuse." Even if they are certain that they have been abused, they may not know whom to call or to trust or may believe that nothing can be done to help them.

Clinician Barriers

Health care professionals such as physicians, nurses, and social workers frequently fail to identify symptoms of elder abuse and, when they do, they often fail to report it (Fulmer, 1989; O'Brien & Piper, 1991). The reasons for this are varied and numerous, despite the fact that, as Kapp (1995) stated, "Failure to diagnose mistreatment may constitute negligence forming the basis for malpractice liability, where prudent similar professionals in like circumstances would have made the diagnosis and taken appropriate management steps that would have prevented subsequent harm" (p. 369).

Physicians may lack the training needed to accurately identify signs of abuse even when they are readily apparent. This task becomes even more difficult when the signs are not so readily apparent (as in the case of psychological abuse or when a physical injury is explained as resulting from an accidental fall). It is also usually the case that physicians are not looking for signs of abuse and therefore may not notice them if they are not salient; this, coupled with the fact that the clinical presentation of elder abuse victims varies widely, makes the task a complicated one.

Physicians are also typically under a great deal of pressure to perform examinations quickly and may not be willing to take the time that a thorough assessment of potential elder abuse would require; also, such extended office visits are not reimbursed at a higher rate by Medicare or Medicaid (O'Brien, 1996). In addition, physicians prefer to be sure about their diagnoses and may be unwilling to label something as "abusive" unless they are certain that this is in fact the case. This preference for certainty, together with the victim's reluctance to acknowledge abuse, may result in undetected and unreported abuse (O'Brien & Piper, 1991). It also may not be clear if the elderly person is the victim or the perpetrator of abuse, thus contributing more uncertainty to an already uncertain situation.

When physicians do detect abuse, it is not uncommon for that abuse to go unreported (O'Brien, 1996). Often, physicians do not know the mandatory reporting laws in their state (Penhale, 1993). These laws state, generally, that if a physician has a reasonable suspicion that elder abuse, neglect, or financial exploitation has occurred or is occurring, he or she must report it to the appropriate agency, usually the adult protective services (APS) agency for that state or the local police department. Far more often, however, physicians choose not to report despite this knowledge (O'Brien, 1996). They may believe that reporting the abuse to the appropriate agency (e.g., the APS agency in that state) may result in more harm than good. For instance, physicians may be skeptical about the availability of effective interventions and resources and fear that social services will remove the victim to an environment that is not suitable or that the victim does not want. They may fear that by reporting abuse against the wishes of the victim they will be jeopardizing a doctor–patient relationship, which they view as a valuable resource for the elderly victim, or that the problem could be better handled by the family or by way of a collaboration of the family members with the physician. It may also be the case that physicians do not believe that the victim's symptoms are serious enough to warrant a report of abuse, even though they know that technically it meets the criteria for abuse.

Another potential reason for physicians not reporting elder abuse is based on the philosophical stance that to override the victim's wishes by doing so is an affront to that person's autonomy. Individuals who take this stance claim, in essence, that to do so is an example of ageism (i.e., using age as a reason for ignoring a person's right to make his or her own choices; Kapp, 1995).

INTERVENTION STRATEGIES

Despite formidable barriers to the detection of elder abuse, it is imperative that efforts be made to prevent and to effectively intervene in cases of actual or potential elder abuse. Efforts to reduce elder abuse will be most successful when primary, secondary, and tertiary intervention strategies are combined and implemented. *Primary intervention strategies* focus on prevention; that is, they reduce the probability that elder abuse will occur by addressing the risk factors that are associated with abuse. Ideally, primary intervention strategies will prevent the initial abusive incident from occurring. *Secondary intervention strategies* focus on identifying abuse when it has occurred and treating the immediate consequences of abuse, such as physical injuries and emotional trauma. *Tertiary intervention strategies* focus on preventing further abuse by addressing those factors that led up to or maintain the abusive situation. Each strategy is discussed here. For a list of useful resources, see Appendix A.

Primary Intervention Strategies

Perhaps the most common primary intervention strategy is education (Wiehe, 1998). Education efforts may be directed toward the general public, health care personnel or other professionals, caregivers, family members, or the elderly victim. By way of public service announcements, advertisements, workshops, published research findings, and other types of awareness-boosting strategies, individuals may learn what elder abuse is and its risk factors and how to report potentially abusive situations. More important, individuals may be educated about the frequency of elder abuse and steps that they can take to prevent a situation from becoming abusive. One example of such an educational program presented information using training videos, expert speakers, group exercises, and information packets that contained information about community resources and readings on elder abuse (Weiner, 1991).

An important role that public education can play is to inform caregivers that they are not alone and that it is not unusual for people in their position to feel overwhelmed. Normalizing the caregiver experience and encouraging them to seek support in any of a number of forms may result in increased use of available resources and a decrease in the number and severity of risk factors. It is important that educational efforts avoid tactics that tend to make caregivers feel guilty, defensive, or patronized, as this will likely result in a caregiver's unwillingness to identify himself or herself as being at risk for abusing.

Educating elderly people about abuse and the resources available for prevention may make them more likely to seek assistance, particularly if this assistance holds the potential for helping their family members who are also the potential abusers. It is also important that education efforts validate elderly people's fears and address the issues of shame and self-blame by reminding them that abuse is in fact not uncommon and that "good" parenting is not a guarantee against abuse.

By educating health care professionals—particularly primary care physicians—about the risk factors associated with elder abuse, the chances that a professional will initiate a discussion with an elderly person, caregiver, or both about the potential for abuse and the resources that are available increase. Health care professionals must, of course, be knowledgeable as to how to conduct such a conversation in a sensitive manner that addresses patient and caregiver concerns and preserves their dignity.

In addition to education, important prevention strategies include providing services that decrease the dependency of the caregiver on the potential victim—and vice versa—and that directly address some of the risk factors for elder abuse, such as substance abuse, stress, or inadequate caregiving skills. Services that may decrease the dependency of caregivers on elderly care recipients may include job training skills or child day care services, as well as psychological treatment targeted at increasing social support, interpersonal skills, or other relevant domains that are interfering with normal adult functioning. Services that may decrease the dependency of elderly people on caregivers may include adult day care services, programs such as Meals on Wheels, home health care services, assistance with personal finances and other household tasks such as shopping and housecleaning, and psychological treatment to address problems (e.g., depression, social isolation) that may make it more difficult for an elderly person to engage in self-care or to find support from someone other than the caregiver.

Alternative services that directly address other risk factors for elder abuse include stress and anger management workshops, caregiver skills training, substance abuse treatment programs, and psychological treatment (e.g., to provide training in communication or problem solving or to address problems that interfere with the delivery of appropriate care such as mental illness and impulsivity). Two examples of service programs that can be offered to caregivers were created by Gallagher-Thompson (1994): "Coping With the Blues" and "Coping With Frustration" were designed to treat caregiver depression and anger. Both of these workshops are group treatment protocols, which maximize cost-effectiveness and efficiency while providing social interaction and support opportunities for caregivers. The "Coping With the Blues" workshop focuses on integrating pleasant events into caregivers' daily routines, with an emphasis on developing plans to overcome barriers to engaging in these activities. The "Coping With Frustration" workshop is designed to teach caregivers relaxation skills, coping skills to use when angry, assertiveness skills, and appropriate ways to express anger and frustration.

In addition to these group approaches, Zarit and Edwards (1999) have shown that caregivers can also benefit from as few as 5–10 individual psychotherapy sessions. This finding is consistent with that found in a meta-analysis of intervention studies conducted by Knight and colleagues (Knight, Lutzky, & Macofsky-Urban, 1993). Family counseling has also been found to be helpful for decreasing caregiver stress and reducing family conflict, as have support groups (Zarit & Edwards, 1999).

Secondary Intervention Strategies

Once the initial abusive incident has occurred, secondary intervention strategies are implemented. The goals of secondary intervention strategies are to treat the victim quickly and to limit the negative consequences of abuse as much as possible. Strategies for secondary intervention include accurate detection and assessment techniques, reporting of abusive incidents, delivering medical treatment when necessary, crisis management to ensure a safe environment for the victim, and brief psychological interventions designed to return the victim to the level of functioning that existed prior to the abuse.

Among the most crucial aspects of secondary intervention are the detection and assessment of the indicators of elder abuse. Without question, the most important individual involved in identifying these signs and symptoms is the elderly person's primary care physician. Although other individuals—such as neighbors or family friends—can also play a key role in detecting elder abuse, it is the primary care physician who generally has the most access to the elderly person, who is likely to be trusted by the elderly person, and who is in a position to intervene immediately.

Given this position, it is unfortunate that many physicians are unfamiliar with the indicators of abuse or do not know how to skillfully assess the patient once abuse is suspected. Because many of the indicators of abuse can easily be mistaken for consequences of the normal aging process (e.g., bruises from falls), it is understandable that these abuse indicators are often overlooked or misinterpreted. Given the prevalence of elder abuse, however, it has been suggested (Pillemer & Finkelhor, 1988) that a standard screening process is warranted whenever an elderly person is examined by a physician. Such screening can be conducted quickly and during the course of a regular physical examination. The screening process need not be overly intrusive; the goal of the screening is simply to determine whether elder abuse is a possibility that should be further investigated. Within the screening process the physician would seek to determine the elderly person's living situation, available resources, and worries; if he or she is dependent on anyone to assist in caretaking or if anyone is dependent on him or her; who makes the elderly person's decisions, and so forth (O'Brien, 1996). By inquiring into the life of the elderly person in an unstructured, caring fashion, the physician will be able to determine if a more directed assessment is indicated. In addition, such inquiries are likely to make the patient feel that the physician cares for him or her, and this may increase the likelihood that a trusting relationship will be established.

If elder abuse is suspected, the physician (or other health care professional) must conduct a more directed assessment that is designed to obtain specific information about what kind of abuse may be occurring. Hwalek and Sengstock (1986) outlined a brief, 10-item assessment tool that asks questions such as "Has anyone tried to hurt or harm you?" "Has anyone confined you at home against your will?" and "Are you afraid of anyone in your home?" These authors suggested that "yes" answers to any of these questions should be explored in greater detail. To assist with this task, several protocols are available that the physician may use to conduct more thorough investigations of elder abuse, including the American Medical Association's (1992) diagnostic and treatment guidelines.

Knowing when and what to assess for with elderly patients is not the same as knowing how to conduct such assessments. Victims of elder abuse, as we stated earlier, tend to be ashamed or afraid to acknowledge that they are being or have been abused. Furthermore, it must be remembered that elderly people have a right to refuse treatment. Therefore, great care and sensitivity must be used in interviewing elderly patients when abuse is suspected. The interviewer should conduct the assessment in privacy and should treat the elderly person with respect; the interviewer should be patient and careful not to respond in a manner that is blaming, either of the victim or of the perpetrator, as this could interfere with the victim's willingness to continue; the patient should be assessed for cognitive impairment; the interview should be conducted in a nonthreatening manner; and the process of reporting abuse and subsequent actions should be explained. It is also a good idea to normalize the experience for the victim, so that he or she is not left feeling alone in his or her experience.

Once a physician or other professional has reason to suspect that elder abuse has occurred, he or she is mandated to report this abuse to an appropriate agency, such as local law enforcement or APS. In cases in which reporting is not mandated (i.e., the person who has detected abuse is not a mandated reporter), reporting is still a crucial element of secondary interventions. Unless a report is made, it is not likely that the elderly victim will receive the services that he or she needs. Earlier we stated that sometimes physicians choose not to report a case of elder abuse because they are not convinced that doing so will result in a beneficial outcome for the elderly victim. Perhaps one reason for this belief is that reporting physicians are not always informed about the outcome of their reporting. If physicians were informed that their reports resulted in positive outcomes for their patients, they may likely be more willing to report the abuse as mandated.

One remedy to this problem could be for APS agencies to establish a procedure for informing reporting physicians of the steps that have been taken to protect the elderly victim and to prevent further abuse and of the outcome of such treatment. Other steps to increase reporting of elder abuse include ensuring that physicians are aware of the reporting laws in their state, including what constitutes elder abuse.

Once a report of elder abuse has been made, it is typically the APS team that is responsible for crisis management. The goals of crisis management are to ensure a safe environment for the elderly person and to restore him or her to a level of functioning that existed prior to the abuse. Techniques used to achieve these goals include (at times) removal from the home of either the victim or the perpetrator and provision of services such as home health care and mental health services. At the level of secondary intervention, mental health services typically include brief treatment for trauma, anxiety, and stress that resulted from the abuse; often, psychotropic medications are prescribed in place of (or in addition to) psychological interventions. Reasons for this include cost containment, unavailability of appropriate or affordable psychological treatment, acceptability to the recipient of services, or all of these.

Tertiary Intervention Strategies

Once the initial crisis has been addressed, tertiary strategies are used to prevent further abuse. Tertiary strategies are designed to address those factors that contributed to the abuse or maintained the abusive situation. Examples of these factors were explicated in greater detail earlier and include depression, substance abuse, family conflict, and dependence. To effectively intervene in an abusive situation, the mental health professional must have knowledge of the variables contributing to and maintaining the abuse, including the potential skills deficits of the victim and the perpetrator, environmental factors such as financial distress, inadvertent reinforcement of abusive tactics, and so forth. The mental health professional must be cognizant that effective treatment often requires the collaboration of both the elderly victim and the perpetrator. As such, he or she must take steps to engage both in treatment, and this requires an understanding that few abuse cases are black and white in terms of who is to blame and who is right or wrong. It is more often the case that both the victim and the perpetrator need to alter their behavior to decrease the probability of abuse; "right" and "wrong" simply do not apply.

Once the initiating and maintaining variables have been identified, they must be targeted directly in treatment. In other words, if the skills deficits of the perpetrator are seen as contributing to the abuse, then supportive counseling is simply not enough; rather, the skills that are lacking must be taught. To assist mental health professionals in targeting specific behaviors and skills, treatment protocols exist that allow treatment to be delivered systematically, either individually or in groups. Protocols are available for both victims of abuse and their abusers, depending on the treatment targets (e.g., depression in the elderly population, posttraumatic stress, stress management, anger management).

Regardless of whether mental health professionals choose to deliver a manualized treatment versus some other form of treatment, a critical component of tertiary treatments that is designed to affect the future occurrence of abuse is follow-up assessment. By assessing the success of treatment (i.e., whether the targets addressed actually changed) and the occurrence or nonoccurrence of abuse, mental health professionals can determine whether more or different treatment is indicated or whether the treatment as delivered has been successful.

CONCLUSION AND FUTURE DIRECTIONS

Significant progress has been made in the past 3 decades in both acknowledging elder abuse as a social problem and understanding some of the possible causes. However, it is clear that much more needs to be done to address the needs of the thousands of elderly people who are being abused every year. Awareness of the frequency and types of abuse must be increased among both professionals and nonprofessionals. As with child abuse, both professionals and nonprofessionals must overcome the desire to avoid the issue simply because it is distasteful to us or because we do not know enough about how to effectively deal with it.

The need for further research in the field of elder abuse is clear. In particular, data is needed on the effectiveness of intervention strategies. Although many interventions currently are being implemented, it is difficult given methodological problems to determine if these interventions are effective, with whom, and even what it means to "be effective." To meaningfully compare intervention programs, researchers in this area also should consider adopting a definition of elder abuse that can be used for research, if not for legal, purposes. This would be useful not just when comparing intervention strategies but also in studies assessing the possible causes of elder abuse. Research in the area of elder abuse must be conducted with greater scientific rigor than it has been traditionally if researchers hope to present data convincing enough to affect public opinion and public policy.

The problem of elder abuse is not going away. On the contrary, with more and more adults approaching late adulthood, it is reasonable to assume that the problem is likely to increase in scope, if not in severity. To effectively address this complex social situation, researchers must address the problem as scientists committed to effecting change. Doing so will require skill and effort; however, the potential rewards are great.

APPENDIX A
SOME USEFUL RESOURCES ON ELDER ABUSE

Protocols

"Coping With the Blues" and "Coping With Frustration" protocols can be obtained by contacting

Dolores Gallagher-Thompson, PhD
Older Adult Center (Mail Code 182/MP) VA Palo Alto Care System
795 Willow Road
Menlo Park, CA 94025

"Ensuring an Abuse-Free Environment: A Learning Program for Nursing Home Staff" can be obtained by contacting

Coalition of Advocates for the Rights of the Infirm Elderly
1315 Walnut Street, Suite 900
Philadelphia, PA 19107

Web Sites

American Law Sources On-line, *www.lawsource.com/also/*
An on-line link to state laws.

Family Caregiver Alliance, *www.caregiver.org/index.html*
A national organization that provides resources to help caregivers of disabled or frail elderly people. Includes an on-line support group.

Findlaw, *www.findlaw.com/casecode/statehtml*
Another on-line resource for state laws.

Mental Health: National Technical Assistance Center for State Mental Health Planning, *www.nasmhpd.org/ntac/index.htm*
Provides technical assistance to state mental health organizations to help them better serve elderly people with mental illness.

National Aging Information Center, *www.aoa.dhhs.gov/naic*
Searchable database of issues related to aging.

National Center for Victims of Crime, *www.ncvc.org*
A resource for all types of crime victims, as well as a discussion forum for victims and professionals.

National Center on Elder Abuse, *www.gwjapan.com/NCEA/*
A rich resource for professionals, caregivers, victims, and others. Includes help in locating assistance in every state, publications, state laws, reporting issues, data, and links to other sites.

REFERENCES

American Medical Association. (1992). *Diagnostic and treatment guidelines on elder abuse and neglect.* Chicago: Author.

Ansello, E. F. (1996). Causes and theories. In L. A. Baumhover & S. C. Beall (Eds.), *Abuse, neglect and exploitation of older persons* (pp. 9–29). Baltimore, MD: Health Professions Press.

Ansello, E. F., King N. R., & Taler, G. (1986). The environmental press model: A theoretical framework for intervention in elder abuse. In K. A. Pillemer & R. S. Wolf (Eds.), *Elder abuse: Conflict in the family* (pp. 314–330). Dover, MA: Auburn House.

Baker, A. A. (1975). Granny battering. *Modern Geriatrics, 5*(8), 20–24.

Biggs, S., Kingston, P. A., & Phillipson, C. (1995). *Elder abuse perspectives.* Buckingham, UK: Open University Press.

Blenkner, M. (1965). Social work and family relationships in later life with some thoughts on filial maturity. In E. Shanas & G. Streib (Eds.), *Social structure and family generational relations* (pp. 46–59). Englewood Cliffs, NJ: Prentice-Hall.

Block, M. R., & Sinnot, J. D. (1979). *The battered elder syndrome: An exploratory study*. College Park: University of Maryland, Center on Aging.

Brody, E. (1985). Parent care as normative family stress. *Gerontologist, 25,* 19–29.

Browne, K. (1989). Family violence: Elder and spouse abuse. In K. Howells & C. R. Hollin (Eds.), *Clinical approaches to violence* (pp. 119–154). London: John Wiley and Sons.

Curry, L. C., & Stone, J. G. (1995). Understanding elder abuse: The social problem of the 1990s. *Journal of Clinical Geropsychology, 1*(2), 147–156.

Eastman, M. (1984). At worst just picking up the pieces. *Community Care, 20*(1), 20–22.

Finkelhor, D. (1983). Common features of family abuse. In D. Finkelhor, R. Gelles, G. Hotaling, & M. Strauss (Eds.), *The dark side of families: Current family violence research* (pp. 17–26). Beverly Hills, CA: Sage.

Fulmer, T. T. (1989). Mistreatment of elders: Assessment, diagnosis, and intervention. *Nursing Clinics of North America, 23*(3), 707–716.

Gallagher-Thompson, D. (1994). Clinical intervention strategies for distressed caregivers: Rationale and development of psychoeducational approaches. In E. Light, G. Niederehe, & B. D. Lebowotiz (Eds.), *Stress effects on family caregivers of Alzheimer's patients: Research and interventions* (pp. 260–277). New York: Springer.

Garcia, J. L., & Kosberg, J. I. (1993). Understanding anger: Implications for formal and informal caregivers. *Journal of Elder Abuse and Neglect, 4*(4), 87–99.

Giordano, N. H., & Giordano, J. A. (1983, November). *Family and individual characteristics of five types of elder abuse: Profiles and predictors*. Paper presented at the annual meeting of the Gerontological Society of America, San Francisco, CA.

Godkin, M. A., Wolf, R. S., & Pillemer, K. A. (1989). A case-comparison analysis of elder abuse and neglect. *International Journal of Aging and Human Development, 23*(3), 207–225.

Goldstein, M. Z. (1996). Elder maltreatment. In S. J. Kaplan (Ed.), *Family violence: A clinical and legal guide* (pp. 181–208). Washington, DC: American Psychiatric Press, Inc.

Gottlieb, B. H. (1991). Social support and family care of the elderly. *Canadian Journal on Aging, 10*(4), 359–375.

Grafstrom, M., Nordberg, A., & Winblad, B. (1992). Abuse is in the eye of the beholder. *Scandinavian Journal of Social Medicine, 21*(4), 247–255.

Haynes, S. N. (1992). *Models of causality in psychopathology: Toward dynamic, synthetic, and nonlinear models of behavior*. New York: Macmillan.

Hotaling, G. T., & Sugarman, D. B. (1990). Prevention of wife assault. In R. T. Ammerman & M. Hersen (Eds.), *Treatment of family violence* (pp. 180–197). New York: Wiley.

Hudson, M. F. (1986). Elder mistreatment: Current research. In K. A. Pillemer & R.

S. Wolf (Eds.), *Elder abuse: Conflict in the family* (pp. 125–166). Dover, MA: Auburn House.

Hwalek, M., & Sengstock, M. (1986). Assessing the probability of elder abuse: Toward the development of a clinical screening instrument. *Journal of Applied Gerontology, 5*(2), 153–173.

Kapp, M. B. (1995). Family caregiving for older persons in the home: Medical–legal implications. *Journal of Legal Medicine, 16*, 1–31.

Janz, M. (1990, September–October). Clues to elder abuse. *Geriatric Nursing*, 220–222.

Johnson, T. F. (1991). *Elder mistreatment: Deciding who is at risk*. Westport, CT: Greenwood Press.

Knight, B. G., Lutzky, S. M., & Macofsky-Urban, F. (1993). A meta-analytic review of interventions for caregiver distress: Recommendations for future research. *Gerontologist, 33*, 240–248.

Kosberg, J. I. (1988). Preventing elder abuse: Identification of high risk factors prior to placement decisions. *Gerontologist, 28*(1), 43–50.

Kosberg, J. I., & Cairl, R. E. (1986). The Cost of Care index: A case management tool for screening informal care providers. *Gerontologist, 26*, 273–278.

McDonald, A. J., & Abrahams, S. (1990). Social emergencies in the elderly. *Emergency Medicine Clinics of North America, 8*(2), 433–459.

O'Brien, J. G. (1996). Screening: A primary care physician's perspective. In L. A. Baumhover & S. C. Beall (Eds.), *Abuse, neglect and exploitation of older persons* (pp. 51–64). Baltimore, MD: Health Professions Press.

O'Brien, J. G., & Piper, M. (1991). Elder abuse. In M. Pathy (Ed.), *Principles and practice of geriatric medicine* (pp. 211–220). New York: Wiley.

O'Malley, H. C., Segel, H. D., & Perez, R. (1979). *Elder abuse in Massachusetts: Survey of professionals and paraprofessionals*. Boston: Legal Research and Services to the Elderly.

O'Malley, T. A. (1987). Abuse and neglect of the elderly: The wrong issue? *Pride Institute Journal of Long Term Health Care, 5*, 25–28.

O'Malley, T. A., Everitt, D. E., O'Malley, H. C., & Campion, E. W. (1983). Identifying and preventing family-mediated abuse and neglect of elderly persons. *Annals of Internal Medicine, 98*, 998–1005.

Penhale, B. (1993). The abuse of elderly people: Considerations for practice. *British Journal of Social Work, 23*, 95–112.

Phillips, L. R. (1989). Issues involved in identifying and intervening in elder abuse. In R. Finlinson & S. Ingman (Eds.), *Elder abuse: Practice and policy* (pp. 197–217). New York: Human Sciences Press.

Pillemer, K. A. (1985). The dangers of dependency: New findings on domestic violence of the elderly. *Social Problems, 33*, 146–158.

Pillemer, K. A. (1986). Risk factors in elder abuse: Results from a case control study. In K. A. Pillemer & R. S. Wolf (Eds.), *Elder abuse: Conflict in the family* (pp. 239–264). Dover, MA: Auburn House.

Pillemer, K. A., & Finkelhor, D. (1988). The prevalence of elder abuse: A random sample survey. *Gerontologist, 28,* 51–57.

Pillemer, K. A., & Wolf, R. S. (1989). *Helping elderly victims: The reality of elder abuse.* New York: Columbia University Press.

Quinn, M. J., & Tomita, S. K. (1986). *Elder abuse and neglect: Causes, diagnoses, and intervention strategies.* New York: Springer.

Ryden, M. (1988). Aggressive behavior in persons with dementia living in the community. *Alzheimer Disease and Associated Disorders, 2*(4), 342–355.

Steinmetz, S. K. (1983). Dependency, stress and violence between middle-aged caregivers and their elderly parents. In J. I. Kosberg (Ed.), *Abuse and maltreatment of the elderly: Causes and interventions* (pp. 134–149). Littleton, MA: John-Wright-PGS.

Straus, M., Gelles, R., & Steinmetz, S. (1980). *Behind closed doors: Violence in the American family.* New York: Doubleday.

Tatara, T. (1993). *Summaries of the statistical data on elder abuse in domestic settings for FY90 and FY91: A final report.* Washington, DC: National Aging Resource Center on Elder Abuse.

Tomita, S. K. (1990). The denial of elder mistreatment by victims and abusers: The application of neutralization theory. *Violence and Victims, 5*(3), 171–184.

Weiner, A. (1991). A community-based education model for identification and prevention of elder abuse. *Journal of Gerontological Social Work, 16,* 107–119.

Whittaker, T. (1993). Rethinking elder abuse: Towards an age and gender integrated theory of elder abuse. In P. Decalmer & F. Glendenning (Eds.), *The mistreatment of elderly people* (pp. 116–128). London: Sage.

Wiehe, V. R. (1998). *Understanding family violence: Treating and preventing partner, child, sibling, and elder abuse.* London: Sage.

Wolf, R. S. (1996). Elder abuse and family violence: Testimony presented before the U.S. Senate Special Committee on Aging. *Journal of Elder Abuse and Neglect, 8*(1), 81–96.

Wolf, R. S., & Pillemer, K. A. (1989). *Helping elder victims: The reality of elder abuse.* New York: Columbia University Press.

Wolf, R. S., Strugnell, E. P., & Godkin, M. A. (1982). *Preliminary findings from the model projects on elderly abuse.* Worcester: University of Massachusetts, Center on Aging.

Zarit, S. H., & Edwards, A. B. (1999). Family caregiving: Research and clinical intervention. In R. T. Woods (Ed.), *Psychological problems of ageing: Assessment, treatment, and care* (pp. 162–189). Chichester, UK: Wiley.

10

EVALUATING PREVENTION PROGRAMS: CHALLENGES AND BENEFITS OF MEASURING OUTCOMES

PAUL A. SCHEWE AND LARRY W. BENNETT

The purpose of the preceding chapters has been to highlight promising directions for the prevention of violence in relationships. These chapters have provided specific techniques and general guidelines for developing successful prevention programs. Although one method of improving preventive services is to learn from the experiences of others, another way is to gather specific and critical feedback about the outcomes of interventions. This chapter provides basic information on why agencies should (and should not) evaluate their programs and how to design and conduct an evaluation that will provide maximally useful information.

WHY IS PROGRAM EVALUATION IMPORTANT?

There are a variety of reasons for evaluating programs. The motivation to evaluate a prevention program may originate from the community, external funders, internal decision makers (i.e., administrators or boards of directors), staff, or participants in the program. Requests for evaluation usually hinge on accountability to a funding source, a board of directors, or an external service network. Funders and board members want to know whether the program is doing what it intended to do, whether it is having the desired effect, and what the effect costs. Requests for accountability may spark frustration with agency staff, who are struggling to provide badly needed services with scant resources. Funders and board members are sometimes viewed as detached from the work and interested only in the "bottom line." Staff may use this perception (often a misperception) to justify their fear or disinterest in evaluation.

Program staff themselves often drive evaluation efforts. Program staff may want to develop and improve the program and may view evaluation as one source of assistance. Knowing "what works" is important to program administrators and direct service providers alike. In some cases, the stimulus for program evaluation is to learn about unexpected effects of programs. Prevention educators are usually aware that certain program elements seem to be more effective than other program elements. Evaluation may shed light on these disparate experiences or even provide evidence that their perceptions are not well founded. Another motivation agencies may have for evaluating prevention programs is their belief that their program is unique and should be showcased. This motivation is a two-edged sword because agency staff may be less likely to accept findings that show no effect, or worse, show a negative effect.

Evaluation also has the potential to increase the effectiveness of the services evaluated, even beyond the "Hawthorn effect" of staff performing better just because they know they are being evaluated. Some practitioners embrace evaluation as a necessary aspect of practice. Admittedly, the mutual reinforcement of evaluation and practice is not the way most staff will view evaluation, at least to begin with. Initially, the link between evaluation and practice must usually be made by modeling, in which experienced and respected staff embrace evaluation. Unfortunately, the opposite effect, in which evaluation is seen as external interference, may also be modeled by experienced staff and administrators.

Linking evaluation to the allocation of funds or other resources is one of the reasons staff and agencies cite for not wanting to evaluate their programs. Service providers might fear that if their program does not show a positive impact in the evaluation, the program might get cut. The reality of these fears should be addressed prior to beginning any evaluation and are just one reason why, particularly in the relatively young field of interpersonal violence prevention, evaluations should be directed primarily at program development and improvement. In interpersonal violence prevention, the most appropriate research questions are usually developmental in nature: "What are the strengths and weaknesses of the program? Who does this program serve best? What kind of an effect does this program have on participants?" rather than "Is this program effective in reducing child abuse, bullying, rape, dating violence, domestic violence, or elder abuse?"

Edleson and his colleagues at the Domestic Abuse Project in Minneapolis identified several motivations for evaluation that may lead to problems (Edleson & Frick, 1997). One of these motivations is using evaluation to postpone making a decision about a program or service that should be made using other criteria. For example, an administrator may use the results of an evaluation to justify eliminating or replacing an existing program. In essence, the decision to alter or eliminate the program shifted to the evaluator. A second problematic motivation to evaluate is public relations or marketing, in which evaluation factoids are used as sound bites and visual bits to entice funders, politicians, and the public to support a program. Along with public relations and marketing, evaluation data may be sought for other issues such as politics, turf, or competition. Although such phenomena are often unavoidable in agency practice, using evaluation to gain an edge is probably a misdirected effort. A mundane, but more important, reason to not evaluate a program is lack of resources such as money or staff and adequate support for evaluation.

For all the aforementioned reasons, staff and administrators may resist evaluation. Practitioner resistance to evaluation usually has roots in lack of familiarity about the mechanics of evaluation and in resentment of the allocation of time and resources to something perceived as not contributing to the prevention of violence. To expect practitioners to overcome their own resistance to evaluation is a mistake akin to blaming the victim. If lack of familiarity and resource concerns are where resistance is experienced, then agencies, funders, evaluators, and other relevant networks must take responsibility for cocreating the conditions that adequately support the evaluation process.

The bottom line in evaluation is accountability: to administrators and prevention educators; to communities and taxpayers; and most importantly, to the participants in the programs whose lives we are hoping to improve. An agency that does not critically examine its effects on those it seeks to help is probably not accountable to its community or its clients.

OUTCOME EVALUATION, PROCESS EVALUATION, AND SATISFACTION SURVEYS

Many staff believe that they already evaluate their programs. Each week they record the number of students they presented to, indicate which lessons they taught and what materials they used, and review the satisfaction surveys they gathered at the end of every class to determine what the students liked and did not like about the program. These are good examples of process evaluation and satisfaction surveys.

Process evaluations reveal the characteristics of clients that receive the services, the number of clients, and the type and content of the service that they received. An example of a thorough process evaluation report might look like this:

> On May 5th I gave a presentation to 25 11th-grade students at Washington school. 53% of the students were female, and 60% were White, 25% were Black, 10% were Hispanic, and 5% were Asian. Students come from a mostly middle- to upper-middle-class community. 45% of the students in the class indicated that they had already experienced violence in their dating relationships. For this presentation, we showed the 10-minute dating violence video, handed out a copy of the "power and control wheel," discussed power and control in friendships and dating relationships for approximately 15 minutes, spent 10 minutes discussing an incident involving a student bringing a gun to school last week, and ended the session by discussing local resources and handing out our brochure and satisfaction survey. 21 of the 25 students returned completed satisfaction surveys. After the class, one student asked to speak to me about a violent relationship, and after speaking with her for a few minutes, I was able to give her referral information for one of our counselors.

Satisfaction surveys are a systematic way of learning about students' perceptions about a program. Typical questions include "What did you like/dislike about the program? Would you recommend this program to a friend? How helpful was this program? As a result of this program, do you feel that you are better able to avoid violence in your relationships?" Results of satisfaction surveys give indications of how well the program was received, suggest aspects of the program that might be modified or expanded, and show whether the program is perceived as being helpful. Also, because the results of satisfaction surveys tend to be positive, they can be a useful tool in increasing service providers' morale and preventing caregiver fatigue.

Extreme caution must be used, however, to avoid confusing high marks on program helpfulness with positive outcomes. In an experiment by Schewe and O'Donohue (1993b), two independent prevention programs were presented to different groups of students. Although both programs received equally high marks on a satisfaction survey covering the credibility and helpfulness of the program, one of the programs was not at all effective in achieving desirable outcomes, and the other program was moderately effective in producing desired changes among program participants. If only the satisfaction survey were used in this study, both programs would have been shown as equally effective. Use of an outcome evaluation, however, revealed that students in one of the programs evidenced positive changes in knowledge, attitudes, and behavioral intentions, whereas students in the other group evidenced almost no change.

Formative evaluation is another type of process evaluation that consists of two kinds of assessment: needs assessment and evaluability assessment. The purpose of *needs assessment* is to aid in the design or expansion of services. In a needs assessment, an agency may survey a community to determine whether there is a need for an intervention, study other unmet needs of the target population, or conduct an audit of staff competence to deliver the intervention.

Evaluability assessment is often the first step toward designing and conducting an outcome evaluation of an existing program or intervention. The purpose of evaluability assessment is to determine whether an agency or institution is prepared for evaluation by focusing on how information is processed, how fully developed the program is, and whether goals are quantifiable. For example, the goal of many media campaigns is to raise awareness about violence. Although this might be a worthwhile goal, quantifying or measuring an increased awareness about violence is difficult. Regarding program development, if a prevention program is not developed to the point at which another agency or educator could replicate it, it is probably not ready to be evaluated. If a program exists only in the mind of its creator or implementor and changes significantly from week to week or setting to setting, the results of any evaluation will be useless because it will not be clear what was evaluated.

Outcome Evaluation

Outcome evaluations seek to answer the question, "Is the program meeting its goals and objectives?" For programs whose goals and objectives are not so clear, an alternate evaluation question might be, "How are students different after participating in the prevention program?"

Measuring Outcomes

Outcomes assessed for prevention programs often fall into the categories of knowledge, attitudes and beliefs, skills, and behavior or behavioral intentions. The category of behavioral intention is included here because those in the field of primary prevention might not be able to measure the presence or absence of the behavior that we are trying to prevent. For example, if the goal of a rape prevention program were to prevent men from raping, trying to measure the success of the program by tracking rape convictions would be nearly impossible (Schewe & O'Donohue, 1998). Moreover, it would be misleading, because the chance a man will be arrested for rape is only a fraction of the chance he will rape, and it is an even smaller fraction of the chance he will think about rape. This issue warrants further discussion.

Researchers evaluating the efficacy of treatments for convicted sex offenders have commonly used police reports of rearrest or reconviction to track the progress of both treated and untreated sex offenders (Marshall, Jones, Ward, Johnston, & Barbaree, 1991). However, tracking incidence rates is not an effective way to measure the outcome of primary prevention interventions. First, this type of research takes years to complete and is extremely costly. Second, there is the problem of measuring incidence. Given a normal or even high-risk population, only a small percentage of men would be expected by chance to ever commit rape. Estimates using the Sexual Experiences Survey have suggested that about 9% of the male population commit acts that meet the legal definition of rape or attempted rape (Koss & Harvey, 1987). Police reports of incidents would be unacceptable because only approximately 10% of all rapes are reported to the police, and only 50% of these reports result in arrest (Missouri Division of Health, 1985). Of those 50% that are arrested, only 66% are prosecuted, and 85% of these result in conviction (M. Cavins, Cook County State's Attorney's Office, personal communication, June 1996). Thus, the probability of finding that a participant has committed rape by monitoring rape convictions is roughly 1 in 1,000.

Studies of domestic violence incidents have revealed a similar ratio of incidents to official detection. One careful study found that the ratio of victim-reported domestic violence to arrest was 35 to 1; that is, for every reported arrest, there were 35 assaultive actions (Dutton, Bodnarchuk, Kropp, Hart, & Ogloff, 1997).

Because of the difficulties in tracking the incidence of violence among study participants, it becomes necessary to use proximal outcome measures to evaluate the efficacy of primary prevention programs. Such proximal outcome measures include changes in knowledge, attitudes, and beliefs that have been associated with the ultimate outcome (behavior) that prevention educators are trying to influence (Schewe & O'Donohue, 1993a). Typically, violence potential has been measured by assessing attitudes and behaviors thought to be relevant to committing an act of interpersonal violence. For example, in the field of rape prevention it is common to assess acceptance of rape myths, acceptance of interpersonal violence, and the extent to which individuals believe that sexual relationships are adversarial in nature (Burt, 1980). Another approach has been to directly ask men to rate their likelihood of committing rape (Malamuth, 1989) or to ask them whether they have committed acts of sexual coercion in the past (Koss & Oros, 1982). Rape potential is then inferred; that is, rape-supportive attitudes indicate rape potential; self-reported future likelihood of raping indicates rape potential; or self-reported past history of raping indicates rape potential. In domestic or dating violence prevention, proximal measures might include attitudes toward women, beliefs about battered women, or beliefs about gender-based power.

Another proxy for measuring target behavior is to track changes in behavioral intention. For instance, if before the program 25% of the students indicate that they might commit rape if they could be assured of not getting caught on Malamuth's (1989) Attraction to Sexual Aggression scale, and afterward only 5% indicate that they might commit rape, then there is at least some indication of the program's success. How confident we are about this success will depend largely on our experimental design, to be discussed later.

In intimate partner violence, common proximal measures may include hostility, alcohol use, or belief in the situational acceptability of violence. It is critical that proximal measures be linked theoretically to the goal of the intervention. This link often engenders considerable debate. For example, some practitioners believe alcohol use is theoretically linked to dating violence, whereas others argue there is no established causal link between drugs and violence (Bennett & Fineran, 1998; Nicholson et al., 1998; O'Keefe, 1997).

Logic Models

To determine what measures to include in an outcome evaluation, prevention researchers regularly rely on *logic models*, or diagrams that outline the prevention program from its process or content to its multiple objectives, to its ultimate goal or goals. An example of a logic model is found in Table 10.1. Logic models are useful tools that can be used in several ways.

TABLE 10.1
Sample Logic Model

Process (what we do for whom)	Strategies	(Measurable) objectives	Impact
Provide a 1-hour rape prevention program to male and female eighth-grade students	Address rape myths	Decrease rape supportive attitudes	Reduce the incidence of rape
	Teach communication skills	Improve intergender communication	
	Portray the negative consequences of rape	Increase empathy for victims of rape	
	Instruct students about how they can help a rape victim	Increase empathy for victims of rape Decrease rape supportive attitudes	
	Provide information about local rape crisis centers	Increase knowledge local resources Increase participants' sense of safety	Increase the number of victims receiving assistance

Commonly, they are used by evaluators to identify the measurable objectives of an existing program. In this case, the logic model is usually built from left to right. The prevention educator starts by describing the process or the practical characteristics of the program. Next, the content or the specific strategies used in the intervention are noted. Then the objectives of these strategies are noted. At this point an effort is made to identify objectives that are specific enough to be measurable. To say that the objective of an exercise is to "increase knowledge about domestic violence" is not very helpful in developing an instrument for measuring that objective. "Increasing knowledge of the causes and consequences of domestic violence, being able to identify risk factors for an abusive relationship, and increasing knowledge of specific resources for victims of domestic violence" are examples of objectives that are much easier to measure. The idea is to provide enough detail about the program content and the intended objectives to develop a measurement strategy.

One danger is that, in some cases, the measurable objectives may have a weak relationship to the ultimate goal or impact of the prevention program. For instance, changing attitudes about a particular behavior has a relatively small influence on actually changing the behavior. Raising awareness or increasing knowledge in a particular area has an even smaller effect on behavior. In determining which objectives to measure, it makes sense to measure those most closely related to the behavior itself.

Another way to use the logic model is in program development. Here the model is generally completed from right to left. We start with the ultimate goal or impact that we hope to achieve. Next, we identify those subgoals or objectives that are empirically or theoretically related to our goal, along with ways to measure those objectives. Finally, we develop a program (strategies) designed to best achieve those objectives.

Building an Evaluation Instrument

After identification of the measurable objectives of a program, the next step is to identify or develop tools for measuring those objectives. Conducting a search of the scientific literature is one way to find existing outcome measures. Asking researchers in that field of practice is another way to learn about appropriate existing measures. The rigor required in selecting measurement tools is linked to how the evaluation will be used. If, for example, program staff want to gain recognition for their program by writing a journal article or conference presentation, they must use valid and reliable measures that can pass at least some level of scientific review. Evaluation measures can be designed locally as well, which is likely to occur and may be necessary if the evaluation results will be used only by staff and local or state funders. If staff must develop their own evaluation instruments to document the specific outcomes of their unique program, then we recommend that they seek outside assistance from someone who has experience in developing outcome evaluation instruments. This assistance will ensure that measures are appropriate to the task at hand and will provide the information needed.

Other Considerations for Measuring Development

Keep Outcome Measures as Simple and Brief as Possible

When researchers develop outcome measures, they are pressured to be as comprehensive as possible so that every positive outcome can be measured and accounted for. Practical constraints such as the amount of classroom time available and the tolerance of the audience to complete long questionnaires necessitate briefer measures. Use of a logic model of the intervention helps focus the evaluation on the major components of the intervention and its intended outcomes. The evaluation should be focused on the primary outcomes; the evaluation does not need to measure every possible positive outcome.

Be Careful of Ceiling Effects

Teenagers and adults today are well informed and may score surprisingly well on knowledge and attitude questionnaires, regardless of high levels of violence in their relationships. A pilot test of the outcome measures should be administered to the intended audience to be sure that there is room for improvement as a result of the intervention.

Measure Behavior Whenever Possible

The relatively weak link between knowledge, attitudes, and actual behavior argues for the use of behavioral measures whenever possible. However, when collecting data regarding criminal behavior (e.g., assault, drug use), using hypothetical situations or asking questions about behavioral intent is one way to protect participants and may allay concerns of review boards.

Be Clear About Confidentiality Issues

Participants will not answer questions honestly unless they can trust the test giver and are aware of the procedures that will be taken to protect the confidentiality of their answers. Although it has never been tested in a court of law, obtaining a "certificate of confidentiality" is an additional step that researchers can take to protect the confidentiality of information from research participants.

After program staff have identified or developed their evaluation instruments, they still need to decide what type of evaluation design to use. Evaluation design decisions are often based on practical considerations such the amount of time and resources that are available and the availability of appropriate control groups, as well as the research questions that are driving the evaluation.

Single-Group, Posttesting Only

This simplest of evaluation designs is useful in two instances. One instance is when program staff gather information in the form of satisfaction surveys. The other instance is when the program is training to mastery. The quizzes and tests that are taken in school are an example of a single-group, posttesting only design. If the program objective is that "participants will be able to identify three characteristics of an abusive relationship," and after the program, 90% of the participants are able to identify three characteristics of an abusive relationship, then there is at least some evidence of the program's success. One problem with this design, especially in the area of interpersonal violence (IPV) prevention, is that a program is usually not trying to teach to mastery but rather dealing with a wide range of attitudes, beliefs, skills, and knowledge, and the aim is often to move people in the right direction rather than getting them to achieve some level of mastery. Another problem with this evaluation design arises when someone asks, "How would the participants have performed on the test if they hadn't had the program?" Perhaps participants already possessed that knowledge or those attitudes before the program. To state that the results of the evaluation are attributable to the program, a more sophisticated evaluation design is necessary.

Two Groups, Posttesting Only

One way to strengthen the argument that a prevention program was responsible for positive findings is to administer the evaluation instrument to a group of people who did not receive the intervention (a no-treatment control group). By using a no-treatment control group, researchers are able to demonstrate how participants in the program are different from a similar group of people who did not receive the intervention. Here, the difficulty is finding a group of people that do not differ significantly on important characteristics from the people who participated in the program. If the groups do differ, then one could argue that the observed differences between the two groups on an assessment instrument might be attributable to the differences in age, gender, race, education, and so forth. One way to increase the likelihood that the two groups are as similar as possible is to randomly assign individuals to the intervention group and to the no-treatment control group.

In this way, any extraneous variables that might affect performance on the outcome measure, such as level of education, should be equally distributed between the two groups. However, random assignment does not ensure that some important characteristic is not disproportionately assigned to one group, and hence differences between groups might continue to exist regardless of the intervention.

Another way to ensure equality between the two groups is to use a matched sample. In this method, pairs of individuals are matched on important characteristics; then one member of each pair is assigned to the treatment group and the other is assigned to the control group. The drawback is that we often do not know what all of the important extraneous variables might be, or there might be so many variables that matching becomes impractical or impossible.

One Group, Pre- and Posttesting

Another way to strengthen the argument that a prevention program was responsible for the positive findings is to administer the evaluation instrument to participants before and after the intervention. When little time exists between the pre- and the posttest, researchers can be more confident that the changes in participants' scores are a result of the program. However, if the program spans several weeks, one might argue that other life experiences might be responsible for the improvement in scores rather than the intervention. Here again, adding a no-treatment control group can increase the level of confidence that the positive outcomes can be attributed to the program.

Treatment and Control Groups, Pre- and Posttesting

The primary advantage of using pre- and posttesting with both treatment and control groups is that researchers can compare scores between the two groups preintervention to determine if any important differences exist that might influence their scores postintervention. If no differences exist preintervention, then any differences postintervention can be confidently attributed to the effects of the intervention. If differences do exist between group preintervention, statistical techniques can be used to help control the effects of these preexisting differences. So finally, there is an evaluation design that allows us to confidently attribute any significant differences between the treatment and no-treatment control groups after the intervention to the effectiveness of the intervention.

Although this level of evaluation design represents the state of the art in the evaluation of prevention programming, several problems exist with this design. One problem is the practical problem of finding a no-treatment control group that is willing and able to complete the assessment instruments at two points in time similar to the intervention group. School administrators who are reluctant to give prevention educators access to students to deliver a service are sometimes more reluctant to allow class time for an evaluation of that service. Another problem with a treatment and no-treatment control group design is that when the study is finished, all that really can be said is that the intervention is better than nothing. This type of evaluation does not show which aspects of the program were responsible for the observed changes and does not allow the statement that this program is better than any other program (unless another program used identical evaluation instruments and similar evaluation procedures). Fortunately, there is an evaluation design that solves both of these problems.

Alternate Treatments, Pre- and Posttesting

The very best control group for an intervention is an alternate intervention (Horvath, 1988). By providing two interventions, evaluators avoid the practical (and ethical) problem of not providing services to a group of participants in the study. Two interventions also strengthen conclusions by allowing researchers to state that not only is Program A effective, but it is more effective than Program B. Then we can begin to examine the differences between programs A and B to determine which components of the program might be responsible for the positive changes. When selecting an alternate intervention, there are several options. The easiest option for a control group is to use an existing program, if there is one. A second option is to provide a program that is similar to the one being evaluated, minus one or two components. This is also known as a treatment dismantling design and allows assessment of the importance of selected components of the program. Another choice is to select a program that might be considered the state-of-the-art in a particular field of IPV prevention. Of course, there is the very real possibility that the alternate program will outperform the program being evaluated. In this case, staff should consider adopting the other program or, at the very least, modifying the current program to draw on the strengths of the alternate. If practical limitations prevent implementation of a similar prevention program, a prevention video or other easily administered IPV intervention could be used.

One potential problem is that both programs might result in equivalent changes on the selected outcome measures. In this case, the better intervention will maintain its effect several months after the intervention, thus creating the need for long-term follow-up assessments.

USING EVALUATION RESULTS

Obviously, the most important aspect of conducting an evaluation is using the results of that evaluation to fulfill its original purpose. When an evaluation study is done correctly, reporting the results is a relatively simple task because the entire study should have been designed with this purpose in mind. For instance, if the purpose of the evaluation is to share positive initial outcomes with potential funders, practitioners should have a good idea of what they want to say in the report before the evaluation begins. For any given service, the agency would probably like to report how many people the program serves; the types of needs that participants in the program generally have; the number of people that successfully complete the program; barriers to program completion; the benefits that participants report; and the gains in skills, knowledge, attitudes, behavior, or health and well-being among participants following the program. The evaluation study, then, is simply a tool to provide some science and objectivity to the evaluation and a means to provide some numbers for the measurable outcomes chosen for evaluation. The type of information presented, and the way that it is presented, will vary depending upon the audience and the purpose of the presentation. This section provides suggestions for the presentation of evaluation results to stakeholders and funders for the purpose of generating additional support for programs, to the community and other stakeholders for the purpose of improving public relations and generating public support for programs, and to service providers and program administrators for the purpose of modifying and improving services. Although there are several other potential audiences for the results of an evaluation, these three groups will be used here as guidelines that can be modified for other potential audiences.

Funders

Written reports and face-to-face presentations use numbers to support the story that the program wants to tell. Presenters should supplement numbers with testimonials and statements from participants, but sparingly. Funders may also want to see the ratio of program effects to program cost (e.g., the cost per unit of attitude change). Such cost–effect analysis may be more useful to funders and agency administrators than to practitioners or community constituents.

Community

Evaluation results may be reported in brochures, web pages, press releases, letters, and memos. Again, if the program has a story to tell, staff will want to use more narrative, using numbers only to highlight important points; using participant statements and testimonials more freely; and using charts, graphs, pictures, and bulleted lists to make the information easy to read and understand. Explanations about programs geared to community members should be simple and to the point, avoiding jargon and avoiding most of the process-oriented detail service providers enjoy.

Service Providers

Written reports, face-to-face presentations, and workgroups can best be used. Service providers and evaluators will need to get into the details of the measurement tools and the raw data. Service providers need to know exactly how and where participants improved and, more importantly, where they did not improve. Evaluation reports need to describe who improved (including age, ethnicity, gender, education, income, family make-up, and types of presenting problems) and who did not improve. In some cases, the results might indicate that the measurement tool was flawed or did not capture the constructs that the program intended to change. In other cases, results might suggest that the program needs to be adapted to accommodate different populations, emphasize different constructs (i.e., skills, knowledge, attitudes, behavior), or modify other aspects of the service delivery (i.e., time, location, language). Service providers want to know about outcome, but they are often equally interested in process evaluations.

SUMMARY

Conducting an outcome evaluation of a prevention program can be challenging and rewarding. Potential challenges include staff resistance to evaluation; practical difficulties regarding the time and effort required to conduct an evaluation; theoretical difficulties linking the specific intervention techniques to the desired goals and objectives; and technical difficulties related to developing outcome measures, experimental designs, and analyzing data. Potential rewards include a significantly improved intervention, documentation of positive outcomes, and a staff that is more motivated and more focused on the goals and objectives of the interventions. Various funding agencies, social science departments of local colleges and universities, state departments of health and human services, the Centers for Disease Control and Prevention, or the National Institutes of Health can assist in conducting an outcome evaluation.

REFERENCES

Bennett, L., & Fineran, S. (1998). Sexual and severe physical violence of high school students: Power beliefs, gender, and relationship. *American Journal of Orthopsychiatry, 68,* 645–652.

Burt, M. (1980). Cultural myths and supports for rape. *Journal of Personality and Social Psychology, 38,* 217–230.

Dutton, D. G., Bodnarchuk, M., Kropp, R., Hart, S. D., & Ogloff, J. R. P. (1997).

Wife assault treatment and criminal recidivism: An 11-year follow-up. *International Journal of Offender Therapy and Comparative Criminology, 41*, 9–23

Edleson, J. L., & Frick, C. (1997). *Evaluating domestic violence programs*. Minneapolis, MN: Domestic Abuse Project.

Horvath, P. (1988). Placebos and common factors in two decades of psychotherapy research. Psychological Bulletin, *104(2)*, 214–225.

Koss, M., & Harvey, M. (1987). *The rape victim: Clinical and community approaches to treatment*. Lexington, MA: Stephen Greene.

Koss, M., & Oros, C. (1982). Sexual experiences survey: A research instrument investigating sexual aggression and victimization. *Journal of Consulting and Clinical Psychology, 50*, 455–457.

Malamuth, N. M. (1989). The attraction to sexual aggression scale: Part one. *Journal of Sex Research, 26*, 26–49.

Marshall, W. L., Jones, R., Ward, T., Johnston, P., & Barbaree, H. E. (1991). Treatment outcome with sex offenders. *Clinical Psychology Review, 11*, 465–485.

Missouri Division of Health. (1985). *Myths and facts about sexual assault*. Jefferson City, MO: Department of Social Services.

Nicholson, M. E., Maney, D. W., Blair, K., Wamboldt, P. M., Mahoney, B. S., & Yuan, J. (1998). Trends in alcohol-related campus violence: Implications for prevention. *Journal of Alcohol and Drug Education, 43*, 34–52.

O'Keefe, M. (1997). Predictors of dating violence among high school students. *Journal of Interpersonal Violence, 12*, 546–568.

Schewe, P. A., & O'Donohue, W. T. (1993a). Rape prevention: Methodological problems and new directions. *Clinical Psychology Review, 13*, 667–682.

Schewe, P. A., & O'Donohue, W. T. (1993b). Sexual abuse prevention with high-risk males: The roles of victim empathy and rape myths. *Violence and Victims, 8*, 336–348.

Schewe, P. A., & O'Donohue, W. T. (1998). Psychometrics of the Rape Conformity Assessment and other measures: Implications for rape prevention. *Sexual Abuse, 10(2)*, 97–112.

CONCLUSION: PAST, PRESENT, AND FUTURE DIRECTIONS FOR PREVENTING VIOLENCE IN RELATIONSHIPS

PAUL A. SCHEWE

Despite the shortcomings of the scientific literature, it is clear that a lot of progress has been made in preventing violence in relationships over the past few decades. As recently as 10 years ago, the majority of prevention efforts focused on assaults by strangers and primarily targeted potential victims for education and skills training. These programs belied the fact that we all are more likely to be assaulted or sexually abused by someone we love and trust than by a stranger. Young children were once taught to look out for "stranger danger"; now children are taught to discriminate between appropriate and inappropriate touches and that inappropriate touch can sometimes come from people they love. Years ago, parents were taught to protect their children from strangers; now parents are taught positive approaches to discipline and how to deal with the stresses of parenting. Rape prevention programs were once presented only to women on college campuses; now rape prevention programs increasingly target men at earlier developmental stages, and women are taught how to avoid being raped by someone they trust. Years ago, domestic violence and wife rape were legal and not talked about; now the laws have changed, and efforts to prevent domestic violence begin with teaching young children social problem-solving skills and talking with teenagers about violence in dating relationships and continue through interventions with adult couples at risk. Elder abuse was once virtually unknown; now a host of services are available for older adults and their caregivers.

Fortunately, the efforts of advocates, educators, and researchers have raised the level of awareness of the problem of intimate violence to the point where services for victims of sexual assault, intimate partner violence, and elder abuse exist in every U.S. state. Students, parents, teachers, mental health professionals, physicians, law enforcement officers, judges, and others now commonly receive education and training regarding the silent epidemic of violence in relationships. Unfortunately, there still is a long way to go. Although training and education programs exist, only a small percentage of those who need the training receive it. And for many people who receive training, it is not enough to overcome a cultural climate that condones violence within relationships. Victims who disclose their experiences with abuse continue to face disbelief, minimization, shame, and accusations from both formal and informal sources of support. The devastation that occurs when people are physically, emotionally, or sexually violated by someone they trust screams out for primary prevention as the only solution to this problem. However, efforts to prevent individuals from becoming violent will truly be effective only when the pathological social climate that perpetuates violence is replaced with strong proscriptions against violence at every level within every system in society.

The increased awareness of the problem of violence in relationships, the changes in laws that now prohibit such violence, the increased availability of services for victims of violence, and the development of primary prevention programs all have occurred relatively quickly. At the same time that researchers were working to identify risk and protective factors for violence, advocates and educators were delivering interventions designed to raise awareness of the epidemic of violence in relationships. Now that more is known about risk and protective factors for violence, advocates and educators are developing prevention programs that target audiences at the earliest possible developmental stages. Now, the primary task for this field is to understand the efficacy of these preventive interventions and to use all available resources to improve on these interventions and to disseminate them to a wider audience. To do so, one needs to know not only whether an intervention is effective but also for whom that intervention is most effective and what characteristics and components of that intervention are responsible for its effects. For years, prevention educators have been responsive to the scientific literature in developing and modifying their interventions. It is time now for researchers to be responsive to the needs of the prevention educators.

The successes in the field of violence prevention over the past 10 years have spurred new questions. To advance, the field must begin to address questions such as

- Is the prevention program able to change the attitudes and behaviors of males in the audience, or only the females?

- How about the males in the audience who are at the highest risk for committing violence? Is the intervention able to change their attitudes and behaviors?
- How about new immigrants to the United States and students from various ethnic and cultural backgrounds? Can a common intervention be effective for each population?
- What about violence among same-sex couples? Are the risk and protective factors the same? How will interventions need to be modified to meet their needs?

While the field of violence prevention struggles with the question "Are our interventions effective at preventing violence?" (which is primarily a dependent variable problem associated with low-base-rate, private events), we also need to be looking at which components and characteristics of interventions are most effective at creating change on proxy measures of violence-related attitudes, beliefs, knowledge, behaviors, behavioral intentions, and skills.

The goal of this book is to summarize the current state of knowledge of interpersonal violence prevention to improve the efficacy of current interventions and to guide the pursuit of new knowledge. Ideally, this volume has provided readers with an overview of important constructs in several areas of violence prevention. If the information found here has motivated new questions, altered interventions, or expanded the scope of work, then it has done its job. The efforts of strong advocates in research and practice have enabled the field of violence prevention to progress so rapidly. As this rate of growth continues, I look forward to seeing what the next 10 years of work will produce.

AUTHOR INDEX

Abbey, A., 142, 143, 144, 147, *155*, 173, *190*

Abel, G. G., 120, *131*, 146, *155*

Abrahams, N., 14, *21*

Abrahams, S., 223, *244*

Acierno, R., 143, *158*

Ahn, H. N., 34, *49*

Ainslie, J. J., 125, *132*

Akman, D., 10, *21*

Albee, G. W., 210, *215*

Aleman, A., 14, *15*, *24*, *29*, *53*

American Association of University Women Educational Foundation, *101*

American Medical Association, 238, *242*

American Psychiatric Association, 121, *131*

Amick, A. E., 139, 140, 145, *155*, *158*

Amick-McMullan, A., 146, *158*

Amir, M., *155*

Anderson, L., 129, *131*, 183, *190*

Andrews, S., 115, *134*, 164, 172, 173, *195*

Anesheshel, C. S., 82, 86, 87, *104*

Angert, L., 15, 18, *22*

Anglin, K., 204, 209, 212, *217*

Ansello, E. F., 223, 230, *242*

Antill, J., 202, *216*

Arias, I., 82, *101*, 110, *131*, 197, *220*

Armentrout, J., 120, *131*

Arriaga, X. B., 80, 81, *103*

Asafi, I., 43, *51*

Asarnow, J. R., 210, 211, *216*

Asendorpf, J. B., 62, *74*

Asher, S. R., 70, 72, *74*

Association for the Treatment of Sexual Abusers, 28, *49*

Astler, L., *53*

Attar, B., 40, *51*

Avery-Leaf, S., 80, *80*, 81, 84, 85, 86, 88, 89, 90, 93, 94, 98, 100, *101*, *102*, *105*

Babcock, J., 200, 205, 206, 208, *210*, *215*, *217*, *218*

Bachar, K. J., 138, *155*, *155*

Bachman, R., 138, 143, 146, 148, *155*, *159*, 200, *215*

Baker, A. A., 223, *242*

Bandura, A., *101*, 110, *131*, 149, 154, *160*

Barbaree, H. E., 144, *160*, 252, *261*

Barling, J., 197, *220*

Bart, P. B., 114, *131*, 144, 145, 146, 154, *155*

Barth, R. P., 14, 15, *21*

Bartini, M., 63, *77*

Bates, J. E., 59, 61, 62, 63, 65, 75, *75*, *78*

Bates, L., 198, 203, 204, *217*

Bauman, K. E., 80, 81, 93, 97, *103*

Beach, F. A., 43, *51*

Beal, L. S., 108, *134*

Beatty, S. B., 204, 209, 212, *217*

Becker, J. V., 28, *49*, 120, *131*, 146, *155*

Beckett, J., 84, *102*

Beitchman, J. H., 10, *21*

Belknap, J., 115, *134*

Bennett, L., 82, *101*, 253, *260*

Berg, D., 41, *52*, 108, 109, 112, 116, 117, 126, 128, *131*, *133*, 139, *159*, 179, 180, *190*

Bergman, l., 81, *82*

Berkowitz, A., 116, *131*, 142, *155*, *164*, 165, 166, 167, 168, *169*, 170, 172, 174, 175, 177, 178, 179, 180, 182, 183, *185*, *191*, *192*, *193*

Berliner, L., 29, 46, *49*, *50*

Bernard, J. L., 88, *101*

Bernard, M. L., 88, *101*

Bernat, J. A., 142, *156*

Berns, S., *217*

Berry, C. J., 86, 87, 88, *105*

Bershuny, B. S., 116, *117*, 119, 129, *133*

Berts, M., 57, *76*

Best, C. L., 140, 143, 146, *158*

Bierman, K. L., 72, 73, *74*

Biernert, H., 69, 70, 71, *74*

Biggs, S., 225, *242*

Billingham, R. E., 82, *101*

Binney, V., 56, 64, 75, *78*

Bird, S., 45, *51*

Birnbaum, M., 170, *191*

Birns, B., 86, 88, *101*

Bischof, G. P., 203, *220*

Bivens, L., *103*

Bjorkqvist, K., 57, 76, 174
Blackwell, L. M., 154, 157
Blair, K., 253, 261
Blanchard, E. B., 120, 131
Blekner, M., 231, 243
Block, M. R., 226, 228, 243
Block, R., 146, 155, 160
Blum, J., 53
Blum, R. W., 28, 50
Blumberg, E. J., 15, 21
Blumberg, S., 204, 209, 211, 219
Blut, K., 111, 124, 133
Bobash, R. P., 83, 102
Bodnarchuk, M., 252, 260
Boell, J. L., 149, 158
Bogat, G. A., 16, 23
Bogyo, G. R., 202, 215
Boivin, M., 58, 60, 70, 74, 92, 96, 97, 98, 103
Bond, C. F., 143, 157
Bonner, B., 27, 54
Bookwala, J., 81, 82, 85, 88, 89
Borden, L. A., 108, 124, 131
Boscoe, J., 43, 51
Bounds, C., 112, 116, 132, 172, 193
Bourg, S. E., 165, 174, 179, 191, 192
Bowers, L., 56, 64, 75, 78
Bowker, A., 67, 77
Bradbury, T. N., 204, 220
Brecklin, L. R., 138, 142, 144, 156, 161, 166, 167, 182, 191
Brehm, S. S., 116, 131
Breitenbecher, K. H., 138, 150, 152, 156, 166, 169, 179–180, 191
Breslin, F. C., 110, 131, 204, 220
Breslin, K. F., 82, 87, 88, 89, 104
Briere, J., 28, 10, 21, 44, 46, 49, 50, 82, 102
Briggs, D., 43, 49
Briggs, F., 15, 21
Bristow, L. R., 33, 49
Broadhurst, D. D., 28, 54
Brockoff, K., 85, 104
Brockopp, K., 201, 219
Brody, E., 230, 243
Brooks, F., 63, 77
Brown, E. J., 28, 49
Browne, A., 28, 49, 139, 140, 150, 158, 161
Bruce, B., 172, 191
Bruce, K., 146, 155
Bruce, S., 175, 183, 192

Buell, M., 108, 134
Bukowski, W. M., 58, 60, 70, 74
Burgess, A. W., 141, 145, 146, 160, 167, 192
Burgess, E. S., 20, 21
Burgess, K. B., 60, 61, 64, 65, 76, 77
Burkhart, B. R., 165, 174, 179, 191, 192
Burman, B., 206, 207, 215
Burnam, M. A., 140, 156, 160
Burt, M., 108, 120, 121, 131, 252, 260
Bushman, B. J., 143, 156
Bussiere, M. T., 45, 46, 51

Cacioppo, J., 135
CA Conduct Problems Prevention
        Research Group, 73, 74
Cairl, R. E., 228, 244
Caldera, T., 202, 216
Caldwell-Colbert, A., 108, 124, 131
Calhoun, K. S., 139, 142, 145, 152, 154, 155, 156, 159
Callahan, J. E., 81, 104
Calvert, J. F., Jr., 20, 21
Calvin, M. K., 38, 52
Campion, E. W., 228, 244
Candell, S., 127, 132, 167, 193
Cano, A., 80, 84, 85, 86, 88, 89, 90, 94, 101
Cantell, H., 43, 51
Capraro, R. L., 164, 183, 192
Carroll, L. A., 14, 21
Carter, D., 141, 145, 146, 160
Cascardi, M., 80, 80, 81, 84, 85, 86, 88, 89, 90, 93, 94, 98, 100, 101, 102, 105, 198, 215
Casey, K., 14, 21, 24
Caspi, A., 90, 104
Cassavia, E., 10, 21
Cate, R., 82, 85, 88, 102, 103
Ceasar, P. L., 216
Chadwick, D. L., 15, 21
Chadwick, M. W., 15, 21
Chance, D. W., 38, 39, 51
Chandy, J. M., 28, 50
Chasan-Taber, L., 38, 39, 48, 50
Chase, K. A., 88, 102
Check, J. V. P., 108, 114, 124, 131, 134, 167, 194
Chen, X., 67, 77
Chew, E., 85, 104, 201, 219
Christensen, A., 205, 216
Christopher, R. S., 82, 85, 88, 102, 103

Cillessen, A. H. N., 58, 60, 61, 62, 78
Clark, M. L., 84, *102*
Clements, M., 210, *219*
Cleveland, H. H., 143, 148, *156, 158*
Clum, G. A., 142, *156*
Coffin, W., 212, *220*
Cohen, E. S., 114, *131*
Cohen, M. A., 152, *156*
Cohen, R., *77*
Cohn, E., 149, *156*
Coie, J. D., 58, 60, 61, 62, 73, 76, 78, 210,
    211, *216*
Coker, A. C., 143, *156*
Coleman, C. C., 57, 58, *76*
Collins, M. E., 20, *22*, 36, *50*
Committee for Children, 20, *22*
Compoz, P., 43, *51*
Connolly, J. A., 81, *102*
Conte, J., 14, 20, *22*, 28, 29, *49, 50*
Conway, A., 175, *183*
Cook, S. W., *195*
Cooks, S. L., 150, *156*
Cooper, C., 214, *219*
Cooper, H. M., 134, *156*
Corcoran, C., 170, 173, 178, 181, 182,
    188, *192, 194*
Cordova, J. V., 207, *216*
Cotton, S., 202, *216*
Cowen, E. L., 209, *216*
Cowie, H., 56, 64, *78*
Cox, G., 207, *216*
Cox, S. L., 140, 146, *158*
Craig, W., 81, *102*
Craven, D., *7, 21*
Crawford, S., 31, *53*
Crick, N. R., 62, *75*
Crossman, R. K., 203, *220*
Crowell, N. A., 167, *192*
Csapo, M., 69, 70, *75*
Cubbins, L. A., 147, *159*
Cumming, G. F., 108, *134*
Cummings, N., 149, *156*
Cunningham, J., 202, *216*
Cunningham-Rathner, J., 28, *49*
Currie, D. W., 86, 88, *102*
Currier, L. L., 20, *25*
Curry, L. C., 226, 230, *243*
Curwen, T., 45, 46, *54*

daCosta, G. A., 10, *21*
Dahlberg, L. L., 31, *53*
Dale, J., *53*

Daleiden, E. L., 36, *52*
Dallager, C., 127, *131*
Darley, J. M., 177, *194*
Daro, D., 14, *21, 22, 24*
Davis, T. L., *169*, 179, 181, 185, *187, 192*
Dawson, E., 36, 41, 42, *54*
Deblinger, E., 46, *50*
DeBord, K. A., 118, 128, *133*, 138, 152,
    157, 167, 169, *193*
DeFronzo, 98, *102*
Deidre, A., 197, 200, *218*
Deisher, R. W., 28, *50*
DeKeserdy, W. S., *196*
Demare, D., 82, *102*
DeMaris, A., 84, *102*
Dimeff, L. A., 143, 149, 150, 153, *159*
Dinero, T. E., 139, 140, 143, 146, *158, 194*
Dishion, T. J., 38, *53*
Dobash, R. E., 83, *102*
Dodge, K. A., 58, 59, 60, 61, 62, 63, 65,
    73, *75, 78*
Dornbusch, S. M., *102*
Dosch, M. F., 91, 96, 97, 98, *103*
Dowdall, C. L., 138, 151, 153, 154, *157,*
    159, 166, *193*
Downes, J., 119, 125, *133*, 167, *193*
Duggan, P., 129, *131*, 183, *190*
DuMont, J., 140, *161*
Duncan, C., 40, *52*
Dungee-Anderson, D., 84, *102*
Dunn, S., 140, *161*
Dutra, S., 38, 39, *51*
Dutton, D. G., 83, *102*, 203, 205, 206,
    216, 245, 252
Dziuba-Leatherman, J., 14, 16, 18, 19, *22,*
    29, 36, *50*

Earle, J., 116, 128, *132*, 166, 167, 168,
    169, 185, *191, 192*
Eastman, M., 226, *243*
Eberly, C. G., 108, 126, *127, 133*
Edleson, J. L., 249, *261*
Edmunds, C. N., 138, *158*
Edwards, A. B., 237, *245*
Egan, S. K., 60, 62, *75*
Eisenberg, N., 70, *75*
Ekman, K., *74*
Elliot, M. N., 180, *194*
Elliott, A., 14, *23*
Elliott, D. M., 10, *21*, 28, *50*
Ellis, A. L., 110, 126, *132*, 167, *192*
Ellis, L., *132*

Ellsberg, M., 202, *216*
Elrod, J. M., 36, *50*
Epidemiology Program Office, Centers for
    Disease Control and Prevention,
    30, *50*
Ernst, A., 198, *216*
Everitt, D. E., 228, *244*

Fabes, R. A., 64, *75*
Farrington, D. P., 208, *216*
Fehrenbach, P. A., 28, *50*
Feltey, K. M., 125, *132*
Fineran, S., 82, *101*, 253, *260*
Finkelhor, D., 14, 16, 18, 19, *22*, 27, 28,
    29, 36, 39, 46, 49, *50*, *52*, 145,
    156, 225, 226, 238, *243*, *244*
Finkenberg, M. E., 149, *156*
Finnegan, R. A., 64, *75*
Fischer, G. J., 116, 124, *132*, 167, *192*
Fisher, D. G., 38, *50*
Fiske, J., 45, *51*
Fitzgerald, L. F., 109, 112, 116, 117, 126,
    131, *139*, *158*, 174, 179, 180, *190*,
    194, 195
Flanagan, T. J., 28, *49*
Fleming, M. F., 203, *220*
Flitcraft, A., 200, *220*
Flores, S. A., 130, *156*, 169, *192*
Floyd, F., 209, 210, *218*, *219*
Foege, W. H., 30, *50*
Fogarty, L. A., 14, 15, 20, *21*, *22*
Follingstad, D. R., 90, *103*
Fonow, M., *132*, 136, 167, *193*
Fontes, L. A., 34, *51*
Foo, L., 87, 88, *103*
Ford, C. S., 43, *51*
Forde, D. R., 138, *156*, 166, 167, 182, *191*
Forehand, R., 38, 39, *51*, 67, *78*
Forsythe, A. B., *156*
Foshee, V. A., 80, 81, 84, 85, 93, 97, 98,
    103, 198, *216*
Foubert, J. D., 109, 110, 115, 116, 128,
    129, *132*, 148, *157*, 170, 179, 182,
    187, *193*
Frame, C. L., 67, *78*, 142, *156*
Franklin, C. F., 14, 20, *25*
Frazier, P., 127, *132*, 167, *193*
Freeman-Longo, R., 45, *51*
Frick, C., 249, *261*
Friday, J., 31, *53*
Fried, C. S., 29, 34, 37, 40, 41, *53*
Friedberg, A., 175, *183*

Friedman, D. H., *219*
Friedrich, W., 46, *51*
Frieze, I. H., 81, 82, 85, 88, 89, *101*
Fujioka, J., 43, *51*
Fulmer, T. T., 227, 229, 233, 234, *243*
Funk, R. E., 178, *193*
Furman, W., 72, *74*

Gaines, J. A., 202, *218*
Galenson, E., 43, *51*
Gallagher-Thompson, D., 237, *243*
Gannon, L., 115, 125, *132*, 165, *193*
Garbarino, J., 18, *22*
Garcia, J. L., 228, *243*
Gaylord, J., 150, *160*
Gazelle, H., 59, 60, 62, 70, *75*
Gebhard, P. H., 43, *52*
Geib, A., 125, *132*
Gelles, R., 197, 198, 199, 200, 201, 213,
    216, 221, 225, *245*
Gershuny, B. S., 138, 152, *157*, 182, *193*
Gibson, L., 18, 19, *22*, 29, *51*, 143, *158*
Gidycz, C. A., 41, *51*, 113, 114, 127, *133*,
    138, 142, 149, 151, 152, *153*, 154,
    156, *157*, 159, 166, 173, *193*, *194*
Gilbert, B., 115, 125, *132*, 165, *193*
Gilbert, N., 16, *22*, 34, 47, 49, *51*
Gilbert, P., 70, *78*
Gillispie, E. I., 20, *25*
Gilmore, G. D., 91, 96, 97, 98, *103*
Giordano, J. A., 230, *243*
Giordano, N. H., 230, *243*
Gleberman, L., 207, *218*
Glenn, N. D., 200, *216*
Godkin, M. A., 220, 226, 227, 229, *243*,
    245
Golding, J. M., 140, 152, 154, *156*, *157*,
    160
Golter, B. S., 72, *76*
Gondolf, E. W., 207, 208, *216*
Good, G., 116, 127, *132*
Goodman, L. A., 139, *158*
Goodyear-Smith, F., 198, 200, 205, *216*
Gordon, L. C., 87, *105*
Gordon, M. T., 149, *157*
Gortner, E., *217*
Gottlieb, B. H., 232, *243*
Gottman, J. M., 72, *75*, 200, 204, 205,
    206, 207, 208, 210, *215*, *216*, *217*,
    218
Goudena, P. P., 14, 15, 24, 29, *53*
Grafstrom, M., 226, 229, *243*

Graham, S., 55, 57, 58, 65, 69, 70, 73, 75

Graham, T. L., 150, *160*

Gray, M., 112, 116, *132*, 172, *193*

Greefeld, L. A., 7, *21*

Greenberg, M. T., 73, *74*

Greene, D., M., 140, 147, *157*

Greene, E., 20, *23*

Greer, J. H., 14, *23*

Griffin, B. S., 146, *157*

Griffin, C. T., 146, *157*

Griffith, L., 14, *23*

Gross, K. H., 214, *219*

Groth, A. N., 120, 121, *133*

Guerra, N. G., 40, *51*

Gullotta, T. P., 210, *215*

Hacquard, L., 116, 127, *132*, 167, *193*

Hahlweg, K., 204, *218*

Hall, G. C. N., 182, *193*

Hamberger, L. K., 207, *217*

Hammond, W. R., 33, 34, 40, *51*, *53*, *54*

Hanson, K. A., 41, *51*, 113, 114, 127, *133*, 138, 149, 152, 154, *157*

Hanson, K. R., 45, 46, *51*

Harlaub, M. G., 169, *192*

Harrington, N. T., 143, 144, *157*

Harris, G. T., 92, *103*

Harris, M. B., 85, *103*

Harrison, P. J., 119, 125, *133*, 167, *193*

Harrist, A. W., 62, *75*

Hart, C. W., 72, *76*

Hart, S. D., 252, *260*

Hartlaub, M. G., 130, *156*

Hartman, S. G., 211, *217*

Harvey, J., 114, *131*, 149, *156*

Harvey, M., 252, *261*

Hastings, J. E., 207, *217*

Hatton, E. W., 167, *193*

Hauer, A., 120, *131*

Hauggard, J. J., 14, *24*, 36, *53*

Hause, E. S., 90, *103*

Hawkins, A., 116, 127, *132*

Hawkins, J. D., 210, 211, *216*

Hawkins, K. A., 167, *193*

Hawkins, R. M. F., 15, *21*

Haynes, S. N., 225, *243*

Hazzard, A., 14, 15, 18, 19, *22*, 29, *51*

Heath, J. L., 80, 81, *103*

Heavy, C. L., 205, *216*

Hecht, M. L., 119, 124, *134*, 167, *194*

Hedges, M., 198, *217*

Hedlund, A. D., I24

Heesacker, M., 115, 125, *132*, 165, 167, *193*, *195*

Hegmen, K. E., 41, *52*

Heidotting, T., 14, *23*, *51*

Heiger, B., 129, *131*

Heise, L., 140, *158*

Helge, D., *23*

Helms, R. W., 93, 97, *103*

Henderson, D. A., 86, *105*

Henry, F., 33, *52*

Henton, J., 82, 85, 88, *102*, *103*

Heppner, M. J., 116, *117*, 118, 119, 127, 128, 129, *133*, 138, 152, *157*, 167, 169, 182, *193*

Heppner, P. P., *196*

Hernstein, R. J., 201, *221*

Herrera, A., 202, *216*

Heyman, R. E., 201, 210, 212, *217*

Hieger, B., 183, *190*

Hildebran, D., 108, 109, *133*

Hill, J. L., 16, *23*

Hillenbrand-Gunn, T. L., 116, 118, 127, 128, *133*, 138, 152, *157*, 167, 169, *193*

Hilliker, D. R., 36, *52*

Hilton, N. Z., 92, *103*

Hodges, E. V. E., 59, 60, 62, 63, 64, 72, *75*

Hogan, C., 48, *52*

Holcomb, D., 127, *133*, 167, *194*

Holcomb, L., 127, *133*, 167, *194*

Holmberg, J., 36, 37, *52*

Holmes, K. A., *136*

Holtzworth-Munroe, A., 198, 201, 203, 204, 208, 209, 210, 212, *217*, *218*

Hong, L., 176, 181, 183, *194*

Hood, J. E., 10, *21*

Horvath, P., 258, *261*

Hotaling, G. T., 203, *217*, 225, *243*

Houry, D., 198, *216*

Howell, J., 146, *155*

Hubbard, J. A., 58, 60, 61, 62, *78*

Hudley, C., 55, 69, *75*

Hudson, M. F., 226, 230, *243*

Hughes, J., 16, *23*, 29, 47, *52*

Hull, J. G., 143, *157*

Humphrey, C. F., 118, 128, *132*, 138, 152, *157*, 167, 169, *193*

Hymel, S., 58, 60, 67, 70, 74, 76, 77

Intons-Peterson, M. J., 111, 124, *133*

Ivie, D. L., 144, *160*

Jacobson, N., 200, 205, 206, 207, 208, 210, *215, 216, 217, 218*
Jaffe, P. G., 92, 96, 98, *103*
Jamison, J., *24*
Janz, M., 225, *244*
Jasinski, J., *103*
Jason, L. A., 16, *23*
Jaudes, P. K., 38, *52*
Jenkins-Hall, K. D., 108, 110, *133*
John, R. S., 206, 207, *215, 218*
Johnson, J. D., *133*
Johnson, J. E., 143, *156*
Johnson, S. D., 143, *158*
Johnson, T. F., 227, *244*
Johnston, P., 252, *261*
Jones, J., 117, 125, *133*
Jones, L. E., 91, 96, *103*
Jones, R., 252, *261*
Jonson-Reid, M., *103*
Jordan, P. L., 212, *220*
Julien, D., 202, *218*
Juvenile Crime Bill, 30, *52*
Juvonen, J., 55, 57, 58, 65, 69, 70, 73, *75*

Kagan, J., 208, *218*
Kaplan, M. S., 28, *49*
Kapp, *234, 235, 244*
Karabatsos, G., *161*
Karr, S. K., 108, 124, *131*
Kashima, K., 108, *134*
Kassin, S. M., 116, *131*
Kast, L. C., 15, 19, 20, *25*
Kathari, C., 108, 109, 116, 128, *133*
Katz, J., 170, 182, 186, *194*
Kaufman, K., 27, 36, 37, *52, 54*
Kaufman, L. G., *103*
Kavoussi, R., 28, *49*
Keita, G. P., 139, *158*
Kellerman, A. L., 198, *218*
Kelly, L., 145, *158*
Kelsey, T., 82, *105*
Kendall-Tackett, K. A., 10, *23,* 28, *52*
Kendziora, K. T., 84, 87, 88, *105*
Kidder, L., 114, *131,* 149, *156, 158*
Killip, S. M., 92, 96, 98, *103*
Kilmartin, C. T., 165, 171, 174, 175, 176, 183, *194*
Kilpatrick, D. G., 138, 140, 143, 146, *158, 158*
King, E., 57, *76*
King, N. F., *242*
Kingston, P. A., 225, *242*

Kinsey, A. C., 43, *52*
Kivel, P., *194*
Kivlighan, D. M., 116, *117,* 119, 129, *132,* 138, 152, *157,* 182, *193*
Klaw, E., 41, *52,* 108, 109, 116, 128, *133,* 139, *159*
Kleck, G., 146, 147, *158*
Kleemeier, C., 15, 18, 19, 22, 29, *51*
Kline, R. J., 116, *133*
Kling, K. H., 129, *131,* 183, *190*
Knight, B. G., 237, *244*
Knight, R. A., 114, *135,* 141, 142, 143, 144, 146, *161*
Knight-Bohnhoff, K., 85, *103*
Knopp, F. H., 45, *52*
Koch, G. G., 93, 97, *103*
Kochenderfer, B. J., 56, 57, 58, 67, 73, 76
Kochenderfer-Ladd, B. J., 57, 58, 63, 73, 76
Kolbe, L., 40, *52*
Kolko, D., 16, *23,* 29, 47, *52*
Kondrick, C. L., 15, *25*
Kosberg, J. I., 225, 227, 228, 229, 232, 243, *244*
Koss, M., 40, *54,* 82, *103, 133, 134,* 138, 139, 140, 142, 143, 145, 146, 147, 148, 150, 152, 155, *155, 156, 157, 158, 159, 160, 161,* 173, *194,* 202, *218,* 252, *261*
Kothari, C., 41, *52,* 139, *159*
Koval, J., 82, 85, 88, *102, 103*
Kraft, S. A., 204, 209, *219*
Krajewski, S. S., 91, 96, 97, 98, *103*
Krans, T. S., 92, *103*
Krivacska, J. J., 18, *23, 24*
Kropp, R., 252, *260*
Kullgren, G., 202, *216*
Kusel, S. J., 56, 60, 61, *77*
Kvaternick, M., 14, 20, *25*
Kyriacou, D. N., 197, 200, *218*

Ladd, B. J., 61, 64, *76*
Ladd, G. W., 56, 57, 58, 59, 60, 61, 62, 63, 64, 67, 69, 70, 72, 73, 75, *76*
Lagerspetz, K., 57, 74, *76*
Laidlaw, T. M., 198, 200, 205, *216*
Landry, S., 43, *52*
Langhinrichsen, J., 198, *215*
Langwick, S. A., 80, 81, *103*
Lanier, C. A., 180, *194*
La Taillade, J. J., 208, *217, 218*
Latane, B., 177, *194*

Laub, L. H., 147, *158*
Lauritsen, J. L., 147, *158*
Lavigne, S. E., *92, 103*
Lavoie, F., 92, 96, 97, 98, *103*
Law, S., *53*
Laye-McDonough, M., *24*
Leanord, K. E., 198, 199, 201, 203, *219*
Leber, D., 201, 210, *217*
Lee, L., 108, 109, 116, 128, *133*
Leitenberg, H., 18, 19, *22, 29, 51*, 143, 144, *157*
LeMare, L., 67, *76*
Lemerise, E. A., 58, 60, 61, 62, *78*
Lenihan, G., 108, 126, 127, *127, 133*, 167, *194*
Leonard, K. E., 202, *218*
Le Prohn, N., 16, *22*, 47, *51*
Lesser, D., 112, 116, 132, 172, *193*
Levant, R. F., 174, *194*
Leversee, T., 43, *51*
Levy, B., 91, *103*, 145, *158*
Lilly, R. S., 182, *193*
Lin, K.-H. 87, *105*
Lindahl, K. M., 200, *218*
Linden, J., 197, 200, *218*
Linden, R., 143, *158*
Linder, G. F., 80, 81, 93, 97, *103*
Linton, M. A., 108, 113, 114, 115, *134*, 147, *159, 194*
Lippmann, J., 46, *50*
Lips, H. M., 82, *102*
Lipton, D. N., 114, 120, *134*
Livingston, J. A., 143, *161*
Lizotte, A. J., 146, *158*
Lloyd, S., 82, 85, 88, *102, 103*
Lochman, J. E., 73, *76*
Loh, C., 151, 154, *157, 159*
Lonsway, K. A., 41, *52*, 109, 112, 116, 117, 124, 126, *134*, 138, 139, 140, *159, 166, 169*, 174, 179, 180, *182, 190, 194, 195*
Lowry, R., 40, *52*
Lutzky, S. M., 237, *244*
Lynn, S., 151, 154, *157*
Lyons, J., 143, *156*

Macgowan, M. J., 94, *104*
MacMillan, A., 14, *23*
MacMillan, H. L., 14, *23*
MacMillan, J. H., 14, *23*
Macofsky-Urban, F., 237, *244*
Madden, M. E., 149, *159*

Mahalik, J. R., 164, *194*
Mahlstedt, D., 170, 178, 181, 182, 188, *192, 194, 195*
Mahoney, B. S., 253, *261*
Makepeace, J. M., 82, 85, *104*, 201, *218*
Malamuth, N. M., 108, 114, 121, 124, *131, 134, 152, 159*, 167, *195*, 252, 253, *261*
Malik, N. M., 200, *218*
Malik, S., 82, 86, 87, *104*
Malone, J., 197, 198, *218, 220*
Malone, M. J., 59, 62, 63, 72, 75, *76*
Maney, D. W., 253, *261*
Mann, C. A., 119, 124, *134*, 167, *195*
Marcus, S., 155, *159*
Margolin, G., 87, 88, *103*, 206, 207, *215*, 218
Marion, G., *160*
Marioni, N. L., 151, 154, *157, 159*, 166, *193*
Markman, H. J., 201, 202, 204, 206, 209, 210, 211, 212, *216, 217, 218, 219*, 220
Marolla, J., 110, *135*
Marriott, K. A., 128, *132*, 170, 179, 187, *193*
Marrs, S. R., 15, *25*
Marshall, W. L., 252, *261*
Martin, C. E., 43, *52*
Martin, S. E., 143, *159*
Martone, M., 38, *52*
Marx, B. P., 152, 154, *159*
Masten, A., 67, *77*
Mazurek, C., 41, *52*, 108, 109, 116, 128, *133, 139, 159*
McAuslan, P., 143, 144, 147, *155*, 173, *190*
McCaughey, M., 149, 150, 153, 154, *159*
McCrady, F., 36, 37, *52*
McDaniel, P., 149, *159*
McDonald, A. J., 223, *244*
McDonel, E. C., 114, 120, *134*
McDougall, P., 67, *77*
McDuffie, D., 143, 144, 147, *155*, 173, *190*
McEwen, M. K., 109, 115, 129, *132*, 170, 179, 187, *193*
McFadyen-Ketchum, S., 59, 62, 63, *78*
McFall, R. M., 114, 120, *134*
McKinnon, J., 47, *77*
McLaughlin, I. G., 198, 199, 201, 203, *219*
McLeod, M., 28, *49*
McMahon, P. M., 33, 34, *52*

McManus, M. J., 214, *219*
McMaster, L., 81, *102*
McMurran, M., 202, *219*
McQuiod, T., 175, 183, *194*
Meier, R. F., 147, *159*
Melton, G. B., 18, *23*
Melzer, A. M., 19, 20, *25*
Men Can Stop Rape, 170, *195*
Mercy, J. A., 30, 31, 33, *33*, 34, *50*, *52*, *53*, 198, *218*
Meyer, S., 86, 88, *101*
Miethe, T. D., 147, *159*
Millenberger, R. G., 14, *21*
Miller, B. A., 142, 147, *160*
Miller, D. S., 38, 39, *51*
Miller, T. R., *152*, *156*
Miller, W. R., 177, *195*
Miller-Perrin, C. L., 10, 11, 13, 14, 15, 19, *23*, *25*, 30, 36, *54*
Mills, R. S. L., 67, *78*
Mills, T., 198, *216*
Missouri Division of Health, 252, *261*
Moffit, T. E., 90, *104*
Molidor, C., 82, *104*
Monastersky, C., 28, *50*
Monson, T. C., 62, *75*
Morgan, S., 172, *195*
Morison, P., 67, *77*
Morison, S., 20, *23*
Morokoff, P., 140, 150, *159*
Morris, M. L., 214, *219*
Moser, J., 16, *23*, 29, 47, *52*
Moyer, M. M., 149, *158*
Muehlenhard, C., 108, 113, 114, 115, 117, 125, *133*, *134*, 147, *159*, 164, 172, 173, *195*
Munsie-Benson, M., 20, *21*
Murphy, B. C., 70, *75*
Murphy, C. M., 89, 97, *104*
Murphy, W. D., 108, *134*

Narang, D. S., 182, *193*
National Center for Missing and Exploited Children, 16, *23*
National Research Council Institute of Medicine, 200, *219*
Navarro, R. L., 140, 147, *157*
Neidig, P., 201, 202, 210, 212, *217*, *219*, *220*
Neimeyer, G. J., 167, *195*
Nelson, E. S., 125, *135*

Neville, H. A., 116, *117*, 119, 129, *133*, 138, 152, *157*, 182, *193*
Nichols, R., 116, 127, *132*, 167, *193*
Nicholson, M. E., 253, *261*
Nick, T., 198, *216*
Norbet, T., 175, 183, *194*
Nordberg, A., 226, 229, *243*
Norris, J., 143, 147, *149*, 150, 153, *159*, *160*
Notarius, C. I., 206, *219*
Nurius, P. S., 140, 143, 149, 150, 153, *159*, *160*
Nyman, N., 16, *22*, 47, *51*

O'Brien, J. G., 234, 235, 238, *244*
O'Brien, M. K., 81, *101*
O'Brien, P., 114, *131*, 144, 145, 146, 154, 155
O'Donohue, W., 14, *23*, 41, 44, *53*, 108, 111, 112, 116, 119, 120, 122, 126, 128, *134*, *135*, 138, 139, 146, 148, 152, *160*, 162, 166, 170, 186, *195*, *196*, 250, 251, 252, *261*
Offord, D. R., 14, *23*
Ogloff, J. R. P., 252, *260*
O'Keefe, M., 85, 86, 87, 88, 89, *104*, 253, *261*
O'Keefe, N., 201, *219*
O'Leary, K. D., 80, 81, 82, 84, 85, 86, 87, 88, 89, 94, 97, 98, 100, *101*, *102*, *104*, *105*, 110, *131*, 197, 198, 199, 200, 201, 202, 203, 204, 210, 212, *217*, *218*, *219*, *220*
O'Leary, S. G., 84, 87, 88, *105*
Olweus, D., 55, 58, 59, 62, 64, 65, 66, 67, 73, *76*
O'Malley, H. C., 228, 229, *244*
O'Malley, T. A., *244*, 227, 228
O'Neill, H. K., 14, *21*
Oriel, K. A., 203, *220*
Oros, C., 252, *261*
Orts, K., 36, 37, *52*
O'Sullivan, C., 110, 126, *132*, 167, *192*
Owens, J. S., 16, 19, *25*
Ozer, E. M., 149, 154, *160*

Paley, V. G., 73, *77*
Pan, H. S., 202, 212, *220*
Paris, J., 181, *196*
Parker, J. G., 72, *74*
Parks, K. A., 142, 147, *160*, *161*
Pashdag, J., 151, 154, *157*, *159*

Patterson, G. R., 38, *53*
Payne, D. L., 180, *195*
Payne, J. P., 129, *131*, 183, *190*
Pederson, P., 82, 84, *104*
Pellegrini, A. D., 63, *77*
Penhale, B., 224, 235, *244*
Pepler, D., 81, *102*
Perez, P. J., 215, *220*
Perez, R., 229, *244*
Peri, C., 113, *135*, 149, *160*
Pernanen, K., 142, *160*
Perry, D. G., 56, 59, 60, *60*, 61, 62, 63, 64, 72, *75*, *76*, *77*
Perry, L. C., 56, *60*, 61, 63, *77*
Peters, R., 43, *52*
Pettit, G. S., 59, 61, 62, 63, 65, 73, *75*, *78*
Petty, R., *135*
Phillips, L. R., 225, *244*
Phillipson, C., 225, *242*
Piche, C., 92, 96, 97, 98, *103*
Pierce, K. A., *77*
Pillemer, K., 215, 220, *221*, 224, 226, 229, 230, 231, 233, 235, 238, *243*, *244*, *245*
Piper, M., 234, *244*
Pithers, W., 108, 109, *133*, *135*
Pleck, J. H., 174, *195*
Pohl, L., 15, 18, *22*
Polek, D. S., 90, *103*
Pollack, W. S., 174, *194*
Pomeroy, W. B., 43, *52*
Popple, K. T., *160*
Powell, K., 40, *52*
Powell, L. B., 31, *53*
Prentky, R. A., 141, 145, 146, *160*
Prothrow-Smith, D. B., 30, *31*, 44, *53*
Proto-Campise, L., 115, *135*
Puett, R. C., 33, 34, *52*

Quigley, P., 146, 147, *160*
Quinn, E., 112, 116, *132*, 172, *193*
Quinn, M. J., 229, *245*
Quinsey, V. L., 142, 146, 149, *160*

Raine, A., 208, *220*
Ramsay, C. A., 181, *196*
Randall, T., 198, *220*
Rasmussen, K., 215, *220*
Ratto, R., 16, *23*
Raud, M. R., 7, *21*

Rawlins, M., 108, 126, 127, *127*, *133*, 167, *194*
Ray-Keil, A. A., 28, *53*
Reitzel, D., 92, 96, 98, *103*
Renick, M. J., 210, *219*
Reppucci, N. D., 14, *24*, 28, 29, 34, 36, 37, 40, 41, *53*
Resnick, H. S., 143, *158*
Resnick, M. D., 28, *50*
Rice, M. E., 92, *103*
Rich, C. L., 154, *157*
Richardson, L., 126, *132*, 167, *192*
Rigby, K., 65, *77*
Riger, S., 149, *157*
Riggs, D. S., 82, 85, 86, 87, 88, 89, *104*, 110, *131*, 204, *220*
Riley, L. A., 214, *221*
Riophe, H., 43, *51*
Risch, G. S., 214, *221*
Rispens, J., 14, *15*, *24*, 29, *53*
Robertson, S., 43, *51*
Rogge, M. R., 204, *220*
Rollnick, S., 177, *195*
Romano, N., 14, *24*
Roscoe, B., 81, 82, *104*, *105*
Rosen, C., 14, *22*, 28, *50*
Rosen, L. A., 127, *131*
Rosenbaum, A., 197, *220*
Rosenberg, M. L., 30, *50*
Rosenthal, E. H., 167, *195*
Roskos-Ewoldsen, B., 111, 124, *133*
Ross, D., 73, *77*
Ross, L. T., 142, 143, 144, 147, *155*, 173, *190*
Rotzien, A., 36, 37, *52*
Rowden, L., 67, *76*
Rozee, P. D., 138, *160*
Ruback, R. B., 144, *160*
Rubin, K., 60, 61, 64, 65, 67, 69, 70, *76*, *77*, *78*
Rubin, R. H., 36, *50*
Ruff, G. A., 140, *158*
Runtz, M., 28, *49*
Rushe, R., 207, 208, 210, *216*, *217*, *218*
Russ, I., *133*
Russell, D. E. H., 138, *146*, *160*
Russo, N. F., 139, 140, *158*
Rutledge, L. L., 90, *103*
Ryan, G., 43, 44, *51*, *53*
Ryan, K., 81, 82, 85, 88, 89, *101*
Rybarik, M. F., 91, 96, 97, 98, *103*
Ryden, M., 230, *245*

Samios, M., 82, *101*
Sampson, M., 34, *54*
Sampson, R. J., 147, *158*
Sandau-Christopher, D., *53*
Sanday, P. R., 148, *160*
Sanders, B., 46, *53*
Sandin, E., 198, 203, 204, *217*
Saperstein, L., 14, *22*, 28, *50*
Sarno, J. A., 15, 16, *24*
Sarvela, P., 127, *133*, 167, *193*
Saunders, B., 46, *49*, 143, 146, *158*
Sayles, S., 146, 147, *158*
Scarce, M., *135*, 138, 150, 152, *156*,
    176, 179, 187, *195*
Schewe, P. A., 41, 44, *53*, 91, *104*, *105*,
    108, 111, 112, 116, 119, 120,
    121, 122, 126, 128, 130, *135*,
    138, *160*, *195*, 250, 251, 252,
    261
Schneider, B., 69, 70, 71, *74*
Schumm, W. R., 214, *220*
Schwartz, B. K., 40, *54*
Schwartz, D., 58, 59, 60, 61, 62, 63, 65,
    73, *78*
Schwartz, M., 84, 87, 88, *105*, *196*
Scully, D., 110, *135*
Sedlak, A. J., 28, *54*
Segel, H. D., 229, *244*
Seibel, C. A., 140, 146, *158*
Senchak, M., 198, 199, 201, 202, 203,
    218, *219*
Seto, M. C., 144, *160*
Seymour, A. K., 138, *158*
Sharpe, M. J., *196*
Sherling, G., 70, *78*
Shermack, R., 28, *50*
Shirley, M., 111, 124, *133*
Shizas, N., 111, 119, 121, 130, *135*,
    195
Shortt, J., *217*
Siegel, J., 140, 145, *156*, *160*, *161*
Sigelman, C. K., 86, 87, 88, *105*
Silliman, B., 212, *220*
Simon, A. K., 181, *196*
Simons, R. L., 87, *105*
Sinnot, J. D., 226, 228, *243*
Skinner, L. J., 146, *155*
Skogan, W., 146, *160*
Skogan, W. C., 146, *155*
Sleet, D., 40, *52*
Slep, A., 81, 88, 89, 94, 98, *102*, *105*
Smith, C., 81, 82, 85, 88, 89, *101*

Smith, J. P., 87, *105*
Smith, K., 67, 78, 116, *117*, 119, 129,
    133, 138, 152, *157*, 182, *193*
Smith, P. K., 56, 64, *75*, *78*
Smith, T., 29, *50*
Smith, W., 28, *50*
Smutzler, N., 198, 203, 204, *217*
Snow, B., 16, *24*
Sockloskie, R. J., 152, *159*
Soled, S., 14, *23*, *51*
Sondag, K. A., 127, *133*, 167, *193*
Sorenson, S. B., 82, 86, 87, *104*, 140,
    156, *160*
Sorenson, T., 16, *24*
Sowards, B., 110, 126, *132*, 167, *192*
Speth, T. W., 15, *21*
Sroufe, L. A., 64, 65, *78*
Stanley, S. M., 204, 209, 210, 211, 212,
    217, *218*, *219*, *220*
Stark, E., 200, *220*
Steele, B., *54*
Steer, R., 46, *50*
Stein, J. A., 140, *156*, *160*
Steiner, Y., 202, *220*
Steinmetz, S., 201, *221*, 225, 230, 234,
    244, *245*
Stermac, L., 140, *161*
Stets, J. E., 86, *105*, 198, 201, *220*
Stevenson, W., 45, *51*
Stewart, S. L., 60, 70, *78*
Stith, S. M., 203, *220*
Stoelb, M. P., 129, *131*, 183, *190*
Stone, J. G., 226, 230, *243*
Stone, S., 197, 200, *218*
Storaasli, R., 209, *218*
Stouthamer-Loeber, M., 38, *53*
Strapko, N., 14, *22*
Strassberg, Z., 88, *102*
Straus, M., 81, *105*, 197, 198, 200, 201,
    213, *220*, *221*, 225, *245*
Strauss, C. C., 67, *78*
Strugnell, E. P., 226, 227, *245*
Stuart, G. L., 207, *217*
Sudermann, M., 92, 96, 98, *103*
Sue, S., 182, *193*
Sugarman, D. B., 203, *217*, 225, *243*
Suitor, J., 200, *221*
Sundine, C., *53*

Tabachnick, J., 36, 38, 39, 41, 42, 48,
    50, *54*
Taler, G., *242*

Taliaferro, E., 197, 200, *218*
Tanaka, J. S., 152, *159*
Tatara, T., 227, *245*
Terry, R., 73, *76*
Teske, J., *53*
Testa, M., 143, *161*
Tharinger, D. J., *24*
Thomas, C. D., 82, 84, *104*
Thomas, L., 111, 124, *133*
Thompson, E. H., 86, *105*
Thornton, T., 31, *53*
Tolman, R. M., 82, *104*
Tomita, S. K., 229, *244*, *245*
Torgler, C. C., 125, *134*
Treboux, D., 88, *102*
Treister, L., *104*
Trower, P., 70, *78*
Troy, M., 64, 65, *78*
Tschan, P., 175, 183, *194*
Tubb, T., 197, 200, *218*
Tutty, L. M., 14, *24*
Tyree, A., 197, 198, *218*, *220*

U. S. Department of Criminal
    Justice, 175, *196*
U. S. Department of Health and
    Human Services, 10, *24*,
    33, *54*
U. S. Department of Justice, 3, *24*
U. S. Government Accounting
    Office, 14, *24*
Ullman, S. E., 113, 114, *135*, 140,
    141, 142, 143, 144, 145,
    146, 150, 152, *156*, *161*
Underwood, M. K., 73, *76*
Upfold, D., 142, 146, 149, *160*

Valentine, K. B., 119, 124, *134*,
    167, *194*
Valtinson, G., 127, *132*, 167, *193*
Van Dyke, D. T., 214, *221*
Veronen, L. J., 140, *158*
Vezina, L., 92, 96, 97, 98, *103*
Villeponteaux, L. A., 140, *158*
Vincent, G. G., *24*
Violence Against Women Act, 30,
    54
Vivian, D., 198, *215*

Waldo, C., 41, *52*, 108, 109, 116,
    128, *133*, 139, *159*
Walker, C. E., 27, *54*

Walker, D. L., 72, *74*
Walker, L. E., 140, 145, 150, *161*
Walls, L. G., 143, *156*
Waltz, J., 200, 205, 206, 208, 210, *215*,
    218
Wambolt, P. M., 253, *261*
Ward, C. A., 174, *196*
Wardrop, J. L., 57, 58, 73, *76*
Warfield, J., 34, *54*
Warr, M., 149, *161*
Warshaw, R., 148, *161*
Watson, J., 100, *105*
Watt, N. F., 210, 211, *216*
Webb, C., 15, 18, 19, 22, 29, *51*
Weher, F., *53*
Weinberg, J., 170, *191*
Weiner, A., 236, *245*
Weinrott, M., 45, *54*
Weiss, S., 198, *216*
Weissberg, R. P., 40, *51*
Wells, S. M., 84, *102*
Wemmerus, V., 126, *132*, 167, *192*
West, S. G., 210, 211, *216*
White, J., 40, *54*
Whittaker, T., 228, *245*
Whitton, S. W., 211, *217*
Wiehe, V. R., 236, *245*
Wiles, K. A., 86, 87, 88, *105*
Williams, J. E., *136*
Williams, J. G., 87, *105*
Williams, L., 10, *23*, *24*, 28, 46, *52*, *53*,
    214, *221*
Williams, M., 1119, 125, *132*, 67, *193*
Williard, J. C., 63, *77*
Wilson, J. Q., 201, *221*
Winblad, B., 226, 229, *243*
Winkvist, A., 202, *216*
Wolf, R. S., 220, 224, 226, 227, 229, 230,
    233, *243*, *244*, *245*
Wolf, S., 29, *50*
Wolfe, V. V., 10, *24*
Women Against Rape, *136*
Woolard, J. L., 29, 34, 37, 40, 41, *53*
Wooldredge, J., 115, *134*
World Health Assembly, *54*
Worling, J. R., 45, 46, *54*
Wurtele, S. K., 10, 11, 13, 14, 15, 16, 19,
    20, *21*, *23*, *24*, *25*, 28, 29, 30, 36,
    54
Wyatt, G. E., 148, *162*

Ximena, B. A., 93, 97, *103*

Yeater, E. A., 138, 139, 146, 148, 152, *162*, *166*, *196*
Yllo, K., 83, *105*, 145, *156*, 201, *221*
Young, D. S., 150, *160*
Yuan, J., 253, *261*
Yung, B., 34, 40, *51*, *54*

Zaia, A. F., 62, *75*
Zarit, S. H., 237, *245*
Zawacki, M. A., 173, *190*
Zetes-Zanatta, L. M., 147, *160*
Zucker, K. J., 10, *21*

SUBJECT INDEX

Abusive men
    power discrepancy and, 205
Accountability
    program evaluation and, 248, 249
Acquaintance rape
    risk factors for, 147
Adolescent
    dating violence in, 80–81
Adult protective services
    elder abuse and, 239
Advocacy
    media violence policy and, 41
Age
    domestic violence and, 200–201
    in elder abuse, 228
    in rape prevention programs, 117
Ageism
    and elder abuse, 226–227
Aggression
    attitude toward and dating violence,
        85–86, 88–89
    marital, 204
    partner violence prevention programs
        and, 94
    in peer victimization, 61, 62
    physical
        in violent couples, 206
    premarital and domestic violence, 197–
        198
Aggressive personality
    dating violence and, 87–88
Aggressive victims
    of peer victimization
        hostile attribution bias of, 61–62
        interventions for, 73
Alcohol use. See also Substance abuse
    domestic violence and, 202–203
    as rape risk factor, 142–144, 147–148,
        151
Anger management
    in dating violence prevention programs,
        100
Anxious–withdrawn behavior
    peer victimization and, 60–61, 62, 70
Assertiveness
    and date rape prevention, 114–115
Assertiveness training
    peer victimization and, 70–71

Attitude(s)
    ageism
        in elder abuse, 233
    of college students at-risk for child
        abuse, 44
    in dating violence prevention programs,
        100
    of men
        in rape prevention programs, 182–
            183
        toward women, 164
    public, child abuse and, 39–40
    rape-related, 138–139 (See also Rape
        myths)
    toward aggression and dating violence,
        85–86
Attribution
    hostile bias in, 61–62
    in peer victimization, 71
    self-blame, 71
Audience
    in rape prevention programs, 116–117

Batterers
    classification by physiological markers,
        208–209
    types of, 207
Behavior
    measurement of
        in evaluation instrument develop-
            ment, 255
Building Relationships in Greater
        Harmony Together (BRIGHT)
    dating violence program for high
        school, 93–94
Bully–victim relationship
    intervention in, 66–67
Bystander approach
    in rape prevention programs, 111–112,
        177, 178

Caregivers
    elder abuse by, 226, 230
    peer victimization and, 64
    supervision and monitoring of
        in prevention of child sexual abuse,
            38–39

Caregiving skills deficit
in elder abusers, 229–230
Centers for Disease Control
and public health model, 30
studies of child sexual abuse, 37
Child sexual abuse (CSA)
collaboration of victim and offender
therapists in, 48–49
consequences of, 10–11
psychological and psychosocial, 28
definitions of, 27–28
fostering children's reports of, 47
incidence of, 28, 29
interventions in
ethnic and cultural diversity and, 34
linkage of victim and offender treatment and, 49
prevention of, 28–30
prevention programs and, 11–19
knowledge gains with, 14–15
negative and positive side effects of,
18–19
parents as partners in, 19–21
reduction of incidence and, 17–18
skill gains with, 15–17
primary prevention of, 36–41
protective factors and, 11, 12–13
as public health concern, 33–34
public health model for
advantages of, 31–33
application of, 34–35
versus criminal justice model, 33–34
dual-track, 32, 34–36
systematic approach of, 30–31
risk for, 11, 12–13
school-based programs for, 9–21, 28–29
criticisms of, 29–30
scope of problem, 9–10
secondary prevention of, 41–44
attitudes of at-risk college students
and, 44
potential abusers in, 42
school in identification of at-risk
behaviors, 42–44
tertiary prevention of, 44–47
treatment of offenders, 45
victim of, treatment of, 46–47
Child sexual offender
college students at-risk as, 44
modus operandi of, 36–37, 38
population of, 36–37
potential, 42

risk and protective factors and, 12
treatment of, 45–46
Choice. *See also* Consent
in male sexual assault programs, 172
Clothesline Project, 184
Coercion
in male sexual assault programs, 173,
174
Cohabitation
domestic violence and, 201
College students
at-risk for child sexual abuse, 44
Communication
and date rape prevention, 114–115
domestic violence and, 204, 206
in domestic violence prevention, 209
in male sexual assault programs, 173
Communication deficits
Prevention and Relationship Enhancement Program and, 209, 210
Community
in child abuse
risk/protective factors of, 13
Community violence
and dating violence, 86
Confidentiality
in evaluation instrument development,
255
Conflict
dating violence and, 89
male role and, 164–165
Conflict management
in domestic violence prevention of, 209
Prevention and Relationship Enhancement Program and, 209, 210
Consent
conditions for, 177, 178
in rape prevention programs for men,
172–173, 185
Coping difficulties
dating violence and, 89
CSA. *See* Child sexual abuse (CSA)

Date Rape Prevention: A Video Intervention for College Students, 186–
187
Dating violence. *See also* Partner violence
prevention
in adolescents, 80–81
attitudinal models and, 85–86
child abuse and, 87
in college, 82–83

feminist theory and, 83–84
gender and, 84–85, 96
in high school, 81–82
in middle school, 81
prevalence of, 80–83
prevention of
  multiethnic middle school program, 94
  Skills for Violence Free Relationships, 91
prevention programs and
  mandatory, 101
  school-based, 91–95
  selection of, 95–101
risk factors for
  acceptance and use of aggression, 88–89
  aggressive personality, 87–88
  child abuse, 87
  community and school violence, 86
  conflict and argument, 89
  coping difficulties, 89
  jealousy, 89
  parental violence, 86–87
  retaliation to "save face," 89–90
  sex roles, 88
  social deviance, 90
Demand–withdraw interaction
  and violence *vs.* wife, 205–206
Dependence, of caregiver on recipient, elder abuse and, 230

Elder abuse
  barriers to identification and reporting of
    in clinicians, 234–235
    social or cultural, 232–233
    in victim, 233–234
  categories of, 224
  contextual risk factors for
    family conflict, 231
    financial difficulties, 231
    social support deficit, 231–232
  crisis management for victim, 239
  definition of, 223
  detection and assessment of victim, 237–238
  education
  as elder abuse intervention
  health professionals and, 236
    public, 235, 236–237
  incidence of, 223
  information sources for, 241–242

interventions in
  primary, 235, 236–237
  secondary, 235, 237–239
  tertiary, 235, 240
perpetrator risk factors in
  caregiving skills deficit, 229–230
  dependence on victim, 230
  psychological problems, 229
  stress, 230
  substance abuse, 229
reporting of
  barriers to, 233–235
  mandatory, 239
theoretical explanations for, 225–232
  ageism, 226–227
  caregiver exhaustion, 226
  external stress, 226
  social exchange theory, 225–226
transgenerational theory of, 225
victim risk factors in
  age, 228
  gender, 227–228
  psychological problems, 228–229
  substance abuse, 228
Emotional factors
  as risk for elder abuse, 228
Empathy. *See* Victim empathy
Evaluation. *See* Program evaluation

Face saving
  dating violence and, 89–90
Family
  in child abuse
    risk/protective factors of, 12–13
  history of violence in
    domestic violence and, 203
Family systems
  bully–victim relationship and, 66–67
  peer victimization and, 65
  school environment and, 65–66
Father
  involvement in child safety programs, 20–21
  peer victimization and, 65
Fear
  of elder abuse victim
    failure to identify and report and, 233–234
Feminist theory
  dating violence and, 83–84
Fraternity Violence Education Project
  violence against women issues in, 187–188

Gender
  and dating violence, 84–85
  in dating violence, 84–85, 96
  and differences in victim empathy, 109–
    110
  domestic violence and, 201–202
  of elder abuse victim, 227–228
  and partner violence, 198
  in partner violence prevention program,
    96
  in rape prevention programs, 116–117
  role conflict of men, 164–165

Health care professionals, failure to
    identify and report elder abuse
    and, 234–235
Hostile attribution bias
  in aggressive victims, 61–62

Interactive format
  in rape prevention programs, 118–119,
    169, 181
Isolation
  of elder abuse victim
    in failure to identify and report abuse,
    233
  as risk factor for domestic violence,
201–202
  as risk factor for peer victimization, 60–
    61
  as risk for elder abuse, 228–229

Jealousy
  dating violence and, 89

Kempe Center
  training curriculum in child sexual
    behavior, 43–44

Limit setting
  and date rape prevention, 115

Mandatory reporting
  of suspected elder abuse, 239
Masculinity
  male perception of and rape, 164, 165,
    180
Media
  advocacy against physical and sexual
    violence in, 41
  attitudes about child sexual abuse and,
    39–40

Men
  as child sexual offenders, 27–28
  gender role conflict in, 164–165
Men Against Violence, 189
Men Can Stop Rape, 189
Men's Program, The, 187
Mental health professional
  elder abuse prevention and, 240
Mother
  peer victimization and, 64, 65
Myth(s)
  male sexuality and sex, 174
  rape, 108–109, 124, 125, 126, 129

Outcome evaluation
  behavioral intention in, 251, 252–253
  evaluability assessment in, 251
  incidence rates and, 252
  instrument development for, 254–255
    considerations in, 255
  logic models of, 253–254
  measurement of outcomes in, 251–253
  proximal measures of, 252–253
  of rape prevention programs, 152–153
  of rape prevention studies
    review of, 124–130

PACT. *See* Physical Aggression Couples
    Treatment (PACT)
Parent–child relationship
  peer victimization and, 64
Parenting style
  peer victimization and, 64
Parents
  in child sexual abuse education, 36
  in identification of child abuse victims,
    20
  role in child sexual abuse programs, 19–
    21
  violent
    dating violence and, 86–87
Partner violence
  consequences for women, 198
  gender and prevalence of, 198
  proximal measures of, 253
Partner violence prevention program(s).
    See also Dating violence
  adult *vs.* adolescent violence in, 96–97
  Building Relationships in Greater
    Harmony Together, 93–94
  Canadian, 92–93

gender in, 96
general *vs.* at-risk populations in, 95–96, 99
implementation recommendations for, 99–101
outcomes of, 94–95
physical *vs.* verbal aggression in, 97
Safe Dates curriculum, 93
selection of, 99–101
selection of implementers of, 98–99
settings for, 99
Skills for Violence Free Relationships, 91
time allocation for, 97–98
Peer victimization
conceptualization and measurement of, 57
consequences of, 73–74
definitions of, 56
effects of
chronic *vs.* isolated, 57
internalizing difficulties, 58
maladaptive social behaviors, 58–59
friendship and, 63
interventions in
at bully–victim level, 66–67
at friendship level, 71–72
at individual level, 67, 69–71
levels of, 68
linkage with adjustment, 58–59
peer rejection in, 63
physical weakness in boys, 62
risk factors for, 59–65
familial, 64–65
individual, 59–63
peer relations, 63
school environment, 59
social–cognitive characteristics and, 61–62
school environment and, 59
self-report *vs.* peer reports of, 56–57
submissiveness and withdrawal of victim, 59–60
Personal safety programs
involvement of parents in, 20–21
parent concerns about, 19–20
Physical aggression
women's use of, 84–85
Physical Aggression Couples Treatment (PACT)
in domestic violence prevention, 212–213

Power, abuse of, in male sexual assault programs, 173
Power relations
in domestic violence, 204–205
PREP. *See* Prevention and Relationship Enhancement Program (PREP)
in combination with Stop Anger and Violence Escalation program, 212, 213
description of, 209
for domestic violence, 209–211
follow-up study of, 210
male battering and, 211
outcomes, 210
safety concerns in treatment strategy and, 210–211
speaker–listener technique in, 209–210
time-outs in, 210
Process evaluation
description and example of, 250
evaluability assessment in, 251
formative, 251
needs assessment in, 251
Program development
logic models in, 254
Program evaluation. *See also* Evaluation design; Outcome evaluation
design in
alternate treatments, pre- and posttest, 258
one group, pre- and posttest, 257
single-group, posttest, 256
treatment and control groups, pre- and posttest, 257–258
two-groups, posttest, 256–257
design of, 256–260
for development and improvement, 248–249
for effectiveness, 248
importance of, 247–249
outcome evaluation, 249–255
problems in, 249
process evaluation, 250, 251
satisfaction surveys, 250
use of results
by community, 259
by funders, 259
by service providers, 260
Program valuation
in rape prevention programs for men, 180–181

Psychological problems
    of elder abuser, 229
Public attitude
    child sexual abuse and, 39–40
Public health model
    in child sexual abuse, 30–41

Race and ethnicity
    domestic violence and, 201
    in rape prevention programs, 117–118
Rape. *See also* Sexual assault
    alcohol use in bar context and, 147–148
    avoidance strategies in, 114
    college
        by at-risk students, 44
        by fraternity members and athletes, 148
    consequences of, 110–111
    contexts of
        bars, 147–148
    decision theory and, 110–111
    false accusation of, 175
    high-risk situation education for women,
        112–113
    hypermasculinity and, 165
    by intimate partners, 148
    juvenile offenders and, 28
    male victims of, 176
    and self-defense strategies for women,
        113–114
    stranger rape theories and, 147
    women's responsibility bias and, 139
Rape avoidance
    alcohol use, perpetrator and victim, 142–
        144
    alcohol use as risk factor and, 142–144,
        151
    interrelationship of situation, rapist,
        victim in, 140–151
    male choice of violence against women
        practice implications of, 151–152
    prevention and risk reduction programs
        and, 152–155
    research needs and
        alcohol use and, 151
        in situational context and intimate
            relationships, 152
    resistance strategies in, 141–142
    risk reduction education programs for,
        140
    self-defense training for, 140
    victim–offender relationship, context,
        outcome and, 142

Rape Myth Acceptance scales, 121, 122
Rape myths
    articles on, 124–126, 129
    presentation and correction of, 108–109
    reasons for belief of, 109
Rape prevention
    learning summary of, 122–123
    research and practice implications of,
        151–152
    self-defense in, 149
Rape prevention programs, 41
    audience in
        age of, 117
        gender of, 116–117
        race and ethnicity of, 117–118
    awareness and knowledge of rape in,
        112
    bystander approach in, 111–112
    in child sexual abuse prevention, 44
    communication, assertiveness, limit
        setting in, 114–115
    confrontational format of, 116
    confrontation in, 116
    cultural relevance in, 117–118
    "dead-man" rule in, 118
    developmentally appropriate, need for,
        154–155
    example of, 120–121
    gender of presenter in, 117
    high-risk situations and, 112–113
    literature review of, limitations of, 121–
        122
    for men and boys, need for, 155
    negative consequences for perpetrators
        in, 110–112
    number of sessions in, 119
    outcome evaluations of, 152–153
    persuasion in, 115–116
    presentation methods in, 118–119
    rape myths in, 108–109
    self-defense strategies in, 113–114
    social psychological barrier component
        in, 150–151
    theoretical orientation of, 120
    victim empathy in, 109–110
    victimization and subsequent rape and,
        154
Rape prevention programs for men
    assumptions of, 170
    benefits of, 167–168
    case example of sequenced, integrated,
        183–184

consent in, 185
developmental model for, 176–184
elements of, 170–176
   alcohol and drugs, 173
   coercion and abuse of power, 173, 174
   communication, 173
   consciousness raising and action, 176
   consent, 172–173, 185
   impact of rape, 175
   legal definitions, 172
   male responsibility, 171
   male socialization, 174
   male victimization and, 176
   myths and assumptions about male sexuality, 174, 176
   responsibility, 175
   risky situations, 172
   sexual activity as choice, 172
format of, 166–176
future directions
   collaboration with female colleagues, 181–182
   comparative evaluations, 180–181
   empathy induction programs, 179
   environmental interventions in, 182–184
   interactive discussions in, 181
   outcome measures, 180
   program design and implementation, 181–184
   subpopulations, 182
interactive process in *vs.* format of, 169
model programs, 184–189
   Date Rape Prevention: A Video Intervention for College Students, 186–187
   Fraternity Violence Education Project, 187–188
   The Men's Program, 187
   Mentors in Violence Prevention Program, 186
   Rape Prevention Program for Men, 185
   Speaking with Men About Sexism and Sexual Violence Trainer's Manual, 188–189
preference for, 168
rationale for, 166–168
stages of change model in
   bystander behavior in, 177, 178
   conditions for consent in, 177, 178

Rape prevention studies
   in review of outcome evaluation research, 124–130
Rape resistance
   alcohol use and, 142–144
   attack–resistance–injury and, 141–142
   barriers to, 149–150
   rapist type and, 145–146
   risky situations and contexts and, 147–148
   victim–offender relationship, 144–145
   victim–offender relationship and context and, 142
   weapons in
      offenders display of, 146–147
      victim use of, 146–147
Rape risk reduction programs
   in rape prevention programs, 153
   victimization histories of women and, 153–154
Reporting
   of child sexual abuse
      reluctance to, 38
   of elder abuse
      barriers to, 233–235
      suspected, 239
   research needs in, 241
Responsibility
   male, in rape prevention, 175
   male, in sexual assault prevention, 171
Risky situations
   in male sexual assault programs, 172
   in rape prevention programs for women, 147–148

Safe Dates
   dating violence program for middle school, 93
Safety
   in child abuse prevention programs, 19–21
   in domestic violence prevention programs, 210–211, 215
Satisfaction survey, 250
School
   and child sexual abuse prevention, 37–38, 42–44
   child sexual abuse programs in, 9–21
   and peer victimization prevention, 65–66
School environment
   dating violence and, 86

in peer victimization
    in intervention for, 65–66
    as risk factor, 59
Screening
    for elder abuse, 238
Self-blame
    in rape victim, 150
Self-defense
    child sexual abuse survivors and, 149
    social and psychological barriers to,
       149
Self-protection
    from peer victimization, 67
    for women, 112–113
Service provision
    for caregivers of elders, 236–237
SES. *See* Socioeconomic status (SES)
Sex roles
    dating violence and, 88
    male conflict and, 164–165
Sexual aggression
    of male adolescents, 85
Sexual assault. *See also* Rape
    bystander behavior in, 177
    in domestic violence, 145
    legal definitions of
       in male sexual assault programs,
       172
Sexual assault prevention
    social action resources for, 189–190
    socialization of men and, 164
    terminology in, 165–166
Sexual assault prevention programs.
       See also Rape prevention
       programs
    coeducational, 166–167
    men's *vs.* women's, 166
    single-gender, 166–167
Sexual behavior
    in childhood
       Kempe Center training program
       and, 43–44
Sexual behaviors, in childhood, 43
Skills for Violence Free Relationships,
    91
Social attitudes
    toward violence, 48
Social exchange theory
    of elder abuse, 225–226
Socialization
    in male sexual assault programs,
       173–174

of men
    sexual assault and, 164
    to violence in
       child abuse and, 40–41
    of women
       rape and, 140
Social-psychological barriers
    to date rape resistance, 149–151
    to self-defense, 149
Social skills training
    in dating violence prevention programs,
       100
    peer victimization and, 69–70, 72
Social support deficit
    elder abuse and, 231–232
Socioeconomic status (SES)
    domestic violence and, 199–200
Solitary behavior
    as risk for peer victimization, 60–61
STAR (Southside Teens About Respect)
    partner violence program, 91–92
Stop Anger and Violence Escalation
    (SAVE) program
    in combination with Prevention and
       Relationship Enhancement
       Program, 212
    in domestic violence prevention, 211–
       212, 213
STOP IT NOW!
    child sexual abuse and
       change in public attitudes, 39–40
       outreach to potential abusers, 42
       social marketing strategies of, 39–40,
       42
Stranger rape, theories of, 147
Submissiveness
    as risk of peer victimization, 60
Substance abuse. *See also* Alcohol use
    in elder abuse
       by perpetrator, 229
       by victim, 228

Take Back the Night, 183, 184, 189–190
Teachers
    as implementers
       of dating violence prevention
       programs, 98–99

Verbal aggression
    dating violence and, 89
Victim blaming
    feminists and, 84

in male sexual assault programs, 174
Victim empathy
    female victim, 109–110
    gender differences in, 109–110
    in male sexual assault programs, 175
    male victim, 109
    in men's rape prevention programs, 179
    in rape articles, 124–126, 128–130
Videos
    in date rape prevention, 119, 186–187
Violence
    change in attitudes toward, 48
    socialization to
        reduction of, 40–41
Violence against women
    Fraternity Violence Education Project
        and, 187–188
Violent couples
    interactions in
        negative reciprocity and, 207

physically aggressive husbands, 206–
    207
self-report data and, 206

Weapons, in rape resistance, 146–147
White Ribbon Campaign, 183, 190
Withdrawal
    as risk for peer victimization, 60–61
Withdrawn children
    peer victimization of
        assertiveness training for, 70–71
        friendship approach with, 71–73
        risk for, 60–61, 62
Women
    abuse of elder, 227–228
    as child sexual offenders, 28
    rape prevention programs for, 165–166
    socialization of and rape, 140
    violence against, 198

ABOUT THE EDITOR

Paul A. Schewe, PhD, is a prevention researcher at the University of Illinois at Chicago. He is a clinical/community psychologist with extensive experience in developing and evaluating school-based violence prevention programs. In recent years, Dr. Schewe has worked on a variety of projects ranging from evaluations of single programs, to community-based collaborations, to statewide initiatives. The focus of these efforts has included sexual assault, teen dating violence, and domestic violence prevention programs, as well as early childhood interventions to promote social–emotional development. Dr. Schewe is a home-schooling father of three children and contributes to his local community as a scout leader and soccer coach.